BIRDS OF TROPICAL AMERICA

Number Five
The Corrie Herring Hooks Series

BIRDS OF TROPICAL AMERICA

By Alexander F. Skutch

Drawings by Dana Gardner

 UNIVERSITY OF TEXAS PRESS, AUSTIN

First Edition, 1983

Requests for permission to reproduce material from this work should be sent to Per-
missions, University of Texas Press, Box
7819, Austin, Texas 78712.

Library of Congress Cataloging in Publica-
tion Data

Skutch, Alexander Frank, 1904–
    Birds of tropical America.

    (The Corrie Herring Hooks series; 5)
    Bibliography: p.
    Includes index.
    1. Birds—Latin America.   2. Birds—
Central America.   3. Birds—Tropics.
I. Title.   II. Series.
QL687.A1S57   1982   598.298   82-8597
ISBN 0-292-74634-2   AACR2

To EDWIN O. WILLIS,
whose indefatigable fieldwork has taught us
much about tropical American birds

Contents

Acknowledgments

For permission to reprint, with revision, life histories that first appeared in their pages, I thank the editors and publishers of the following journals and book. Full citations of the original papers appear in the bibliography.

Animal Kingdom and the New York Zoological Society for the chapter on the Great Tinamou (1959a).

The Auk and the American Ornithologists' Union for part of the chapter on the Rufous-tailed (Black-chinned) Jacamar (1937) and the chapters on the Mountain (Mexican) Trogon (1942), Prong-billed Barbet (1944b), Blue-throated Green Motmot (1945), Turquoise-browed Motmot (1947b), Collared Trogon (1956b), Groove-billed Ani (1959c), and Rainbow-billed (Keel-billed) Toucan (1971b).

The Condor and the Cooper Ornithological Society for the chapters on the Resplendent Quetzal (1944c), Marbled Wood-Quail (1947a), Black-headed (Citreoline) Trogon (1948b), Ruddy Ground-Dove (1956a), Amazon Kingfisher (1957), Collared and Fiery-billed araçaris (1958b), and Little Tinamou (1963b).

The Ibis and the British Ornithologists' Union for the chapters on the Vermilion-breasted (White-tailed) Trogon (1962) and Blue-diademed Motmot (1964b) and part of that on the Rufous-tailed Jacamar (1963c).

The Living Bird and the Cornell Laboratory of Ornithology for the chapter on the Common Potoo (1970).

The Nuttall Ornithological Club and its editor for part of the chapter on the Emerald (Blue-throated) Toucanet (1967).

The Wilson Bulletin and the Wilson Ornithological Society for part of the chapter on the Emerald Toucanet (1944a) and for those on the Black-breasted Puffbird (1948a), Black-throated Trogon (1959b), Gray-headed (Chestnut-winged) Chachalaca (1963a), Scaled, Red-billed, Short-billed, and Band-tailed pigeons and White-winged Dove (1964a), Squirrel Cuckoo and Lesser Ground-Cuckoo (1966), and Broad-billed and Rufous motmots (1971a).

I am grateful to Holly Carver for her painstaking and discriminating editing.

Artist and author are grateful to the Western Foundation of Vertebrate Zoology for providing facilities for making the drawings.

Preface

Nature captivates us by her beauty, then challenges us to discover her secrets. She does so most compellingly with the loveliest of her animate creations: the birds so colorful in plumage, graceful in form, melodious in voice. Above all, the birds of tropical lands charm us with their gorgeous plumage, while they cunningly conceal the secrets of their lives in epiphyte-laden evergreen forests, in scarcely penetrable thickets, in treacherous swamps, and on heart-straining mountain peaks. In the second decade of this century, when I fell under the charm of tropical American birds, they had long been famous for their splendor, but few of the secrets of their lives had been revealed. I accepted the challenge implicit in their beauty and, for over half a century, have spared no effort to learn how they live. What I have discovered about them has been told chiefly in books and journals published by the ornithological societies of North America and Great Britain.

As I planned this book for a wider circle of readers, the forms of all the loveliest and most interesting birds that I have watched flitted through my memory, as though pleading to be included. Unfortunately, to include them all would make far too bulky a tome; selection was inevitable. The criteria that I have used for inclusion are, first, the intrinsic interest of the birds themselves and, second, the fact that my readers may be far from any library with long series of ornithological journals of already published accounts of these birds. Since books tend to be more readily procured than the journals of thirty or forty years ago, I have omitted all the species included in the three-volume *Life Histories of Central American Birds*, published

from 1954 to 1969 by the Cooper Ornithological Society, and (with one exception) in the three smaller books, with various titles, published by the Nuttall Ornithological Club from 1967 to 1981. The Cooper series is devoted wholly to passerine birds, from finches to woodcreepers, and to woodpeckers. The Nuttall Club publications range more widely over the orders of birds but do not include species whose life histories I had already published elsewhere, unless I had important new information about them. Accordingly, biographies of many of the most fascinating birds that I have intimately known remain widely scattered throughout periodical publications, dating back to the 1930s. Among these are birds that most challenged my perseverance in disclosing their secrets because so little was known about the way they live— tinamous, wood-quails, trogons, kingfishers, motmots, jacamars, puffbirds, barbets, and toucans, among others.

Without unique opportunities that may never be repeated, much that these birds revealed to me might never have been disclosed. They seem to have placed me under an obligation to make their lives more widely known. To bring their life stories together in a single volume, thereby making them readily accessible to the growing number of people interested in tropical nature, is the aim of this book. To accomplish this, I have carefully revised the original accounts, in the process omitting details that no longer seem important and adding whatever new information has become available over the years.

The science of ornithology has grown so rapidly because the poetry of birds has led so many people to study them. Wholly to divorce the science from the poetry would injure the science. The rewards of the serious study of living birds in their natural settings are many and varied, including the loveliness of the birds themselves, the charm of the places where they dwell, the excitement of finding cunningly concealed nests and disclosing well-guarded secrets, the facts about them that patient dedication accumulates, and, above all, the enduring satisfaction of knowing how the patterns of their lives integrate with their ancestral habitats. Scientific reports of ornithological investigations, increasingly mathematical and statistical, concentrate upon facts to the exclusion of almost everything else. Popular accounts emphasize the beauty of birds and the excitement of

finding or watching them but often fail to tell us much about the way they live and reproduce. In this book, I have tried to do justice to both aspects of bird study, the scientific and the aesthetic. I have also thought it proper to share with the reader some of the frustrations and disappointments of studying tropical birds, arising in part from the shyness and elusiveness of the birds themselves but chiefly from the heavy predation that prematurely destroys so many of the nests that have been found after long, diligent searching. How well I have succeeded in conveying all these aspects of the study of living birds in tropical America the reader of the following accounts will be the best judge.

BIRDS OF TROPICAL AMERICA

When the name of an organism is cap-
italized, the scientific equivalent will be
found in the index.

1. Great Tinamou

Tinamus major

I stood on a wooded ridge, amid palm trees whose slender, soaring trunks thrust feathery crowns into the high canopy of the rain forest. Around me grew clusters of low spiny palms, with ribbed fronds that tapered to tips beneath which brown hermit hummingbirds fastened their downy nests. My eyes followed the graceful curve of a woody vine upward to the lofty bough from which it hung, like a tree trunk that had lost the power to stand erect. The forest dripped after the heavy afternoon shower of early May; but the sun, dropping toward the wooded summit of the opposite ridge, sent nearly horizontal rays through a gap in the massed clouds.

Far above me in the sunlit treetops, a party of Chestnut-mandibled Toucans were singing their vespers, throwing their great yellow-and-chestnut bills skyward as they began each high-pitched verse. A Black-faced Antthrush, walking daintily over the leaf-strewn ground, whistled thrice in a full mellow voice. From the ferny undergrowth came a Thrushlike Manakin's exquisite whistle, ascending in three stages. A sweet, slight call revealed the presence of a Black-striped Woodcreeper, clinging unseen to some high trunk. The cicadas, which through the dry early months of the year had filled the woodland with their strident sounds, mingled their sharp sizzles with the liquid notes of the birds. Doomed to perish beneath the hard rains now beginning, these insects introduced a note of mutability and death into the joyous woodland chorus.

Suddenly a strong, solemn voice swelled through the forest, overpowering all slighter sounds as sunshine dims a lamp. Now on one side, now on another, the organ peals were repeated, saturating all the woodland with pure sound. In songs consisting of one or more phrases, each composed of a short note followed by a prolonged, ascending, sometimes slightly quavering note, the Great Tinamous were heralding the approach of night.

No other inhabitant of these forests has a voice so strong and full, yet so soft and mellow. If, as many hold, the true function of art is to awaken emotion, and if the highest art is that which stirs the strongest, purest feeling by the simplest means, then these birds are supreme artists, for with a musically simple utterance, lacking all the involutions of the best performances of songbirds and depending for effect on tone quality alone, they arouse a flood of emotion. All the beauty of the tropical forest, all its mystery, all its aeonian striving toward higher forms of life, all the tragedy, too, of the strife among its denizens and of its relentless spoliation by humans find expression in these exquisite notes.

For a few minutes the tinamous' whistles pealed intermittently through the woodland; then they fell silent for the night. As I walked homeward along a narrow fern-bordered path, the last of the Pyrophorus fireflies, creatures of the drier weather, traced brilliant, erratic courses between the trunks of the great trees—my trees. Recently I had bought this forest, along with the adjoining clearings and small plantings of a farm newly carved from the wilderness in the Valley of El General in southern Costa Rica, and close beside it, at an altitude of about 2,500 feet (760 meters), I had built the house that has been my home for many years.

Sometimes, as I followed a forest path at

Los Cusingos (as I named my farm), I met a Great Tinamou, a bird the size of a Guinea Fowl, with a stout, lightly barred, olive-brown body, a slender grayish neck, a small chestnut head with large dark eyes, a straight bill of moderate length, and a negligible tail. After walking ahead of me for a short distance, picking fruits and seeds from the ground, the tinamou would quietly vanish into the surrounding undergrowth. These birds were almost always alone, although once I met a parent who led three half-grown chicks for a good way down a forest road before they veered into the underwood.

More often, especially while walking through pathless woodland, I would become aware of a tinamou, not by sight but by a startlingly loud burst of wingbeats as the heavy bird emerged abruptly from amid screening herbage and, rising to a height of 15 to 20 feet (4.5 to 6 meters), flew with a whistling sound between the tree trunks, to alight at some point beyond my view. This sudden noise often evoked a sharp whistle from a Rufous Piha, a solitary cotinga the size of an American Robin, high in the trees. The same response could be elicited by a shout, a sneeze, a blow with the machete, almost any sudden, sharp sound, although the piha usually refused to answer twice in swift succession. The tinamou's sonorous wingbeats, followed by the piha's penetrating whistle, formed one of the characteristic sequences of sounds in the forests of El General while they were still unspoiled.

Although the abrupt rising of the heavy tinamou seems to demand an effort too violent to be well controlled, I have never known the bird to strike an obstacle, as, according to Hudson (1920), the Spotted Tinamou of the open pampas of Argentina frequently does, with fatal results. Any tendency of a forest-dwelling bird to collide with the trees that closely surround it would be sternly suppressed by natural selection. In Panama, Chapman (1929) saw a Great Tinamou fly up in this way when stalked by a Tayra, a large black weasel that preys heavily on domestic fowl.

One does not often watch a bird as large and shy as the tinamou at ease in its natural setting; but years ago, in the forest of Panama, I enjoyed this unique experience. I was passing the morning in a little wigwam of brown cloth, watching a Yellow-thighed, or Red-capped, Manakin attend her eggs, when I noticed the tinamou about 30 feet (9 meters) off. For a long while it walked around in small circles, from time to time picking up something edible but never quitting that one small area. I wondered what the attraction of this particular spot could be, but I did not wish to emerge from my blind to investigate.

Presently a Plain-brown Woodcreeper, next a pair of Spotted Antbirds, arrived to accompany the tinamou; from tree trunks or saplings they dropped to snatch something from the ground, then rose at once to their observation posts. This behavior, typical of followers of army ants, assured me that these insects were present, long before they came close enough to be distinguished. The tinamou was evidently eating the insects and other small creatures driven out of the ground litter by the hunting ants. Although this method of foraging by a variety of small birds had long been known, to see a big tinamou so engaged was unexpected. Gradually the swarm of restless brown ants drifted toward my blind, as did the smaller feathered attendants. But the tinamou, suspicious of the unfamiliar object set amid the undergrowth, remained farther away. After a while it sat on the leaf-carpeted ground, resting with its under tail coverts fluffed out to reveal the whitish tips of the feathers.

I had known the tinamou for years before I saw it anywhere but on the ground or on short, swift flights when disturbed. As I passed through the forest at Los Cusingos one afternoon in September, a tinamou rose from the undergrowth to a stout horizontal limb of a tall tree, 40 or 50 feet (12 or 15 meters) up. Here it stood for so long that I thought it had gone to roost, although an hour of daylight remained, but when I returned ten minutes later it had vanished.

The following April I stood quietly in the forest as day waned, watching a low globular nest into which I hoped to see an elusive Nightingale Wren retire for the night. As the light faded, a tinamou flew into a neighbor-

Rain forest in the Valley of El General, Costa Rica, home of the Great Tinamou, Marbled Wood-Quail, Short-billed Pigeon, Vermilion-breasted Trogon, Black-throated Trogon, and Fiery-billed Araçari.

ing small tree, to settle on a nearly horizontal bough a few inches thick and about 20 feet (6 meters) up. This was at the enchanted interval of twilight, when the tinamous were raising their voices here and there in the distance, but the bird in the tree stood silent and motionless.

When the Chestnut-mandibled Toucans had finished their vesper chorus and it was nearly dark in the underwood, I advanced cautiously toward the tinamou's tree. Since the bird gave no sign of alarm, I approached nearer. Throwing my flashlight's beam upon it, I moved all around and beneath it, keeping it always in the circle of light. Its only movement was to turn its head. The reflection from its eyes was white, not ruby like that of the Pauraque of the neighboring clearings; to judge by the brilliance of its eyeshine, the tinamou sees fairly well at night. Finally I departed, leaving the bird resting

peacefully in the very spot where it first alighted.

Formerly, when I was wakeful at night and heard a tinamou call in the nearby forest, I was troubled by the thought that it wandered over the ground, exposed to many perils. Now I pictured it resting on a high bough in relative security. The Great Tinamou participates little in the dawn chorus, and it sings only sporadically throughout the day, as it does in the night. I hear it most often in the evening twilight.

The Eggs and Incubation

One day in June, as I walked through open woodland near a rivulet, three big, intensely turquoise-green eggs caught my eye from a distance. Except for the Morpho butterfly's satiny sky-blue wings, these were the most vivid objects in the underwood. They lay near the top of the low bank on the farther side of the stream, at the base of a clump of tree ferns. Although slightly screened by the heart-shaped leaves of a terrestrial aroid, they were so inadequately concealed that I could see them from a hundred feet (30 meters) away.

Refraining from approaching for a closer inspection of these lovely eggs, I marked with a stick the most distant spot from which they were visible. The next day I cautiously returned to my marker, hoping to glimpse the parent bird, whatever its kind, as it covered the eggs. But alas! they had vanished; now only a few fragments of glossy shell were scattered around the spot where they had rested on the ground, with no sign of a nest. From descriptions that I had read, I knew they were eggs of the Great Tinamou, which nests in humid lowland forests from southern Mexico to northern Bolivia and Amazonian Brazil and upward, sparingly, to 4,000 or 5,000 feet (1,200 or 1,500 meters).

In later years, at Los Cusingos, I found five more nests of the Great Tinamou. Usually their presence was revealed by the explosive departure of the incubating parent as I walked unsuspectingly by. At each nest three to five lovely blue or turquoise-green eggs, averaging 61 by 48 millimeters, lay in a shallow depression in fallen leaves, at the base of a tree or stump, sometimes in a recess between its plank buttresses, or beside fallen branches. Elsewhere as many as twelve eggs have been reported, but they may have been contributed by several females mating with a polygynous male. With one exception, all my nests were either abandoned or destroyed by predators, which appears everywhere to be the usual fate of any Great Tinamou nests that people find. I did not see the successful nest until after the eggs hatched, leaving five empty shells from which chicks had obviously emerged. Although once in February, higher in the mountains, I was led to see a nest in which, my guide assured me, big blue eggs had been present a few days earlier, at Los Cusingos Great Tinamous lay from April to August.

So conspicuous to the human eye are these glossy eggs that they seem to invite predation.

On the other hand, the incubating parent blends so well with the ground litter that it would more often escape detection if it remained steadfastly at its post as one passes by. Do the parent or parents keep the eggs continuously covered if undisturbed, as many other birds do, thereby decreasing the advantage of laying cryptically colored eggs?

To answer this question has not been easy. Years ago, I found four eggs at the base of a tree, close beside a little-used woodland path. The incubating parent fitted closely in the niche between the buttresses, where it consistently sat facing inward. Since it did not take fright when I walked along the path without seeming to notice it, I decided to make frequent visits instead of watching continuously from a blind, the presence of which might increase the risk of desertion or predation. Although the sexes of the Great Tinamou look alike, and I was not sure whether one or both sexes incubate, I did not try to place a distinguishing mark on this touchy bird, as I had earlier done with the calmer Little Tinamou. However, an almost daylong rain helped me determine whether both parents shared incubation. The downpour left the dark feathers of the sitting tinamou's rump matted together and covered with a white deposit, conspicuous where spots of sunshine fell upon it. Evidently this deposit consisted of salts leached from the bird's plumage and dried by the heat of its body. At noon on the day after the rain, the tinamou appeared not to have moved or preened its feathers since the rain began about twenty-seven hours earlier. Frequent inspections throughout the afternoon always revealed the same easily identified individual sitting with head inward.

I returned the following dawn, hoping, by checking the nest at short intervals throughout the day, to profit from this unusual opportunity to study incubation by a marked Great Tinamou. As I came in view, a whitish object lying beside the bird caught my eye in the dim light. With a noisy burst of wingbeats, the tinamou flew up when I looked at it, as it had not done on preceding days. The three eggs that remained in the nest were wet and cold, indicating that the parent had returned to them only a short while before my arrival. The animal that attacked it in the night, tearing out a tuft of pale downy feathers and leaving an empty eggshell with a network of red lines on its white inner surface, had made the bird more wary. The three remaining eggs, two intact and one dented, lay upon blood-stained leaves, which I replaced with clean dead leaves. One of the undamaged eggs was eaten during the day, and the single surviving one was deserted. Evidently the animal that plundered the nest, possibly a weasel, was too small to eat more than one of these big eggs at a time.

One August I discovered three eggs at the base of a tree, amid tangled vegetation close beside the grassy road into Los Cusingos. To my surprise, the tinamou continued to incubate them while a thick trunk that had fallen across the road, about 75 feet (25 meters) away, was cut into logs by a shrieking chain saw. Later, the parent remained sitting while a horde of army ants passed so close that some of the scouts might have reached it and attendant birds flitted all around it. After I had watched from a good distance for an hour and a half, the tinamou calmly arose and walked away, leaving the eggs uncovered. After an absence of three to four hours, it returned to resume incubation. Unfortunately, that rainy afternoon two visitors with umbrellas passed along the road on their way into and out of the farm, and this, added to the other disturbances, caused the tinamou to desert.

From these fragmentary observations, it appears that the Great Tinamou sits continuously for long intervals, especially in rainy weather, but also takes prolonged recesses. It leaves the eggs exposed, although it might easily conceal their shiny shells by dropping a few dead leaves upon them. Probably the eggs are not so conspicuous to their chief predators, evidently small mammals who may hunt by scent rather than by sight and by night rather than by day, as they are to us who are gifted with full-spectrum vision. Although I did not succeed in learning the sex of the parent who incubates the eggs and leads the chicks, studies of several other species of tinamous point to the conclusion that this is always the male.

Postscript

Despite the vulnerability of their lovely eggs, despite all the poachers who, year after year, prowl through the forest at Los Cusingos, and despite the marauding dogs that make the woodland hideous with their yelps, Great Tinamous have managed to survive in fair numbers. Since the Crested Guans disappeared years ago, they are the largest birds continuously present. It is easy to understand why the mainly terrestrial tinamous have survived better than the arboreal guans. When guans are alarmed, they perch conspicuously well above the ground and clamor absurdly in high-pitched voices, behavior which is probably discreet enough when hunting Ocelots, Pumas, Tayras, or other mammals disturb them but which is suicidal in the presence of anyone who can kill at a distance. But the tinamous rise so unexpectedly from the undergrowth, and fly so rapidly away, that the hunter who would shoot them must be exceptionally quick. The incautious guans have vanished; the wary tinamous remain.

Although, like other small sanctuaries in the midst of farms, our forest has lost much, it has not yet been despoiled of all its treasures. A troupe of White-faced Monkeys still roam through its treetops, and most of the smaller birds remain. Perhaps most important of all, as night falls the stirring chorus of the Great Tinamou still rings through the woodland, expressing its beauty, mystery, and vitality.

2. Little Tinamou

Crypturellus soui

For millennia, the magnificent rain forests where Great Tinamous roam have been felled and burned by farmers—destruction which in recent decades has been proceeding at an alarmingly accelerated pace. When, after a few crops of maize or beans are harvested, the fields are abandoned, straggling shrubs, creepers, and young trees soon cover them so densely that one can hardly move through the tangled growth without vigorous use of the machete. Such impenetrable thickets are the home of the Little Tinamou, which, over a vast range from southern Mexico to Bolivia and the Guianas, has profited by the Great Tinamou's loss of habitat and consequent decline in numbers. Little Tinamous also frequent bushy growth at the forest's edge, neglected pastures, and weedy plantations of maize, coffee, bananas, cassava, or sugarcane. From the lowlands they extend upward, in diminishing numbers, to about 5,000 feet (1,500 meters) in southern Central America and northern South America, and in especially favorable localities they have been found as high as 5,600 feet (1,700 meters). Amid dense, concealing vegetation, the Little Tinamou walks over the ground, gathering many seeds and berries, along with a few insects, an occasional small frog, and much gravel for grinding its food. It prefers to escape pursuers by walking rather than by flying, but, if surprised or closely pressed, it rises with an explosive burst of wingbeats and shoots out of sight. Never flocking, it is usually found alone.

I rarely enjoy a good view of a Little Tinamou unless I watch from concealment or see one briefly as it crosses a road or path amid thickets or weedy plantations. Then I behold a stout, dull-colored, short-winged, almost tailless bird, about half the size of the Great Tinamou. The top of its head is slaty black, its cheeks sooty gray. Its unbarred back is grayish brown. Its ventral surface is whitish on chin and throat, becoming deep grayish brown on the chest and grayish tawny on the abdomen. It has brownish yellow eyes, a short, straight, blackish bill, and greenish yellow legs and feet. As in the Great Tinamou, the sexes are nearly or quite alike.

As in the dim light of early dawn I walked through dense, tall grass, a Little Tinamou arose from my feet with an alarmingly sudden whir of wings. Apparently, it had slept on the ground, as this species and the related Variegated Tinamou do in Guyana, according to information which Beebe (Beebe et al. 1917) received from an Indian hunter. Beebe watched a Great Tinamou ascend into a tree to roost, as I did in Costa Rica. He correlated this difference in the manner of sleeping of the two genera with differences in the posterior surface of the leg, smooth in the Little Tinamou, rough in the Great Tinamou, apparently to give the latter better support when it squats on a broad branch.

The Little Tinamou is a member of that select company of birds scattered through the "songless" orders whose notes are so full, so pure, so charged with feeling that as music they often seem to rank higher than the more complex performances of all but a few of the most gifted of the true songbirds. The exquisite notes of this tinamou are heard occasionally throughout the year, at all hours of the day and even in the night, but, like those of the Great Tinamou, they are most frequent as darkness settles over the thickets within which these birds move unseen. To rest amid tangled growth while daylight fades, hearing the tinamous' sweet voices sound back and forth from the lush verdure, is a deeply moving experience.

The Little Tinamous' whistled songs vary considerably in volume and structure, but whether these differences are associated with differences of sex or of motivation I cannot tell. As daylight waned, a tinamou whom I watched incubate, presumably a male, broke his daylong silence with short, subdued whistles that gradually, with numerous repetitions, grew in volume. Presently a second tinamou, perhaps the incubating bird's mate, heard these notes and answered from amid a nearby thicket with a long series of full, clear, slightly trilled whistles, beginning low in the scale and increasing slightly in pitch with each repetition—the incomparably beautiful, soul-stirring song of the tinamou. As though encouraged by this response to his first tentative notes, the bird on the eggs re-

plied with a whistle that was louder and longer yet not so full as those which issued from the thicket.

On another evening, a tinamou uttered a mellifluous crescendo, followed by a beautiful prolonged whistle, full yet tenuous, which neither rose nor fell in pitch. Another song was a single long-drawn-out, exquisitely modulated tremulous whistle. Once, when at the day's end I sat in a blind amid second growth near high forest, the twilight chorus included the voices of both Great and Little tinamous. Among the more varied songs of the latter were some that resembled those of the former, but the notes of the larger bird were more powerful and stirring. Doubtless, the Little Tinamou's lovely notes will continue to adorn the more prosaic setting of plantations and scrubby growth, long after the Great Tinamou has vanished together with its lofty forests.

The Eggs and Incubation

In the Valley of El General, I have seen eggs of the Little Tinamou in every month except March, June, and July but most often in dry February and rainy September. The measurements of sixteen of the glossy, oval, vinaceous lavender eggs averaged 43.1 by 32.4 millimeters, with extremes of 40.5 to 45.6 by 31.8 to 33.3 millimeters. These eggs are laid on the ground, from which they may be separated by a few leaves or other fragments of vegetation, which appear to have been already present rather than placed there by the tinamous.

These lovely eggs nearly always lie amid such dense vegetation that they and the parent who covers them are invisible just a few feet away. Of the seventeen nests that I have seen, I found only two; the rest were found by laborers cleaning weedy plantations or pastures. Seven of these nests were in small patches of sugarcane that were being cleaned by hand. Others were in plantings of coffee, cassava, bananas, and maize or in bushy pastures. One was in a tangled opening amid tall second-growth woods, one in primary forest near its edge. Even when the laborer cleaning a plantation or pasture spares the nest and leaves a sheltering patch of herbage, it has usually been more or less exposed before he noticed it, so that, even if the parent does not desert, the eggs are likely to be discovered and destroyed by some prowling animal. Of the seventeen nests that I have seen, thirteen contained two eggs. In two instances, the parent continued for several days to incubate a single egg, which may have been the full set. In Trinidad, where Little Tinamous also breed through most, if not all, of the year, they also usually lay two eggs (ffrench 1973). In Guyana, where "the nesting period seemed interminable," single eggs were incubated (Beebe et al. 1917).

Unlike the Great Tinamou, the obscurely colored Little Tinamou sits closely on his eggs, in the shade of the lush vegetation that clusters densely around him. Often he has remained steadfast while I bent over him, my head low above his own. Frequently I found the tinamou crouching with his foreparts depressed, his head near the ground, his posterior end elevated until the rudimentary tail and under tail coverts stood almost erect, revealing the dark pencilings on the light gray feathers of the latter—a posture often assumed by incubating doves when alarmed. It is questionable whether the tinamou gains anything by crouching forward, for, to the human eye, the bird is certainly no less conspicuous than when incubating in the usual position. Moreover, the elevation of the hindparts often leaves the eggs more or less exposed, and these glossy, richly colored objects are more eye-catching than the bird himself.

Although incubating Little Tinamous permit such a close approach, I have never been able to touch one, as other people have sometimes done. While my slowly advancing hand was still a foot or two away, rarely closer, the birds have taken flight with explosive suddenness and skimmed low over the ground, to plunge into the herbage a short distance away and vanish. Often, however, the incubating tinamou permits himself to be touched with the end of a stick a yard or so long. By attaching a paint-soaked tuft of cotton to a stick, I have placed identifying marks on several tinamous. In each instance, repeated visits revealed only the single marked parent covering the eggs. I did not learn the sex of this parent, but, as in other tinamous, it was doubtless always the male.

At noon on November 25, 1936, I entered a blind which on the preceding day I had set 6 feet (1.8 meters) from a nest in a small canefield. The two eggs were then uncovered and cold, and they remained so until, at 12:44, the marked parent approached from the side opposite the blind, walking calmly through the weeds that flourished among the sugarcane. Reaching the eggs, he adjusted them with his bill while standing over them, then settled down to incubate. All through the dim cloudy afternoon the same bird remained quietly on the eggs, only at long intervals shifting his position or rising to turn them. He was much annoyed by mosquitoes and other small flies that buzzed around his head, which he frequently shook to drive them away. As night approached he grew restless, and in a few minutes he shifted his position on the eggs more often than he had done in the preceding hours. After the crepuscular Pauraques had begun to fly and call in the dusk, I heard the voices of tinamous for the first time since I started to watch. One among the sugarcane sang enchantingly, while from the neighboring thickets came the melodious whistles of others. But the patient bird so close in front of me neither called nor murmured.

I watched for the incubating tinamou to tuck his head back among his feathers and fall asleep, but in the gathering darkness he faded from sight with his head still exposed. After I could no longer see the bird by light from the sky, I directed the beam of my flashlight upon him from time to time, but each time he was awake, sitting with his head depressed near the ground. Thus he rested when, at six o'clock, I carefully emerged from the blind and left him.

At daybreak, the marked tinamou was still covering the eggs. In the dim early light, while Orange-billed Nightingale-Thrushes sang, the tinamous in the canefield and off in the thickets whistled sweetly, then lapsed into a silence which they did not break after the light grew strong. Throughout the early morning, the bird in front of me sat quietly and patiently until, at 7:05, he rose and walked deliberately away through the weeds. Then the hours slipped by without the arrival of a parent to warm the now thoroughly chilled eggs. They were still unattended when I went for lunch at 11:30, but by 1:00 the marked tinamou was again incubating. He sat motionless and apparently unperturbed while I removed the cloth blind close in front of him. In my twelve hours of watching, no other tinamou came within my restricted field of vision.

On the following day, November 27, the marked tinamou was on the nest at 7:25 A.M. and 3:56 P.M., and on November 29 he was present at 9:15 A.M. Two days later the eggs were broken, evidently by some animal.

In a later year, I made frequent visits, over an interval of fifteen days, to a nest situated in second-growth woods. On all but one of twenty-eight visits at various times between 7:15 A.M. and noon or a little later, I found the eggs unattended. The single occasion when the parent was present in the forenoon was at 8:10 on the fourteenth day after I discovered the nest. On each of nine visits in the afternoon, which at this season was often rainy, the parent was covering the eggs; on no visit after 12:30 did I find him absent. My observations at these two nests showed that the tinamous habitually left the eggs in the early morning and, after an absence of four or five hours, returned at midday to incubate throughout the afternoon. On occasional inspections of several other nests, I found the eggs unattended in the forenoon.

Although incubating Little Tinamous usually seem to take a single long recess covering most of each forenoon, this schedule is not invariably followed. We have already noticed that one bird was on duty at 9:15 A.M., another at 8:10. At the end of February 1937, I made half-hourly visits to a nest in a canefield, where I had marked the attendant tinamou in the manner already described. At 7:25 A.M. and on eight subsequent visits, including one at 11:30, the marked bird was sitting on the single egg. At noon and on five later inspections, including one at 2:30, the egg was unattended. By 3:00, this egg had completely vanished, probably into the maw of a Zopilota, a large shiny black snake that I had glimpsed among the surrounding sugarcane. Another tinamou, found after he had started to incubate, sat for sixteen more days before an egg hatched. The full incubation period is probably about three days longer than this, as in other small tinamous.

The Chicks

In early September, a little boy led me to a tinamou's nest that his grandfather had found while cleaning a small and very weedy coffee plantation. The old man had permitted the sheltering herbage to stand uncut for about 2 feet (60 centimeters) around the nest. When I revisited this nest two weeks later, the parent sat until I almost touched him, then flew off in the usual abrupt manner. But within 4 or 5 feet (1.2 or 1.5 meters) he alighted, turned about ninety degrees, and slowly and deliberately walked past me with relaxed, quivering wings. His gait was steady and regular; he did not limp, drag his body, or act like an injured bird, except for the helpless attitude of his wings. In this manner he walked into the neighboring thicket, after giving me the only distraction display that I have seen any tinamou make.

In one of the two eggs which this bird had just left, the chick had already pierced the thick shell with a small hole and was peeping softly. When I returned from my cabin with my blind, the parent was again sitting on the eggs. The only spot where I could advantageously set the brown wigwam was just 4 feet (1.2 meters) from the incubating bird, who remained watching me while I arranged it. It seemed absurd to hide myself from a bird so confiding, but for observing his unconstrained behavior it was better to screen myself from his view.

When I finished setting up the blind and seated myself on a campstool within it, the hour was a few minutes past two in the afternoon. Soon the threatening rain fell and continued to fall through most of the afternoon. The drops that landed upon the tinamou's dark compact plumage gathered into crystal spheres and rolled off or, on the flat surface of his back, remained as shining beads, unable to spread and wet his well-oiled feathers.

For over two hours, the tinamou sat as motionless as a painted bird. Only the occasional blinking of his eyes revealed that he was alive. Finally, at five o'clock, he ended his long period of immobility, shook the glistening drops from his back, and rotated about forty-five degrees to his right. Darkness descended early beneath a heavily overcast sky. In the waning light, the tinamou started to whistle on the nest, at first faintly, then with increasing volume, while another tinamou answered with stronger notes from the neighboring thicket, without approaching the nest. After the bird in front of me had continued to whistle intermittently for about twenty minutes, he faded from view, and I stole away in the gloaming.

At dawn I resumed my vigil. Although I had not marked the tinamou at this nest, the bird now covering the eggs appeared to be the one that I had left at nightfall. He sat almost as motionless as on the preceding afternoon, but he turned his head more often and at times moved his body very slightly. Soon I heard the soft peeps of a chick. After a while, the newly hatched tinamou ruffled the feathers of its parent's side. Occasionally I glimpsed its bill or the top of its head, pushing up briefly through the outfluffed plumage that sheltered it.

In midmorning, the parent ended his long interval of quiescence. He shifted his position on the nest and vigorously preened his feathers, while the chick called more loudly. The parent's movements pushed out from beneath himself half of the shell from which the chick had emerged. After arranging his plumage for a few minutes, the adult stood up on his stout greenish yellow legs and revealed the chick, a cottony ball of softest down. With careful, deliberate steps, the parent advanced through the plantation toward the thicket, repeating at short intervals a low soft whistle. When he had covered about half the distance to the thicket, he stopped to look around and see whether his chick was following; but the latter, still hardly able to stand, was tumbling about in the tall weeds surrounding the nest and had made scarcely any progress. Accordingly, the parent returned to the nest and settled down to brood.

After covering the chick for a few minutes, the parent rose again and walked slowly toward the thicket, repeating the same low whistle at intervals of a few seconds. The downy one tried bravely to follow but was impeded by every slightest obstruction; when the parent reached the thicket, the chick was hardly clear of the tangled herbage that enclosed its natal spot. The parent walked a short distance into the thicket, then emerged to see how the little one was progressing. He did this twice more, constantly repeating his low whistles, while the chick answered with soft, rapidly delivered peeps. After every tumble it valiantly picked itself up and struggled toward its parent, but when about 4 feet (1.2 meters) from the nest it fell upon its side into a slight depression among decaying weed stems. Here it lay, trapped and unable to proceed.

Finding that his notes had lost their power

to draw the chick onward, the parent again returned from the thicket and settled on the nest, while the downy one continued to lie on its side and call. After sitting for about two minutes, the parent arose and walked back to the thicket. He did not again leave the shelter of the tangled bushes and creepers but walked around beneath them, frequently coming to the edge to look out and never ceasing to utter his magnetic whistle. At times he was answered by the full song of the other tinamou who frequented the thicket and was perhaps the chick's mother. However, as far as I saw, this bird took no maternal interest in the chick at this critical stage of its life.

When the chick, after struggling out of the little hollow into which it had fallen, was again approaching the thicket, the parent in charge came to a clear space at the edge and picked a small insect from the ground. He moved it between the tips of his mandibles while he uttered low coaxing notes; then, as well as I could see, he laid it on the ground, all much in the manner of a domestic hen calling her chicks to food. But the downy tinamou was still too far away, and too absorbed in the task of reaching the thicket, to respond to its parent's solicitation. Whenever it came to a little level ground, it ran ahead with mincing steps for a few inches, until it tripped over some slight obstruction or bumped into a higher one that blocked its progress and made it stagger around until it found an opening and could push onward. A medium-sized fallen banana leaf proved to be a major barrier and long delayed the chick, who had been out of the shell for much less than twenty-four hours. But, pushing dauntlessly forward, it at last gained the edge of the thicket where the parent awaited it, having taken more than half an hour to traverse 8 feet (2.4 meters) of uneven ground. It had not yet eaten.

For another half hour, I stayed in the blind and continued to hear the parent's low whistle and the chick's answering peep, without again seeing either of them. Finally going to the thicket to investigate, I found the parent sitting, as though brooding, in a little opening amid dense vegetation. When he arose at my approach, the expected chick was not beneath him. After a long search, I found it between two thin rotting logs that formed a trap into which it had fallen. It might have died there had I not picked it up and placed it where its parent had been sitting. Then I left. When I returned a few hours later, both parent and chick had vanished. The latter seemed excessively small and weak to face the perils of rough ground covered with rank tropical growth in which snakes and other enemies lurked, yet that a fair proportion of young survived this severe test was evident from the abundance of Little Tinamous in the valley of the Río Buena Vista (a tributary of the Río General), where I watched this absorbing episode.

After the single chick's departure, the second egg in this nest was abandoned. When convinced that it would not hatch, I opened it and found a well-formed embryo that had apparently died before the other egg hatched, rather than as a result of desertion.

While I held the downy chick admiringly in my hands, after rescuing it from the trap between the logs, I was tempted to make a drawing of its rather intricate markings. Then I remembered that, a few years earlier, I had sketched a tinamou chick in Guatemala, so I had no reason to keep this one from reaching its parent. I had found the

Little Tinamou: head of downy chick. Drawn by Gene M. Christman from author's field sketch.

Guatemalan chick a little before sunset on an evening in mid March, as I walked between a banana plantation and a second-growth thicket in the Motagua Valley. At my approach, the parent flew to a clear space about 50 feet (15 meters) ahead. When I reached the spot whence he had arisen, I detected the chick trying to hide among fallen banana leaves. It did not resist when I picked it up.

No bigger than a newly hatched domestic chick, the young tinamou was softly clad in long, dense, silky down. It had bright black eyes, a black bill, and black feet, each with a very short hind toe. The down on its back was dark, almost fuscous, with tawny spots, and its lower surface was chestnut. Its head was marked with certain conspicuous tawny areas, outlined in black, as in the accompanying sketch—markings wholly lacking in the adult tinamou. While I sketched, holding my notebook on my knee with my pencil hand and the chick in my left hand, it grew impatient and struggled mildly to escape, uttering a few weak peeps. When I had finished its portrait and set it on the ground, it proceeded to walk off alone. I retired a short distance and watched. After a few moments, the parent emerged from the bushes and led the chick off through the banana plantation. This occurred nearly fifty years ago. Although in most of the intervening years I have dwelt where Little Tinamous are abundant, I have not again seen a parent with young, except the one whose hatching I watched.

3. Gray-headed Chachalaca

Ortalis cinereiceps

Although most of the thirty-eight species of the tropical American guan family inhabit heavy forests, chachalacas prefer lighter vegetation. From eastern Honduras through eastern Nicaragua and the rainier parts of Costa Rica and Panama to extreme northwestern Colombia, Gray-headed Chachalacas and Little Tinamous are neighbors in light second-growth woods, tangled thickets almost impenetrable by humans, bushy abandoned fields, and forest edges. Although the tinamou is strictly terrestrial, the chachalaca is highly arboreal. Thickets where scattered, rapidly growing trees have succeeded in rising well above the riotous growth of scrambling shrubs and vines that would bear them down are especially attractive to this guan. How elegantly slender these long-tailed birds appear as, with graceful ease, they walk along a thin horizontal branch of one of the emergent trees or stand, two or three together, silhouetted against the sky in statuesque immobility! Their heads and upper necks are gray, their dorsal parts and breasts grayish brown, which becomes paler on the abdomen. Their grayish brown tail feathers are broadly tipped with dull white or buffy gray. The short thick bill is a pale bluish horn color. Each yellowish brown eye is surrounded by naked slate-colored skin, and the bare skin of the throat is red. The strong legs and toes are gray. Only when spread in flight do the wings reveal large areas of chestnut.

Sociable birds, chachalacas live at all seasons in parties of six to a dozen or more individuals. They do not travel in compact flocks, like many parrots, but straggle along one behind another, like toucans. When flying downward, they flap a few times, then set their spread wings for a long descending glide that displays the rich chestnut. On an upward course, they rarely fly far but ascend by short flights or leaps from branch to branch.

Fruits and foliage form the bulk of the chachalacas' diet. I have watched them peck away fragments or swallow whole green leaves of the Tuete, a tall shrubby com-

posite that in the dry season displays broad panicles of white flower heads. Another species of Compositae on which they browse is the yellow-flowered shrub *Oyedaea verbesinoides*. Leaf eating appears to be widespread in the guan family, as in other gallinaceous birds. I once watched three Crested Guans stuff themselves for half an hour with the tender young foliage of a vine that draped a tall dead tree at the forest's edge.

I have seen the chachalacas eat the hard, green, oily, olivelike drupes of the Olivo tree; the yellow fruits of tall Muñeco trees; the small red or black berries of *Hamelia patens*, a red-flowered shrub of the madder family; and the still smaller berries of *Miconia hyperprasina*, a shrub or small tree of the melastome family. They enter our dooryard to feast on fragrant Guavas, eating fruits that hang in the treetops rather than those that litter the ground. They share with a great variety of smaller birds the fingerlike green fruiting spikes of spindly Cecropia trees. When Pokeweed grows rankly in a recently burned clearing in the forest from which maize has been harvested, the chachalacas descend into the dense low growth to gather the small juicy black berries, then fly up into the trees at the edge of the clearing to rest and preen in the sunshine. Although they avoid the depths of closed forest, they enter its edges to pluck fruits from high treetops.

At intervals the chachalacas visit the nearest river. They walk along branches that stretch far out over the channel and stand upon boulders that rise above the rushing current. I once watched one pluck a large insect from a rock over which water was shallowly flowing. They gather from exposed patches of sand or gravel small objects that could be seeds, insects, or pebbles for grinding food in their stomachs. In the dry season, chachalacas who live high up on ridges descend in loose flocks, in the morning and again in the evening, to drink at the river. Their thirst quenched, they return to the second-growth thickets where they feel safer. In the rainy season, they seem to find enough water without visiting the larger streams.

Anybody who undertakes to describe the utterances of the Gray-headed Chachalaca wishes that at least one of them was as easily paraphrased as the stentorian *cha-cha-lac* of its northern relative, the Plain Chachalaca, or the similar call of the Rufous-vented Chachalaca of northern South America. But, curiously enough, these birds that occupy an intermediate range have no comparable note, nor do they engage in the bouts of calling in which many individuals over a wide area participate, the vocal outbursts surging back and forth perhaps for miles, in the dramatic fashion of certain of their congeners. There appears to be no good reason why Gray-headed Chachalacas cannot shout as loudly as any of them, for the males have the same elongated trachea, looped far back between the skin and the body before it enters the thorax.

Nevertheless, Gray-headed Chachalacas are noisy birds with a variety of utterances, most of them difficult to characterize. Frequently they deliver loud, rather high notes which seem like surprised complaints, disappointing to one who expects to hear a vigorous assertion similar to that of the northern species. Sometimes this chachalaca gives high-pitched, long-drawn-out squeals that sound like *oooeee* and are occasionally intensified to piercing screams. Or it may repeat a high soft *white white white white*. A flock of chachalacas resting and preening in the sunshine after their morning meal mingled loud harsh notes with others that were soft and low, including a sort of purr or rattle such as a domestic hen makes when she settles down to brood her chicks. Heard in the distance, the calls of this chachalaca have sometimes reminded me of the notes of the domesticated Guinea Fowl.

The Nest and Eggs

I have seen nests of the Gray-headed Chachalaca only from February to May; but its breeding season is longer than this, for I have watched half-grown birds in late January. The six nests that I have examined were situated in vine-draped bushes and small trees, in tangles of creepers, or in a large heap of dead branches, in or near the dense thickets which these birds frequent. These nests were from 3 to 8 feet (.9 to 2.4 meters) above the ground; three of them were between 4½ and 6 feet (1.4 and 1.8 meters) up. Broad shallow saucers, 9 to 12 inches (23 to 30 centimeters) in diameter, the nests were substantially made of a variety of coarse materials. The chachalaca builds with whatever suitable material is most easily available and often uses green vegetation. One nest suspended in a tangle of vines was composed chiefly of slender lengths of vine. Another was made of coarse sticks, pieces of vine, inflorescences, and, chiefly, leaves. Many of these leaves had apparently been plucked and placed in the nest while green, and in drying they had matted compactly together. The largest sticks were 13 inches (33 centimeters) long and as thick as a lead pencil. The lowest nest was composed chiefly of leafy grass stems, which seemed to have been gathered while green. The builder had also twisted into her structure the tops of some long slender grasses that grew beneath it; these remained alive and green.

Four nests held three eggs and two nests had two, but these small sets may have been incomplete, as they were in areas that had been disturbed by agricultural operations, in at least one case while laying was in progress. The large eggs are dull white, with a rough shell that is often heavily pitted. The depressions in the surface of the shell vary in size and density even in eggs of the same set; they may be small, deep, and crowded or larger and more scattered. Large and small pits are mixed together on some eggs, and I have seen sets without pits visible to the naked eye. One egg was sprinkled all over with embossed flecks of pure white, which varied in size from mere dots to flakes nearly a quarter of an inch (6 millimeters) in diameter and appeared to be composed of nearly pure lime. The second egg of the same set bore hardly any of these flecks, but it was much more densely pitted than the first egg. Even when devoid of visible pits or flakes, the shells are rougher than those of any other kind of egg that I have seen. Often chacha-

lacas' eggs, like those of Squirrel Cuckoos and anis, are heavily stained by the green vegetation on which they lie. Ten eggs averaged 58.2 by 40.3 millimeters, with extremes of 55.6 to 61.9 by 38.1 to 42.5 millimeters.

Incubation

By moonlight I entered a blind set in a bushy pasture. Dawn revealed a chachalaca incubating her three eggs in a nest 5 feet (1.5 meters) up in a vine tangle at the edge of the neighboring thicket, 30 feet (9 meters) away. When the beams of the rising sun fell upon her, she turned to face it. Soon she panted, her bare red throat distended and prominent. At intervals she preened. At 7:31 she left the nest for a recess that continued for an hour and a quarter. At 8:45 she returned alone, approaching her nest inconspicuously through the dense vegetation behind it. For the rest of the morning she sat without interruption, often panting with her neck stretched up, for this day in late March, the height of the dry season, was warm. Extremely sensitive to heat, the chachalaca continued to pant even when her nest was shaded. I had intended to watch throughout the day, but, soon after noon, smoke arising not far away caused me to leave the blind to assure myself that the fire was not on my land.

I watched this nest through most of the following day. Around sunrise, a flock of about six chachalacas passed twice through neighboring trees, calling softly. The bird on the nest seemed indifferent to these intruders, whose presence suggested that pairs of chachalacas do not defend territories; perhaps these birds are polygamous. Soon after the flock had passed, the incubating chachalaca left for the first of her daily outings, which lasted for an hour and two minutes, from 6:59 to 8:01. Her second recess was slightly longer, an hour and seventeen minutes, from 4:20 to 5:37 P.M. As the sun set, a Chestnut-mandibled Toucan sang in the top of a Cecropia tree behind the nest, then chased a chachalaca, perhaps the sitting bird's mate, from the treetop. As daylight faded, I left the parent sitting calmly.

After each outing, the chachalaca returned

to her eggs silently and alone. In watches totaling twenty-three hours, I had no indication that a second individual was interested in the nest, although the incubating bird was closely associated with her flock. She took a recess in the early morning and another in the late afternoon. The three that I timed lasted from sixty-two to seventy-seven minutes.

The Chicks

During the chachalaca's afternoon absence from her nest, I examined her eggs. The shells were not yet pipped, but I heard peeping and tapping sounds within them. Accordingly, early the following morning, I reentered the blind to witness their hatching. After sitting quietly for an hour and a half while the sun was low, the parent became restless, moving around on the nest and repeatedly rising to look beneath herself. Soon she picked up a piece of empty shell and laid it on the side of the nest. At 8:50 I first glimpsed a downy chick in front of her breast, and I heard soft peeps. An hour later, two chicks emerged in front of her, and in another ten minutes I saw three, their down already dry and fluffy. Now the parent sat high, with raised wings, and panted in the hot sunshine. When the chicks emerged in front of her, she gently nibbled the down on their heads. By 11:00 the restless chicks were often venturing out to move around beside her, panting as she did.

Soon after, the parent left the nest to eat berries from some bushes of *Hamelia patens* that grew a few yards away. She plucked both black ripe berries and red unripe ones, sometimes hanging head downward to reach them. The chicks peeped softly while she left them exposed. After an absence of four minutes, she returned to the nest, her bare red throat distended with berries. She moved a red berry forward to the tip of her bill and held it there for several seconds while she mashed it, then took it back into her throat. She did this again and again. Her chicks moved around in front of her and pecked at the berry in the tip of her bill, but, as far as I could see, they did not eat. Five minutes after

her return, the mother seemed to swallow all the berries, then panted.

Presently a chick climbed to a slender dead vine about an inch above the nest's rim and perched there, but it had difficulty keeping its balance, and in less than a minute it returned to the nest. At 12:52 the mother again left the nest to eat more berries of the *Hamelia*. In five minutes she returned to the nest, her throat swollen with berries, and again moved one to the tip of her bill. A chick reached up and appeared to take and eat the berry. The mother swallowed the remainder.

At 1:10 the parent left the nest and slowly climbed down through the tangled vegetation to the ground—a mode of departure that I had not previously witnessed. I did not see the chicks follow her. After an interval, I emerged from the blind to remove a vine that had slipped down and obstructed my view. The parent was on the ground a few yards from the nest, walking slowly away and calling softly. Without going near enough to see whether the chicks were still in the nest, I quickly returned to the blind and continued to watch intently. But, when nearly an hour had dragged by without another glimpse of a chick, I went to investigate. The chicks had vanished, leaving two empty shells in the nest and another beneath it. Evidently, they had left the nest along with their mother. Since, despite close watching through my binocular, I did not see them leave, I cannot tell whether they jumped down, climbed down through the tangled vegetation, or perhaps were carried down clinging to their parent. I was certain that she did not carry them down in her bill.

After such long and hopeful watching, it was exasperating not to have learned how the chicks left their nest. But, if I had set my blind closer or cleared away all the vegetation that impeded my vision, the chachalaca might have deserted her nest, and it would have been more visible to predators. (Often, when setting a blind before a nest, the watcher must weigh the desire for a near, clear view against the risk of endangering the nest.) At least, I had learned that the chicks left the nest considerably less than twenty hours after their escape from the eggs and that their mother led them away over the ground. How the chachalaca chicks reach the ground is the detail that remains to be elucidated. The other parent did not come to assist at this critical event, a fact which supports my conclusion that only one parent was interested in the nest.

At another Gray-headed Chachalaca's nest, found after incubation had begun, the chicks hatched twenty-two days later. The incubation period of the Plain Chachalaca in Texas is most often twenty-five days, with extremes of twenty-four and twenty-seven days (Marion and Fleetwood 1978).

On the evening after the departure of the three chachalaca chicks, I watched to learn whether they would return to their nest to be brooded. Neither parent nor chicks came near it. Whether the latter are brooded on the ground or, as with other guans, on a perch beneath a parent's sheltering wings I do not know.

After her chicks become mobile, the parent rejoins her flock with them. At first she seems to lead them over the ground, although ordinarily chachalacas forage chiefly in bushes and trees. While passing through second-growth woods in April, I met a chachalaca walking over the ground, followed by several young chicks, who vanished before I could see them well. A number of grown chachalacas were among neighboring trees.

Downy chicks, apparently only a few days old, hop and flit through close-set boughs and vines. One April a flock of chachalacas, frequenting my dooryard to eat Guavas, were sometimes accompanied by three young, each about the size of a Black-faced Antthrush. While the adults were in the Guava trees, the young birds waited in the nearby hedge, where they walked dexterously along slender branches, rapidly repeating a sharp, clear *pip pip pip*. Chachalacas are fed by their parents until they are quite large. In late January, I watched a half-grown chachalaca perch close beside an adult in a Tuete bush, while the latter plucked pieces of leaf and passed them to the juvenile. Later, the young bird foraged for itself. Parents appear also to help the young drink. One morning I watched an adult stand on a rock in midstream, with a half-grown bird, well feathered and with a conspicuously long tail, close beside her. Several times, when the adult raised her head after dipping into the river, the juvenile touched the adult's bill, evidently picking off drops of water, although I was too distant to see this detail.

Of the five chachalaca nests that I have followed, two produced three chicks each, and two were abandoned when the surrounding vegetation was cleared away to plant maize. The fifth nest was invaded by termites, which deposited much clay on the three eggs. The parent continued to incubate even after her eggs were heavily encrusted with soil, but after a few days they vanished.

Postscript

The shifting agriculture long practiced in the tropics, which destroys old forests but permits fields to lie unplanted until they become covered with thickets and light woods, has favored chachalacas at the expense of guans that require heavy forests. But, with swelling human populations, more intensive land use, and increasing mechanization of agriculture, fewer thickets and second-growth woods remain. Although chachalacas should survive after the forest-dwelling members of their family vanish, their future, too, is uncertain.

4. Marbled Wood-Quail

Odontophorus gujanensis

Rarely now, after the vesper song of the Great Tinamou has pealed through the forest, I hear, emerging from the darkening woodland, a flow of notes so beautiful and so expressive of mystery and urgency that, whatever I happen to be doing, I must pause and listen. *Burst the bubble burst the bubble burst the bubble* a full mellow voice seems to command many times over, so rapidly that I wonder how any creature can continue so long without running out of breath. Actually, the rapid performance is an antiphonal duet, the two partners singing alternately, fitting their notes together so exactly that the liquid undulatory flow seems to issue from a single throat.

Although the Marbled Wood-Quails' song is now so rarely heard, years ago, when the forests of El General were much more extensive and less ravaged by hunters and their dogs, it was one of the characteristic sounds. Most frequent in the gloaming, after most diurnal voices had been hushed for the night, it might be heard at any hour of the day, on a moonlit night, and more rarely on a dark and moonless night. I never succeeded in watching the quails as they sang, but sometimes their notes issued from the underwood into which I saw them disappear, only to cease before I could come in sight of the performers. Chapman (1929), watching a captive pair of wood-quails of a different race, noticed that "as one called *corcoro* the other added *vado*. The syllables were uttered rapidly, the timing was perfect, and the performance clearly revealed the method by which the song of this species is produced."

Here in the Valley of El General, near the northwestern limit of a range that extends to Bolivia and Amazonian Brazil, Marbled Wood-Quails were formerly abundant up to an altitude of about 3,000 feet (910 meters). A few decades ago, I often met them as I wandered through the forest. Usually they traveled in single file, in small coveys of from five to eight grown birds—I never encountered more. As I approached, they walked or ran rapidly away. They seemed reluctant to fly, but if I surprised them at close quarters, as when I suddenly loomed above them at a bend in a forest trail, they rose with a loud whir of wingbeats, ascended rarely higher than my head, and flew a short distance to vanish in dense undergrowth. At other times, they tried to escape detection by squatting amid brown leaf litter, with which they blended well; they remained immobile while I searched for them, to rise explosively when I came near. I was told that, when alarmed by man or dog, wood-quails rise to a low perch and freeze, sometimes permitting the intruder to approach and seize them by hand. Only the last solitary quail that I met, a few years ago, behaved this way. I did not try to catch the poor survivor of a vanishing race.

Nearly always, when I tried to follow a covey of wood-quails, they walked off through the dark underwood more rapidly than I could force my way through the tangled growth of bushes, vines, and the climbing fern *Salpichlaena volubilis*, so interesting to the botanist, so annoying to the bird watcher. In contrast to this elusiveness, on several occasions when I met quails at the forest's edge or a short way beyond it, they were amazingly confiding, affording unique opportunities to study their behavior.

The first of these encounters that I treasure in memory occurred over forty years ago, in the dry month of February. While roaming through a small grove of bananas, plantains, and coffee shrubs shaded by *Inga* trees, I fell in with a covey of five well-grown wood-quails, probably a family group. After a short, unhurried retreat, they paused to forage. Here in bright light, I saw them much better than I had on earlier meetings in dim forest. They were stout, compactly built birds, slightly larger than the Common Bobwhite. At a distance, they appeared rather bright brown, but a closer inspection revealed varying shades of browns and buffs, exquisitely blended in an intricate pattern that was flecked and vermiculated with black. Their breasts and bellies were finely and irregularly barred with buff or cinnamon-brown and black. Each quail had an erectile crest of long deep brown feathers. Each dark eye was surrounded by bare bright orange-red skin, deeper in hue on the male than on the female, who was also slightly smaller. All had short, stout, blackish bills and lead-colored legs.

As these wood-quails became accustomed to my presence, I approached closer, and soon I was following them at a distance of only 3 or 4 yards (2.7 or 3.6 meters), watching how they raked away the ground litter with long deliberate strokes of either foot, but never of both together, and picked up anything edible that they uncovered. At intervals one scrutinized me with large dark eyes and raised crest; but, after a few moments of this inquiring attitude, it calmly resumed its foraging. The quails advanced by short runs, with outstretched necks. Remnants of fallen bunches of green bananas, which had dried hard during many rainless weeks, provided much of their food. Industriously they pecked the white pulp from shriveled black skins. Apparently, they also ate insects attracted to these decaying fruits.

I was impressed by the amity that prevailed among these five birds, who usually foraged in a compact group, although at times one or two would wander off alone for a few yards. I did not notice the slightest display of aggressiveness or ill temper. No objection was raised when one individual approached to pick up food in a space which another had cleared, often while standing close beside the latter or even in contact with it and plucking the morsel almost from beneath its body. When one quail found something too big to swallow at a gulp, such as a small dry banana, it did not scurry off with its prize to escape the pecks of greedy neighbors, in the manner of domestic chickens, but ate in peace where the food happened to lie or amicably shared it with its companions. When a quail did carry a large piece of food, it was to follow its friends rather than to escape them. While they searched and ate, the quails constantly murmured low, soft, liquid sounds.

While I watched these wood-quails pecking at the remnants of a bunch of bananas long since fallen, a squirrel in the crown of a nearby banana plant noticed me and shouted harshly in alarm. Instantly four of the quails squatted down on the dry leaves in plain sight of me, while the fifth ran off behind the clump of bananas. I stood motionless, and soon the birds rose up to resume eating. Becoming bolder, the squirrel descended to the ground and approached the blackened remains of the raceme, for he also liked the hard white remnants of unripe pulp within the shriveled rinds. The quails hardly feared him. After the mammal approached within a foot of the nearest, it directed a peck toward him, and he withdrew slightly. When he again advanced, the nearest quail struck out with a wing in his direction and retreated a few inches; the squirrel stopped short; and the birds continued to eat. After they moved on, the rodent nibbled at what they had left.

For more than an hour, I accompanied these wood-quails closely until, in the failing light, they circled back to the forest's edge. Here they foraged for a while, then drifted farther inward, where tangled bushes and vines held me back. I could not discover how these wood-quails passed the night; but, higher in the mountains, I watched two orange-crested Spotted Wood-Quails fly at nightfall into a large tree, then rise from branch to branch until they were lost to my view in the high crown. Probably Marbled Wood-Quails likewise roost in trees, instead of sleeping on the ground, like bobwhites in the United States.

A few years later, I came upon six or seven Marbled Wood-Quails, all well grown if not mature, scratching among fallen leaves at the very edge of tall second-growth woods, beside a pasture. All stayed close together in friendly fashion, uttering soft, pleasant, contented notes. Presently one jumped upon a log, and soon another hopped up beside it. The second then bent down and billed its companion's legs and the feathers of its abdomen. After this had been repeated a few times, the first hopped upon a slender inclined trunk, up which it walked to a point where the trunk was horizontal, about a yard above the log. The other promptly joined it there, and they perched side by side, each alternately preening its own and the other's feathers. Each billed the plumage of its companion's head and of the abdomen between the legs, and each sometimes seemed to run its bill over the legs as well. Again and again, each bent forward to perform this service for its companion. After a while, a third quail joined the two on the stem and proceeded to preen as they did. The one in the center, in addition to its own, billed the feathers of both its neighbors and received this attention from each in turn. One of the end birds reached past the middle one to bill the legs of that on the other end. Soon a fourth joined the preening party on the slender trunk, while on the ground two others helped one another arrange their plumage.

As far as I could learn, these wood-quails lacked a pecking order, such as has been studied in domestic chickens and certain other birds, chiefly in the artificial situation of a poultry yard or a well-attended feeder. If a dominance hierarchy prevailed in the flock of wood-quails, it was subtle and well concealed. The cohesion of the group was preserved not by aggressive interactions but by sharing food and reciprocal services, such as mutual preening—friendly acts that seem much better fitted than aggression to hold individuals together. Similarly, in a flock of eleven Spotted-bellied Bobwhites that I watched closely, I noticed no suggestion of enmity.

The Nest and Eggs

The six nests of the Marbled Wood-Quail that I have seen in the Valley of El General held eggs from early January to June, but a family with downy chicks in mid October revealed that the breeding season continues into the rainiest months. Each nest was on the ground, beside a mound of earth raised by an uprooted tree, at the foot of a slope, beside a rock, or between projecting roots of a huge strangler fig tree. Usually the nest was in a deep accumulation of fallen leaves and twigs. In form it ranged from a domed structure with a side entrance to a pocket or even a tunnel, up to 11 inches (28 centimeters) long, with a diameter of about 5 inches (13 centimeters). The opening was about 4 inches (10 centimeters) wide. Often the eggs rested on finer dead leaves and other vegetable fragments below ground level, but whether the wood-quails scooped out a hollow or found one already made I could not learn. The leaves and twigs that thickly roofed the nests blended so well with the surrounding ground litter that the nest could have been formed simply by burrowing into this accumulation of forest debris, but green uprooted grasses in the roof of one nest indicated that at least some of the material had been placed there by the quails, perhaps in the manner of which I shall soon tell.

These nests were so excellently concealed, and the incubating parent sat so steadfastly, that one could walk close by them without suspecting their presence. While I searched for a nest between the sinuous woody ridges formed by the roots of a great fig tree, not without unpleasant thoughts of lurking venomous snakes, a trespassing dog came running up, and with a whir of wings the quail rose almost under its nose. I had passed unsuspectingly close in front of her nest without making her flee. On several occasions, the presence near the nest of the incubating quail's mate or companions caused me to search until I found it.

Two of my nests were visited by predators before the sets were complete. Three other nests held four eggs, and one had five. The eggs were laid at intervals of one or more days. At the nest with the largest set, the fifth egg was laid four days after the fourth, possibly by a second hen, as three individuals were closely associated with several of the nests. The eggs, which taper strongly toward the small end, are pure white and at best only slightly glossy. Brown stains result from contact with damp leaves. Eighteen eggs that I measured averaged 38.9 by 28.5 millimeters, with extremes of 36.5 to 42.9 by 27.4 to 30.2 millimeters.

Incubation

Only the first of my nests was successful, rather surprisingly, as it was in the most disturbed area. The forest on the ridge between the Río Buena Vista and the Río Chirripó, where it was situated, had been thinned by lumbering; and, not far away, two men worked almost daily, noisily ripping boards with a long saw from logs raised upon a scaffold. The parent quail continued to sit while I looked at her with my head hardly a yard from hers, and she permitted me to place a white spot on her breast with paint-soaked cotton on the end of a stick, as I did with the Little Tinamou. Likewise, she sat motionless while I arranged my blind only 8 feet (2.4 meters) in front of her. After she had been incubating a week, I arrived at dawn to find her absent, her four eggs cold but intact, the forepart of her roof torn away, and a few downy feathers scattered around the entrance. Evidently, she had been attacked in the night, but the absence of bloodstains gave me hope that she had escaped without serious injury. Later that day, she resumed incubation.

Beginning in January 1937, in twenty-six hours of watching from the blind, and on many visits of inspection, I found only the marked female in this nest. She sat so deeply in the depression in the earth, always facing outward, that her head was level with the ground in front. Peering intently into the blackness framed by the round doorway, even when the sun was bright, I could discern little more than the orange-red skin around her eyes and the shiny ridge of her bill. On cloudy afternoons she was nearly or quite invisible, so close in front of me. Leaves lying loosely before her doorway often improved her concealment, but the effectiveness of this screen varied from day to day, for reasons that will presently appear. She always incubated in perfect silence. When I arrived at dawn, my flashlight revealed that she slept with her head turned back among her feathers.

Each day, around sunrise, this female's mate came to call her from the nest, uttering a prolonged *caaa caaa caaa* (the *a* as in *draw*) which, when first heard, I surmised was the voice of some bird calling from much farther away. After this had continued for some minutes, the female would arise and walk straight toward me, then, with a sudden whir of wings, rise steeply and fly over my blind or, after she became more accustomed, walk past it. In either case, she called *witty witty witty*, sometimes followed by *caaa* notes, and appeared to join her mate. With more *caaa*'s and low, liquid notes of greeting, they walked off through the forest together.

After stepping from her nest, the female often picked fallen leaves from the ground in front of her and, with an upward toss of her head, threw them over her back, so that some fell on the roof of the nest behind her but, as she continued to move forward and toss, others fell short. Sometimes this random procedure improved the nest's concealment, but on other days it removed screening leaves and left the doorway more exposed. Such sideward tossing is widely used by birds who build artless nests on the ground (Skutch 1976).

On four mornings, the female left her nest at times ranging from 6:07 to 6:15. The hour of her return fluctuated from 7:55 to 9:10. Her single daily absence varied from one hour and forty minutes to three hours and three minutes, during which her eggs became quite cold. Her mate always escorted her to near the nest, repeating his low *caaa caaa caaa*. As she walked toward her doorway, the female voiced her liquid *witty witty witty* or, more rarely, *caaa*'s in rising sequence. Then she settled on her eggs, facing outward, to sit quietly for the remainder of the day. I never found her absent after midmorning. Even many small brown ants crawling over her head, as I noticed one day, hardly disturbed her. Her only movement was to blink her eyelids when ants walked over them.

When he came to call the female from her

eggs at sunrise or escorted her back to them, the male (whom I learned to recognize by the larger area of bare skin around his eyes) always stopped short several yards from the nest, thereby reducing the risk of betraying its location. Often I heard his voice but failed to see him. Toward the end of the incubation period, I noticed on several mornings that he was accompanied by a third grown wood-quail, whose relationship to the mated pair I could not learn. After the female's return from her morning outing, the male and his companion stayed beyond sight and hearing for the remainder of the day.

On frequent visits to two other nests, I consistently found the parent absent early in the morning but always sitting on the eggs after midmorning. One wood-quail sat behind a big yellow fallen leaf that completely covered her doorway, leaving nothing to reveal her presence amid a deep accumulation of dead leaves.

The Chicks and Their Departure

Early on February 11, I found all four eggs in my first nest slightly chipped. Holding them to my ears, I heard tapping sounds and weak peeps. By the following morning, the peeps and tapping sounds were more frequent and stronger, the shells more extensively fractured, but none was yet pierced. Arriving at dawn on February 13 to watch the emergence of the chicks, I found the hen sitting quietly, but with her head and foreparts much more exposed than on previous mornings. Soon after six o'clock, the male's subdued *caaa caaa caaa* announced his arrival. For many minutes he continued to call and to move around in the undergrowth, as I could tell by the sounds of rustling leaves, without coming into view of the blind. At half past six, the first level rays of the rising sun darted between the tree trunks and cast bright circles here and there upon the foliage in front of me. Overhead, a Garden Thrush proclaimed his presence in triumphant song— the year's first. After a while, the male wood-quail punctuated his numerous *caaa*'s with a note new to me: a low deep *cahoo*, several times repeated.

After the male had been calling and waiting patiently beyond my view for over half an hour, his mate at last answered. She whispered *caaa*, then murmured softly in a liquid voice. Now his excitement increased; he moved more rapidly through the undergrowth, as I could tell by the rustle of dry leaves. Then, revealing himself for the first time, he passed quickly behind the nest, closely followed by the third quail.

Now the female quail, with more low murmuring, rose and pushed halfway out of the nest. The chicks, who had escaped from the shells since her return to resume incubation on the preceding morning, needed no urging to leave. One pushed out beneath her while she paused in the doorway, picking up leaves and sticks from the ground in front of her and tossing them backward upon the roof. Then she stepped forth quite clear of the nest, and four downy chicks tumbled out around her. As she advanced, uttering her low, liquid *witty witty witty*, she continued to pick up dead leaves and toss them backward. It appeared that she did this to clear a path for her chicks' first steps; more probably, she merely persisted in an old habit. Yet she continued to throw back the leaves until she had advanced at least 4 feet (1.2 meters) from the nest, much farther than I had seen her do this before.

The chicks were tiny chubby creatures, clad in soft down marked in a pattern of black and buff. The top of the head and the back were blackish, with a narrow white line along either side of the back. The cheeks and sides of the neck were buff. I could not distinguish the pattern on the underparts. As their mother walked slowly forward, uttering her liquid notes, the chicks easily followed, with an intermittent and jerky movement compounded of short forward runs and brief pauses. The male, murmuring excitedly, advanced into the clear space to meet his family. The third quail took less interest in the proceedings.

The mother turned to her right and crossed a long, low, decaying log. After a few ineffectual trials, three of the chicks managed to scramble over its sloping, creviced side and dropped down to clear, level ground beyond. But the last was arrested by this obstacle that stretched for a long way to right and left. Apprised by the chick's weak peeps of its distress, the father returned to it, while the mother continued slowly onward with the other three. He stood upon the log, looking down, while the chick struggled along the barrier, first to one side and then to the other, until at last it found a spot where pits in the decaying surface helped it scramble up and over. Then, following its father, it hurried after the rest of the family.

As they crossed a level space carpeted with fallen leaves, the father scratched the litter aside and called to his chicks, but they did not try to pick anything up. All too soon, they passed beyond my narrow circle of vision in the dense undergrowth.

I had brought drawing paper to sketch one of the chicks, should opportunity arise. I was sorely tempted to hurry from my blind and catch the chick who was delayed by the log, to make a drawing of it, then release it. But I desisted, remembering that the tiny chicks would be exposed to countless perils during their first day of wandering through the forest and that any disturbance would diminish their chances of survival. I preferred to remember them as, unaware that they were being watched, their parents led them forth upon their perilous career, to the accompaniment of the soft murmurous music of subdued liquid voices. This comfortable, soothing crooning of the parents continued to reach me for a while after the family had vanished; but soon it, too, was extinguished by distance and the denseness of the foliage.

The incubation period at this nest was between twenty-four and twenty-eight days. I am aware of no other determination of this period for any species of *Odontophorus*, but that of the Common Bobwhite is generally given as about twenty-four days.

After leaving the nest, the downy young are led through the forest by their parents, often in company with the covey; I repeatedly saw recently hatched chicks traveling with five or six grown quails. When accompanied by young, the adults are more than ordinarily shy and difficult to watch, but I suspect that all the grown birds help the chicks find food. Whenever I approached a group of quails with chicks, an adult remained behind, running back and forth through the undergrowth at no great distance from me and seeming to try to draw attention to itself without incurring too much risk, while the others led away the downy ones and quickly vanished amid the vegetation. If a chick lagged behind or was cut off from the flock, usually a single adult remained and tried to lead it to safety. This strategy usually succeeded, and it was exceedingly difficult to catch a downy chick. Sometimes, when the adults' behavior left no doubt that they were accompanied by young, I searched in vain for them, while a grown bird moved around just beyond reach, showing the greatest solicitude for the chicks that I could not see. From the behavior of the pair whom I watched as they led their brood from the nest, I believe that the female walks off with the chicks, while the male stays behind to distract the attention of hostile eyes and take care of laggards.

One midday in early November, a loud, clear, rapidly repeated whistle made me search until I found a wood-quail where I never expected one—on the rafters above a porch. Less than half-grown but fully feathered, it had evidently sought refuge there when pursued by intruding hounds that had been making a hideous din in the nearby forest. On the lawn beside the house, more exposed than I had ever seen a wood-quail, an adult continued to call softly, trying to induce the youngster to come down. But the terrified young bird remained aloft until I climbed up to rescue it, when it managed to squeeze between a wall and the roof and escape. Then the faithful adult led it back to the woods.

Postscript
Although a few Marbled Wood-Quails linger in the old forest and taller second growth, they have become so excessively shy that I no longer have the intimate meetings with them that I formerly enjoyed. Such charming birds, so devoted to their young, deserve a better fate than the near extinction to which they have been reduced over the wide areas where, not long ago, they were abundant.

5. Scaled Pigeon

Columba speciosa

Although beautiful in their softly blended neutral colors, the pigeons of the western hemisphere cannot vie in splendor and ornateness with those of the islands of the southwestern Pacific and neighboring regions. One of the most handsome of the American representatives of the family, however, is the Scaled Pigeon. The male is clad in rich shades of chestnut and brown, glossed on the neck with purple and green, with scalelike markings of black and white or cinnamon-rufous on the neck, upper back, and breast. The female's colors are similar but paler. Both have brown eyes ringed with bare red skin and red bills, legs, and feet. Although individuals from the same region exhibit considerable diversity in plumage, throughout its immense range from southern Mexico to Paraguay the species is so uniform that no geographical races are recognized. An inhabitant of the wooded lowlands of continental America, this 12-inch (30-centimeter) pigeon ranges upward to 4,000 or 5,000 feet (1,200 or 1,500 meters) in southern Central America and northern South America.

Todd and Carriker (1922) mentioned a flock of no fewer than one hundred Scaled Pigeons, which in early November roosted on a scrubby hillside at an altitude of about 1,500 feet (450 meters) in the Santa Marta region of northern Colombia; but such concentrations appear to be rare even there. In northeastern Venezuela this pigeon was found in small flocks of fewer than ten individuals, always in the rather heavy woods of the ravines which cut back into the savanna of the mesa (Friedmann and Smith 1955). In the Valley of El General and other parts of southern Pacific Costa Rica, which seems to be the only section of the country where the Scaled Pigeon is somewhat common, I have usually met it singly or in pairs—once I saw six flying together, never more. Here I often see the splendid bird perching conspicuously on a dead limb at the very top of a tall tree at the forest's edge, with the sky as its background, or flying swiftly and directly across a clearing, above reach of the hunter's gun. This bird is largely frugivorous and appears to find most of its food high in trees. Recently I watched a single Scaled Pigeon spend many minutes gathering berries at the top of a small tree of the melastome family, in the midst of the forest. I have never seen it on the ground.

The Scaled Pigeon's call, heard chiefly in the dry season and the early part of the wet season, from January to April or May, is a deep, full, far-carrying *cooo-cu-cooo*, several times repeated. Comparing this booming sound to the lowing of distant cattle, Friedmann and Smith state that in northeastern Venezuela it has earned the bird the appellation *paloma tora* ("bull pigeon"). In the Valley of El General, however, it is called *paloma morada* ("purple pigeon").

Nesting

Strangely enough, this pigeon that spends most of its life high in the giant trees of the rain forest often nests near the ground, in secondary vegetation. I have often watched a solitary bird struggle to break a twig from a high dead branch at the forest's edge, then fly down into a neighboring second-growth thicket with its single piece. Sometimes the pigeon has traveled over the low tangled growth for 200 or 300 yards (180 or 270 meters) before vanishing amid the foliage, where doubtless its mate was waiting to receive the contribution and arrange it in the growing nest. But the almost impenetrable density of the rank intervening vegetation, often a two- or three-year-old growth on a resting grainfield, discouraged my attempt to find the nest by following the flight of the building pigeon.

Over the years, however, I have discovered thirteen of these nests in the Valley of El General, between 2,500 and 3,000 feet (760 and 910 meters) above sea level. Two of the nests were situated at a height of 15 feet (4.5 meters) in Sotacaballo trees growing on the shore of the broad, rushing Río Buena Vista. One was far out on a lower branch, the other in a tangle of vines that had overgrown the tree. Possibly in former times, when forests were more continuous, Scaled Pigeons built their nests amid such streamside vegetation; now many have taken to nesting in the low second-growth thickets that soon cover abandoned croplands and neglected pastures. Of the eleven nests not beside a river, five were built at heights ranging from 7 to 15 feet (2.1 to 4.5 meters) in tangles of vines covering bushes and small trees in second-growth thickets. One nest was lower and more exposed, only 2 feet (60 centimeters) above the ground on the leaning stalks of a cluster of Bracken fern, in a bushy field from which maize had been harvested only seven months earlier.

The last five nests were in very different situations. Four were from 50 to 150 feet (15 to 45 meters) up in the tops of trees so densely covered with lianas that the nests were hardly visible from the ground. Three of these nests were in a small grove of secondary woods between coffee plantations, about 600 feet (180 meters) from the nearest forest, whence the materials for building at least one of them were carried across an intervening pasture. The highest nest was at the vine-smothered top of a huge Mastate tree in the forest. Another nest was about 40 feet (12 meters) up on a spiny frond of a Pejibaye palm in a coffee plantation, so well concealed near the center of the palm's crown that I could detect only a red-rimmed eye of the incubating pigeon.

The accessible nests were broad, slightly concave platforms composed of fine twigs and branched dry inflorescences, in one instance of the Burío, a tree with very soft wood. Nearly always thin, some of the nests were so slightly constructed as to be hardly more than latticework for supporting the egg. In one nest, the largest stick measured 10 inches in length by 3/16 inch in diameter at its thicker end (25 by .5 centimeters).

Five of these nests held a single white egg each, and three had solitary nestlings. The earliest nest contained an egg on February 21, 1937, and the latest of the accessible nests had an egg on May 22, 1936. A high nest was built in July, two others in August. At one of the latter, the pigeons were incubating or brooding young in early September. Single eggs are laid in Belize, Surinam, and aviaries (Russell 1964; Haverschmidt 1968; Goodwin 1967). Belcher and Smooker (1936) reported two sets of two eggs in Trinidad, where a number of species of birds occasionally or regularly produce larger sets than I have discovered in Costa Rica. The nests described by these authors were fairly substantial platforms of twigs, from 30 to 40 feet (9 to 12 meters) up in smallish trees in the forest of Trinidad. The eggs measured 37.4 to 40 by 29.1 to 29.9 millimeters.

When I visited a pinfeathered chick at one of my low nests, it tried to intimidate me by an impressive display. It rose in the nest, stretched up its neck, puffed out its breast, and lifted its wings, all of which made it look much bigger than it did while resting quietly. In this attitude it swayed upward and backward, downward and forward, and with each forward and downward movement it made a low clicking or clacking sound with its bill. As long as it felt itself menaced, the nestling continued to perform rhythmically in this fashion. The clack was produced in a peculiar manner. The lower mandible was pushed slightly forward, until its apex rested against the downwardly bent tip of the upper mandible. The bill was then slightly open. Apparently, the two mandibles were pressed together until the lower one slipped back into its normal position; and the two, striking together along their entire length, emitted the

sharp sound. The nestling also darted forward to peck my intruding hand with its bill; and, after its feathers began to expand, it struck with its wings. Taken in hand, it struggled vigorously, without ceasing to clack its bill, and at the same time it hissed slightly. Doubtless, all this belligerent display intimidates small animals, yet some nestlings are taken by predators.

During the first week or so after the nestling hatches, the parents apparently remove its droppings, for the frail platform remains clean, although the empty shell may be left

there for several days. Later, the adults relax their attention to sanitation, with the result that a nest from which the young pigeon has just flown is foul with excrement. I do not know the length of the nestling period; but one nestling, who appeared to be only a few days old when first found, was found two weeks later resting a yard from its nest, well clothed with feathers. It watched me come near, then flew well. Its plumage was a warm shade of brown but lacked the light markings that impart a scaly appearance to the adults.

6. Red-billed Pigeon

Columba flavirostris

Viewed in sunshine, the prevailing deep vinaceous purple of the Red-billed Pigeon, contrasting with the bluish gray of its rump and upper tail coverts, makes it outstandingly beautiful. At least as applied to the Costa Rican race, the Latin *flavirostris* is more accurately descriptive than the English "Red-billed," for in the field the bill appears pale yellow rather than red. The eyes are orange or reddish orange, the legs and toes dark red. This 13-inch (33-centimeter) pigeon ranges from the lower Rio Grande Valley in Texas to central Costa Rica. In the north it inhabits more or less arid country, mainly below 3,500 feet (1,050 meters). At the southern extremity of its range, it spreads from the semi-arid lowlands of Guanacaste to the central valley of Costa Rica and over the surrounding deforested mountains, up to about 7,000 feet (2,150 meters). It has even become estab-

lished in clearings in the heavy rain forest on the wet Caribbean slope. In 1938, on the excessively wet northern side of the Cordillera Central, I did not find this pigeon between July and March, but at the end of the latter month a pair arrived in the subtropical forest where I dwelt. These pigeons perch high in the trees, singly or in pairs, rarely in larger groups. Their song is loud, deep-toned, and far-carrying: *woooo, c'c'coo, c'c'coo, c'c'coo.* A shorter version consists of a long-drawn-out, sonorous, ascending note followed by three shorter notes: *cooo cu cu coo.* Their food includes mistletoe berries, other small fruits, acorns, and buds.

Nesting
In the valley of the Río Pejivalle, on the Caribbean slope of Costa Rica at an altitude of about 2,100 feet (640 meters), I found a pair

building a nest on April 15, 1941. Their site was about 80 feet (24 meters) up in a crotch of a tall dead tree standing beside a stream that flowed through a pasture. Here it was above the foliage of all the surrounding streamside trees but well screened by the ferns, bromeliads, and other epiphytes that grew on the dead tree. In midmorning, one member of the pair went to the nest with an empty bill, then promptly left, perched on the end of a dead branch, and called with deep resonant notes, which soon drew its mate. The first pigeon then flew up beside the new-comer and crouched, and after a while the latter acceded to this invitation and mounted its companion. Presently they reversed roles, the one who had been below mounting the one who had been on top. Thus, to my regret, I could not distinguish the sexes by their positions in coition. Soon they proceeded to

build. While one member of the pair sat continuously on the nest, the other made five trips, each time bringing a single fairly large twig and delivering it to the stationary partner for arrangement in the structure. In this same locality, a week later, I noticed another pair building high in a clump of thorny Pejibaye palms growing in a field of sugarcane on a hillside. Screened by the clustered, plumelike fronds, the nest was wholly invisible from the ground.

From 1937 to 1954, I found seven nests at the hacienda Las Cóncavas, a few miles east of Cartago, at an altitude of about 4,500 feet (1,370 meters). Here the breeding season was long, for one pair seemed to be incubating as early as March 26, 1952, while in other years eggs were present as late as mid August. One nest was in a *Callistemon* tree in the garden; one was in a young cypress in a hedgerow; and the remaining five were in a long narrow plantation of half-grown cypresses in the midst of open pastures. This dense planting was a favorite site—here I discovered three nests on June 28, 1937, two on August 14 of the following year. The nests in the young cypress trees were built on slender horizontal branches from 7 to 15 feet (2.1 to 4.5 meters) above the ground, and that in the garden was 25 feet (7.6 meters) up. These nests, made of coarse sticks, were thin frail platforms, one of which measured 7 by 9 inches (18 by 23 centimeters) in diameter. I never found more than one egg or chick in a nest, and this is the number which the Redbill lays in the northern parts of its range. One pure white egg measured 40.5 by 26.6 millimeters.

Nests with still featherless young were quite clean, although sometimes a few droppings, probably from the parents, lodged on the supporting branch beside them. But, when older, feathered nestlings were present, the nest was heavily soiled around the edges although clean in the center. From this it appears that parent Red-billed Pigeons, like parent Scaled Pigeons, attend to the sanitation of the nest while the nestlings are young but neglect this after they are older. When disturbed, feathered nestlings rose up, stretched out their necks, and made clacking sounds with their bills, not so loud as those of young Scaled Pigeons. They struck and bit my intruding fingers, not hard enough to hurt.

The parent Red-billed Pigeons were most attentive, and on several visits I found one of them brooding, or at least resting beside, a well-feathered nestling. The situation of the nests in the cypress plantation surrounded by broad open fields was favorable for distraction displays, and these parents made the most of it. While brooding, they permitted me to come very close; sometimes I had to shake their tree to make them reveal what they were covering. Leaving the nest, they fluttered across the open pastures, beating their wings loosely as though scarcely able to fly yet skimming over the short grass at a good speed. Thus they led me for 100 feet (30 meters) or more, until they reached a bush or low tree, where they alighted but continued to flap their wings in a loose and apparently uncoordinated fashion, while they watched my advance. When I came closer than they deemed safe, they dropped down and again flew low over the pastures until they came to the next bush that offered a limb for perching, and here they paused and fluttered their wings as before. At times they made still a third fluttering flight, before at last they flew off in their normal way, leaving me several hundred yards from the nest where I had disturbed them. A parent of a feathered nestling, who had lured me away in this fashion, returned while I examined its nest ten or fifteen minutes later, perched at the top of a neighboring cypress tree, and flapped its wings loosely, as it had done while tolling me off in the first place.

A more spectacular performance was given one day when a dog followed me into the cypress plantation. At my approach, a pigeon dropped from beside its feathered nestling almost to the ground. As it descended, the dog jumped toward it, and to save itself the bird had to flee more rapidly than it could do while fluttering over the ground in the usual distraction display. But it flew slowly, only a foot or so above the grass, and tolled the dog, which continued to follow with a high hope of catching the pigeon, until the two had passed over the boss of the hillside and were beyond my view.

7. Short-billed Pigeon

Columba nigrirostris

Above the cicadas' strident chorus of sizzles and chirrs, which fills the Central American rain forests through the dry early months of the year, sounds a far-carrying melodious call of four syllables that, to one who has wandered much through these majestic woods, becomes indissolubly associated with them. I learned long ago from a great lover of these forests, Frank M. Chapman, to paraphrase this most distinctive pigeon's song as *O je t'adore*. Less romantic was the interpretation of the boys who used to help me collect plants and find birds' nests in the

Valley of El General: they insisted that the pigeon proclaimed *tres tontos son* ("they are three fools"). Both of these renderings fit the call so well that I rarely hear it without mentally repeating one or the other. Eisenmann's (1952) paraphrase, *ho, cu-cu-coóoo*, is equally accurate but less easy to remember. Sometimes, when I have heard two of these pigeons answering each other with similar phrases, the voice of one, probably the male, has sounded deeper than that of his mate. A growling *grrr* is sometimes interspersed with the more melodious notes.

From southern Mexico to northwestern Colombia, the author of this appealing song is the most abundant pigeon in the upper levels of many of the wetter forests, from the lowlands up to about 4,500 feet (1,370 meters) in southern Central America. Becoming rarer at the higher altitudes, it mingles with, and is then replaced by, the Ruddy Pigeon of the epiphyte-burdened mountain forests, which is confusingly similar in both appearance and voice, although its notes are harsher. One of the smaller members of the genus

Columba, the 11-inch (28-centimeter) Short-billed Pigeon is nearly everywhere warm brown, tinged with purple on its neck and back and with vinaceous shades on its breast. Its bill is black, its eyes bright red, and its legs and toes coral red. Similar in plumage, the male and female live in pairs throughout the year. Perching close together, they nibble the feathers of each other's head and neck. I have never seen these pigeons in flocks.

From the upper levels of the rain forests that are their true home, Short-billed Pigeons enter neighboring clearings to eat the small green or orange berries of mistletoes that often parasitize the scattered trees, as well as the tiny black berries of *Miconia minutiflora*, an arborescent melastome. To break pieces from the dangling green fruiting spikes of Cecropia trees, they sometimes hang head downward. They descend low to eat berries of the Pokeweed, which springs up profusely on scorched land from which a crop of maize has been harvested. Rarely, these pigeons of treetops drop to the ground to gather fallen berries. Once I watched a pair alight on a sandy patch of shore beside a mountain torrent, to pick up small objects which may have been gravel or insects.

Nesting

Early on a March morning, I watched a Shortbill break pieces from old inflorescences of a Burío tree that stood in tall second-growth woods, about 100 yards (92 meters) from the old forest. To detach part of a many-branched dry panicle was strenuous labor, and sometimes the pigeon tugged at branch after branch before he found one that yielded to his efforts. Having procured a branching piece of inflorescence, he flew down into a dense tangle of vines, shaded by taller trees, at a point about 25 feet (7.6 meters) above the ground. After much moving through the resisting undergrowth, I found a spot whence I could glimpse this pigeon's mate, who sat amid the vines, received the pieces that the other brought, and worked them into what obviously was the foundation of a nest. In two hours, the active partner presented at least seventeen contributions, but never more than one branching piece on

a journey, as far as I could see. Sometimes he seemed to stand on the other's back while he delivered it, but obstructing vegetation did not permit a clear view of the transaction. The partner who took charge of arranging the material remained on the nest continuously throughout the two hours that I watched. At the end of this interval, I was forcing my way rather noisily through the undergrowth toward the neighboring road, when the member of the pair who had been fetching material began to call *O je t'adore*, while the mate answered from the nest with a throaty, growling note. This strengthened my conclusion that the more active partner was the male, as in a number of other pigeons and doves where the sexes differ in appearance.

On August 10 of the following year, I watched a Short-billed Pigeon break twiglets from a dead branch at the top of a small tree in the forest. He had chosen a Cacique, a tree of the myrtle family which has very tough wood, and he struggled hard to detach pieces, trying twig after twig, sometimes hanging head downward with spread wings while he threw all his weight against the obstacle. With indomitable persistence, he continued until he secured a fragment of the branch, which he then promptly carried up to the crown of a tall Mastate tree that grew nearby, into the midst of which he vanished. Soon he returned to the same dead branch for another twiglet. Several that were easily broken off he dropped, but at last a satisfactory one was obtained and borne up into the same great tree. Here, somewhere about 100 feet (30 meters) above the ground, his mate was evidently sitting to receive and arrange the materials which he continued to bring to her, but she was perfectly concealed amid the heavy masses of foliage into which the pigeon each time disappeared.

Nests placed as high as those of the Short-billed Pigeon, amid such dense foliage, are not often found after completion, when the parents' visits to them are much less frequent. The single egg of which I have found a record, collected at Almirante in northwestern Panama, was plain white and 36.3 by 24.7 millimeters (Wetmore 1968).

8. Band-tailed Pigeon
Columba fasciata

Standing in statuesque immobility on the topmost bough of a towering tree, its stout grayish body silhouetted against the sky, the large Band-tailed Pigeon is a vision of alert freedom, fit to quicken and inspire the spirit of a poet. Its deep mellow *c'coooo c'coooo* fills all the air. A good binocular reveals, even at this great height, the white crescent on the bird's nape and the narrow blackish band across the middle of its tail, the apical half of which is much paler than the gray base. A closer approach is needed to see that its eyes are yellow, its bill yellow with a dark tip, and its legs and toes deep yellow. With loudly flapping wings, the wary bird takes flight and, making a rattling sound that seems to be vocal, swiftly crosses the valley to the opposite ridge. Would anyone sensitive to nature's grandeur trade such a vision for a pot of flesh?

From Vancouver Island and southwestern British Columbia, Band-tailed Pigeons range through the mountainous west of the United States, Mexico, Central America, and northern and western South America into northwestern Argentina. Although near their northern limit they occur at low altitudes, throughout the tropics they are confined to the mountains and, as with other widely distributed highland birds, the discontinuity of the mountain ranges has favored the evolution of a number of geographic races. In Arizona and New Mexico, these pigeons nest above 7,000 feet (2,150 meters) and have been found as high as 11,000 feet (3,350 meters). In Middle America and northern South America, they live chiefly between 5,000 and 10,000 feet (1,500 and 3,000 meters) but occasionally descend to 3,000 feet (910 meters) and, rarely, a few hundred feet lower. In northern Central America, they prefer the zone of mixed woodland, where pines grow amid oaks and other broad-leaved trees. I found them also about the margins of the vanishing forests of great cypress trees on high mountain tops. South of Nicaragua, where native pines and cypresses are absent, they are closely associated with the oaks that dominate the forests above 5,000 or 6,000 feet (1,500 or 1,800 meters). In large flocks they spread over the cold paramos above the tree line in search of berries, and at lower altitudes they are often seen in clearings with scattered trees.

Band-tailed Pigeons eat a variety of small fruits, often descending almost to the ground to gather them from low shrubs. In Guatemala I watched them plucking the berries of mistletoes and surprised them in fruiting bushes of *Fuchsia arborescens* and a species of *Cestrum*; but they were too wary to continue eating the small black berries of the first, or the white berries of the second, while I watched. While walking over the open summit of Cerro de las Vueltas in the Talamancan range of Costa Rica in March, I saw hundreds of these pigeons, attracted by the small fruits of a bushy Pokeberry that flourished there.

When acorns are available, they appear to be the Band-tailed Pigeons' preferred food.

In late September, when the abundant oak trees on the Sierra de Tecpán in Guatemala were laden with ripening acorns, flocks of these pigeons settled in the treetops and tried prematurely to pluck them. Perching precariously near the ends of the twigs, they grasped the acorns in their bills, making strenuous but, as far as I could see, always unsuccessful attempts to detach them. While trying to pull the acorns from their cups, the heavy birds often lost their balance and moved with loudly flapping wings to another perch. A party of a score or more made a great commotion in the treetops. Six weeks later, when the ground was littered with fallen acorns, the pigeons still gathered them from the treetops—the birds stood far out on the twigs, plucked the acorns from their sockets, and swallowed them whole. Now that the fruits were so easily detached, the birds foraged so silently that I might pass beneath a tree where a dozen were feasting without becoming aware of them until, alarmed by my presence, they noisily took wing. What strong stomachs they must have to digest acorns without first removing the embryos from their hard coats, as jays do! Although I have never seen a Band-tailed Pigeon on the ground, in widely separated parts of their range they are reported to resort to stubble fields and glean fallen grain.

High on the northern slope of Volcán Irazú in Costa Rica, we found several Bandtails near a stream of hot water that welled out of the mountainside into a pasture. My companion, Roderich Thun, told me that he had seen the pigeons taking warm baths.

Nesting

Scarcely any nests of Band-tailed Pigeons have been reported from the tropics. The only one that I have seen was on a bushy slope on the Sierra de Tecpán, at an altitude of about 9,000 feet (2,750 meters). The loosely made platform of coarse sticks, about 8 by 7 inches (20 by 18 centimeters) in diameter, rested on a nearly horizontal branch, in contact with the main trunk, 20 feet (6 meters) above the ground—a site similar to that of northern Bandtails. When found on March 13, 1933, this nest contained a single white egg, which was almost equally blunt on the two ends and measured 42.9 by 28.6 millimeters. No other egg was laid in the following days. Throughout their range, as far as is known, Band-tailed Pigeons nearly always incubate one egg, although sets of two are sometimes found, as in a nest in the Santa Marta region of Colombia (Todd and Carriker 1922).

I spent the whole of one day and parts of three others watching the pigeons attend their egg in the pine tree. When I began at 5:50 A.M. on March 15, it was still too dark to distinguish the nest. As daylight grew stronger, the female on the nest became increasingly restless until, at 6:20, she flew away. After an absence of only a minute, she returned and sat quietly until her mate replaced her at 8:23. He incubated without interruption until the female came back at 3:57 in the afternoon. She sat steadily until she faded out amid the pine needles and I stole away, at 6:40. At daybreak the next morning I reentered the blind, and when there was enough light I saw that the female was still on her nest. At 6:13 she took an outing that lasted about one minute, then sat until her mate relieved her at 8:31. On March 17, he was already present when I began to watch at 9:00, and he covered the egg until the female arrived at 4:00 in the afternoon. On March 18, the male was present at 8:40 in the morning. That afternoon I watched the female replace him at 3:30. She remained until nightfall.

These pigeons, then, incubated on a simple schedule, well adapted to a bird able to sit for long periods without eating. The female went to the nest between 3:30 and 4:00 in the afternoon and, if undisturbed, sat continuously until soon after 6:00 the following morning, when she went off for about one minute, probably to stretch her wings and avoid soiling the nest; she was not absent long enough to find food. Returning, she remained on the nest until, between 8:15 and just after 8:30, the male came to take charge of the egg. He sat without a break for seven or eight hours, until his mate returned in the afternoon. If the pigeons were not disturbed, their egg was left exposed for less than two minutes in the course of a day. At a Band-tailed Pigeons' nest in California, the male did not arrive until after 10:00 A.M. The female also came later in the afternoon, usually after 5:00 (Peeters 1962).

The changeover was effected without ceremony. The newcomer flew into the pine tree with no sound except the loud wing flaps that broke its momentum as it alighted on a branch at a distance from the nest. Then the partner on the egg stretched up its neck, slowly arose, walked out along the supporting branch, and, when in a clear space, noisily beat its wings as it launched itself into the air. Neither bird gave any greeting or other sign of recognition to the other. After the departure of its mate, the new arrival flew to the supporting branch, walked along it to the nest, and settled down on the egg. At first it held its neck stretched up and looked around, as though to assure itself that no enemy lurked near. If it saw nothing alarming, it gradually sank its neck down between its shoulders. Then it shifted to a more comfortable position, perhaps turned the egg, and was ready for a long period of continuous sitting.

Often one's attention is drawn to the nest of a pigeon or dove by the bird's loud abrupt flight as one unwittingly approaches. The bird's swift departure gives the impression that it burst wildly from the nest, so that one wonders how the egg escaped being thrown from the shallow receptacle by this sudden movement. But long watching from concealment corrects the impression that pigeons are flighty birds who jeopardize their eggs by panicky departures. The Band-tailed Pigeons in the pine tree were very reposeful, sat for long intervals without shifting their position, and rarely turned their egg. The male rotated on the nest and stretched his wings even less than the female. When perfectly at ease, each kept its head between its shoulders, turned to the left. Distant noises were usually disregarded by the sitting pigeon, except when very loud and sharp. Sounds from a nearer source caused it to stretch up its head and look around. If the noises became more alarming, the pigeon rose in the nest, prepared to flee. But if the approaching animal proved to be only a horse or a cow, snorting or treading on dry sticks that snapped loudly, the bird settled down again; then slowly, very slowly, its neck contracted and its head turned leftward. Thrice, while I watched, men searching for cattle or gathering firewood passed beneath the nest without frightening away the incubating pigeon, who lifted its head, took in the situation, and decided to risk remaining.

These pigeons seemed to know that their departure in the presence of an intruder would draw attention to their nest. I admired the cool judgment, the careful weighing of risks, that kept them at their post until the last moment compatible with their own safety and, indirectly, that of their offspring, who could not survive without them. Except when suddenly alarmed, pigeons do not take wing without first stepping from their nests, which might be damaged by the birds' taking off directly from them, as hummingbirds do. The loud wingbeats, which give the impression of immoderate haste, are the necessary accompaniment of a heavy bird's launching itself into the air and are not indicative of a panicky departure.

A few days after I completed my study of incubation, the egg vanished from the nest in the pine tree. Fortunately, Neff and Niedrach (1946) provide details of the care and development of a nestling in Colorado. For twenty days after it hatched, the parents brooded it almost continuously, leaving the nest only rarely for short intervals, up to thirty minutes, to drive away an intruder or fly to a nearby spring for water. While

brooding, they followed much the same schedule that the Guatemalan pair did while incubating: the male came to the nest between 8:45 and 9:30 in the morning and took charge of the nestling until his mate returned between 3:45 and 5:15 in the afternoon. Once, when the male failed to appear, the female sat throughout the day. Until the twentieth day, the male alone fed the nestling, during the first week giving it three meals daily, between noon and 3:00 P.M., while in the second week the number of meals was reduced to two, delivered between noon and 1:30 P.M. Only after she ceased to brood, on the nestling's twentieth day, did its mother feed it. It left the nest when between twenty-seven and thirty days old. At the nest studied by Peeters in California, parental care followed much the same pattern.

Postscript
Of all the Central American pigeons, the Bandtail seems most in need of legal protection, not only because its large conspicuous flocks are very vulnerable but also because it lives in the highlands where the human population is densest. In the Cordillera Central of Costa Rica in the dry season of 1963, I watched loose flocks fly down the mountain in the morning, evidently to forage at lower altitudes, then return upward in midafternoon. As they flew laboriously up the slopes, often into a head wind, they fell easy prey to gunners stationed in the open pastures over which they passed. This slaughter continued in the nesting season.

9. White-winged Dove

Zenaida asiatica

In the more arid regions of Middle America, where the harsh *no hope, no hope* of the countless Inca Doves sounds all day long, a more complex and melodious song floats at intervals through the hot dry air. *Cuu-cu-c'c' cu cuu c'cu cuuu* it goes, as well as I can express it in human syllables. Anyone tracing this arresting utterance to its source may be surprised to find a grayish dove of medium size perching on an organ cactus, on an opuntia, or in the sparse shade of a thorny tree or shrub. One does not expect such a prolonged, varied song from a pigeon. As the dove takes flight with loudly flapping and whistling wings, it exposes a large and lunate white patch on the coverts of each black wing, as well as white, black-bordered tips on the outer tail feathers. A nearer view reveals the prominent black patch below and behind each eye, the bronzy iridescence on the sides of the neck, the orange or red eye circled by naked blue skin, and the red or pink legs and toes.

Sometimes known as the Singing Dove or, in Guatemala, as El Cantorix, this exceptionally melodious dove has a wide but discontinuous range. It is found from the southwestern United States through Mexico and the more arid parts of Central America, especially along the Pacific coast and in the arid interior valleys in the Caribbean drainage, to northwestern Costa Rica. A curiously isolated population inhabits the mangrove swamps around the shores of the Golfo de Parita in central Panama. After a wide gap, White-winged Doves appear again in southwestern Ecuador; they continue down the arid Pacific coast of South America to northern Chile. They are also found in Cuba, Hispaniola, Jamaica, and the southern Bahamas.

White-winged Doves that nest along the southern border of the United States migrate southward in winter, and local migrations occur within the tropics. In Guatemala the birds range far upward into the zone of oaks and pines, occasionally as high as 9,000 feet (2,750 meters). On the Sierra de Tecpán, they nested at about 8,500 feet (2,600 meters) in March and April, when the weather was severely dry. After the rainy season began in mid May, they vanished; I saw none either on the mountain or on the plateau at its foot, about 7,000 feet (2,150 meters) above sea level, until late the following November—a month after the advent of the dry season, when heavy frosts whitened open fields at the end of every clear, windless night. Evidently these doves sought drier regions while cold rains drenched the heights. After their return toward the end of the year, they sang much, suggesting that they belonged to the local breeding population and were not winter visitors from farther north, which are abundant along the Pacific coast. In Costa Rica, where the high mountains are more continuously wet than in Guatemala, White-winged Doves are rarely seen above 4,000 feet (1,200 meters). Even when heard in a frost-whitened clearing amid highland oak forests, the Whitewing's long-drawn-out song carried my thoughts back to the hot, cactus-studded lowland valleys where I first heard it.

Unlike the highly arboreal pigeons that we have considered, White-winged Doves forage over the ground and, in regions naturally forested, are found chiefly in open woodland and pastures, along roadways, and in other areas of sparse vegetation. Large numbers gather in stubble fields to pick up fallen grain, especially wheat. Berries of various kinds and the fleshy fruits of cacti, plucked from the plants that bear them, enrich the diet, which also includes insects. Their hunger satisfied, the birds fly up to rest in neighboring trees, singly or in groups.

Nesting

In the southernmost United States, White-winged Doves nest, or formerly nested, among mesquite thickets in great colonies spread over many acres, with thousands of breeding pairs loosely spaced, rarely more than two or three in a tree, rather than closely packed. Their slight structures of dead twigs, weed stems, and straws—placed from 4 to 25 feet (1.2 to 7.6 meters), mostly 8 to 10 feet (2.4 to 3 meters), above the ground—contain two eggs, very seldom one or three. The impressive choruses of these colonial-nesting doves are well described by Wetmore (in Bent 1932).

In Central America, as in Ecuador (Marchant 1960), White-winged Doves nest singly rather than in colonies. None of the three nests that I found was in sight of another of its kind. The first of these nests was 9 feet (2.7 meters) up in an organ cactus in a pasture near El Rancho in the Motagua Valley of Guatemala, at an altitude of about 1,000 feet (300 meters). The second was 8 feet (2.4 meters) up among the close-set shoots of a pollarded *Viburnum* tree growing beside a rivulet that flowed between a pasture and a rather open thicket, at an altitude of about 8,500 feet (2,600 meters) on the Sierra de Tecpán. The third was about 25 feet (7.6 meters) up, far out on a branch of a cypress tree that stood in an open pasture in the same locality. Each of these nests was a frail shallow saucer of coarse sticks, about 4½ inches (11.4 centimeters) in diameter. The two highland nests were liberally lined with pine needles, material unavailable to the doves who built the lowland nest. Each of these slight structures rested upon a rather solid foundation. The first was on the flat surface of a fallen cactus branch that had lodged horizontally among the close-set limbs of the cactus tree. The second, in the *Viburnum*, was built upon an old nest, apparently of the Rufous-collared Thrush, by arranging coarse

sticks around the rim and pine needles in the bowl. The nest itself rested solidly on the cut-off end of the trunk, amid clustered sprouts. The foundation of the nest in the cypress tree appeared to be an older dove's nest.

Each of these nests contained two eggs when found, that in the Motagua Valley on June 25, 1932, those in the highlands on March 25 and April 14, 1933, in the driest part of the year. Four of the pure white eggs averaged 29.7 by 22.1 millimeters, with extremes of 27 to 31.8 by 19.4 to 23.8 millimeters.

Before daybreak on March 30, I walked by starlight over fields where the frozen herbage crunched underfoot. As I entered my blind near the nest in the *Viburnum* tree by the rivulet, a many-voiced dawn chorus of Rufous-collared Thrushes swelled through the cold thin air of the high mountains. The slowly increasing light revealed a dove sitting calmly on the nest. Doubtless this was the female, although I could not distinguish the sexes by appearance. When finally the rays of the rising sun struck the hillside behind the nest, five minutes was long enough to melt the white frost from the sparse brown grass of the pasture, where soon Rufous-collared Thrushes and Steller's Jays were foraging with evident success. But the warming rays were slow to reach the spot where I sat in shade, and it was nearly noon before the numbness left my hands and I ceased to be chilly. In this boreal setting, I passed the day watching the nest of a bird that I had come to associate with the hottest and driest regions of the lowlands.

Arriving at 8:32, the dove's mate found her sitting motionless, just as dawn had revealed her. He alighted on a nearby Raijón bush and approached the eggs by walking over a long, naked, nearly horizontal branch which passed through the *Viburnum* tree close by the nest. As he drew near, the female rose, walked to the other side of the nest tree, took wing, and flew out of sight. Reaching the nest, the male settled slowly on the eggs. Neither partner had uttered a syllable; the changeover was accomplished in perfect silence, save for the whistling of wings in flight and the loud flaps of the male as he arrested his course and of the female as she launched forth into the air.

For nearly five hours, the male sat in the position into which he had settled on his arrival. Although sometimes he preened and shifted the eggs beneath himself, he never rotated on the nest. But toward the middle of the afternoon he grew restless, shifted his position from time to time, stretched his wings, and preened more often than in the forenoon. In intervals of drowsiness, he closed his eyes briefly as though asleep; but after a second or two, or four at the longest, he would open them to look around. Finally, when the sun sank low over the mountains and the thin air rapidly cooled, his looked-for relief arrived. At 5:15 the female alighted on the Raijón bush and waited there while her

mate, who had incubated continuously for eight hours and forty-three minutes, slowly stepped from the nest, walked to the outside of the tree, and took wing. Then with mincing steps she walked 12 feet (3.6 meters) over the long horizontal branch to the nest. As she stepped into it, I heard a subdued version of her queer polysyllabic song. Then she slowly settled on the eggs, where she remained without moving while the stars and a crescent moon shone forth, and a Whip-poor-will called from a perch in the Raijón bush close by her.

It was interesting to observe the doves' reactions to their many visitors. Early in the morning, the incubating dove seemed indifferent to a Steller's Jay gathering material for a nest from the ground nearby. Toward

noon, a pair of black-eared Bushtits discovered some downy feathers, apparently shed by the doves, among the branches below the nest and gathered billfuls with much small twittering, at times coming within a foot of the sitting dove, who paid no attention to these tiny bustling visitors. When two horses waded up the stream beneath the nest, the dove merely raised his head to learn the source of the sounds he heard. He was equally unperturbed when a bull and three cows came running noisily down the slope toward him, then drank and waded in the stream and cropped the lusher herbage on its banks, sometimes directly below him. Yet even using the utmost stealth I could not approach within 25 feet (7.6 meters) of the nest without sending off the sitting bird. Like the Band-tailed Pigeons, these doves were alert to sounds, looked around for their source,

assessed the threat, and stuck to their nest as long as this seemed prudent. They knew what to expect of the creatures amid which they lived, but whether this resulted from direct experience or hereditary wisdom I could not tell.

On April 2, the incubating dove, departing from its usual practice, remained on the nest while I approached in full view to within 10 feet (3 meters). Then, courage failing, it flew directly from the nest with such force that it nearly rolled out an egg. One of the two eggs was pipped. When I returned on the following morning, the nest was empty.

Certain authors have doubted whether the male White-winged Dove shares incubation (Goodwin 1967). My long day's vigil proved conclusively that he does, as in all other pigeons, as far as is known.

10. Ruddy Ground-Dove
Columbina talpacoti

Recently, in May, I took my ornithology class from the University of Costa Rica down the valley of the Río Térraba from San Isidro to Palmar Sur near the Pacific coast. As we rode along the Inter-American Highway, a constant succession of Ruddy Ground-Doves rose ahead of our car, happily all in time to avoid being struck—we saw no corpses along the road. These doves and the equally numerous Blue-black Grassquits who mingled with them, picking up unidentified objects from the asphalt, were by far the most abundant birds that we saw in this valley, where the

splendid rain forest that I knew long ago has been almost wholly replaced by pastures, plantations of coffee and sugarcane, and scrubby growth. The males of these pretty sparrow-sized doves had light blue-gray heads, cinnamon-brown upper plumage, warm reddish chestnut wings with black bars, and pinkish cinnamon underparts. The females were paler, more grayish and brown, with usually only a suggestion of the males' ruddy color on breast and wings. Black in shade, the eyes of both sexes were red when viewed in a strong light. Their bills were light horn color with darker tips, their legs and toes reddish pink.

Travelers along many a road from southern Mexico to eastern Peru and northern Argentina are likely to see these widespread doves, which from the lowlands range in diminishing numbers up to 4,500 or 5,000 feet (1,370 or 1,500 meters) in Central America and northern South America. Although they prefer the more humid regions, where rain forest or moist forest is the natural vegetation, these birds avoid the interior of closed woodland but may abound in clearings, including bushy pastures, plantations, parks, rural dooryards, suburban gardens and vacant lots, and light second-growth thickets. In drier regions with sparser vegetation, they tend to be replaced by the even more widespread, scaly plumaged Common Ground-Dove, while in intermediate types of country

the two species may intermingle. Their relative abundance depends largely on rainfall, as was strikingly demonstrated on a farm in north central Venezuela where I studied birds for several months. Here numerous ground-doves of both species, with Blueblack Grassquits, rose a few yards ahead of me as I walked through weedy fields and pastures, where they foraged unseen beneath low herbage. In March and April, when drying vegetation was freely shedding seeds, Common Ground-Doves were much more abundant than Ruddy Ground-Doves. By late June, when frequent rains had covered the fields with lush verdure, many of the latter remained, but the former had vanished from the farm, although I found them in Tocuyito, the nearest town.

Preferring to forage in open areas, Ruddy Ground-Doves abandon neglected fields and

other clearings when the swiftly springing vegetation of rainy regions becomes dense enough to exclude sunshine from ground level. They are strongly attracted to bare earth around rustic cabins and cow sheds, where ten or twenty may gather in a flock, sometimes with a few Blue Ground-Doves. Up to a hundred or more Ruddy Ground-Doves foraging together have been reported. It is difficult to learn what they so industriously gather from the ground, but apparently they pick up small seeds, with perhaps a few insects.

A soft *kitty-woo* is the most frequent call of both sexes. Sometimes a simple low coo is uttered, and I have heard males deliver a phrase that sounded like *too-oo-wooo*. The male's voice is somewhat deeper and fuller than that of the female. A female brooding nestlings called *t'cuwu t'cuwu*.

In the village of Buenos Aires in southern Costa Rica, one December, I found a number of Ruddy Ground-Doves roosting amid the bases of the broad crowded leaves of the arborescent *Dracaena fragrans* that bordered the pathway leading up to the little church. Here they slept in company with many wintering Baltimore Orioles. The male of a pair that nested in a dense hedge of *Stachytarpheta* behind our house slept in the hedge not far from the nest where his mate incubated. Another male roosted for several nights amid the dense foliage of a sour orange tree, about 20 feet (6 meters) from his nest in a Calabash tree. He did not sleep with his head turned back and buried in the plumage of a shoulder, in the manner of many birds, but held it forward and exposed, the bill pointing slightly downward—the usual sleeping posture of doves.

The mutual attachment of mated Ruddy Ground-Doves is strong. In a mountain pasture, one morning in May, I watched a male and a female perched in a small tree, so closely pressed together that the female held up her wing on the side next to her mate, as though there were not space for it between them. Presently they began to preen, and the female gently billed the feathers of her partner's neck. After a while both turned to face the other way, pressed as close together as

before, but with different sides in contact. They remained resting side by side in this affectionate fashion for nearly an hour.

The Nest and Eggs
In Colombia, Ruddy Ground-Doves begin to breed in December, for on January 3, 1941, I found a nest with two eggs near Cali in the Cauca Valley. In southern Costa Rica and adjacent regions of Panama, the long breeding season starts at least as early as January. The nest is usually placed in a tree, shrub, or herb growing in a low thicket, bushy field, pasture, plantation, dooryard, or hedgerow. In western Panama, I found nests built upon the topmost hand of a bunch of green bananas hanging in a plantation, where the upturned fruits prevented their slipping off. Occasionally the slight structure rests upon a stump or the abandoned nest of some other bird. One pair used as their foundation the remains of an old Blue Tanager's nest in an orange tree; another pair built upon a nest of the Golden-masked Tanager; and a third pair placed their nest atop the bulky edifice of sticks made by Slaty Castlebuilders. Another exceptional site was a leaf of a pineapple plant, one of a dense cluster growing close beside our house. Here the nest was in an exposed situation, with no foliage above to shade it from the morning sun and little to screen it at the sides. Thirty-two nests ranged from 1 to about 30 feet (.3 to 9 meters) in height, but those lower than 2 feet (60 centimeters) or higher than 20 feet (6 meters) were exceptional. Two-thirds of the nests were between 4 and 8 feet (1.2 and 2.4 meters) above the ground.

A most surprising nest was about 125 feet (38 meters) up in a towering Surá tree in a clearing in the Caribbean rain forest of Costa Rica. The nest was hidden amid the epiphytes that heavily burdened the tree, but I saw the male carry to it many billfuls of material that he gathered from other epiphytic growths high above the ground. Unlike the Common and Plain-breasted ground-doves, the Ruddy appears rarely, if ever, to nest on the ground.

The shallow, saucer-shaped nest is built by the male and female working in closest coop-

Ruddy Ground-Dove: nest with two young, on a bunch of green bananas.

eration. On January 3, 1941, I watched a pair build one about 20 feet (6 meters) above the ground in a crotch of a jacaranda tree growing in a vacant lot, close beside a motion-picture theater on the outskirts of Cali, where this dove was exceedingly abundant. The female was sitting in the nest, arranging the material. Her mate picked up sticks and straws from the ground, then flew up to the nest and stood on her back while he laid them beside her. After he had done this thrice, the female flew away; then he sat on the nest himself, arranging the material with his bill. This method of building, with one member of the pair sitting on the incipient nest while the other brings material to it, is widespread among pigeons. Whenever the sexes are distinguishable, observation reveals that, usually, the male brings most or all of the material, while the female sits on the nest and arranges his contributions.

About seven o'clock on the morning of June 13, 1943, I noticed a pair of Ruddy Ground-Doves starting a nest on a thick branch of an Annatto tree beside the house at Los Cusingos. Only a few straws and the like had been placed in this attractive site. About 2 feet (60 centimeters) away, nearer the center of the tree, was a still smaller collection of straws, evidently another beginning of a nest. The surrounding foliage was open, so I enjoyed an unusually favorable view.

Although the female dove was absent when I started to watch, the male twice brought material and sat on the nest to arrange it. Then she returned and settled on the nest. Twice more the male came with a straw, and each time he stood on her back while he laid it in front of her; when she was present, he almost always stood upon her to deposit his contribution. After he flew off, she put the straws and twiglets in order. After receiving the second piece, she left, probably frightened by a movement that I made; and the male brought two more straws, one at a time, and arranged them himself. Then his mate returned and sat while he carried seven straws to her. After placing the last of these, she flew away, for no apparent reason.

When next the male brought a bit of nest material, instead of going to the site where the pair had been building, he went to the other accumulation of material nearer the center of the tree. Here he deposited his burden and settled down to shape the nest. Soon the female, returning with an empty bill, went directly to sit on him, until he moved off the incipient nest and left her resting there alone. But when, after a short absence, he again brought a straw, he ignored his mate, went to the outer pile of straws, placed his load, and settled down to shape the nest. He remained there until the female deserted the inner position and came to him, sitting half upon him until he made way for her. Here she stayed, putting things in order, while he brought her three more straws. Her readiness to build in whichever of the two locations her mate preferred suggested that the choice of the nest site rested with him. Continued watching convinced me that he took the initiative in nest building and that his mate followed his lead. That morning they worked intermittently until 9:10.

The next morning I began to watch at dawn, but neither member of the pair appeared in the Annatto tree until well after sunrise, at 6:44. Then the male arrived alone and sat on the nest to arrange its material, pausing once in his work to call *kitty-woo, kitty-woo, kitty-woo*. Three minutes after his arrival the female flew up, as usual bringing

nothing. She walked over the male on the nest, then stood beside him and reached over his back to arrange material on the opposite side. Then she walked over him again. Since he refused to yield his place to her, after a minute she flew away, and he soon followed.

At 7:09 the pair returned together, both with empty bills. The male went to sit on the nest. His mate came and stood first upon him, then at his side. After a minute or two he flew off, and she settled in his place. In the next nineteen minutes he brought six contributions, including straws and rootlets—as before, he deposited this material while standing on his partner's back; then she shuffled it into place with her bill. They made a pretty picture in the old Annatto tree, which had been cut back in successive harvests of pods until it had a shapely rounded dome of light green foliage, at this season covered with delicate pink blossoms and prickly developing pods of a light shade of red, all aglow in the golden beams of early sunshine.

At 7:30 the male dove vanished and remained out of sight for nearly forty minutes. During his long absence the female stayed on the nest, at first busily pushing the straws into a more compact mass, later resting quietly, preening a little, or desultorily shoving the material around. When at last her partner returned, his bill was empty; nevertheless, he stood beside her and went through the motions of placing a straw by her breast. Then he dropped down to the lawn and returned promptly with a contribution. Now he began to bring things to his mate in rapid succession, for he found a liberal supply of straws and grass rootlets—during the next quarter hour he took ten pieces to the nest. Among his contributions were fine fibers and one brown curled Annatto leaf, which the female accepted and worked into the structure, although it resembled nothing else there. He carefully selected the single piece that he took each time to the nest, picking up and dropping many articles until he found one that was satisfactory.

In another interval of concentrated activity, the male brought eleven pieces in sixteen minutes. At 8:53, while he was beside the nest depositing a straw before her, the female, who had been sitting continuously for almost two hours, abruptly stepped from the nest and walked to the end of the supporting branch. The male himself placed this last contribution, then went to stand close beside his companion. Two minutes later, both flew away; they had not returned by 9:30, when I ended my watch. Long before sunrise the next morning, an egg was present in this nest. Nearly all the work of building it had been done on two mornings between about seven and nine o'clock, and I had the good fortune to watch most of its construction.

Another nest in our garden was completed in three or four days. In Surinam, Haverschmidt (1953) also watched Ruddy Ground-Doves finish a nest in two days. Here, also, the doves carried one piece of material at a time. Although nest-building passerine birds often gather a whole sheaf of straws or fibers in their bills, all the pigeons that I have watched carried only a single piece. This restriction to one item at a time is understandable in the Scaled, Short-billed, and Red-billed pigeons, who break twigs or inflorescence branches from high in trees, often struggling hard to detach them. It would be difficult for these birds to pull away one stubborn piece while holding another. Ruddy Ground-Doves and others that glean loose bits of vegetation from the ground do not have this difficulty. Possibly their habit of bringing only a single piece was inherited from ancestors who built their nests with material gathered in trees. In any case, the ability to seize something with the bill while holding something else is not so useful to pigeons, who feed their young by regurgitation, as to small passerines, who profit greatly by this ability when they gather a generous load of insects or other items for their nestlings.

The Ruddy's nest is a firm, shallow, saucer-shaped structure, sometimes scarcely more than a platform with a central depression. It is composed of straws, fine twigs, and weed stems and lined with bits of dry grass and rootlets. One nest measured 3 by 2¾ inches (7.6 by 7 centimeters); another,

much bulkier, was 4½ by 4 inches (11.4 by 10 centimeters). The nests are about 2 inches (5 centimeters) high, and the hollow that contains the eggs is about 2½ inches in diameter by 1 inch deep (6.4 by 2.5 centimeters). Although barely big enough to hold the eggs, the nests of Ruddy Ground-Doves are usually substantial, with thick walls; yet some, especially those on a broad supporting surface, are flimsy. The nest of this dove can often be distinguished from that of the Blue Ground-Dove by its more solid construction.

The Eggs

The first egg may appear on the day after the nest is finished. In two cases, the female came in the evening to sleep on the empty, newly completed nest; when she flew off, in the dim light of dawn the next morning, she left the first egg. At four nests, the second egg was laid on the day after the first appeared; at one nest, two days intervened between the laying of the first and the second eggs; and at another nest the interval was three or four days. Even when the eggs are laid on consecutive days, the interval between the first and the second may be greater than twenty-four hours, for in several instances the second egg was deposited considerably later in the morning than the first. Thus, at one nest, the first egg was laid before 5:30 A.M. At 6:35 the next morning the male was sitting on the single egg. The female was on the nest at 7:20 and 7:40; and, since I did not wish to risk disturbing her in the act of laying, I did not learn when she deposited the second egg, but it was certainly more than twenty-five hours after the first. At another nest, the first egg was laid before 5:20 A.M., the second between 6:00 and 8:55 the next morning. At a nest in Surinam, the first egg was laid before 6:30 A.M., the second between 7:00 A.M. and 4:30 P.M. the following day.

The Ruddy Ground-Dove's full set nearly always consists of two eggs. I found a few nests with one egg, but sometimes an egg is rolled from the shallow nest if the dove is frightened and darts away suddenly. However, at a nest that I checked frequently during the period of laying, I never found more than one egg, which was abandoned soon after it was deposited. Haverschmidt likewise found that only one egg was laid in a nest that he watched closely. In Guyana, Beebe, Hartley, and Howes (1917) found occasional nests of this species with one egg and even some with three eggs, which is most unusual in the pigeon family.

The Ruddy's eggs are pure white and ellipsoidal, with little difference in shape between the two ends. Sixteen eggs averaged 23.2 by 17.1 millimeters, with extremes of 21.8 to 25.4 by 15.7 to 17.9 millimeters.

In the Valley of El General, eggs were laid in twenty-nine nests as follows: January, one; February, four; March, six; April, eight; May, one; June, four; July, two; August, one; September, two. Most nests were found in the rainy season, which extends from March or April to December or sometimes January. It is perhaps significant that three of the four February nests were found in the unusually wet February of 1937. At Palmar Sur near sea level I found nestlings on September 20, 1947, and a pair were building on October 20 of the same year. In Trinidad and Tobago, nests have been found in all months, with a peak from July to September, an interval of high rainfall.

Incubation

Incubation begins with or—if a paradox is permissible—even before the laying of the first egg, for we have seen that the female may sleep on the nest before she has laid, and she sits there for long periods while building is in progress. Until the second egg appears, the first is almost constantly covered by the parents, who thereby probably reduce predation, because when sitting motionless they are less conspicuous than the shining white object that they conceal. Since, from laying to hatching, pigeons' eggs are rarely left exposed, natural selection has not promoted pigmentation that would make them less conspicuous in the open nests, except in a few species such as the Ruddy Quail-Dove, who, unlike many other pigeons, fails to keep its first buffy egg covered.

On the day the first egg is laid, the male and female Ruddy Ground-Doves sit according to a schedule quite different from that which they will follow after the second egg appears. At the nest on the pineapple leaf beside our house, the female flew off, leaving the single freshly laid egg, at 5:30 A.M. At 6:05 I found the male covering the egg. The female was sitting at 7:27, 9:18, and 10:55. The male was again in charge at 12:15 and 3:30, but the female was back at 5:30. The next morning, at 6:35, the male again covered the egg.

Later in the season, at the nest that I had watched the doves build in the nearby Annatto tree, the treatment of the single egg was different. This egg was laid before 5:20 A.M. on June 15. At 6:00 I found the male covering it and began to watch the nest. At 6:24 he called *kitty-woo* several times, and a moment later I noticed his mate approaching. She stood over him, and after a brief delay he relinquished the nest to her. At 7:37, after sitting quietly for an hour and twelve minutes, she left spontaneously. Her absence was short, and at 7:44 she returned to the egg. At 8:16 she cooed, then departed, as her mate approached with a straw in his bill. He laid it on the nest and sat on the egg, from time to time arranging the material around him. Meanwhile, a Bananaquit carried off straws from the nest that the doves had started but left unfinished, about 2 feet (60 centimeters) away. The male dove sat until after 9:00, when I ended my three-hour vigil. Returning at 1:35, I found the female on the nest. She was still present at 2:05, but at 3:20 the male was again sitting.

Thus, at the nest on the pineapple leaf, the male dove took at least two turns on the egg in a single day, and at the nest in the Annatto tree he took three, in each case with intervening sessions by the female. After incubation had continued for a few days, I never found a male sitting as early as six in the morning, nor (save most exceptionally) did I find a female sitting in the early afternoon.

The incubation pattern of the Ruddy Ground-Dove after the clutch is complete is similar to that of other pigeons. The male and female replace each other on the nest only twice each day. The female settles on the eggs in the afternoon and remains until her mate relieves her the next morning. He is then in sole charge through the middle of the day, until the female returns in the afternoon. Each partner sits continuously until replaced by the other; or, if it interrupts its long session, whether spontaneously or because disturbed, it usually returns in a few minutes. Thus, the eggs are rarely left uncovered unless the doves are often molested. The times of the changeovers vary from nest to nest and even at the same nest from day to day; but, as a rule, the male is to be found covering the eggs from somewhat before the middle of the morning until about the middle of the afternoon, the female during the late afternoon, night, and early forenoon.

During the incubation period, I made no continuous watch of the nest on the pineapple leaf beside the house, but I looked at it frequently to learn which sex was in charge of the eggs. The latest hour of the morning at which I found the female on the nest was 7:55, the earliest at which I found the male there was 8:05. In the afternoon, the latest record of the male's presence was 3:00, the earliest for the return of his mate 2:50. Accordingly, the male covered the eggs from approximately 8:00 A.M. to 3:00 P.M. or over an interval of seven hours each day, during which I never failed to find him at his post.

At the nest in the Annatto tree, which apparently belonged to the same pair of doves, I made many observations from the porch, since the birds seemed indifferent to my presence. Here the latest hour at which I found the female on the two eggs in the morning was 8:40, the earliest at which the male was present 8:27. The changeover usually occurred in the half hour between 8:15 and 8:45. In the afternoon, my earliest record for the female's return was 2:45, but this was the day when she laid the second egg. Thereafter, I did not see her on the nest before 3:15; by 3:30, on an afternoon without heavy showers, she was usually to be found covering the eggs. On afternoons of the hard and long rains frequent at this season, she might arrive very late. Once she did not return until 4:13 and, on another wet afternoon, not until 5:01. In each instance, the male sat faithfully, if impatiently, until relieved of duty. At most he might absent himself for a minute or two,

probably to avoid soiling the nest, and from time to time while sitting he called his tardy partner with soft coos. At this nest, too, the male usually incubated for about seven hours a day, but on wet afternoons his session might be prolonged to eight or almost nine hours.

Less methodical observations at other nests in southern Costa Rica showed that the incubation schedule of this pair was fairly typical of the local Ruddy Ground-Doves. Only once have I found a female on the nest as late as 9:35 A.M. after the set of eggs was complete.

At Colomba on the Pacific slope of Guatemala, as I spent all the daylight hours of July 21, 1935, in a blind watching a nest where the doves had been incubating for at least six days, I found a very different schedule. The female passed the night on the nest and sat continuously throughout the morning until she heard her mate approaching at 12:38, except for one spontaneous absence of only two minutes, from 11:03 to 11:05, when possibly she went to drink. As the morning wore on and her partner did not come to relieve her at the conventional hour, she called softly over and over, *kitty-woo, kitty-woo*, and once received an answer from the distance; but this exchange of greetings did not lead to her prompt release from incubation. The male went on the nest at 12:43 and sat continuously for five hours less two minutes. Like his mate, he frequently closed his eyes while sitting, but only for an instant. Silent at first, around 5:30 he grew impatient of his mate's continued absence and began to coo in a voice somewhat fuller than hers. At 5:41 the female came for the night session, and he flew off. In this instance, the female's arrival was not delayed by inclement weather, for the afternoon was fair; apparently, she returned late because she had left late.

On subsequent days, I found the male dove on this Guatemalan nest earlier in the morning—at 11:00 on July 22 and at 9:10 on July 23—but on July 24 the female was still on the nest at this hour, although the male had come by 10:00. Between 9:00 and 9:30 seemed to be his usual time for coming to the nest during the last few days of incubation.

The female, having been relieved late in the morning, commonly kept her mate sitting far into the afternoon: 4:35 was the earliest hour at which I found her present, and twice more I found the male covering the eggs as late as 5:15. His daily session, from roughly 9:00 A.M. to 5:00 P.M. during the final days of incubation, lasted about eight hours.

The male Ruddy Ground-Dove studied by Haverschmidt in Surinam almost invariably came to the eggs between 10:00 and 11:00 in the morning and sat until the female returned between 3:00 and 4:00 in the afternoon. Sometimes the incubating bird was so reluctant to leave that the incoming partner had to push it from the eggs.

Approaching or leaving the nest, the doves do not fly directly to or from it, as do hummingbirds and other small birds with well-made nests and precisely controlled flight. On the contrary, when arriving the doves usually alight on a branch a foot or more away and walk to the nest. Similarly, to leave they carefully step from the nest and walk out along the supporting limb before they fly. Thus, they are less likely to knock or shake the eggs from the shallow nest. Only when suddenly alarmed do they fly directly from the eggs, sometimes causing their loss.

Less concerned with cleanliness than many birds, the doves sometimes soil the nest with their excrement while they incubate, a not unnatural result of their very long periods of uninterrupted sitting. At times they appear to leave the nest to void their droppings at a distance, for their absence of a few minutes is hardly long enough for foraging, although it might suffice to go for water.

Rarely I have seen doves add a few pieces to their nests after they had been incubating for a number of days. I found a Ruddy female bringing material to a nest in our garden only three days before her eggs hatched. Between 9:30 and 10:00 A.M., while her partner incubated, she brought at least seven pieces and placed them on the rim beside him. She walked over the lawn, bobbing her head in typical pigeon fashion and plucking at dry straws and fallen twigs until she found one loose and light enough to be moved, which she then picked up and carried to the nest. She also brought the fibrous remains of a half-decayed leaf. Similarly, I once watched a female Blue Ground-Dove take a number of twigs to her nest, between 9:00 and 9:15 in the morning, while her mate sat on the two eggs. The female's activity in carrying material to the nest during the course of incubation is surprising because, when the nest is originally built, I have seen only the male of these two species take material to it, while the female sat on the nest to receive and arrange his contributions. Both sexes of the Ruddy Quail-Dove often bring a leaf or twig when they return to the nest to incubate, but I have not seen them make special trips to add to their slight nests after the eggs were laid (Skutch 1949, 1981).

While incubating, the male Ruddy Ground-Dove is usually more steadfast than his mate; at times he remains at his post while a person approaches and almost touches him. A few females are almost equally staunch. A female in Surinam stayed on her nest while Haverschmidt removed the nestlings from beneath her for weighing, but none that I have known has been so confiding.

I have rarely seen Ruddy Ground-Doves give distraction displays, probably because the low thickets where they so often nest are too dense to permit injury feigning; and even in plantations the ground is frequently covered with weeds too tall to permit a convincing performance. At times, when disturbed, the dove leaves the eggs and drops toward the ground as though to alight upon it, but seeing the dense herbage it decides otherwise and skims off over the tops of the grasses and forbs. But while I stood in a scrubby pasture near Cali, around noon on a day in January, a ground-dove burst abruptly from a compact, spiny *Xanthoxylum* bush a few yards from me. Dropping to the ground, he walked away slowly and haltingly, with raised, quivering wings that appeared to be painful and useless. I followed slowly, and he continued to drag himself along on a wavering course until beyond my sight among the bushes. Returning to the thorny shrub, I found his nest with two eggs.

One morning I found a male Ruddy

Ground-Dove brooding two newly hatched nestlings 10 feet (3 meters) up in a Costa Rican thicket. He sat steadfastly until I raised my mirror to the nest; then he dropped to the ground in the midst of the thicket. Here he stayed for about a minute, beating his wings noisily against the surrounding vegetation. Although the foliage between us was so dense that I could see little of him, the sounds revealed unmistakably that he was flapping his wings. It was the best demonstration that he could make amid such tangled vegetation.

At two nests, each with two eggs, the incubation period was twelve days or a little less, counting from the laying to the hatching of the last egg. At two other nests, the period was thirteen days. In four nests, both eggs hatched on the same day; in two, the eggs hatched on consecutive days. In Surinam the incubation period of this dove was twelve days at one nest and thirteen days at two nests. The eggs of these small doves of open country and secondary vegetation require a day or two more of incubation than those of the larger Ruddy Quail-Doves of heavy forest, but they hatch in considerably less time than those of many pigeons of northern lands.

The Nestlings

Newly hatched Ruddy Ground-Doves have pink skin with sparse, buffy, hairlike down; and their eyes are tightly closed. The shells from which they escaped promptly vanish from the nest, but whether eaten by the parents or carried off I have not learned.

Because of the special way that pigeons feed their young, one may watch for hours without seeing any feeding activity. To learn how many times nestlings are fed and how long the meals take, very long watches, preferably continuous through the day, are needed. Of all my Ruddy Ground-Doves' nests, that on a pineapple leaf beside the house was best situated for studying the care of nestlings. When I sat on a campstool atop a box inside the blind, I was higher than the nest and could see very well all that happened, except when the parents turned their tails toward me. I watched this nest for nearly thirty hours while it contained nestlings, until they were taken by a predator. Although I learned much, my study was not as thorough as I had hoped to make it.

When the nestlings were one and two days old, they were brooded almost continuously, the parents occupying the nest according to much the same schedule as while they incubated. The father, who now came earlier than he did during the incubation period, covered the nest most of the day and was the chief provider of nourishment. When he arrived at about 7:30 in the morning, he had a seemingly inexhaustible capacity to secrete "pigeon's milk," which he regurgitated into the mouths of the nestlings at short intervals throughout the morning and until 2:10 in the afternoon. He did not need to go off and hunt food to replenish his supply; his absences from the nest, lasting only a few minutes, were apparently for the purpose of drinking.

The male always fed the sightless nestlings alternately. Taking a nestling's bill into the side of his mouth, he regurgitated into it for a fraction of a minute or, intermittently, for five and once for ten minutes. Regurgitation appeared to require great muscular effort and was accompanied by jerky movements of his body that gave the little one's head a good shaking. When, early in the afternoon, the young were slow to rise up and take nourishment, he aroused them by gently seizing the tips of their bills. He trembled and panted much, even in the early morning when the sun was low and the air cool. After the female returned in midafternoon, she did not feed the nestlings; but the next morning, before taking food herself, she was able to regurgitate into one for four minutes and into the other for two minutes.

Each day, the male came to the nest earlier in the morning. His bouts of regurgitation were less frequent but continued longer, once, when the nestlings were four days old, intermittently for seventeen minutes. Thereby he exhausted the contents of his crop earlier each succeeding day and was no longer able to respond to the nestlings' subsequent requests for nourishment. When they rose up and silently importuned him for food, he might take their bills in his mouth, only to drop them without giving anything. When, at the age of three or four days, the nestlings' eyes opened and they could see to place their bills in a parent's mouth, they were often fed simultaneously, one on each side, instead of alternately, as at first.

As the days passed, the male remained away longer in the early afternoon. When only three days old, the nearly naked nestlings were left exposed to a shower that began soon after midday. The female dove returned to the nest progressively earlier each afternoon, and, when the nestlings were a week old, she fed them at this time. When the nestlings were four days old, the male began the habit of returning to replace his mate about the middle of the afternoon; he now took two turns on the nest each day, whereas formerly (during incubation and when the nestlings were a day or two old) he had not returned after his partner replaced him in the afternoon. He fed the nestlings, brooded them for about an hour, then was relieved by the female, who also fed them once more and stayed with them until nightfall. When the young were a week old, the parents came to the nest, after long absences, twice as often as when they were newly hatched yet at the same time gave them fewer meals, apparently because each was more liberal and the contents of their crops were sooner exhausted. At nests of the White-fronted Dove, Blue Ground-Dove, and Ruddy Quail-Dove, I also found decreases in the number of feedings and the total time devoted to regurgitation as the nestlings grew older; and, in an extremely careful study of the parental care of Mourning Doves, Luther (1979) recorded similar trends, with minor fluctuations from day to day.

The parent Ruddy Ground-Doves approached and left their nest by walking along the arching pineapple leaf that supported it. As they passed each other at the changeovers, they bobbed their heads and twitched or vibrated their wings without spreading them. Once, facing each other across the nest, they continued these movements for a minute or two. When bright sunshine fell upon the nest, they stood to shade the nestlings instead of brooding them. Often they stepped upon the tender young, who seemed to suffer no ill effects from this careless treatment. Once the brooding male exchanged calls with another male who perched about 100 feet (30 meters) away. Sometimes the brooding female gently pecked or touched her nestlings with her bill. While a small brown grasshopper walked over the nest's rim, she paid no attention to it; but, when it crept up her breast, she gave it a sharp peck that made it hop away.

As darkness fell, I left the mother dove covering her week-old nestlings. She appeared so calm and secure amid the spiny pineapple leaves that I did not doubt that she would be there in the morning. At daybreak I returned to the blind, prepared to watch until midday. But the slowly growing light revealed the distressing fact that the nest was empty. Probably a snake had swallowed the nestlings. Happily, their mother escaped, and later in the morning she was seen with her mate near the blighted nest.

At other nests, more fortunate although less favorably placed for watching, I traced the development of young Ruddy Ground-Doves from hatching until they flew. When they escape the shells they are, as we have seen, pink, blind, and thinly covered with buffy hairlike down. Their skins darken so rapidly that when two or three days old they are nearly black. At the age of three or four days, they open their eyes. Pinfeathers now sprout and become conspicuous on five-day-old nestlings. The little doves now peep softly. At the age of eight days, they are nearly clothed with expanded feathers. Alert and active, they preen and vigorously exercise their wings. A day later, the nestlings' bodies are well covered, although their heads are still spiky with unopened pinfeathers, each terminated by a little tuft of buffy bristles. Nine-day-old doves can fly a little and will leave the nest if alarmed, although if undisturbed they remain from three to five days longer. When I attempted to lift from the ground a dove who had fluttered prematurely from the nest, it raised its wings above its back in a defensive attitude. Eleven-day-old doves may hop from the nest and perch a few inches away, returning later to be brooded.

The nest, sometimes lightly soiled by the

incubating parents, becomes increasingly dirty after the eggs hatch, for the adults do nothing to keep it clean. Before the nestlings fly, it is heavily laden with their dried droppings. Other doves, such as the White-fronted and the Ruddy Quail-Dove, are better housekeepers: they keep their nests scrupulously clean by swallowing all droppings until their young fly.

Parent Ruddy Ground-Doves spend much time on the nest with well-feathered young twelve days old. But, as while the nestlings are nearly naked, the parents are not consistent; although they often cover the young in fair weather when this seems superfluous, they may leave them exposed to heavy rain. The female broods them throughout the night until they are twelve or thirteen days old. When sleeping on the nest, as when roosting on a branch, she does not turn her head back among the plumage of a shoulder but lets it droop forward until her bill touches the fluffed-out feathers of her breast, as I noticed repeatedly on nocturnal visits.

On an early morning visit to a nest in an orange tree, I found the male parent brooding two twelve-day-old fledglings. As he flew off, one of them followed, flying easily to a tree about 25 feet (7.6 meters) distant. When I raised a mirror to see whether the other fledgling remained on the nest, it flew to a neighboring thorn, then back to the rim of the nest. At noon this nest was empty, and the fledglings were in neighboring trees. Although able to fly well, they had difficulty alighting, sometimes missing the intended perch and fluttering down to the grass. That evening both returned to their heavily soiled nest to be brooded by their mother. When I visited the orange tree the following evening, both young doves flew out. Apparently they were returning, after two days of activity among the surrounding trees, to sleep once more upon the nest. As far as I could learn without making another disturbing visit to this nest well screened by foliage, they did not again return that evening; but their mother flew from the nest when I approached it before sunrise the next morning.

At another nest a single nestling, who likewise left at the age of twelve days, failed to return for an additional night's brooding. From a third nest, two young doves departed at the age of fourteen days. Haverschmidt found the nestling period of Ruddy Ground-Doves in Surinam to be eleven to twelve days. Recently fledged Ruddy Ground-Doves roost in a tree or shrub, sandwiched between their parents, much as I have found young White-fronted Doves roosting (ffrench 1973).

Doves are sometimes supposed to be less flexible and adaptable than songbirds, but this is not always true. While a laborer pruned a banana plantation in Panama, he cut down a plant bearing a bunch of green fruits, without noticing that it supported a Ruddy Ground-Doves' nest with two flight-less nestlings. Fortunately, the nest was not thrown from the falling fruits, nor the young from the nest. I placed nest and nestlings in a corresponding position on a younger bunch of bananas in the same cluster of stems. Two hours later, I was pleased to see the female dove brooding her offspring in the new location. I have known songbirds of several species to feed but fail to brood callow nestlings whose situation was similarly changed.

A second brood often follows swiftly after the first. One pair of doves, whose single nestling departed successfully on April 1, had by April 8 already covered the old nest with fresh straws, and on the following day the female laid the first egg of a new set. Another pair, whose fledglings flew from the nest on March 14, had relined the old structure by April 3, and the following day they had an egg. A pair whose nestlings took wing on August 31 were building a new nest a yard from the first on September 17, but they failed to finish it, probably because of the lateness of the season. In a nest in Surinam, three broods were raised between October 25 and the following February 24, and five consecutive broods were produced in a nest in Trinidad (Haverschmidt 1953; ffrench 1973).

In Central America, the Ruddy's breeding season covers most of the year. Since the whole breeding cycle is completed in about five weeks, a single pair might raise six or seven broods in the long nesting season of eight to ten months. However, I doubt that any pair produce, or even try to raise, so many broods in a year; I have no evidence for more than two broods in the same breeding season.

Of the thirty-seven nests that I have seen, I know the outcome of twenty-one that were found before the eggs hatched. Nineteen of these were in the Valley of El General, two on the Pacific slope of Guatemala. These twenty-one nests contained forty eggs, of which twenty hatched. Of the twenty nestlings, eight fledged from five nests. Thus, 20 percent of the eggs yielded fledged young, and 24 percent of the nests produced at least one fledgling. The only predator that I caught in the act of pillaging a Ruddy Ground-Doves' nest was a Fiery-billed Araçari, who late one September afternoon ate the two eggs from a nest in front of our house. As for the other causes of loss, one nestling died in the nest, one egg fell from the nest, and one nest with a single egg was abandoned.

Postscript

Most of my studies of Ruddy Ground-Doves were made from 1942 through 1944; my first three full years at Los Cusingos, when these birds nested freely in my dooryard and the adjoining pasture; in 1943 I had seven nests. Since then I have found only two nests in this same area, both thirty-two years ago. After that, these doves deserted us, although they remain fairly abundant in other parts of the valley more intensively farmed. I do not know why they remain away, unless it is because two larger ground-feeding doves, the White-fronted and the rufous-naped race of the Gray-chested Dove, have become numerous, attracted in part by the maize that they share with the domestic chickens. Although I have never seen any interaction between these bigger doves and Ruddy Ground-Doves, perhaps the latter cannot compete with them for food.

11. Squirrel Cuckoo
Piaya cayana

The nearly cosmopolitan cuckoo family is well represented in the western hemisphere on the continents from Canada to Argentina, in the Antilles, and on many other islands. Among the American cuckoos are species that breed in single pairs, communal nesters, and brood parasites. Most are birds of distinctive character, easily recognized—none more so than the subject of the present chapter. Nearly 11 of the Squirrel Cuckoo's 17 inches (28 of 43 centimeters) are occupied by its great tail. Above, it is rich chestnut, paler on the head, deepening to bay on the tail, the strongly graduated feathers of which are broadly tipped with white. Its throat and chest are pinkish cinnamon, its breast and belly gray, deepening to slate-gray on the flanks and thighs and still darker on the lower surface of the tail, except the white tips. Its bill and the bare skin around its big

deep red eyes are yellowish green. Its legs and feet are light bluish gray. The sexes are alike.

From central Mexico to northwestern Peru, northern Argentina, and Trinidad, the Squirrel Cuckoo is a familiar bird, found in a wide variety of habitats. I have most often met it in light open woods and cultivated areas with scattered trees, including hedgerows, coffee plantations with light shade, pastures, dooryards, and abandoned clearings where here and there a taller tree, almost overwhelmed by a heavy burden of creepers, has managed to struggle up above the disorderly welter of swiftly springing vegetation. It often hunts through the tangle of vines at the forest's edge and even amid the crowns of trees a short distance within the forest, but it rarely ventures far into heavy rain forest and it consistently avoids the dark undergrowth. In more arid regions, Squirrel Cuckoos are most likely to be found among the taller trees along watercourses and at lower ground levels. An adaptable bird, it ranges up to 7,000 or 8,000 feet (2,150 or 2,440 meters) above sea level, but it is most abundant in the warmer life zones below 4,000 or 5,000 feet (1,200 or 1,500 meters).

I cannot recall having seen a Squirrel Cuckoo undertake a long flight. It proceeds from tree to tree and bough to bough, with now and then a swift dart across an open space. It prefers to gain altitude by working from limb to limb rather than by a single effort. When it finds itself at last far up a hillside or high in the crown of a tree and wishes to return to lower levels, it sets its short wings and, its great tail streaming, makes a long downward glide, uttering sharp metallic notes as it goes. Squirrel Cuckoos never flock but live in pairs at all seasons. Mates do not, as a rule, keep close company either in flight or while hunting through vegetation but straggle along one behind the other, often several trees apart, and keep in contact by their voices.

I have seen Squirrel Cuckoos eat only caterpillars and winged insects, chiefly orthoptera, but other observers have recorded an occasional spider or lizard in the diet. This cuckoo hunts among the trees, bushes, and vines in a fashion all its own, which combines deliberate motion and careful scrutiny with sudden darts and leaps of sometimes amazing length. Keeping itself usually well concealed by foliage, it turns its head slowly from side to side and scans the surfaces of leaves with wide eyes until it spies something to tempt it into activity. Then with a sudden pounce it makes the prey its own. A caterpillar crawling over the underside of a leaf above its head may cause the cuckoo to leap upward for a distance of several feet. When it has deftly seized its victim, it returns to a convenient perch, against which it may beat its prey into quiescence before gulping it down, or it may merely mash the insect between its yellow-green mandibles. Then it sits quietly or hops in a leisurely fashion from bough to bough, all the while scrutinizing the foliage until something else excites it to more vigorous action. Or it may run with short hops or longer bounds along a horizontal or ascending limb, thereby earning for itself the name *pájaro ardilla* ("squirrel bird").

One morning I watched a Squirrel Cuckoo capture a phasmid, or walkingstick, about 4 or 5 inches (10 or 13 centimeters) long. The insect was gray, with short wings, the under pair bright pink. When it slipped from the bird's bill and fell to the ground, the captor dropped down to recover it, carried it to a neighboring branch, and pounded it before swallowing it whole. With incredulous amazement, I have from time to time watched a Squirrel Cuckoo pluck a spiny green caterpillar from foliage. Some of the most prolonged and excruciating pain I have suffered was caused by accidentally touching the venomous branched spines which cover such caterpillars. Yet, after mashing them somewhat in its bill, this cuckoo nonchalantly gulps them down!

The Squirrel Cuckoo has such a varied vocabulary that, for years after I became acquainted with the bird, I continued to hear notes that mystified me until I traced them to this versatile source. A frequent call sounds like *jícaro* (pronounced *híc-ǎ-ro*), the name of the useful Calabash tree. As I write this, I hear a cuckoo calling so in a dry and seemingly derisive voice. This call may be loud and far-carrying or given intimately in an undertone. Another common utterance is a loud mocking disyllable, *eee-kah* or, as some have paraphrased it, *keep-rear*. A very different vocalization, heard chiefly in the breeding season, consists of a monosyllable repeated many times in a measured cadence, *whip—whip—whip—whip*, or sometimes the note has sounded more like *wic*. This may be either loud and sharp or low and soft; or the notes, at first loud and clear, may become progressively fainter until the last are whispered. Quite different again, and less frequently heard, is a prolonged churr or rattle, delivered with the bill widely opened and the lower mandible vibrating. On a long downward glide, the cuckoo repeats a loud, sharp, metallic monosyllable—perhaps an expression of anxiety by a weakly flying bird exposed under the open sky.

I have only once seen Squirrel Cuckoos quarrel. One January morning, I watched two of them perched a few feet apart in a lone tree, shaking or twitching their long tails with a vigorous movement of slight amplitude, twitching up their wings barely above their backs, and repeating *jícaro* over and over in a low voice. At intervals they slightly changed their positions. After this had continued for some minutes, one darted at its opponent, who moved to avoid contact.

Then both resumed tail shaking. Again, one lunged at the other and may have seized its tail—the only actual or apparent physical contact that I saw. Presently they flew to a neighboring tree and resumed their altercation. About a quarter of an hour after I found them already engaged in this quarrel, one, evidently admitting defeat, flew to neighboring light woodland, while the victor stayed in the same tree and emitted a long low rattle. The two continued to call *jícaro* back and forth but did not again approach one another. As in many another dispute that I have watched among tropical birds of various species, not a feather was lost by either party. A third Squirrel Cuckoo, who remained nearby while the other two argued, was apparently the winner's mate, as the two stayed together after the conclusion of the contest.

Over the years, I have repeatedly seen a Squirrel Cuckoo give an adult insect or caterpillar to its mate. Early on a sunny April morning, while watching the birds of many kinds that swarmed among the shade trees of a small coffee grove, my attention was drawn by a cuckoo who bounded along a branch in characteristic fashion, holding in his bill a green insect. He presented this to his mate, and, as she grasped it, he mounted upon her back. Continuing to hold the insect at the same time as she, he stood on her back for the better part of a minute. Then he attempted the nuptial embrace, leaning far over sideways and crossing his long tail beneath hers. The size of his tail made it necessary for him to lean much farther than other small birds do in coition. The grasp on the insect which both members of the pair retained gave him essential support; without it, he might have lost his balance.

A little later, I noticed this pair of cuckoos perched side by side on a horizontal bough, tugging at a green caterpillar, which stretched between them. Finally, it broke, the major share remaining with the male, while the female retained and ate only a tiny end. A minute later, I learned how this tug-of-war had probably begun. The male found another green insect and offered it to the female, at the same time trying to mount her. Not ready for more of this, she sidled away from him, this time retaining and swallowing all the prize. In Africa, a male Emerald Cuckoo presented a large hairy caterpillar to a female, displayed, then mounted her (Haydock 1950).

The Nest
The eight Squirrel Cuckoos' nests that I have seen ranged in height from 30 inches to about 40 feet (.76 to 12 meters). That neither extreme is unusual is evident from the fact that two nests were less than 4 feet (1.2 meters) from the ground and four pairs were either building or incubating high in trees. The lowest nest was in a tangle of Bracken fern and the straggling composite *Eupatorium vitalbae*, in a field where corn had been planted the preceding year. The next highest was in a similar situation in a neglected pasture. Two nests were about 40 feet (12 meters) up in an arching spray of a timber bamboo. Another, about equally high, was set between tank bromeliads on a leafy horizontal branch of a large tree in a clearing, near forest. A nest at an intermediate height was 8 feet (2.4 meters) up in a dense hedge of lemon trees, beside a grassy road used by pedestrians, horseback riders, and oxcarts. Another was 18 feet (5.5 meters) high, on the frond of a tree fern overgrown with vines. Most of these sites were well screened by foliage.

To build the nest, one partner sits in the site to arrange materials that the other brings to it. These materials are generally coarse or fine twigs which the more active partner breaks with its bill from trees and vines well above the ground. Occasionally it brings a dead or dying leaf and, more rarely, a leafy twig. The sitting partner often takes the contribution directly from the bringer's bill. Although usual, this division of labor is not invariable, for both members of the pair may bring materials; and, after the sitting partner leaves, the one who has been supplying sticks may stay on the nest to arrange them. Anis and pigeons build their nests in much the same way.

Because the nests tend to be well screened, I have only occasionally been able to observe the finer details of building. A pair of Squirrel Cuckoos who tried to build high in a mango tree, in the laboratory clearing on Barro Colorado Island in the Panama Canal Zone, were exceptionally easy to watch. They worked chiefly in the second half of the forenoon and at intervals throughout the afternoon, sometimes continuing until sunset. While one member of the pair, probably the female, rested in the chosen site, the other industriously brought long fine twigs and dead leaves, all gathered high in trees, and presented them to his mate, who took them in her bill and stuck them beneath herself—whereupon they promptly fell to the ground. The mango tree's coarse branches offered no adequate foundation. Periodic changes in site, all within the same tree's spreading crown, gave no better results. After a week of strenuous effort, the cuckoos had nothing to show for their labor but a litter of dead twigs beneath the tree; every site where they had tried to build remained bare. Probably these were young birds who had not learned that their nest needed a foundation of fine, closely set branches or vines. When, at about five o'clock on an evening at the end of May, the female laid an egg while perching on the branch from which she had most recently been dropping materials, the egg promptly followed the sticks to the ground.

I do not know how long these cuckoos would have stubbornly persisted in their fruitless project if I had not come to their aid. By tying forked sticks together, I made a basketlike framework that I fastened in the top of the mango tree. After several days of neglect, one member of the pair sat in it while the other brought sticks—which slipped out of the basket. To give these hardworking but inept birds a better start, I gathered a handful of the dropped twigs and interlaced them in the framework so that they would stay. Later that day, the cuckoos added sticks and leaves, until by evening they had a promising beginning of a nest. To my regret, my busy sojourn on Barro Colorado ended before I could learn the outcome of this undertaking, but I like to believe that the cuckoos completed the nest that I had started for them in the mango tree and raised a family there.

When finished, the Squirrel Cuckoos' nest has a loose foundation or framework of long, straight, inflexible sticks. Upon or within this is a great mass of whole leaves, brown or green, interspersed with a few fine twiglets, the whole forming a shallow concave platform. These nests measure 6 to 7 inches across (not including the projecting ends of long twigs) and 2½ to 4½ inches high (15 to 18 by 6.4 to 11.4 centimeters). The shallow depression in the top is about 3½ inches (9 centimeters) wide.

The Eggs and Incubation

In the Valley of El General, I have found Squirrel Cuckoos incubating in both the dry and the wet seasons, from January to August. Each of my four accessible nests contained two eggs or nestlings. The hour of laying is irregular. I have already told how a bird without a nest dropped an egg in the evening. Another female, with a proper nest, laid her first egg between 12:00 and 2:30 P.M. and her second before 11:00 A.M. the following day—an unusually short interval between eggs. The eggs are ellipsoidal, with scarcely any difference between the two ends. When freshly laid they are pure white, with a slightly rough chalky surface. The measurements of four eggs averaged 35.1 by 25.9 millimeters, with extremes of 34.1 to 36.5 by 25.4 to 26.2 millimeters.

A day or two after they are laid, the eggs' immaculate white surface becomes stained with brown from contact with the leaves on which they rest. The discoloration increases from day to day, until long-incubated eggs are mottled with deep stains. May not the function of the green leaves which the cuckoos continue to bring until the nestlings hatch be to cause these stains, which mask the glaring whiteness that makes newly laid eggs so conspicuous in their shallow open nest? By this device, the cuckoos compensate for the failure of their oviducts to secrete pigment for the shells.

The great tail of an incubating Squirrel Cuckoo, held tilted upward at a sharp angle, is also a conspicuous object. Usually the bird sits steadfastly and permits a close approach, sometimes even allowing me to touch the tip of its tail before it jumps from the nest. Then it may perch close by and twitch its tail in a most peculiar fashion, while it watches the intruder. I have never known a Squirrel Cuckoo to protest my visit to its nest by vocalizing or any more vigorous demonstration; it flies a good way off before calling to its mate.

One cuckoo continued to cover its eggs while I set up a blind 5 or 6 yards (4.5 or 5.5 meters) away, an operation which necessitated cutting a certain amount of vegetation. I was confident that I would have no difficulty studying incubation at this nest; but, for all its staunchness while attending its eggs, the cuckoo is canny. Stealing away without scaring the bird from its nest, I left the blind in place the greater part of that day and throughout the following night. When I returned at dawn with high anticipation of passing an interesting day learning things I had long wanted to know about the elusive Squirrel Cuckoo, I found, to my dismay, the eggs unattended, cold, and wet. The birds had not resumed incubation by midmorning, when I removed the blind. The next day the eggs had vanished, apparently taken by some predatory animal. At my other low nest, where I touched the tail of the sitting cuckoo, the dense stand of Bracken fern made it necessary to place my blind very close and to disturb the surrounding vegetation more than I wished. As long as the blind was present, the birds stayed away from their eggs, but they returned after it was removed.

Years later, I watched incubating Squirrel Cuckoos at a timber bamboo in sight of my study window. Although the sitting cuckoo's body was invisible from the ground, its tail often revealed its presence. In the evening of the day when I found this pair actively building, one of them was on the nest, where it remained throughout the night. On the following three days, I frequently saw a cuckoo sitting; but sometimes, if present, it was invisible because its tail projected on the far side of the nest. On January 26, I watched continuously from dawn until nightfall. The parent who passed the night on the nest stayed until replaced by its mate at 6:50 A.M. The latter then sat continuously for six hours and twenty-three minutes, or until 1:13,

when it silently left. After only twelve minutes of neglect, the eggs were covered by one member of the pair. Now began a period of restlessness, the two partners replacing each other four times in the next two hours. The bird who settled on the eggs at 3:29 sat continuously until nightfall.

I also watched this nest through the whole of January 28 and from daybreak until late in the afternoon of January 30. After the routine of incubation was well established, the two partners replaced one another only twice each day and kept their eggs constantly attended. On January 28, the changeovers occurred at 7:46 A.M. and 3:35 P.M., so the day shift lasted seven hours and forty-nine minutes. On January 30, the changeovers were made at 9:01 A.M. and 4:12 P.M.; the day shift continued for seven hours and eleven minutes. The partner who went on the nest in the afternoon stayed until relieved by its mate the next morning. I could not tell whether the Squirrel Cuckoo who incubated throughout the night was the female or, as in anis and some other cuckoos, the male.

Sometimes the partner arriving to begin its long spell of incubation brought a leaf or a stick, but at other times it came with an empty bill. The changeover was effected in silence or with a low *jícaro*. Although it usually incubated silently, occasionally the sitting bird called a soft *whip—whip—whip*, at the same time twitching its long tail feathers. These calls were most often heard as the time for its relief approached. Rarely, the cuckoo rose from its eggs to hop around the nest and resettle on it, facing in a different direction.

At my lowest nest, both eggs were pipped eighteen days after the second had been laid. The next day both shells had been pierced by the bills of the chicks trying to escape. Then the eggs were inexplicably deserted and never hatched. These observations would make the period of incubation about nineteen days, but possibly it was lengthened by the disturbances caused by my unsuccessful attempt to use the blind and by the daily passage of farm workers along a nearby path.

The Nestlings

After the desertion of these eggs on the point of hatching, ants entered through the perforations in the shells and killed the chicks within, if they had not already died from exposure. I opened an egg and found the dead chick's blackish skin sparsely sprinkled with hairlike downy feathers, much like the natal down of the Yellow-billed Cuckoo and its relatives in the genus *Coccyzus*.

I did not learn just when the eggs hatched in the high nest in the bamboo, but by February 13 the parents were bringing food. In the first five and a quarter hours of the morning, they came only four times, on each visit bringing a single massive insect. This regimen of infrequent but surprisingly large meals was maintained as long as the young remained in the nest. After another week, I often saw a single feathered nestling as it stood up to exercise its wings or rested on the nest's rim, never two nestlings, although two may have been present at the beginning. From dawn until eleven in the morning on February 19, this nestling was fed only four times, by both parents, in five and a quarter hours; in the same interval of the following day, it received five meals. The winged or larval insects, most often green but sometimes of a darker color, were often badly mangled when the parent arrived with them. One meal consisted of a large green caterpillar bristling with stinging spines. After it was feathered, the nestling flapped its wings vigorously while taking its food on or beside the nest. Its open mouth revealed a bright red interior, although the inside of the adult's mouth is black. Occasionally, after delivering food, the parent carried away a dropping.

I first glimpsed the nestling when it rose to receive a meal on the morning of February 19. It was already well feathered, with conspicuous white tips on its short tail feathers. Nevertheless, the parents continued to brood it much, throughout the night, in the morning until well after sunrise, in the late afternoon, and whenever it rained. On the showery afternoon of February 21, I saw a parent brooding it for the last time. The following day the young bird was out of the nest.

The young Squirrel Cuckoo's separation from its nest was a gradual process. As early as February 19, it sometimes rested beside rather than in the nest or hopped rapidly around or over it, amid the close-set bamboo twigs. While perching on the rim, it spent many minutes assiduously preening and scratching; then it would settle down in the nest out of sight. By February 22 it seemed to pass most of the day perching or hopping amid the crowded bamboo shoots near its nest, to which from time to time it returned. After it had spent two days in this manner, it moved away.

Half-grown fledglings that have just left the nest rather closely resemble their parents in plumage, but their tails are still rudimentary. Their eyes are brown instead of red as in the adults, their bills are grayish horn color, and the bare region around their eyes is gray instead of yellowish green. At intervals these young cuckoos call *eee-kah* sharply. A nest and its surroundings were soiled only slightly by the droppings of the young cuckoos who had recently abandoned it, but this may have been in part a result of washing by torrential rains. The wet leaves in the lower part of the nest harbored many ants, a variety of insect larvae, and other small creatures.

12. Lesser Ground-Cuckoo

Morococcyx erythropygus

Travelers ascending the valley of the Río Motagua in Guatemala notice great changes in climate, vegetation, and birdlife. For many miles inland from the river's mouth on the Caribbean coast, they pass through a region of heavy rainfall, where remnants of magnificent tropical rain forest stand amid banana plantations, lush pastures, and the impenetrable thickets that cover abandoned clearings. Farther from the coast, in the rain shadow of the lofty Sierra de las Minas, which intercepts the moisture-laden trade winds, the valley becomes increasingly dry. Soon one enters an arid land, where cacti and low thorny trees thinly cover sterile slopes, and dry watercourses wind through stony hills. The birdlife has changed as much as the vegetation. Only the most adaptable species of the lower valley venture into this parched region, where they seek the lusher growth along the river. Noisy White-throated Magpie-Jays replace the vociferous Brown Jays of the coastal lands; Inca Doves hunt over open ground in place of Ruddy Ground-Doves; one hears the mellow notes of Rufous-naped Wrens instead of the dry voices of Banded-backed Wrens; and the flocks of parrots that fly noisily overhead consist of White-fronted instead of Red-lored amazonas.

While I stood in this hot dry valley on a morning in mid July of 1932, watching a pair of Rufous-naped Wrens build their pocketlike nest in a thorny *Pereskia* tree, a low weak whistle, repeated over and over, drew my attention to a bird of unique aspect walking over the ground beneath the spreading, orange-flowered tree. By its slender form, long tail, bare skin around the eyes, and curved bill, I at once recognized this bird new to me as a cuckoo, a conclusion

strengthened when it flew up to a perch and I noticed that on each foot two toes were directed backward.

Since this was years before an illustrated field guide to Guatemalan birds was available, I wrote down a description that would help me identify the cuckoo when I could consult the ponderous volumes, without colorplates, of Ridgway's *Birds of North and Middle America*. This strange bird was about 10 inches (25 centimeters) long. The general tone of its upper plumage, including the wings and tail, was brown, with bronzy and greenish glints on its long central rectrices. The under plumage, from the chin and sides of the neck to the abdomen, was tawny-rufous. Each dark eye was surrounded by a yellow orbital ring, in front of which was a triangular area of bare yellow skin, and behind the ring was a similar area of bright blue bare skin. Each eye and its surrounding featherless region was framed by black lines, which diverged from the base of the bill, to meet again near the ear. To complete the striking color pattern of this bird, a blackish band ran along the ridge of its yellow bill, and its legs and toes were bright orange-tawny. Months later, I learned from Ridgway's very detailed description that this was a Rufous-rumped Cuckoo. Since the rufous on the rump is hardly noticeable, the bird's name has been changed to Lesser Ground-Cuckoo.

The cuckoo walked sedately over patches of bare ground between low scattered bushes, picking up whatever it could find to eat; once it jumped several feet straight into the air, to snatch an insect from foliage. At intervals the bird paused and, raising its head, uttered a low mellow whistle that seemed to come from far away, although it was not 20 feet (6 meters) from me. While calling, it hardly opened its bill. From the distance came a faint answering whistle. Not in the least shy in my presence, the cuckoo continued to forage with no sign of constraint while I watched, fully exposed to its view, only 6 or 8 yards (5.5 or 7.3 meters) away.

After a while, the cuckoo jumped into some bushes, where it rested a few minutes before it descended to the ground on the other side and toyed with fallen twigs. Finally, it selected some very thin ones and walked away with them in its bill. I was elated by the prospect of finding a nest still under construction, but my new bird dropped its burden before it vanished among low shrubs. Disappointed, I followed through the bushes until, from a low shrub on my left, a bird burst forth so suddenly that I had only a fleeting glimpse of it. Here on the ground was a nest well hidden beneath the densely branched bush rounded by browsing cattle, beside a dry watercourse in a pasture. The shallow bowl, loosely made of dry petioles and slender sticks, was lined with fine herbaceous material, mostly in short lengths. The inside of the bowl was 3¼ inches in diameter by 1¾ inches deep (8.3 by 4.5 centimeters). It held two white eggs, with a chalky surface that I could scratch off with a fingernail. They measured 27 by 20.6 and 27.8 by 21 millimeters. This nest, discovered near El Rancho in the Motagua Valley, at 900 feet (270 meters) above sea level on July 15, 1932, is the only nest of the Lesser Ground-Cuckoo that I have seen or of which I have found a record.

Incubation

The chalky eggs in the crudely constructed receptacle left little doubt that I had found a cuckoo's nest; but I had only the most fleeting glimpse of the bird that fled from it, so to confirm the identification I returned cautiously a quarter of an hour later. A Lesser Ground-Cuckoo was covering the eggs, and it remained steadfast while I bent over it for a closer view. Then the bird ran rapidly from the nest; but, after going only 3 yards (2.7 meters), it abruptly slowed down and

walked deliberately away, as though with a painful effort. On a fallen log 5 or 6 yards (4.5 or 5.5 meters) from me, the cuckoo paused, to remain quiet while I wrote a description of the nest and measured the eggs.

When I revisited the nest in the afternoon, the incubating parent did not leave until my inclined head was almost above it. This time it walked away even more deliberately, with little mincing steps, until it reached a bare sandy area beneath an organ cactus. Here it stopped, puffed out its feathers to make itself look bigger, relaxed its wings, and moved back and forth several times with short, slow steps. Although it did not grovel, beating the ground with its wings in a typical act of injury simulation, it was clearly trying to lure me from its nest by a distraction display. When I approached, it slowly retreated through shrubbery and passed beyond my view.

A few days later, a parent (whether the same I could not tell) gave a different display when my intrusion drove it from the nest. This time it walked unhurriedly away for several yards; then, still in full view, it crouched on the ground with fluffed-out plumage and spread, depressed tail. In this attitude, it vibrated its relaxed wings, beating them against its own body instead of the ground, which it seemed to scratch with its feet. When I followed, the cuckoo moved off until out of sight. On another of my visits, the bird left the nest by jumping 2 feet (60 centimeters) into the air, then alighted on the ground and walked away.

Since I could not distinguish the two parents, I tried to mark one by the method that had been successful with another member of the cuckoo family, the Groove-billed Ani. I covered the end of a short twig with cotton, soaked the cotton in white enamel, and stuck this improvised paintbrush into the nest, with its end projecting over the eggs. When I returned fifteen minutes later, my brush had been carried away, probably by the cuckoo who was now sitting on the eggs with no visible sign of white on its plumage. A second attempt to mark a parent by the same procedure had the same outcome. Later, I noticed that, while removing the paintbrush,

one of the parents had acquired a white spot at the base of its bill. I designated this bird A and its mate B. I was eager to learn whether, as in anis, the male sat on the nest by night, but I was uncertain how I could determine the sexes of A and B without watching one of them lay an egg for a subsequent brood.

I set up my blind before the nest and watched continuously from 7:00 A.M. to 2:12 P.M. on July 16. Cuckoo A, who had left the nest as I entered the blind, returned at 7:43. At 9:30 it turned the eggs and shifted its position, very slightly, for the first time in nearly two hours. It did not move when a half-grown calf walked within a yard of the nest. At 10:15 it began to whistle, the notes at first very low but gradually becoming louder. At intervals, its mate answered from the distance, and after a while these whistles sounded nearer. At 10:24, B approached from the bushes to my left, flying low across the arroyo beside which the nest was situated. The newcomer landed several feet from the nest, its bill full of fine material, and A left. Cuckoo B continued to approach the nest by walking, but when about 2 feet (60 centimeters) distant it seemed to suspect my blind, turned around, and marched away. But, about a quarter hour later, B returned afoot, now with an empty bill, and covered the eggs.

Cuckoo A had incubated continuously for two hours and forty-one minutes when B arrived to replace it. Cuckoo B now sat for three hours and twenty-six minutes, never shifting its position or turning the eggs in all this long interval. In the early afternoon, when the sun's nearly vertical rays reached the bird through the branches of the sheltering shrub, it panted with open bill. Finally, at 2:07, B deliberately arose, walked from the nest, and, after proceeding a few steps, called to its partner, whose voice had been sounding in the distance for several minutes. At 2:12, A arrived, marching over the ground with a billful of fine material, which it added to the nest's lining. After the newcomer was comfortably settled on the eggs, I left.

My observations at this nest were interrupted by a bout of fever, which for much of the next two days kept me in bed. The day

after I resumed my study, the eggs vanished—only a broken shell on the bare sand a few feet away was left. Before this loss, I had learned that cuckoo A, who sat more steadfastly than B, passed each night on the nest. Apparently, incubation followed a simple schedule, with A in charge of the eggs most of the time, while B took a turn of three hours or more in the middle of the day. Before I could confirm this conclusion by finding another nest, continuing fever drove me up into the more healthful highlands. In the many years that have elapsed since I made these fragmentary observations, nothing more appears to have been learned about the breeding of this interesting bird, the only species in its genus.

Postscript

Like a number of other members of the arid tropical avifauna of Mexico and Central America, on the rainy eastern side of the continent the Lesser Ground-Cuckoo has a spotty distribution, being largely confined to deep valleys, such as the middle reach of the Río Motagua, where enclosing mountains intercept the rain-bearing winds and dry conditions prevail. On the more uniformly arid Pacific side, the cuckoo extends more continuously from the state of Sinaloa in Mexico to the Gulf of Nicoya in Costa Rica. Altitudinally, it ranges upward to 4,000 or 5,000 feet (1,200 or 1,500 meters). At the southern limit of its distribution, on the peninsula of Nicoya and around the gulf, I found the ground-cuckoo amid vegetation much lusher than that of the valley where I discovered its nest, including low dense thickets on abandoned patches of cultivation, neglected pastures, and the more open parts of light woods. It was also present in thorny thickets just inland from the beach, as well as beside a mangrove swamp. At the edge of a thicket on the Nicoya Peninsula, a cuckoo perched a few feet above the ground while it tirelessly repeated a full, deep, pensive whistle. Then it delivered a high, clear, stirring, trilled whistle, clacking its mandibles together while it emitted the notes—a performance quite different from any that I heard in Guatemala.

13. Groove-billed Ani

Crotophaga sulcirostris

It seems proper to admit at the beginning that one of the most interesting and endearing birds that I know is not beautiful. Yet it is not absolutely ugly for, being a bird, it wears feathers, and, as Grey of Fallodon wrote about another not very comely bird, having feathers it cannot avoid a measure of beauty. The Groove-billed Ani is lean and lank and appears loosely put together. Its long tail, nearly always frayed and worn, seems so inadequately attached to its body that it is in danger of being brushed off as the bird pushes through the tall grasses and weeds where it forages. In facial expression this ani is especially unfortunate. Its black bill is narrow and high, with the upper mandible strongly arched and furrowed lengthwise by parallel curving ridges and channels. Its black face is largely naked, and prominent lashes shade its dark beady eyes. Its plumage is everywhere black; but the feathers of its neck appear scaly, while greenish and purplish glints play over its body and wings in the sunshine and redeem its black monotony.

In voice, the anis are hardly more attractive than in appearance. Members of the cuckoo family, they are not songbirds, and they lack even the stirring calls of some of their relatives. The call note of the Groove-billed Ani is well paraphrased by one of the common names given to it in Guatemala: *pijúy* (pronounced *pe-whó-e*) or *pichúy*. This call is uttered as the anis perch or fly. Usually given three times together in a soft high-pitched voice, it is neither unpleasant nor melodious, and it is usually preceded by a few throaty clucks, audible only when the bird is near: *tuc tuc tuc pijúy pijúy pijúy*. A Costa Rican name for the ani, *tijo tijo* (*téeho téeho*), represents another attempt to re-produce its peculiar call in human words. These notes are more attractive than the high-pitched whine of the Smooth-billed Ani. Where the ranges of these two black birds overlap, as in much of South America and Panama, they are more readily distinguished by voice than by appearance.

Other utterances that I have heard from Groove-billed Anis include a full, prolonged, mournful call, soft but deep, an expression of anxiety or distress, which one individual delivered while I examined its nest and another uttered after it had been repeatedly repulsed by some Smooth-billed Anis that it tried to join; a harsh rasping *grrr*, voiced as the birds attacked intruders at their nests; and a cackling sound which parents used while coaxing a fallen nestling to return to its nest.

In northern Venezuela, where Groovebills coexisted with the slightly larger, more aggressive Smoothbills, they impressed me as being much quieter, more subdued than I had found them in Central America, where Smoothbills are mostly absent. The *tuc tuc* that Central American Groovebills voice in flight was here reduced to a scarcely audible *tic*; and the soft high-pitched *pijúy* was represented by a slight, shrinking splutter or a sibilant note or, at loudest, a wheezy *pitchu*.

Although anis lack beautiful plumage and a melodious voice, they have been amply compensated in other ways. They have an extraordinarily affectionate nature, adaptability which enables them to thrive in a greater range of environments than many other birds, and nesting habits that make them second in interest to none. Few birds crave the close company of their kind more constantly than the anis. I have never seen them quarrel or fight. When one is separated from its flock, it calls and calls until it finds its companions. Even in hot weather, when it is hardly necessary to huddle together for warmth, from two to fifteen perch side by side as closely as they can press. If one of the inside birds of such a group flies away, the others promptly close the gap. When an ani wishes to pass from one end of the row to the other, it may walk over its companions without provoking hostility, or a new arrival may alight upon the perching birds until they open a space for it in the middle of the row. While one stretches up its neck, its neighbor carefully bills and nibbles at the feathers, possibly searching for insect pests; and, when the first has finished its kind office to the second, the latter reciprocates the favor.

When not nesting, anis associate in flocks of usually ten to twenty-five individuals, who travel over their home range in a leisurely fashion, foraging as they go or pausing to rest on low perches, singly or in compact groups. They do not, like some birds, move in a compact flock that seems to be motivated by a single will, but they straggle along singly or a few together, often strung over a distance of a few hundred feet, and keep in contact by their voices. Sometimes one ani starts off on an expedition only to find that its companions will not follow, in which case, after vainly calling to them, it rejoins the main party.

The ani's flight is as characteristic as any other of its peculiar habits. A long journey, much in excess of a hundred yards (92 meters) is seldom made by a continuous flight. On the contrary, the bird advances with frequent pauses in conveniently situated trees and bushes. As it alights on one of the lower branches, the momentum of its tail carries this long appendage forward above its head with a jerk. Recovering its balance, the ani delays here for a short while, looking cautiously around and calling in its high-pitched voice. Then, satisfied that the way ahead is clear, with a *tuc tuc tuc pijúy pijúy pijúy* it launches itself on the next stage of its journey. A few rapid strokes of its short wings suffice to impart the requisite momentum; then it sets them for a glide, by which it may cover a surprisingly long distance, on a

slightly descending course, without further muscular exertion. If its destination is a certain branch of a tree or shrub, it often alights on a limb considerably lower. Then, by a few queer, rapid, sideward hops along the bough and some bounds or, better, bounces from limb to limb, it gains the desired position, where, most likely, it spreads its wings to the morning sunshine.

In cool wet weather of the rainy season, the anis are a picture of misery as they huddle together on a perch, heads drawn in among damp bedraggled feathers. Although they dislike wetness, they must often seek food amid drop-laden grass and foliage. Then, to dry themselves, they perch atop a fence post, stake, or bare limb and patiently hold their wings spread to the sun's rays, looking very much (if they will pardon the comparison) like miniature vultures. This habit of resting in the sunshine with outstretched wings is best developed in birds with black or blackish plumage; in tropical America the species that I have most often seen sunning themselves in this manner are the Turkey Vulture, Black Vulture, Anhinga, and anis. Because not only in plumage but also in this mannerism the ani resembles a vulture, in Costa Rica it is sometimes called *zopilotillo*, the diminutive of *zopilote* ("vulture").

The variety of habitats acceptable to anis is great; their chief restriction seems to be that they do not tolerate closed woodland. Birds of open country, they appear nearly indifferent to its type. In cultivated parts of the humid coastal regions of Central America, they are one of the most conspicuous species. Their favorite habitats include bushy pastures, orchards, light open woods, lawns with shrubbery, and clearings around the huts of squatters. Marshland is almost as acceptable to them as a well-drained hillside. I found them numerous in such extensive stands of saw grass as those surrounding Toloa Lagoon in Honduras, where they probably did not venture far from some hummock or ridge that supported a few low trees or shrubs in which they could roost and nest. In the semidesert regions of the interior, where their associates in the coastal lands, if present

at all, are as a rule rare and confined to moist thickets along rivers, anis are abundant, living among thorny cacti and acacias as successfully as amid the rankest vegetation of districts watered by 12 feet (3.6 meters) of rainfall in a year.

In altitude, Groove-billed Anis range upward to about 5,200 feet (1,580 meters) above sea level in northern Central America and 7,500 feet (2,280 meters) in Costa Rica, but they are not nearly so abundant in the highlands as in the lowlands. In Panama and Venezuela, where the ranges of Groovebills and Smoothbills overlap, the former appear not to have been reported above 2,500 feet (760 meters). This restriction in altitudinal range appears to be associated with a restriction in habitat. In northern Venezuela, where I found Smoothbills conspicuously abundant in pastures and open fields and along roadsides, the more retiring Groovebills lived chiefly in canebrakes and streamside thickets. From these retreats they ventured into adjoining pastures and weedy fields, to hurry back to sheltering tangles when alarmed.

The anis' food consists largely of insects, which they procure both from the ground and amid the foliage of bushes, and to a much smaller extent of berries and other fruits. They vary their diet with an occasional small lizard. Often they hunt grasshoppers and other creatures amid long grass or tall weeds, where they are completely hidden except when, from time to time, they leap a foot or so above the herbage to snatch up an insect that has tried to escape by flight. Whether they run or hop in such dense vegetation it is scarcely possible to learn; but, when they forage over bare ground or the short grass of a lawn, one can see that they progress both by running and by hopping with feet together, as best suits the occasion. Sometimes they course swiftly after an insect and finally overtake it by a bound into the air.

Anis' favorite method of foraging is beside a grazing cow, horse, or mule. Several birds remain close to the head of the quadruped, progressing by awkward hops as it moves and barely avoiding its jaws and forefeet, ever alert to seize the insects stirred up from the grass by the passage of the herbivore. Rand (1953) showed by careful counts that the anis catch more insects per minute when foraging with cattle than when hunting alone and that the quadrupeds are especially helpful to them in the dry season, when insects are relatively scarce. Similar results were obtained by Smith (1971).

It is frequently stated in books, and affirmed by residents of the countries where anis live, that they alight upon cattle and pluck ticks and other vermin from their skins—whence the name *garrapatero* ("tick eater"), given to them in parts of Central America. It is told that a Costa Rican minister of agriculture, having heard that anis relieve cattle of ticks, imported some from Cuba (the Smooth-billed species), apparently unaware that his own country was well populated with Groove-billed Anis! While it is doubtless true that anis sometimes eat ticks, I have watched Groovebills near cattle from Panama to Guatemala, and only with extreme rarity have I seen one alight upon a cow. Since the ani associates so much with cattle without alighting upon them, and the Giant Cowbird, another black bird of about the same size, does frequently perch on them and relieve them of parasites, I suspect that the ani often receives credit for the good offices of the cowbird, especially since the latter is shier and less known. People who have assured me that the ani plucks ticks from grazing animals were unaware of the existence of the Giant Cowbird. At a distance, such an unobservant person might suppose that the birds upon an animal's back were the same as those of the same color about its feet; and, since a closer approach would leave only the latter, the error would probably persist. Rand failed to see anis perch on cattle in El Salvador, and only once did he see one of these birds pluck a tick from a cow.

Frequently I have come upon a group of anis, perhaps a dozen or more, clustered together on the ground or low among bushes, calling excitedly and jumping around in a lively, apparently aimless way, as though they were mad. Such animated assemblies generally indicate that the birds have discovered a battalion of army ants and have flocked to the feast. It is difficult to see just what the anis do, for often the vegetation is dense, and if one approaches too near they melt away. Anis are canny birds, more or less indifferent to the presence of a person who does not too obviously pay attention to them but shy and restless if they discover that they are being watched. Yet I have little doubt that on these occasions they seek not the ants but the cockroaches, spiders, and other small creatures driven from their hiding places in the ground litter by the horde of hunting ants. If they preyed upon the ants themselves, so much excitement and apparently aimless jumping around would be inexplicable, for they could stand beside a moving column and pick up multitudes of ants without much exertion. The mixed parties of antbirds, woodcreepers, Gray-headed Tanagers, and other birds that accompany army ants in lowland forests behave in much the same manner, and it is often obvious that they prey not upon the ants but upon the hapless creatures driven from concealment by them.

In Venezuela, I watched Groove-billed and Smooth-billed anis foraging with the same large swarm of army ants in a pasture near a stream. Although most of the time the two kinds of anis remained in separate flocks, occasionally they intermingled without signs of aggression, which surprised me, as the two species do not fraternize. In these mixed parties, the Smoothbills made most of the noise, but the Groovebills quietly gathered their share of the booty. Thus, the adaptable anis employ creatures as diverse as oxen and ants to rouse up their small prey.

Anis forage among bushes, vine tangles, and low trees as well as on the ground. It is amusing to watch them jump from branch to branch with an apparent clumsiness that conceals their real agility. Going either up or down, they progress by short hops from twig to twig and pluck small invertebrates from the foliage. If an insect tries to escape by flight, they may dart into the air and catch it on the wing. When the wet season's first showers send the termites' winged broods into the air in countless multitudes, one may watch the anis everywhere foraging like flycatchers, making ungraceful darts, not exceeding a few feet, from low twigs and fences; but the weakly fluttering insects are then so numerous that the birds can seize many without quitting their perches.

Thus, in an unhurried manner, the flock of anis visits each day its favorite hunting grounds, the pasture where the birds forage at the heads of cattle, the dooryard where they search for insects amid the shrubbery, more rarely a bush or vine that supplies ripe berries. In the warmest hours of the afternoon, they rest close together in the shade. Toward evening they forage more actively again, and before sunset they gather for the night at their roost, preferably a citrus tree whose dense dark green foliage and branches armed with formidable thorns offer both concealment and protection or, this failing, a tangle of vines at the edge of a thicket. One night my flashlight's beam picked out eleven sleeping in a compact row on a horizontal branch of a lemon tree, all facing the same way—a sight to remember.

The History of a Solitary Pair
Although several pairs of Groove-billed Anis often lay eggs in the same nest, fortunately I began my study of their nesting with a single pair and could learn details which are less clear when two or three pairs attend a nest. On June 21, 1930, a student at the Lancetilla Experiment Station in northern Honduras found a nest while he was spraying a small orange tree, amid whose dense foliage it was well concealed, 7 feet (2.1 meters) above the ground. When he showed it to me two days later, two eggs rested on the bed of fresh green leaves that lined the shallow, rather bulky cup of coarse sticks. I pulled out one of the longest sticks, which measured 34 inches (86 centimeters). Although I often saw an ani on the two eggs by day, they were left uncovered at night. On June 27, four days after the second egg was present, the third and last egg of the set was laid. Even then, these erratic birds left the eggs exposed during the night. Perhaps they awaited a fourth egg, since this is the usual number, but, if so, they waited in vain. By day, they incubated and

brought fresh green leaves to the nest. Finally, in the evening of June 29, the third after the last egg had been laid, a bird remained on the nest.

The male and female of this pair were so similar in appearance and voice that, to learn their respective parts in incubation, I needed to place a distinguishing mark on one of them. This was long before the days of mist nets. I had never marked a bird; and my naïve scheme was to approach the nest stealthily at night, dazzle the sitting ani by suddenly flashing a beam of light in its eyes, and deftly place a spot of white paint on its plumage. The last hour of darkness seemed the best time for this attempt, for it appeared unwise to risk driving the bird from its nest early in the night, when, if it fled, the eggs would be exposed to prolonged chilling. Before dawn, I climbed the stepladder that I had set beside the nest on the preceding afternoon. Unfortunately, the ani slept more lightly than I had anticipated; the slight rustle of the foliage against which I brushed in the dark frightened it from its nest before I could reach it. Foiled, I stuck my little brush between the sticks so that the ani might rub against the paint-soaked bristles when it returned, and, greatly disappointed, I went back to sleep until daybreak.

After breakfast, I entered my blind to see the results of my experiment. On the breast of one member of the pair was a tiny white spot, difficult to detect. I dipped the brush into the paint again and set it with the bristles projecting farther over the shallow nest. The ani who soon returned appeared not to notice the brush but, with unexpected carelessness, bumped right into this conspicuous object, marking the right side of its bill and head, as well as its breast. I feared that it even got paint in an eye, but, if so, this soon vanished with no ill effects. The enamel dried quickly and stuck well, and for the next three months it was easy to recognize the clumsy bird, whom I named Whiteface. Its mate, by way of contrast, I knew as Blackface. Since Whiteface always occupied the nest at night, I assumed that this bird was the female. All through the first nesting of this pair, I attributed the wrong sexes to

these two birds. Only after they started their second brood did I correct my error, as will be told in due course. But it will simplify the following account if I say at once that Whiteface was the male and Blackface the female.

These two anis were paragons of conjugal affection. It was pleasant to see, on the morning when I first set a blind before their nest, the one driven from the eggs by my operations fly straight to its mate, who was perched on an exposed branch drying its wings. The two sat as close together as they could press, and each billed the other's plumage. They showed their mutual attachment in many little ways. They were continually calling to each other, even as they entered or left the nest; and sometimes, while sitting, one answered the call of its mate in the distance. Both took turns on the nest, but they were at first most impatient sitters, frequently replacing each other. In seven hours of watching during the first six days after the completion of the set, thirty minutes was the longest session on the eggs that I witnessed. Sometimes an ani sat for only a minute or two before the other flew up to relieve it; and sometimes, at the call of its mate, the sitting bird would leave the nest unattended to go and perch or forage with its partner. Often they flew together to the nest, which had been left unguarded for from a few minutes to nearly half an hour while they enjoyed each other's company. Then one settled on the eggs while the other, after delaying a moment beside it, went off again. From 7:10 to 10:32 A.M. on July 2, Whiteface incubated for four periods ranging from two to nineteen and totaling fifty minutes; Blackface incubated for five periods ranging from less than one to twenty-two minutes and totaling sixty-nine minutes; and the eggs were unattended for seven intervals ranging from two to twenty-seven and totaling eighty-three minutes.

Many times each day, when they came to take their turns on the eggs, the anis brought fresh leaves plucked from neighboring trees or shrubs. They tucked these beneath the eggs; since they never removed the old ones, a thick layer of dead leaves covered the inside of the cup before the eggs hatched. Usually each bird placed the leaf that it brought, but sometimes it gave it to the sitting mate, who arranged it in the nest. The eggs were never covered by the leaves but always lay above them. Even when a parent departed spontaneously, leaving the nest unattended, it did not conceal or protect the eggs beneath the leaves. Occasionally the anis also brought sticks and straws, and while incubating they sometimes arranged the material around them.

As the days slipped by, Whiteface and Blackface shared the common experience of newly mated couples and became less eager for one another's company. The one who was free stayed at a greater distance from the nest, and they called back and forth less frequently. At first, one was rarely out of the other's sight; before their eggs hatched, they had settled into a humdrum routine. Although at the beginning of incubation they sat on the eggs for from one to thirty minutes at a stretch and often left them uncovered, by the last two days of incubation their sessions had lengthened greatly and were seldom less than half an hour. When one partner saw that the other had left the nest, it went immediately to occupy it, often plucking a green leaf on the way. In over five hours on July 9 and 10, Whiteface took three sessions lasting 51, 26, and 53 minutes and totaling 130 minutes; Blackface took four sessions lasting 30, over 46, 36, and 59 minutes and totaling over 171 minutes; the nest was unattended only twice, each time for about a minute.

One of the three eggs vanished soon after it was laid. On July 11, fourteen days after the last egg appeared, I held one of them in my hand while the chick worked its way out. When I picked it up, a gap in the thicker end extended about a third of the way around the circumference. The chick's short thick bill was in the gap, so pressed out of alignment that the lower mandible projected beyond the upper one—a temporary condition. At intervals, the struggling prisoner drew its bill farther into the egg, then abruptly pushed it outward, bringing the keeled ridge, equipped with a rather insignificant egg tooth, against the edge of the shell at one end of the hole, breaking off a small fragment.

Groove-billed Ani: Whiteface incubating in a sprayed orange tree.

The squirming chick, propelling itself in a manner that remained obscure to me, rotated imperceptibly slowly in the shell in such a way that its head, turned under a wing, moved backward and the ridge of the bill was constantly brought to bear against a fresh part of the shell, chipping it off at the next outward thrust. From time to time, the struggling chick emitted a weak cry. Thus, bit by bit, the ragged gap was lengthened until it extended two-thirds of the way around the egg, when the chick's struggles succeeded in cracking the remainder and the thicker end of the shell fell off like a cap. Then the naked creature wriggled out into my palm, where it lay exhausted by its sustained effort.

The two hatchlings were blind and black-skinned, with no trace of feathers—differing from the Yellow-billed and Black-billed cuckoos, which at birth bear rudimentary down in the form of long, rather stiff bristles. Whiteface and Blackface showed more solicitude for their newly hatched young than they had ever done for the eggs. Both flew very close to me, calling *pijúy pijúy*.

At first, the nestlings were brooded almost continuously. Usually one parent remained covering them until the other arrived with food, when it made way for its mate, who stood on the nest's rim to place an insect into a widely opened mouth. Then, often after delaying several minutes on the rim, the parent settled down to brood until its partner returned. Rarely, the nest was left uncovered for short intervals. The nestlings' eyes opened within two days after they hatched, and their pinfeathers sprouted rapidly. The parents cleaned the nest by swallowing their droppings.

On the morning when the nestlings were six days old, both bristled with long pinfeathers. On one, apparently the older by a few hours, the true feathers were already escaping from the ends of the sheaths. While I was at the nest, the parents, bolder than ever before, circled around and alighted in the small nest tree only a few feet away, calling loudly. Darting close by my head, they uttered a harsh threatening *grrr* and snapped their strong bills with a loud clack. Whiteface far outstripped his mate in these demonstrations, venturing much closer to me and voicing louder complaints.

When I approached later that same day, the older nestling jumped from the nest, climbed quickly down through the thorny branches, and dropped to the ground. It hopped out of the circle of bare earth that surrounded the tree and pushed through the tall grass beyond until it vanished completely. I searched but, fearing that I might step on the young ani unseen in the herbage, I soon abandoned the fruitless quest. When I returned to see whether the other nestling had remained at home while I searched for the truant, it, too, climbed out and hopped along a branch, but only for a short distance. All the while, the parents displayed the greatest excitement.

Leaving the young where they had betaken themselves, I disappeared into the blind to watch further developments and muse upon the oddness of what I had witnessed. In Pan-

ama, I had seen featherless nestlings of the Smooth-billed Ani climb from their nest and crawl through the grass in the same manner. I had read of Hoatzins, strange relatives of the cuckoos who live in trees and thickets bordering lowland rivers and tidal estuaries in tropical South America. When alarmed, their fuzzy, flightless nestlings drop into the water beneath their nests; when all is quiet, they climb back to them, using bill and feet and primitive claws on their wings to raise themselves from twig to twig (Beebe et al. 1917). Later, I learned from Herrick (1910) that young Black-billed Cuckoos climb from the nest at about the same age and stage of development as the anis. But nearly all other altricial nestlings, especially those reared in trees, cling tightly to their nests in the face of danger until their feathers have expanded and they can fly or at least flutter away. It is not that these nestlings are immune to alarm until they have well-developed plumage, but, until they can use their wings, a threat only makes them crouch and cling to their nests.

Meanwhile, Whiteface and Blackface were becoming more composed. They flew around, constantly calling, and looked through the branches of the orange tree and the grass around it for the lost nestling, who remained quietly hidden. After ten minutes, Blackface sat in the empty nest while the other nestling perched in full view before her, but soon she left to resume searching and calling. Soon the younger nestling moved back to the edge of the nest. Blackface returned and pecked at the leaves on the bottom, as though she expected to find her lost offspring beneath them. Not succeeding in this search, she abandoned it and moved over to brood the other, not in the nest but beside it. Later, Blackface returned to rummage again among the leaves that lined the nest, now all brown and dry, for no new ones were brought after the eggs hatched. Then she flew off and found an insect, which she gave to the nestling in the tree. After about an hour, this young ani entered its nest, to be fed and brooded by both parents in the usual manner.

By this time, the parents had become calm again. After an hour and a half of quiet secrecy amid sheltering grass, the truant nestling emerged into the bare circle at the base of the orange tree and called in a weak infantine voice. Blackface, brooding the other nestling 7 feet (2.1 meters) above, seemed not to notice these cries; but, when Whiteface returned, he promptly discovered it and gave excited calls which immediately brought his mate from the nest. Both flew around and above the young ani, calling and making low cackling notes, evidently trying to coax it up into the tree. They seemed powerless to help it, and Whiteface soon began to brood the other nestling. For almost an hour, the young ani on the ground moved about in the grass, climbing up the stalks and stretching up as far as it could toward the lowest branches of the tree, from which its parents looked down as though to encourage it. At intervals it peeped softly. Finally, it reached the trunk and tried to climb up. But the bare smooth column, which rose a foot to the lowest branch, offered it no support; it repeatedly slipped back from the flaring base. After ten minutes of fruitless effort, the young ani returned to the grass, where the tree's lowest limbs were tantalizingly close above it.

Although the parents continued to be much concerned about the nestling on the ground, the stay-at-home received most of their attention. The latter was brooded and fed seven times in two and three-quarters hours, while I saw the former receive only a single meal. Possibly it was given a few more insects, for sometimes, when a parent approached, the young bird was so low in the grass that I could not see just what happened. At least, they were much more attentive to their fallen offspring than those European songbirds which permit their own nestlings to starve before their eyes, while they continue to feed and brood the young Cuckoo who has thrown them from the nest. At last, tired of being left alone and more or less neglected, the young ani climbed as far as it could up a grass stalk, beat its wings, and launched itself into the air. Needless to say, it promptly fell to the ground, but its attempt to fly was not as ridiculous as it seemed to me at the moment.

I had not examined the young ani since

Groove-billed Ani: nestling about six days old, with feathers just beginning to unsheathe.

Groove-billed Ani: the same nestling as in the previous photograph, twenty-four hours later.

morning and remembered it as a nestling that bristled with long pins from which the feathers had just begun to protrude. When finally, convinced that it would not regain its nest without my help, I went to rescue it, I hardly recognized it as the same individual. The feathers had escaped their sheaths with such amazing rapidity that it was already well clothed. Its back and underparts, except a naked strip along the middle of the latter, bore soft downy black plumage. The flight feathers of both its wings and its tail now had broadly expanded tips, the most advanced of which were from one-half to three-quarters of an inch (13 to 19 millimeters) long; when the young bird flapped its wings, they did indeed exert a lifting force, although insufficient for its need. As I replaced the truant in its nest, Whiteface twice struck me on the back, not hard enough to hurt. The restless youngster would not stay at home but climbed upward among the branches. I left it to follow its fancies, and later it returned to the nest. At dusk, I found Whiteface quietly brooding his two restless offspring.

The next morning both young anis, now well feathered, climbed from the nest as I approached. Instead of dropping to the ground, as the older one had done on the preceding day (which, as I learned later, is not the usual procedure), the week-old birds turned their courses upward and went hopping vigorously from twig to twig, hooking a bill over a branch to catch themselves when a leap fell short of its goal. The stronger nestling gained at least 3 feet (90 centimeters) above the nest, then jumped when I tried to capture it. Down through the thorny boughs it hurtled, in danger of impaling itself on those cruelly sharp spines, until it arrested its descent on a lower branch.

Taken in hand, the young ani protested with sharp rasping sounds that resembled the threat calls of its parents. When I set it down on a path, it hopped along at a good pace until it gained the long grass, in which it tried to hide. After recapturing it, I offered it an outstretched finger as a perch. For a minute, it seemed to forget where it was and spread its newly feathered wings, with its back toward the morning sun, a miniature of the adults. Soon it jumped down and tried again to escape. As I replaced it in the nest, one of the parents—Whiteface, I believe—bumped the back of my head. After I left, both young settled down in the nest, to be brooded as though they had never been beyond its rim.

Whiteface covered his offspring for the last time that night, when they were between seven and eight days old. On the next two nights, they stayed in the nest tree but did not return to the nest to sleep. They could not yet fly and had entered a half-scansorial, half-terrestrial stage. When they were ten days old, I tried to catch them for a photograph; but they hopped from limb to limb with such agility that, protected as they were by sharp thorns, I could not capture them. While I went for a ladder to try to reach them in the treetop, the parents, who had been interested spectators of the chase, led them to a smaller orange tree about 50 feet (15 meters) distant. Since the young birds were still incapable of sustained flight, they must have crept through the tall grass, which they could do very well, and hopped up to the low branches of the tree. They were now so adept at hiding amid the roots of grasses and clambering into the densest foliage of bushes that it was extremely difficult to find them. When eleven days old, the anis could make short flights from branch to branch of the same shrub or tree. Their bills were smooth, without grooves, and their cheeks were bare of feathers.

On August 11, three weeks after their nestlings left the orange tree where they hatched, Whiteface and his partner began a second nest in a nearby lime tree. Of the identity of Whiteface I have no doubt, for his distinguishing marks were still prominent. The faint white stain on his mate's breast, if she was in fact the same individual, had vanished; but, in the absence of contrary evidence, I may be permitted to call her Blackface. The pair had been too strongly attached to be easily separated. From my blind, I watched them build in a desultory, halfhearted fashion. Whiteface brought most of the material, consisting of green leaves and sticks in about equal numbers, to Black-

face, who sat on the nest to receive and arrange them. Whiteface sometimes undertook
this work, too, and occasionally the pair
were on the nest together for brief intervals.
The leaves that they brought could hardly
have been intended for the lining, as the nest
was still no more than a frail platform that
had not yet become bowl-shaped. Thus, the
nest was becoming a pile of intermingled
sticks and leaves. But doing things in a definite stereotyped sequence is not the way of
Groove-billed Anis. They line their nest before it is built, then often continue to build
after it has been lined and the eggs have been
laid. Although, for many kinds of birds, each
stage in the complex series of reproductive
activities leads to another and each early
stage's characteristic acts seem to be forgotten, anis sometimes anticipate stages which
should come later or revert to activities that
belong to an earlier phase.

After the third day, I no longer saw the
pair at this nest and I found no more fresh
leaves in it. They appeared to have abandoned their half-finished structure, probably
because it was in a situation more than ordinarily exposed and they sought privacy. A
few days later, I saw Whiteface carry a green
leaf to the old nest where the first brood had
been reared. Later, he and his mate brought
more leaves, which they laid over the old
ones, and sticks to build up the rim. Many of
the latter were removed from the unfinished
nest, which fast dwindled away, in the
neighboring tree.

The pair devoted four days to refurbishing
the old nest, before the first egg appeared in
it. For two months I had been calling Whiteface the female because "she" warmed the
eggs by night; but when I saw that, while
building, Blackface sat in the nest to arrange
material that the other brought, I doubted
the correctness of this ascription. I resolved
to determine the pair's sexes beyond all
doubt by observing which laid the eggs.
Early the following morning, I entered the
blind to watch for the appearance of the next
egg. Both birds sat on the single egg for intervals not exceeding fifteen minutes. They
brought a few sticks and leaves to the nest,
but neither laid another egg. The second day

Groove-billed Ani: fledgling eleven days old.

passed like the first. Early in the morning of
the third day I resumed my vigil, confident
that I would witness the laying of an egg.
Both Whiteface and Blackface sat in the nest,
the latter more often than the former. In midmorning, while Blackface sat, Whiteface
worked harder than I had ever before seen
either partner work. In twenty-one minutes
he brought thirteen sticks, some of which
were transferred from the remnant of the unfinished nest in the lime tree, others picked
up from the ground beneath the nest now in
use. Many of these sticks were much longer
than Whiteface, who had much trouble pulling them up through the close-set spiny
branches of the orange tree. All were given to
Blackface, who arranged them on the nest.

When I left the blind at 11:10 A.M., the nest
still held a single egg. Returning from lunch
at 12:30, I was chagrined to find that an egg
had been laid in my absence. I had spent the
better part of two and a half days, mostly
monotonous because the anis were out of
sight, sitting on a hard box in a stuffy blind,
and in the end I had missed the event that I

had waited so long to see. But at least I now knew in what part of the day it occurred, and with this knowledge it should be relatively easy to observe the laying of the third egg. The chief difficulty was that the interval between the deposition of successive eggs was irregular—it appeared to vary from one or two to four days.

When I returned to the nest the following morning, an ani was sitting in it, but the eggs had vanished; only some fragments of shell lay on the ground below. I began to despair of solving the question of Whiteface's sex; but the birds, not so easily discouraged, turned their attention again to the dismantled second nest, of which only a few sticks remained in the lime tree. The very next day they resumed work on it, bringing more sticks and leaves. I noticed this time that the sticks were not always gathered from the ground. With their bills, the anis broke long slender dead twigs from nearby eucalyptus trees. Such was their industry that three days after the destruction of their eggs the new nest was ready to receive its first egg, which was laid between 12:45 P.M. and sunset on August 29.

At a few minutes before twelve o'clock on September 1, I entered the blind before the new nest with its single egg. I had not long to wait until Blackface flew up with an empty bill, calling, and entered the nest. While she sat, Whiteface brought sticks and green leaves, which she arranged in the nest. After sitting for eighteen minutes, Blackface left the nest, and I hurried up to look in. A second spotless white egg lay beside the first on the bed of dark green leaves. So Blackface was the female; and Whiteface, who incubated every night, more boldly defended the young, and brought sticks and leaves while the other sat in the nest—Whiteface to whom for nearly three months I had applied the feminine pronoun—was the male!

I might at any time after the first nesting have settled this point by shooting either member of the pair and performing an autopsy, which would have taken ten minutes instead of the several days that my watching cost me. But many considerations weighed against the latter course, the first and most irrefutable of which was sentiment. I owed a large share of the joy that this discovery brought me to the fact that I had made it with no sacrifice of life, after having developed an appropriate procedure. Moreover, if I had chosen the easier way of learning Whiteface's sex, I would have missed some of the most exciting revelations which this family made to me.

Three days had elapsed between the laying of the first and the second eggs at this nest, but only two intervened between the second and the third, two more between the third and the fourth. The fact that Blackface had laid six eggs in almost unbroken succession (only four days had elapsed between the laying of the second egg in the rehabilitated nest and of the first in the new nest), when the normal set consists of only four eggs, is an example of a bird's marvelous power to control an intricate physiological process in response to external events.

Again, Whiteface was responsible for the eggs at night. I believe that he would have incubated throughout the night before the last egg was laid; but, when I approached close enough to see whether he was on the nest, he flew off through the twilight to join his mate in the bamboo grove where she roosted. Birds as sociable and affectionate as anis must feel keenly the loneliness of passing the night on the nest, far from companions who sleep amid dense vegetation; at the outset of incubation, any slight disturbance makes them desert their eggs and fly to their comrades, if there is still enough light to find them. Likewise on the following evening, as I entered the blind, Whiteface flew from the nest and would not return, although much daylight remained. But later, when he had become more attached to the nest, he would return even if driven off in the dusk, if I retired to a moderate distance or slipped into the blind, before it was quite dark. I subjected him to these annoyances because I wished to be sure that it was always he who covered the eggs at night.

Years later, in Panama, I watched a nest of the Smooth-billed Ani attended by three adults, whom I had marked with paint by the method I used for Whiteface. One day two of these birds each laid an egg between 12:30 and 1:53 P.M. Since these females laid fertile eggs, the third member of the group was evidently a male. He, too, occupied the nest by night, while his partners roosted amid bushes on the neighboring shore of Gatún Lake (Skutch 1966).

The home life of Groove-billed Anis is beautified by the affection that persists between all members of the family. One of the juveniles of Blackface's first brood was the constant companion of his parents while they attended their second brood. Of his identity I had no doubt; although he was nearly as large as his parents, his bill was smooth except for traces of grooves at the base. I do not know what befell the other young ani. The survivor frequently rested on the nest's rim, beside his incubating parent. Once, while Blackface sat, he flew to the nest with a roach in his bill. I watched eagerly, expecting to see something unprecedented in my experience with birds: a juvenile feeding a parent. Doubtless, if it were the habit of the female Groove-billed Ani as it is of females of the Smooth-billed Ani (Köster 1971) and many other species of birds, to receive food from her mate while she incubates, Blackface would have accepted the insect from her offspring, who held it in his bill for a full minute before he swallowed it. Later, while Whiteface was in the nest, the young ani arrived with a small lizard. He held it within reach of his father, possibly offering it to him, but the latter was not interested. The juvenile carried it away, only to bring it back a minute later. Still, Whiteface showed no desire for the lizard, and the young ani finally ate it. I never saw a breeding ani approach the nest with food in its bill while its mate incubated. Sometimes Whiteface and the young bird perched side by side, nibbling each other's feathers in the manner of adults. When I visited the nest, the juvenile flew around me with his parents, sharing their excitement and adding shrill protests to theirs.

On September 18, three of the four eggs hatched. The one which was deposited last hatched thirteen days after it was laid; if it had been warmed during its first nights in the nest, it might have hatched in twelve days. Davis (1940) found the incubation period of the Smooth-billed Ani to be about thirteen days, although sometimes it was as long as fifteen days. The eggs of the parasitic Cuckoo of Europe hatch in twelve or thirteen days.

From what I had seen of the young ani's behavior while his parents incubated their second complete set of eggs, I was hardly surprised when I first saw him, at the age of seventy-two days, give a small lizard to one of his younger brothers and sisters—on the contrary, for some weeks I had been eagerly waiting to see this happen. Yet this occurred two years before I found yearling helpers at Brown Jays' nests, and such precocious participation in parental activities was wholly new to me. The young ani fed the nestlings regularly, although not as frequently as did the parents. In four and a quarter hours, Whiteface, always the more attentive parent, brought food to the three nestlings twenty-nine times, Blackface fourteen times, and their young helper eight times. The juvenile not only fed the nestlings but protected them zealously, flying up close to me with an angry *grrr-rr-rr* whenever I went near them. When the parents were absent, he tried to defend the chicks alone. He was already a more spirited guardian than Blackface, and from his early ardor I surmised that he was a male, for his father was much bolder than his mother when their family seemed to be threatened. Juvenile Smooth-billed Anis also feed nestlings of the second brood, sometimes beginning when only forty-eight days old, as Davis (1940) saw. A hand-raised Smoothbill engaged in building activities at the age of six weeks (Merritt 1951).

Of the further history of Whiteface's family I have little to record. When the three nestlings were nine days old and clothed with plumage, they left the tree where they hatched. The identifying marks gradually vanished from Whiteface; if I saw him again, I could not distinguish him from others of his kind. The glimpses I had received of the intimate details of this pair's lives deepened my affection for all of their race and guided me through the intricacies of the communal nests.

Communal Nests

Throughout the early months of the year, from February to May, when neighboring birds of other species are mating and building nests, Groove-billed Anis usually live in small flocks and give no indication of being paired. Two often perch in contact, each in turn billing the other; but, even more frequently, one sees three or more birds sitting in a compact row, and these little coteries seem not to be founded on the attraction of opposite sexes. In May and early June, however, the anis pair off and are then more often seen two by two instead of in the larger groups which prevailed earlier in the year. Mated birds are inseparable, foraging together, perching side by side, preening one another's feathers, and calling persistently to each other if they happen to become separated. They give every indication of being monogamous, and one rarely sees mates more attached.

In June 1932, I watched the construction of a communal nest in a small orange tree behind the plantation house at Alsacia, in the Motagua Valley of Guatemala. Although I sometimes saw five pairs near this nest, the birds were not marked, and I was not certain that more than three pairs participated in building it. They worked in pairs, never all together. A mated male and female flew to the nest tree, sometimes side by side, sometimes one in advance, calling *pijúy pijúy pijúy*. One member of the pair settled on the little pile of dry weed stems and leaves in a fork, while the other perched nearby or at times sat beside its mate on the incipient structure. They often tarried quietly in either of these positions for many minutes, doing no work; but at other times the partner on the nest arranged the material with her bill or shaped it with her body. More rarely, when they approached the nest, the male bore a stick or green leaf in his bill. After his mate had settled on the nest, he passed it to her, to be worked into the growing structure. I use these pronouns advisedly, because at the earlier nest of the solitary pair it was usually Whiteface, the male, who delivered material to his mate on the nest.

While one ani remained on the nest, the other brought sticks and green leaves to her. The sticks were often found in the nest tree, where they had been dropped among the close-set branches on earlier occasions; but many were gathered from the ground or broken from a bush in the neighboring pasture. The richly branched dead inflorescences of a shrubby composite were frequently pulled off and taken to the nest. Green leaves were usually plucked from the nest tree and mixed at random with the sticks, even while the nest was in its earliest stages.

Males disliked adding sticks to the nest in the absence of their mates. Once, when a supposed female happened to leave the nest just as her partner approached with a stick in his bill, he followed, still carrying his burden, and dropped it at a distance. At another time, I saw an ani break a dead flower stalk from the composite bush in the pasture, fly with it to his mate perching in the hedgerow, then proceed to the nest, evidently expecting her to follow. When he reached the orange tree and found that she had not budged, he took the stalk back to her, then returned to the nest, calling to her as he went. Finding that she was still not inclined to come, he placed his burden on the nest and rejoined her in the hedgerow.

Groove-billed Anis of the same group seemed almost incapable of quarreling among themselves. Two or three pairs often perched amicably in the same bush. Each pair preferred to work alone at the nest; if a second pair flew into the nest tree, the first often quietly withdrew. However, sometimes one member of the second pair (probably the female) entered the nest beside one of the first pair, while their two mates perched nearby or else brought sticks to them. Rarely, three pairs were in the nest tree simultaneously. Once three birds tried to sit on the unfinished nest together; but these, I believe, were a mated male and female and a female of another pair. Whiteface and his mate, working alone and in a hurry, had built a serviceable nest in three days; but these three pairs, beginning early and proceeding at their leisure, took about three weeks to build theirs. At the end of a month, when I was obliged to leave them, no egg had been laid in it. Nevertheless, the anis continued to take an interest in the nest and to bring fresh leaves for its lining.

In Chiapas, Mexico, Alvarez del Toro (1948) watched nest building by a trio of Groove-billed Anis, consisting of one male and two females. Possibly this deviation from monogamy was caused by the isolation of these three birds, which made it impossible for each of the females to find a separate mate, as was true of the three Smooth-billed Anis in Panama who nested in a small clearing, separated by wide expanses of forest and water from others of their kind. Here the polygynous relationship appeared to be an adjustment to the disparity of the sexes in a small isolated group. However, the Smooth-bills that Davis (1940) studied in Cuba exhibited monogamy, polygyny, and polyandry, all in the same neighborhood.

One of the Groovebills' communal nests most satisfactory to watch was situated in a small orange tree at Birichichi, beside the Río Ulúa in Honduras. It was composed largely of tufts of grass, straws, and stems of herbaceous plants, many with roots attached, suggesting that they had been pulled from the ground by the birds. Not many woody twigs were included in it because the nest tree grew in a field where few were to be found, and the ani, being an adaptable bird, manages with what is available. Since this nest was too far away for me to visit it daily, the man who showed it to me kindly made a record of the dates on which eggs were laid, which of itself, when it is recalled that a female ani usually lays at intervals of two or more days, shows that at least two females were involved:

July 22	1 egg
July 23	2 eggs
July 24	3 eggs
July 25	4 eggs
July 26	5 eggs
July 27	6 eggs
July 28	6 eggs
July 29	8 eggs

Four of these eggs were relatively long and narrow, the other four shorter and broader; they appeared to be two separate sets.

Groove-billed Ani: nest of two pairs with eight eggs resting on green leaves.

A week after the last of these eggs had been laid, I tried to mark the attendants with white paint or, rather, to make them mark themselves, in the same manner that White-face had received his distinguishing characteristic. After three of them had touched the paint-soaked brush, acquiring white blotches adequate for recognition, there remained a fourth, whom I did not deem it necessary to daub.

All four of these anis took turns on the eggs, in no regular order and with no fixed duration. Sometimes one had been on the nest for less than a minute when another came to sit beside it. Without protest, the first always departed almost immediately, leaving the latest arrival in full possession. The longest interval that I saw two individuals cover the eggs side by side hardly exceeded a minute. The ani so promptly displaced by another gave no indication either of resentment or of satisfaction at being free again; often it perched quietly in the nest tree while the newcomer incubated. One afternoon, an individual warmed the eggs for an hour and eighteen minutes, with only a single brief interruption, when it jumped off the nest to chase a small lizard that came near. This was longer than I saw Whiteface or Blackface incubate, although one would have expected the turns on this nest to be shorter, since four birds shared them. At the other extreme, on the following morning, just after I had entered the blind, leaving the anis excited, each of the four took a short turn on the eggs in less than ten minutes. At night, one ani covered the eggs alone.

At a neighboring nest, also of two pairs, two anis were busy bringing pieces of dead vines and dried bases of grass tufts to be arranged by a third individual, who covered the eight eggs. This was a belated spurt of nest building, for on the next day a nestling hatched. These anis hatched all eight of their eggs over an interval of four days, with the result that the youngest nestling was naked and blind while its siblings had long pinfeathers. A single parent brooded the eight nestlings at night.

Just as the parents cooperate in incubating the eggs, so do they all join in attending the nestlings. I watched three nests, each belonging to two pairs, while they held young. Two of these nests were certainly attended by four adults, but at the third I could not convince myself that more than three participated. Possibly some mishap had befallen the fourth member of this association, or possibly I failed to recognize it, since the anis at this nest were unmarked and indistinguishable. I found it almost impossible to make the parents rub against a paintbrush except while they incubated their eggs. If I stuck a brush into a nest with young, the insatiably hungry nestlings tried to swallow it. At one of the nests, I learned to recognize all four parents by their tail feathers, which were frayed and broken in diverse patterns.

When hungry, the nestlings made a loud sizzling sound, as of something frying in grease, and tried to swallow everything in reach—a finger that I presented to them, a stick, or a thorn projecting above their nest's rim. At the age of five or six days, they scrambled out of the nest and hopped away through the branches of the nest tree when alarmed. Since they could support themselves hanging by one foot, they rarely fell. While the young tried to escape, their parents vigorously buffeted my head, continuing this as long as I remained by the nest and at times almost knocking off my hat. At some of the communal nests, I received many more bumps than at Whiteface's nest. Except while the nestlings were very small, the parents did not clean the nest, but the young squirted their excrement over the side. Thus, the nest was kept more or less clean, much as with hummingbird nests, from which the parent also removes with her bill droppings of very small nestlings, while older ones eject their excreta over the rim. Although this method is adequate to keep a hummingbird's compact cup sanitary, the long projecting sticks of an ani's nest are fouled by the ejected droppings, and the nest soon acquires a characteristic odor that betrays its presence.

Anis become active late in the morning, for they dislike wetting their plumage by hunting amid herbage heavy with dew. While early birds are busy stuffing their young, anis prefer to rest on exposed perches, spreading their wings to the slanting rays of the rising sun. Meanwhile, one of the parents remains brooding the little ones in their nest. It is eight o'clock or later before they begin to feed their nestlings actively, but then they do so with great energy. The three or four attendants of the above-mentioned nest brought food to eight nestlings sixty-six times in two hours or at the rate of about 4.1 meals per nestling per hour. Unfeathered young often climb upon their nest's rim, the sooner to receive a meal. Their diet consists largely of grasshoppers, but also includes cockroaches and other insects, spiders, an occasional small lizard, and a rare berry.

Very small nestlings manage to swallow surprisingly large grasshoppers; but sometimes two parents, standing on opposite sides of the nest, prepare a particularly large morsel by pulling it apart between them, and each gives its half to a nestling. Although parent birds of many kinds try patiently for minutes together to induce a nestling to swallow an item beyond its capacity, few cooperate with their mates to reduce the size of such an article, as anis do.

The efforts of parent anis to separate a lizard into swallowable pieces are not always successful. Once I saw an ani bring a lizard of moderate size, already dead, and offer it to a nestling, whose efforts to swallow it were of no avail. The parent took it up again and perched with it in the nest tree, calling for help, until another attendant arrived. Standing on the rim of the nest, the two tried to tear the lizard apart between them, but they succeeded only in pulling it out of each other's bills. Then one again presented it to a nestling, with no better result than before. Next it carried the victim to a clear space on the ground and, for ten minutes, struggled vainly to shake and beat it into pieces. Tiring of this fruitless effort, it again took the reptile to the nest and offered it to a nestling; but it had scarcely diminished in size, and none of the brood could swallow it. Now another parent carried the lizard to the ground and tried to accomplish what the first had failed to do, but after five minutes it abandoned the attempt and brought it to the nest for the fourth time. Now a nestling made a brave effort to swallow the lizard, but this was still impossible. Finally, a parent flew away with the corpse, and I saw it no more.

Sometimes a young ani manages to gulp down all of a small lizard but the tail, which then projects into the air and waves from side to side with the nestling's movements, until at last it disappears. On the whole, birds save energy and feed their young more efficiently when they avoid items that cannot be easily swallowed or readily broken apart.

A General Survey of Nesting
Throughout Central America, Groove-billed Anis nest late, after the majority of their neighbors of other families have raised one or two broods. They wait until the dry season has ended and rainfall has caused the herbaceous vegetation to spring up lushly, increasing the abundance of grasshoppers and other insects that, flourishing in it, are a large part of the anis' diet. In waiting for the rains to refresh the vegetation before they begin to breed, Groove-billed Anis resemble Smooth-billed Anis, which nest sooner in years when the dry season ends early than when it is prolonged (Davis 1940).

The earliest occupied Groove-billed Anis' nest that has come to my attention in Central America was found at Los Cusingos on April 26, 1942, when it already held four eggs, which vanished a few days later. In the following year, on April 4, a pair of anis started to build in an orange tree in our garden, but they abandoned the vicinity before completing their nest. In both years much rain fell in March, and by April the herbage was already lush. About this time, the population of Groovebills in the Valley of El General began to diminish, as invading Smoothbills became more numerous, and I have not again found the former nesting in this region. Elsewhere in Central America, I have not seen anis building before late May or June.

For its nest site, the ani prefers a densely foliaged tree or bush standing in an open space or, at least, near a grassy area where the bird can forage. Orange trees with crowded thorny branches and profuse foliage, or other kinds of citrus trees, are highly favored. Nearly half of the thirty nests that I have seen were in orange, lemon, or other varieties of citrus trees. Thorny plants of other kinds are frequently chosen: one nest was in a dense clump of low, spiny palms; another was in a compact thorny bush of *Randia*; in arid regions, an organ cactus or an opuntia bristling with needlelike spines is often selected to support the nest. Where a well-armed compact tree or shrub is not available, anis often build in a dense tangle of vines that have overgrown a tree standing in the open or near the edge of a thicket. One nest, in the most impenetrable second growth, was about 25 feet (7.6 meters) from a neighboring grassy plantation and 13 feet (4 meters) above the ground. Sometimes the nest is placed in a clump of bamboo. One pair of anis refurbished an ample, cup-shaped nest that a Great-tailed Grackle had abandoned by adding a few sticks to the rim and lining the bottom with fresh green leaves, but such appropriation of nests of other species is unusual. In height, the nests that I have seen ranged from 4 to 25 feet (1.2 to 7.6 meters) above the ground, but two-thirds were from 5 to 10 feet (1.5 to 3 meters) up. In El Salvador, Miller (1932) found a nest only 2 feet (60 centimeters) up. Anis' nests are nearly always well concealed by foliage and not easily found.

The nest is a bulky, usually shallow, bowl-shaped structure, open above. It is composed of coarse material, including woody twigs, lengths of dead herbaceous vines, weed stalks, tufts of grass, often with roots attached, strips of palm leaf, rather coarse roots, and the like—varying considerably according to what the locality affords. The lining always consists of small leaves, plucked while fresh and green and never removed after they wither. The first of these leaves are brought at an early stage of construction, and others are added daily until the eggs hatch, so that finally a thick layer of dead and dying leaves covers the bottom of the nest. It is difficult to give the overall dimensions of such a structure, for one does not know how far to measure along the projecting ends of twigs, some of which are nearly a yard long. Often the body of the nest is about 1 foot (30 centimeters) in diameter. The internal diameters of six nests varied from 4¼ by 4½ to 6 by 6½ inches (10.8 by 11.4 to 15 by 16.5 centimeters), while in depth these nests ranged from 2¼ to 4¼ inches (5.7 to 10.8 centimeters). The widest nest was also the deepest, but the narrowest was of about average depth, 2¾ inches (7 centimeters). Nests more than 3 inches (7.6 centimeters) deep are exceptional. My records do not reveal whether structures built and occupied by several pairs are consistently more capacious than those of solitary pairs. As is evident from the foregoing histories, the time taken to complete a nest is most variable; with pressing need, a single pair finished a nest in three days, but three or more cooperating pairs took about three weeks.

The eggs, as we have seen, are laid around noon or soon after midday. The interval separating the laying of successive eggs by the same female is variable, usually two or three

days. It is difficult to learn with accuracy the number of eggs deposited in an ani's nest. More often than with any other bird that I know, one finds either whole or broken eggs lying on the ground below the nest, and these must be added to those still within the nest to give the full number that were laid. One can never be sure that all the eggs that somehow fell from the nest have been counted. I do not know just how these eggs are removed from the nest. Most anis' nests are so well built that they could securely hold a dozen eggs. Perhaps the birds carelessly knock them out, but possibly this is done by a predator that is attracted by the appearance of the eggs but, after sampling one, finds them unpalatable (see also the end of this chapter).

The number of eggs in apparently complete sets that I have seen has ranged from three to twelve, but one set of fifteen was reliably reported to me. I have found no mention of a larger set in print. The Groove-billed Ani does not produce such big nestfuls as the Smooth-billed Ani, several females of which may lay as many as twenty-nine eggs in a nest (Davis 1940). Nests of Groovebills attended by a single pair contained from three to five eggs, but usually a single female produces a set of four. One nest with eight eggs was attended by four adults, and another set of eight eggs was cared for by at least three anis. In all, I have watched (rather than merely found) five nests in which two pairs took an interest; but in three of these nests laying had apparently not been finished, or some of the eggs or nestlings had been lost. I once watched at least six anis, or three pairs, build the same nest, and that which contained twelve eggs seemed to belong to three pairs. The apparently complete sets in my records were of the following composition (including, in two instances, an egg found beneath the nest): one set of three, seven sets of four, one set of five, three sets of eight, one set of eleven, one set of twelve, and one reported set of fifteen. According to Davis, the female Smooth-billed Ani in Cuba lays from four to seven eggs, and this agrees with my more limited experience with this species in Panama.

The Groove-billed Ani's eggs are bluntly ovate in shape. When newly laid, they are uniformly covered with a chalky white deposit, which is readily scraped away with a fingernail and, in the nest, is scratched off by the birds' bills or toenails or by the projecting sticks. The removal of this superficial deposit reveals the blue or blue-green of the underlying shell, which is equally evident on the inner surface. Not only is the chalky layer readily scratched away, it is also stained by the dying or dead leaves on which the eggs rest, so that, by this combined action of scratching and staining, the shells soon lose their original whiteness and are far less conspicuous on their bed of green leaves. One can estimate how long they have been in the nest by the degree of their discoloration. The measurements of fifty-six eggs which I temporarily removed from nests averaged 32.1 by 24.2 millimeters, with extremes of 28.6 to 35.7 by 22.2 to 25.4 millimeters.

In nineteen nests in the Caribbean lowlands of northern Central America (Honduras and Guatemala), eggs were laid as follows: late June, three; July, eleven; August, four; early September, one. In Costa Rica's central valley, from 4,000 to 5,000 feet (1,200 to 1,500 meters) above sea level, I have found eggs from June to November. Some pairs raise two broods in the long nesting season.

Relations with Smooth-billed Anis

Although Groovebills and Smoothbills coexist over wide areas of South America and Panama, the southern Pacific quarter of Costa Rica is the only region farther north where I have found the two similar species together. In 1936, my first full year in the Valley of El General, Groovebills were sparingly present; but I saw no Smoothbills until March 1940, when I found a few following cattle in a pasture near the cabin I then occupied toward the head of the valley. Early in April, I was surprised to see one of this flock chasing another black bird and to hear the unmistakable soft *pijúy pijúy* of the Groove-billed Ani coming from the fugitive, while the pursuer voiced the whining *ooenk ooenk* of the Smoothbill. While the latter continued to

drive the Groovebill away, two other Smoothbills rested in a bush, where the third joined them after the would-be intruder had fled to a satisfactory distance. Two perched side by side, by turns preening each other's plumage. The soft-voiced Groovebill, hungering for the company of the only other anis in the vicinity, repeatedly tried to join them. Every time it approached, one of the Smoothbills drove it off again; and it fled, voicing the subdued calls so different from the notes of the pursuer.

Through the remainder of April and most of May, or for no less than six weeks, the lone Groove-billed Ani persisted in its efforts to attach itself to the little flock of Smoothbills; but it was always as ungraciously repulsed. Meanwhile, I had found a party of about seven Groovebills high on the slope of the mountain at whose foot this little drama of thwarted affection was being acted. A belt of forest possibly a thousand feet (300 meters) wide, in addition to open fields, separated this group from the solitary individual of their kind and the three Smoothbills. Since anis are poor fliers and avoid forest, it was not likely that the isolated bird would soon find others of its own species. A long circuitous course might have taken it to the flock of seven, without passing through or over woodland; but I had little hope that it would join them.

Day after day, the lonely Groovebill hovered in the vicinity of the three Smoothbills and was driven off innumerable times. Once I saw one of the latter take over the chase after another had grown tired; the solitary bird aroused the antagonism of more than one of the trio. But the Smooth-billed Anis were no better fliers than the Groovebill, who easily eluded the pursuers, ever and again circled around to rest once more in their neighborhood, and was driven away anew when it ventured too near. In the evening, I sometimes found it perching all alone in a bush in the pasture, after the others had retired to sleep together amid the denser shrubbery beside a brook. A bird of companionable disposition, it yearned for company at the roost but could find none—it was a poignant example of a social being unable to find congenial companionship.

At the end of April, a fourth Smooth-billed Ani arrived and perched near the other three, while the soft-voiced outcast hovered in the offing, to be driven off whenever, uttering its alien call, it attempted to come too near. That evening, while watching the flock go to roost, I learned that the fourth Smooth-bill had not been wholly accepted by the original trio. After much moving around, three of the Smoothbills retired into a loose clump of bushes and young trees in the midst of the open pasture. When the fourth individual of their kind tried to join them there, one of the others sallied out and chased it beyond the rivulet a hundred yards (92 meters) away, then returned to its companions, while the intruder remained out of sight amid shrubbery. On the preceding day, I had noticed signs of antagonism between the Smoothbills, yet they all seemed to agree with one another better than with the Groovebill.

The Groove-billed Ani, who as usual had been driven around during the late afternoon, perched quietly at the top of a small shrub, while the three Smoothbills settled down for the night after driving away the fourth. Then, flying from bush to bush, sometimes voicing a soft *tijo tijo*, the Groovebill gradually approached the clump where the three that it desired as companions rested. When it had nearly reached the bushes, one of the Smoothbills emerged and chased it back to the rivulet. Among the bushes on the steep slope bordering the brook the Smoothbill continued to chase the Groovebill, who now stubbornly refused to retreat farther but circled and doubled around, easily eluding the chaser. Sometimes the Smoothbill alighted in the same bush where the fugitive had paused; for a brief interval the two black birds caught their breath while perching close together in apparent amity; then the Smoothbill would renew the pursuit. I never saw one strike or grapple with the other.

After prolonged circling around among the bushes along the rivulet, the Smooth-billed Ani desisted from the useless pursuit and returned to the clump where the others were resting. Now the Groovebill perched conspicuously on top of a bush and uttered soft mournful notes, full and continuous, unlike anything that I had ever before heard from an ani. After a long pause here, while daylight swiftly faded, it approached the clump by slow degrees, flying from bush to bush, pausing on the top of each to look around and repeat its mournful cries. By this gradual approach it had almost reached the clump where the others roosted, when one of the three flew out and drove it away. This time, pursuit was not long continued; the assailant soon turned back to the clump, leaving the solitary Groovebill perching atop a low shrub at no great distance. After this latest rebuff, the poor bird had no heart to try again to join the exclusive Smoothbills. After pausing a while in the failing light, it turned about and flew down to sleep alone by the rivulet, softly calling *pijúy* as it went.

As so often happens in such cases, the ani would not, or could not, disguise the feature in which it differed most conspicuously from those with whom it wished to associate—its voice. For a long while, I suspected that it was not permitted to join the three Smooth-billed Anis because it was of a different species and spoke a different language. But later, when the fourth Smoothbill was repulsed, it became evident that these anis were clannish to a degree that I had not suspected of them. The Groove-billed Ani was in much the same situation as the Smooth-billed Ani who had not been accepted as a member of the flock.

First noticed in Costa Rica near the Panamanian border in 1931, the Smooth-billed Ani has continued to spread westward and northward along the Pacific slope, its advance favored by the appalling destruction of the heavy rain forest since that date. By 1940 it had reached the head of the Valley of El General, and by the 1960s it had almost displaced the less aggressive Groove-billed Ani. Now Smoothbills are abundant in the valley and Groovebills rare. Here the two species seem not to coexist as well as they do in Venezuela, where they have had much longer to adjust to each other and occupy different ecological niches.

The Origin of Communal Nesting

The origin of the anis' communal nesting has excited much speculation. Some have tried to relate it to the parasitic habits of the European Cuckoo and many other members of the family. Others have believed that the absence of sharply delimited stages or phases in the nesting cycle predisposes birds to other irregularities. We have noticed how slowly Groove-billed Anis work up to full constancy of incubation, how they may lay eggs before the nest is finished or build up the nest when the eggs are about to hatch. However, by no means all birds, even of species in which monogamous pairs breed in solitude, complete their nests before they start to lay and cease to bring material after incubation has begun, as is usual among songbirds. Among passerines, species of horneros and becards continue to add to bulky or elaborate nests until their eggs hatch, and even a few songbirds, including certain titmice and wrens, have this habit. Yet the absence of sharply delimited phases in the nesting operations does not lead to communal nesting or parasitism in these groups.

Although it is tempting to relate the communal nesting of anis to the nest parasitism of many other members of the cuckoo family, perhaps regarding the several pairs at a joint nest as parasitic one on another, it is more enlightening to consider such nesting in relation to the increasing number of cooperative breeders that are being discovered among birds permanently resident in the warmer parts of all the continents. Among the behaviors that anis share with other cooperative breeders are territorial defense by groups (often parents with full-grown offspring) rather than by single pairs, resting and sleeping in contact, mutual preening, rarity or absence of aggressive behavior among group members, feeding of younger siblings by older nonbreeding siblings, and defense of the nest and of fledged young by all the grown members of the group. Even when the group contains several individuals of both sexes, the breeding pair tend to be monogamous, although exceptions are known.

Anis possess these traits in high degree. Few birds are more strongly attached to each other than members of an ani group. I never saw Groove-billed Anis act aggressively toward their associates. Their monogamy is very evident as the breeding season approaches and while they build, although it is less apparent at a joint nest while they incubate and attend young with no distinction of mine and thine. Far from showing any relaxation of parental care, they defend their nests with a zeal rarely equaled by other small birds, often attacking anyone who appears to jeopardize their young. Thus the communal nesting of anis appears unrelated to the brood parasitism of a number of other cuckoos; rather, it seems to be a wholly independent development in an ancient, widespread, and exceedingly diverse family of birds. Just as anis are more strongly attached to their companions than are certain other cooperative breeders, so they have carried cooperative breeding a step farther than most, several pairs laying in the same nest and attending their progeny together rather than, as is more usual, a number of nonbreeders assisting a single reproductive pair. From a painstaking study of Smooth-billed Anis in Colombia, Köster (1971) likewise concluded that communal nesting is not a trend toward brood parasitism but a consequence of these birds' strong sociability.

Aside from satisfying the anis' strong social impulses, the value of their system of communal nesting is problematic. The bustling activity at communal nests is more likely to attract predators than the more widely spaced parental visits at nests of solitary pairs. To compensate for this, the greater number of watchful eyes at the joint nests may sooner detect an approaching enemy, which, if not too powerful, may be deterred by the four or more bold and resolute attendants. Unfortunately, we do not know which of these opposing tendencies outweighs the other. When a larger number of adults share incubation, each enjoys more time to forage or loaf than when only two parents warm the eggs, but it is doubtful whether they need this extra time to stay well nourished.

Among the advantages of the more widespread system of cooperative breeding, in which a single reproductive pair are assisted by nonbreeding helpers, is the greater ratio of food-bringing grown birds to dependent young. This appears to be especially beneficial after the young leave the nest and scatter, when, if the helpers are sufficiently numerous, each fledgling may be fed and guarded by one or more attendants. This advantage is not gained by communal nesting, in which the ratio of adults to young may remain the same as at nests of solitary pairs of the same species, unless the eggs become so numerous that hatching is inefficient—which is likely to be true if more than two females contribute more than eight eggs, as appears to occur in only a minority of Groove-billed Anis' nests. Perhaps for this reason communal nesting, as practiced by anis, is known in only a few species of birds.

Another aspect of the anis' breeding system—the participation of young nonbreeding individuals, as at Whiteface's second nest—allies it to the more widespread type of cooperative breeding. Here the advantages are less doubtful. The juvenile is safer with its parents than if thrown upon its own resources at an early age, as happens with many birds; and, by helping at the nest, it gains experience that will later make it a more efficient parent. Likewise, it increases the ratio of attendants to callow young.

Despite several careful studies of the two more common species of anis, much remains to be learned about them. Prolonged observations of individually recognizable birds are needed to reveal how the several members of a group are related, whether single or joint nestings are more successful, how new groups arise, and other details that are still far from clear. Although we may question the efficiency of some aspects of the anis' social system, we cannot doubt that both the Groove-billed and the Smooth-billed anis are highly successful species, which singly or together are spread over almost the whole of tropical America at low and middle altitudes.

Postscript

Soon after I typed this chapter, I received copies of three important recent papers on Groove-billed Anis. The first (Vehrencamp 1977) reveals that, at a nest belonging to two or more pairs, each female tosses out all eggs present before she herself begins to lay—which explains why eggs are often found on the ground. The alpha, or highest-ranking, female, who is the oldest, lays last, so that none of her eggs is ejected and a larger number of them are incubated; but early laying, subordinate females compensate for their tossed eggs by continuing to lay. By reducing the time-spread of effective laying in a communal nest, egg tossing decreases the disparity in age and size of the nestlings and appears to benefit the group as a whole. The second paper (Vehrencamp 1978) examines the reproductive success of nests with different numbers of attendants in diverse habitats and, likewise, adult mortality. The alpha male, mate of the alpha female, incubates most assiduously by day and is alone responsible for the nest at night, with the result that alpha males suffer higher mortality than subordinate males and females. An advantage of communal nesting appears to be the reduction of the cost of parental care, because one male assumes the high risk of nocturnal incubation instead of two or more. The third paper (Vehrencamp et al. 1977) shows that in Guanacaste, Costa Rica, Groove-billed Anis are the chief victims of the large carnivorous bat *Vampyrum spectrum*. The statistical studies presented in the first two of these papers supplement the largely behavioral study of the present chapter.

14. Common Potoo

Nyctibius griseus

One's first meeting with a bird outstanding for beauty, song, or habits is always an unforgettable experience. Of the many birds that I have known, none was first seen or heard in circumstances more romantic and stirring, more treasured in memory, than those attending my introduction to the Common Potoo. While I studied birds on Barro Colorado Island in Gatún Lake in the Panama Canal Zone, Frank M. Chapman, the most famous American ornithologist of his time, promised that if I spent the night with him at a cabin across the island from the main buildings I would hear the potoo. By narrow forest trails, we reached the cabin, beautifully situated at the head of an inlet. While we waited, listening, the full moon rose above the trees that crowded around the solitary cabin, but we heard only the chorus of frogs from the marshy cove below us. Finally, despite the irritating ticks and red bugs that I had picked up along the trail, I fell asleep.

Chapman, who was more than twice my age and therefore slept more lightly, heard the bird while I slept soundly. At his call, I sat up on my cot and looked out the window upon a forest bathed in the yellow light of the sinking moon, reflected in myriad spears of light from glossy leaves wet after a passing shower. The frogs continued their chorus; and from the distance came, subdued but clear, the most melancholy notes that I had heard from any bird. The wildness of the setting, the pale moonlight that contrasted so strongly with the dark shadows beneath the great trees, intensified the mournful quality of an utterance that in any circumstances would have sounded forlorn. The soft plaintive notes brought to mind a phrase from

Shelley's *Adonais*: "most musical of mourners." It was not difficult to imagine that through those deep shadows, where venomous serpents and predatory quadrupeds lurked, wandered a grief-crazed maiden bereft of her lover or a mother whose beloved children had been torn from her side. *Poo-or-me, O, O, O, O* the mysterious voice seemed to cry, the notes strongest at the beginning of each phrase and falling away toward the end. Soon we noticed that two potoos were answering one another in the distance.

It was easy to understand why imaginative country people in Trinidad called the author of this plaint Poor-me-one, which means "poor-me-alone," but probably they attributed the voice to a sloth rather than to a bird. This widespread persistent error was already recorded by the Spanish chronicler Fernández de Oviedo, in the sixteenth century. When, after thirty years in the Valley of El General, where the potoo is of rare and sporadic occurrence, I first heard it there, I was amazed to learn that the local girl who worked in our house ascribed the notes to the *perico ligero*, or sloth, which is also rare in the valley.

As I have heard it in Costa Rica, Panama, and north central Venezuela, this song varies little and has everywhere the same melancholy charm. In other regions, quite different calls have been ascribed to the potoo, a matter well discussed by Smithe (1966). A recording by Paul Schwartz reproduces well both the sweetly plaintive character of the song and, likewise, how loud and piercing the opening notes may sound when not mellowed by distance. As with other nocturnal birds, the potoo is heard most frequently on moonlit nights and in the late twilight of moonless nights. In Trinidad, Johnson (1937) heard it sing, during the ten or fifteen minutes before dark, on almost every evening from February to early August. On Barro Colorado, Chapman (1929) heard it almost nightly from December 21 to March 3; and I heard it, first with him and then alone, sparingly from March 20 to May 21. Here in the Valley of El General, we have heard the potoo only at long intervals, sometimes at the height of the rainy season in October. In early November, when a pair were preparing to nest, they sang in the morning as well as in the evening twilight.

This bird—so much easier to hear than to see, known so much better by its voice than by its appearance—is one of five species in a small family, the Nyctibiidae, confined to tropical America. They are closely related to the nightjars or goatsuckers, which they resemble in their mottled plumage, capacious mouths, and small bills; but they may be distinguished by their manner of resting with the body more or less upright, rather than horizontal, as is usual in nightjars. The most widespread member of this family, the Common Potoo is a large bird about 15 inches (38 centimeters) long, with a wingspread of 3 feet (90 centimeters). Its intricately patterned plumage is a blending of browns, buffs, grays, black, and white, producing a general grayish brown tone. The bird has blackish marks on the head and back and black spots in a broken band across the breast. Its long tail is irregularly banded with blackish and grayish, and its large eyes are bright yellow or orange. The sexes are too similar to be distinguished with certainty.

The Common Potoo ranges over continental America from southern Mexico to Peru, Bolivia, northern Argentina, the Guianas, and Trinidad; in the Antilles it inhabits Jamaica and Hispaniola. Most abundant in warm lowlands, in Central America it extends upward to about 5,000 feet (1,500 meters), in northern Venezuela to nearly 6,000 feet (1,800 meters) (Meyer de Schauensee and Phelps 1978). Tolerant of ecological conditions, it inhabits rain forests, especially their edges, dry forests, mangrove swamps, tall second growth, savannas, and other open country with clumps of trees. Nevertheless, this potoo is widespread rather than common, being by no means uniformly distributed in apparently suitable habitats throughout its vast geographical range. Even after becoming familiar with its unmistakable song, I have failed to find it in many apparently suitable localities. Here in El General, I first became aware of the potoo (by sight rather than hearing) on August 31, 1959, nearly twenty-four years after I began the study of the birds of this valley. My failure to discover the potoo during so many seasons is the more surprising since it was found in El General in 1908 (Carriker 1910). This suggests that the potoo's distribution is spotty or discontinuous in time as well as in space.

By day, the potoo rests in light or sometimes heavy woods, often near the edge, from which it sallies forth in the dusk to catch insects over clearings or neighboring bodies of water. In the daytime, it is usually seen perching at a moderate height, quite upright, with its feathers all compressed, its neck stretched up in line with its vertical body and tail, and its head inclined strongly upward. Some upstanding feathers above its eyes simulate low horns, and its ear coverts are puffed out. Its large eyes are closed to the narrowest slits, which from time to time widen slightly to inspect what is happening nearby. Even with closed eyes, two small notches in the upper eyelid, one near each end, apparently permit the bird to detect objects, both in front and behind, through widely dilated pupils (Borrero 1974). In this linear, vertical posture, the potoo remains quite motionless as long as it knows that it is being watched. If one moves around beneath it, the bird does nothing except turn its head and occasionally shift the orientation of its body, when the observer's eyes are turned away. If, as sometimes happens, the potoo is resting on the end of an upright stub of the proper thickness, it appears to be a continuation of the stub and is difficult to detect; and on any perch it looks more like a truncated branch or a piece of dead wood than a bird. Even when in plain view, it often escapes notice by the uninitiated. In Mexico, this ver-

tical stance wins for the potoo the names *pá-jaro estaca* ("stake bird") and *bienparado* ("well erect").

Although the potoo is usually seen and is pictured by artists and photographers in this vertically elongated, horizontally compressed pose, it would be wrong to suppose that it maintains this strained attitude all day long. If you can manage to see the potoo before it sees you, you will find it still perching vertically but shorter and stouter, with its bill directed forward rather than upward. The moment it suspects that it is observed, however, it elongates its body, compresses its plumage, and raises its head, all so gradually that no movement is perceptible. If its support is gently shaken, it may open its great eyes and lower its head to look around, without taking flight. A potoo drowsing on a fence post at midday in Colombia almost permitted one of my companions to seize it in slowly advancing hands before it flew. The potoo's flight is swift and direct, with regular beats of its long wings, which on a downward course may be set for a prolonged glide. Viewed in flight against the night sky, it resembles a large hawk, especially a *Buteo*.

As the evening twilight deepens, the potoo stations itself on the end of a stub, an exposed branch, a fence post, or even a corn-stalk, from which it flies out to catch insects, often circling broadly around to return to the same lookout. The insect is usually captured in the air, flycatcher-fashion, but sometimes it is plucked from foliage, the bark of a tree, or even low herbage. I once watched a potoo weave an intricate course through the open branches of a tree in pursuit of insects. Bee-tles seem to be its principal food in Jamaica (Gosse 1847) and elsewhere, and large fire-flies are a favored fare in Trinidad (Johnson 1937). The remains of moths accounted for 83 percent of the food of a potoo in His-paniola, and it had also eaten eighteen locustid eggs and seven beetles (Wetmore and Swales 1931). With a gape 2 inches (5 centimeters) or more wide, it can swallow such large items as a White-collared Seed-eater, which had apparently been frightened from its perch in the night (Alvarez del Toro 1971).

The Nest Site and the Egg

In the drizzly evening twilight of November 9, 1967, I heard the song of a potoo. Then a large dusky bird, evidently the one I had heard, alighted in an Aguacatillo tree in the hillside pasture behind our house. After a minute or so there, it flew to a dead Guava tree higher on the slope, where it perched upright on the end of an ascending stub about as thick as its own body. In the dim light, I could hardly distinguish it from the broken-off branch; until the bird flew away and the branch suddenly grew shorter, it was hard to believe that it was there. While the potoo rested on this stub, another flew up and tried to alight beside or upon it but, not succeeding, it continued over the brow of the hill and vanished.

These potoos were evidently selecting a nest site. On December 1, and again on the following day, a potoo was resting in the very open crown of the medium-sized Aguacatillo tree every time I looked. I did not disturb it; and, when it spontaneously left in the eve-ning twilight of December 2, I saw that it had been covering an egg, in the exact spot where the potoo had alighted over three weeks earlier. The single large egg rested about 30 feet (9 meters) above the ground on the thick, almost vertical main branch, in a slight depression left by the decay of a thin-ner branch, so shallow that more than half of the egg was exposed above the rim of the hollow. This knothole was situated at a sort of elbow in the branch, which bent to the opposite side, then curved upward again, so that it did not interfere with the incubating bird, who always sat facing it.

Such a shallow knothole at an elbow in an ascending limb, at heights of 10 to 60 feet (3 to 18 meters), seems everywhere to be pre-ferred by the Common Potoo for its single egg, as is evident from photographs taken at points as far separated as Surinam and Mex-ico (Haverschmidt 1958; Alvarez del Toro 1971). A slight depression in the top of a fairly thick erect or slightly inclined stub also serves to hold the egg (Borrero 1970). It seems impossible for an egg to remain for weeks in such precarious situations without being glued in place, like a palm swift's egg to its narrow shelf beneath a hanging palm frond, but apparently this is not true. I did not jeopardize the egg in the Aguacatillo tree by trying to reach it. Viewed from the hill-side above the nest tree, where I was not far below it, the egg appeared white, with faint markings. According to those who have han-dled Common Potoos' eggs, they are white, speckled all over or chiefly on the thicker end with dark brown, lilac, or shades of gray. The few reported measurements from widely separated countries show a range of 35.9 to 41.5 by 25 to 32 millimeters.

Our "nest" was clearly visible from 100 yards (92 meters) away. From the back of our house, even with the naked eye we could see the potoo sitting on it, while through a field glass its movements could be followed. By night, in the beam of a flashlight, its bril-liant orange eyeshine revealed its presence from afar. For nearly three months we con-tinued to keep watch over this nest, some-times from our dooryard, sometimes while standing or sitting on the hillside near it, and during several nightlong vigils. Our near ap-proach, whether by day or night, appeared to have no effect upon the potoos, other than to send them into the elongated alarm posture, from which, if we watched quietly, they soon recovered. Throwing the beam of a flashlight upon them in the night did not interfere with their activities, such as feeding the nestling.

Incubation

We could depend upon seeing a potoo covering the egg at any hour of the day or night, with the exception of a brief interval at dawn and a longer period just after nightfall. I made no daylong watch; but I spent much time in view of the nest while studying a nearby hummingbird's nest and on other occasions, without witnessing a changeover or, indeed, ever seeing a second potoo anywhere in the vicinity in full daylight. I have no doubt that the same individual, who according to an observation of Alvarez del Toro would be the male, remained continuously on the egg all day. I watched throughout the night of December 16 to 17, when the moon was full but unfortunately hidden much of the time by clouds, which before dawn covered the whole sky darkly. Since the nest tree was silhouetted against the sky, I believe that I would have noticed a changeover even while the sky was overcast, but I saw none. Evidently the nocturnal session, like the diurnal session, was continuous.

In the earliest light of dawn, while stars still shone brightly, the potoo who had incubated throughout the night flew from the nest, usually down the hillside toward the river. This morning departure occurred at times ranging from 5:00 to 5:06 on nine mornings between December 3 and 18. When I resumed observations in early January, toward the end of the incubation period, the departure took place, on three mornings, between 5:12 and 5:18. The egg remained exposed, in the dim light, for from 0 to 15 minutes; for eleven mornings, the average period was 7.6 minutes. While the brighter stars still shone and the first tints of dawn suffused the eastern sky, a potoo flew up and settled on the egg. Since the sexes were so similar, I could not tell whether this was the bird who had left a short while ago or its mate. The brief interval of neglect, sometimes only one to four minutes and evidently too short for a potoo to satisfy its hunger

Common Potoo: adult incubating in the elongated cryptic posture.

after an all-night fast, favored the view that the other bird had come to warm the egg. This was certainly true on January 2, when at 5:14 I witnessed the only changeover that I saw while the potoos incubated. On this occasion, the sitting potoo did not go until its mate, flying up swiftly through the twilight, was almost on top of it. The egg was left uncovered for only an instant, the newcomer settling on it the moment the other departed, never wavering in its swift, smooth approach until it came to rest on the egg. This changeover was effected while I stood only 50 feet (15 meters) away, in full view.

It was certain, then, that both sexes incubated, one sitting by night and the other throughout the day. The daytime shift began at times ranging from 5:04 to 5:23 and lasted from twelve and one-half to twelve and three-quarters hours. The potoo who had been incubating all day nearly always flew from the egg in the rapidly fading light, on twenty-nine evenings between 5:42 and 5:54, with two exceptions. One of these occurred on December 11, the first clear afternoon and evening in many days. Then the potoo left its egg, apparently enticed away by a passing insect, at 5:38. After catching the insect, it continued to a neighboring stub, where it stretched and preened. It returned to the egg at 5:45, and ten minutes later it left for a longer absence. On December 12, a dark and drizzly evening with flashes of distant lightning, the potoo remained incubating until 6:22. On the rainy evening of December 17, the potoo did not leave for its customary crepuscular outing but apparently remained until its mate replaced it in the darkness. On a number of evenings, I noticed that the potoo left its egg from one to eight minutes after the Pauraques began to sing.

After the evening departure, the egg remained exposed for from forty-five to ninety-five minutes, usually for about an hour. On December 27, when the potoo left at 5:47, the egg was already covered by 6:32. At the other extreme, on December 4 the diurnal session ended at 5:48 and the nocturnal session did not begin until 7:23. At the nest studied by Johnson in Trinidad, the egg was left exposed for "many hours" after darkness fell. Usually, especially during the latter half of the long incubation period, the potoo taking the night shift at our nest arrived before 7:00. The return to the nest displayed admirable control of flight. With amazing precision, the potoo flew right into the incubating position, folding its wings as it alighted. After it came to rest, no further adjustment to the egg seemed necessary. Such superb control of the approach saved the egg from being knocked out of its shallow receptacle; adjustments on the nest, such as many birds make, would almost certainly have dislodged it.

The potoos always incubated facing the supporting branch, with the long axis of the body vertical, the base of the abdomen covering the single egg, and the end of the long tail touching the branch below. When the bird was at ease, its body was contracted, the feathers fluffed out, making it appear stout, the head horizontal, and the minuscule bill inclined somewhat downward. At times the ventral feathers were so puffed out that I was sure a nestling was hidden among them, although it had not yet hatched. The potoo's eyelids were in continual movement, like those of an incubating Pauraque—opening the merest slit, then closing tightly for a moment, then opening a trifle, rarely revealing much of the large yellow eye. Evidently, with the aid of the notches in the eyelids, a scarcely discernible opening was wide enough for the potoo to see what was approaching. The sparsely foliaged tree afforded scant shade, and much of the time the incubating bird was in strong sunshine. Sometimes it panted with its huge mouth slightly open. Or it might assume a more inclined posture, its long tail slanting outward from the trunk, its wings half spread sideward, apparently sunbathing. After its sunbath, it sometimes preened. Beneath a hard shower, the potoo sat with its body contracted and its plumage fluffed out.

The visible approach of anything larger than a small bird caused the incubating potoo to compress and elongate its body, at the same time raising its head until it inclined strongly upward in the line of the body and tail. The eyes were closed to the merest slit. The change from the plump resting posture to the slender alarm posture was slow and steady rather than abrupt, taking about ten to fifteen seconds. Since rapid movement is always revealing, a too hasty change of attitude would have defeated the very purpose for which it was made. The bird's readiness to assume the cryptic posture varied greatly with circumstances. In full daylight it reacted most readily to the sight of any moving object: a person walking at a distance, a Turkey Vulture or a wintering Broad-winged Hawk flying overhead, would cause it to stretch upward to its full length.

In the morning or evening twilight, the potoo often stretched upward only partly, or not at all, when I approached; and, in the beam of my flashlight at night, it often retained its contracted posture. However, there were exceptions, and on moonlit nights my approach to the base of the nest tree might make the sitting bird elongate itself fully. Once, after the nestling hatched, I saw the brooding parent suddenly stretch upward into the cryptic posture at three o'clock in the morning. My flashlight's rays picked out the eyeglow of a small animal, probably an opossum, in the roadway 50 or 60 feet (15 or 18 meters) below the nest. As the animal moved farther along the road, the potoo sank down into the resting posture, which it maintained when, a little later, a skunk rummaged on the slope below the nest. Could the potoo distinguish these similar-sized animals in the night, and was it aware that opossums climb trees to plunder nests but skunks remain on the ground?

As the potoo was most ready to assume the alarm posture in full sunlight, so it then took longest to resume the resting posture. When, after walking beneath the nest to make the bird stretch up, I watched through a binocular from afar, it might require nearly a quarter of an hour to return to the resting attitude. In the evening, if I stood close beneath the nest, perhaps waving my arms to make the potoo elongate itself fully, it might resume the resting posture in as little as two and a half or three minutes, while I sat watching in full view on the hillside, hardly 50 feet (15 meters) away. Even when most rapid, the contraction of the elongated body was imperceptibly slow.

Since I never came near the incubating potoo, I never saw the threat display which Haverschmidt (1958) witnessed when he tried to touch a potoo covering its egg in Surinam. The bird fluffed out all its feathers, relaxed its wings, spread its tail, opened its big yellow owllike eyes, and, with huge mouth gaping widely, snapped at the approaching hand, causing its prompt withdrawal. Then the potoo slowly resumed its cryptic posture. Haverschmidt cited an earlier observation of a potoo feigning injury on the ground, but neither he nor I saw such a display.

Sometimes at sunset I found the potoo drowsing on its egg in a very contracted posture, seeming about two-thirds as long and

twice as fat as when in the full alarm posture. As daylight faded, the bird became active—opening its great yellow eyes, turning its head from side to side to look around, yawning cavernously, stretching its broad wings alternately sideways or both together above its back, spreading its tail, preening, and perhaps giving once or twice a subdued version of its song, consisting usually of not more than four notes. Tempted by some insect that flew past or crawled over a neighboring branch, it might dart out, apparently seize the creature, which I could not see, then return immediately to its egg—a momentary absence that I did not consider to terminate the long diurnal session. All these activities were not performed every evening, only a selection of them.

Finally, as twilight deepened, the bird would leave, falling away from the egg, as it always did. Often it went to alight on a neighboring dead stub of a Cecropia tree, into which a female Red-crowned Woodpecker had already retired for the night. Here it might repeat some of the activities that had preceded its departure from the egg, such as stretching, preening, and singing briefly, or it would perform some that it had omitted to do. Soon it would fly beyond my sight, toward the forest or the river. Rarely, its mate would appear at this time; but, until after the egg hatched, it was exceptional to have two potoos in view at any hour of the day or night. Throughout the nesting, scarcely any song was heard from either parent, except the few notes uttered as they were about to fly away at nightfall or daybreak.

I never saw a potoo turn the egg or even touch it with its bill. To do so might have dislodged the egg from the shallow depression where it rested. Toward the end of the incubation period, I noticed a conspicuous dark spot on the shell, whether dirt or some other marking I do not know, which was always in the same orientation. I never made the potoo leave its nest in order to see whether the egg had hatched. Indeed, to do so might have been difficult, for later, when the nestling was a few days old, a parent continued to brood it, in the full alarm posture, while we fitted a wide band of sheet metal around the trunk to prevent predatory animals from climbing up. The operation, which included driving nails through the resounding metal, was necessarily noisy. Alvarez del Toro was able to climb to a nest and touch the incubating bird before it flew.

The potoo's departure at dawn on January 4 revealed the egg still intact. By evening, it had been replaced by a downy nestling. Since I first noticed the egg on December 2, the incubation period was thirty-three days or more. In Trinidad, an egg hatched in twenty-nine or thirty days (Johnson 1937). Behind the nestling was the larger part of the empty shell, with a very jagged edge. By the following evening, it had vanished. I searched in vain for a fragment on the grass beneath the nest.

The Nestling

The newly hatched potoo was everywhere densely covered with short whitish down. It already rested facing inward, as the parents did while they incubated or brooded, an orientation that it rather consistently preserved through nearly all of the long nestling period. It soon developed a decidedly prognathous physiognomy, with a tiny bill at the end of a conically projecting mouth covered with whitish down, like the rest of its body.

When the nestling was eleven days old, I first noticed its eyegleam, which was still faint. At this time, too, I first became aware of its voice, a sort of hoarse buzz, uttered at mealtime. When it was sixteen days old, I saw it flap its stubby wings in the twilight. It was now becoming browner on its back and wings, and dark shaft streaks were evident on the ventral feathers. The next day, when for the first time I found it alone in full daylight, it sat upright, with its head drawn in, in much the same posture as the parents assumed when drowsing on the nest. My approach did not make it change its attitude; but, when I stood directly below it and made a noise, it stretched up its body and elevated its bill to an angle of about thirty degrees with the horizontal. Thus it made an approach to the cryptic posture of the adults but did not assume it fully, and it maintained this posture only briefly. When the nestling

was nineteen days old, I found it resting in front of its parent on the nest. As I came near, the parent stretched up in the alarm posture and the young potoo did the same. Its rudimentary tail now projected over the edge of the stub.

On January 30, when the nestling was twenty-six days old, its wing coverts as well as its tail feathers were appearing through the abundant down that still covered its body. Hornlike feathers were appearing above its eyes. To assume the cryptic posture, it required a stronger stimulus than the adults, in the form of a closer approach or a noise, and it did not elongate itself so fully. On this day, I first saw it away from the knothole where it had hatched. It had climbed up the thick ascending branch beside the nest for a distance of about 1 foot (30 centimeters), and it rested there in its customary upright posture. In the evening, it returned to its usual place. When it stretched and flapped its wings in the evening twilight, I noticed that its remiges were expanding, but when its wings were folded these feathers were concealed by the downy covering of the body.

By February 8, when the nestling was thirty-five days old, it was well feathered, much in the pattern of the adults—even to the dusky malar stripes—but the general tone of its plumage was much lighter. The "horn" above each eye was now quite prominent. I had not again seen it climb up the branch beside its nest. By night it was inactive, except at mealtime.

By February 18, the forty-five-day-old nestling was becoming more active. Late in the morning it was resting on the ascending branch about 2 feet (60 centimeters) above the nest—higher than I had seen it before—and it stayed there all afternoon. As it grew dark, the young potoo stretched its wings alternately, flapped them a little, then sidled down the branch to the nest. Here it vigorously flapped its well-developed wings. It repeatedly seemed to pick something, perhaps a bit of bark or lichen, from the branch and eat it. A parent came and fed it while it made a harsh buzz. Two days later, it took its first short flight.

Brooding the Nestling

For the first two weeks of its life, the nestling was brooded most of the time, day and night. It was left alone chiefly during the first hour of the night, when the egg had been left uncovered, and more briefly as the night ended. Thus, on January 4, the day it hatched, it was left exposed for thirty-four minutes, from 6:13 to 6:47 P.M. In the next two nights, when both parents were bringing food, its periods alone were shorter, rarely exceeding fifteen minutes.

My son, Edwin, and I watched alternately throughout the night of January 14 to 15, when the moon was full but the sky was overcast much of the time until midnight. At 6:01 P.M., the parent who throughout the day had brooded the ten-day-old nestling left for the first time. From then until 7:05, the nestling was brooded only twice, for two minutes each time, and left exposed three times, for two, twenty-two, and thirty-six minutes. Then, from 7:05 until 5:12 the next morning, or through the greater part of the night, it was brooded continuously. In the early dawn it was left exposed for three minutes, brooded for five minutes, then left exposed for four minutes, after which a parent settled on the nest for the day at 5:24. From the beginning of activity by the potoos at 6:01 P.M. on January 14 to its cessation in the waxing daylight on January 15, the nestling was left uncovered only sixty-seven minutes, during which it was frequently fed. Both parents brooded, and in the course of the night we saw them change over five times. Spells of brooding by one parent ranged from 2 to 234 minutes. Johnson believed that the chick in Trinidad was "never left exposed" during the first three weeks of its life.

At first, the brooding parent always sat facing inward, as it had incubated, with the nestling in front, covered by the adult's abdominal feathers. As the nestling grew bigger and stood erect, it formed a bulge in front of the parent that was especially abrupt and noticeable when the latter stretched up tall and slender in the cryptic posture. When the nestling was 12 days old, I noticed its head protruding from the parent's feathers for the first time in full daylight. Through much of the following day, the parent brooded facing sideways, having rotated about ninety degrees from its usual position, and the nestling had turned the same way, since it usually faced in the same direction as its brooding parent. This sideward orientation was occasionally chosen by the attendant parent in the following days.

Early in the afternoon of January 21, I saw the nestling, now seventeen days old, alone for the first time in full daylight. During the next week, however, a parent was always found on the nest in the daytime, often with the young bird resting in front of it rather than within its feathers. On January 28, a parent accompanied the nestling much, if not all, of the day; but on January 29, when it was twenty-five days old, it was alone, as thenceforth we always found it until its departure nearly a month later, except when it was fed. The last time a parent was seen brooding in darkness was on the night of January 22 to 23. Since long before diurnal brooding ceased the nestling seemed to have enough plumage to keep it warm on the mild January days, probably the chief service rendered by the attendant parent was to shield the chick from the strong sunshine, for the Aguacatillo tree was rapidly shedding its foliage. Moreover, the parent had better protective coloration than the nestling, whose plumage was too pale to match the bark of the nest tree, although it was scarcely lighter than some of the dry lichens that encrusted it.

We never saw a parent remove a dropping, which it could hardly take in its bill without hovering conspicuously beside the nest. Some deposits on the herbage and fallen leaves beneath the nest tree suggested that the young bird shot its droppings free of the supporting trunk, probably while the parents were absent, but we never saw this act.

Feeding the Nestling

I first saw the nestling when, in the evening twilight of January 4, the parent who had covered the nest throughout the day flew out to seize a passing insect in the air, then at once returned. Twice more the parent flew out to catch insects, once from the air and once from the foliage of the nest tree, each time returning to the nest. After its third return, it bent down to feed the nestling, who stuck its head out from its parent's abdominal feathers to receive its first meal. The parent made jerky movements with its neck, as though regurgitating, and seemed to feed the nestling several times more. Between feedings, the nestling mostly stayed out of sight, although occasionally the tip of its bill projected from the parent's abdominal feathers.

At 6:13, much later than usual while it incubated, the parent flew away through the dusk. The nestling remained alone until 6:47, when a parent flew up and brooded it. At first the adult seemed to be disturbed by the beam of my flashlight, but soon it moved its neck as though regurgitating and bent down to feed the nestling, who stuck its head out as before. The feedings continued for about five minutes, but I could not see details as well as I wished. After the series of feedings, the parent sat quietly in the light of the crescent moon.

The next morning I resumed watching at 5:00, when the east was brightening, and continued until 5:35, when the day was bright. One parent stayed continuously on the nest, save for three momentary sorties to catch insects. After the last, it fed the nestling once, then settled down to brood throughout the day.

That evening, as daylight faded, the nestling, not yet a day and a half old, stuck its head through the feathers of the brooding parent's abdomen, as though expecting a meal. A day later, it could stretch up so far that the parent, standing erect in the brooding posture, needed to bend down only a little to reach its mouth. The nestling turned its head sideways to receive the food. Until the end of the nestling period, the chick was always fed while standing in front of the parent on the nest, at first with only its head projecting from the parent's feathers, later with its whole body exposed.

As days passed, the delivery of a meal became more rapid. Although on the first evening a feeding had continued for about five minutes, from the second until the ninth it lasted only about two to four seconds. When the nestling was ten days old, the delivery of a meal rarely took as much as a second or two; usually it was momentary. From the nestling's second to sixteenth day, a parent returning with food would occasionally deliver it in two or three installments or separate acts of regurgitation; but, during the second half of the nestling period, the meal was delivered all at once. Alighting on the nest with the chick in front of it, the parent alternately stretched and contracted its neck, as though bringing up something that appeared to be quite large and was probably a mass of compressed insects. To pass this to the nestling took only an instant, after which the parent flew away, a fraction of a minute after its arrival.

From at least its eleventh day onward, the nestling made a hoarse buzz at mealtime, often starting as its parent approached and continuing after it had received the meal and retired into the parental feathers or, at a later age, until after the parent had left. The hungrier the nestling appeared to be, the more it buzzed. This sound helped us detect the feedings on dark nights, since we did not keep the flashlight beam trained on the nest continuously, only occasionally and at mealtime.

During the nestling's first ten days, it might receive from three to six meals during the parents' first hour of activity, at the beginning of the night, and as many more between the first dim light of dawn and fairly bright daylight. After this, the number of meals in each of these intervals was reduced to one or two. On the night of January 14 to 15, when until midnight the full moon was obscured by clouds much of the time, the nestling was fed fifteen times between sunset and sunrise. Two of these meals were delivered in two installments. Eight meals were delivered before midnight, seven after midnight. During the night of February 8 to 9, when the waxing moon set at about 1:30 A.M., the nestling was fed only ten times, eight before midnight and two after midnight, when, beneath a clear starry sky, the night had become uncomfortably chilly. Each meal was now delivered in a single, almost instantaneous act. We had abundant evidence that both parents fed the young, although we could not learn their respective roles.

The Fledgling's Departure

On the afternoon of February 20, the young potoo, now forty-seven days old, climbed up the slanting branch above the nest. As it grew dark, the young bird stretched both wings broadly, alternately, then sidled down to the nest, where it stretched its wings more and flapped them vigorously. It appeared to pluck things from the bark, and it looked around a great deal, as though seeking a place to which it could fly. Then, at 6:07, in deep twilight, it launched forth on its first recorded flight. After going only a few yards, it circled around and alighted on a neighboring upright branch with a lateral projection, in a site quite similar to that of the nest and only a few feet from it. Here it plucked lichens, liverworts, or bits of bark and swallowed them, as was evident from the movements it made. It did this again and again, as though hungry. Ten minutes after the juvenile's flight, a parent silently arrived and alighted on the nest. The young potoo began its hoarse buzz and continued until the parent flew across and fed it while standing in front of it, in the usual manner, then flew away. A few minutes after this meal, the first it was seen to receive away from the nest, the juvenile flew back to the nest, where it flapped its wings very vigorously while clinging to the branch, then settled down to pass the night there. Its eyeshine was now only slightly less brilliant than that of the adults, but a bit more yellow, less orange.

Each evening the young potoo became more active and took longer flights. On the evening of February 22, it made six flights before it received its first meal. All were between branches of the nest tree itself, the longest about 20 feet (6 meters), from one side of this tree to the other. Sometimes the young potoo headed outward, as though to begin a longer journey, but after going a few yards it returned to its natal tree.

After passing the night of February 22 to 23 on the nest, the young potoo flew at dawn to the similar site a few feet away, and here it passed the day. This was the first time that I saw it in full daylight away from the branch on which it had hatched. On the evening of this day, the juvenile made fourteen flights in fifteen minutes before it was fed. Some of these flights were short, between the nest and the similar site where it had passed the day—two points of attraction between which it now frequently alternated. But at times the fledgling flew far out from the crown of the tree, 40 or 50 feet (12 or 15 meters), only to veer around and alight on a branch of the nest tree. Once it flew halfway around the tree's crown, to enter it from the opposite side. It never alighted anywhere except in the Aguacatillo tree in which it grew up. I could not ascertain whether it caught insects on any of these flights, but, at the various points where it alighted, it plucked many things from the bark, as on previous evenings. It stretched, shook itself, and preened. Finally, it settled on the nest for its last night there.

As the first promise of dawn brightened the eastern horizon on February 24, the young potoo became active, sidling up the branch beside the nest and appearing to pluck things from it. At 5:04 it was fed on the nest. As the undersides of the eastern clouds became tinted with rose, it flapped its wings and picked more things from the bark. After another meal, it flew to the next branch, then made long circling flights, out from the nest tree and back again. Finally, at 5:30, it flew out once more. Now for the first time it did not turn back but continued across the road and down the hillside into the light second-growth woods, where it vanished. After breakfast, I searched a long while without finding it there.

Since the young potoo flew away while its parents were out of sight I wondered how it would establish contact with them. Would it return to the nest to be fed? That evening I watched in a slow drizzle. In the gloaming, a parent alighted on the nest, as though expecting to find its offspring there, as on past evenings. After delaying a short while, it flew to the nearby Cecropia stub from which it had often caught insects. Then it went to other exposed perches, and twice more it came to the nest. Several times it called in a soft melodious voice. Finally, ten minutes after its arrival, it flew down into the woods where the juvenile had disappeared at daybreak. Possibly it had heard the young potoo's voice, although I failed to detect it.

Soon a potoo, probably the other parent, alighted on the nest. After flying around a while but not calling, this one also flew to the woods to which the fledgling had gone. So the chick probably received its supper— or, more correctly, its breakfast—despite its departure without its parents' knowledge. I never saw it again.

If we count from the hatching of the egg to the first time the young potoo was seen anywhere but on the nest or the branch beside it, the nestling period was forty-seven days (January 4 to February 20). If we count from hatching to its departure from the nest tree on February 24, the nestling period was fifty-one days. Add to this at least thirty-three days for incubation, and we have at least eighty-four days for the total occupancy of the nest. This is a long while for a vulnerable bird and its defenseless young to remain on an exposed stub or branch of a tree in or near tropical woodland where predators abound, and it speaks eloquently for the protective value of the potoos' "dead stub" pose. With the exception of the Black Vulture, no other land bird that I have studied in tropical America, not excepting hole nesters, has such long incubation and nestling periods. The chick studied by Johnson in Trinidad remained on the nest only forty days.

Since this nesting had terminated successfully so early in the year, long before most birds had started to reproduce, I thought it might be followed by a second brood. In early March I left the farm for three months, but I asked my caretaker to keep an eye on the nest site, which was in plain view of his house. He never again saw a potoo sitting there. In the dozen years that have elapsed since the young potoo flew, we have found no other nest, and we have heard potoos only at long intervals.

15. Black-headed Trogon

Trogon melanocephalus

Through long rainless months in Costa Rica's northwestern province of Guanacaste, the northeast trade winds blow steadily and hard, after dropping most of their moisture before they pour through the low passes between the volcanoes of the Cordillera de Guanacaste. Subject to such stress, many trees shed their leaves, giving a wintry aspect to the light, warm woodland. On flatlands with a high water table, the heavier forest remains more verdant, with denser undergrowth. In such a forest, in mid March, many Black-headed Trogons were noisily forming pairs. When they perched well above my head, these thick-billed, pigeon-sized birds appeared to be largely dull black, with orange-yellow bellies fading into dull white against the slate color of the chest. Only when a male rested low, in a spot of sunshine, could I enjoy the loveliness of the

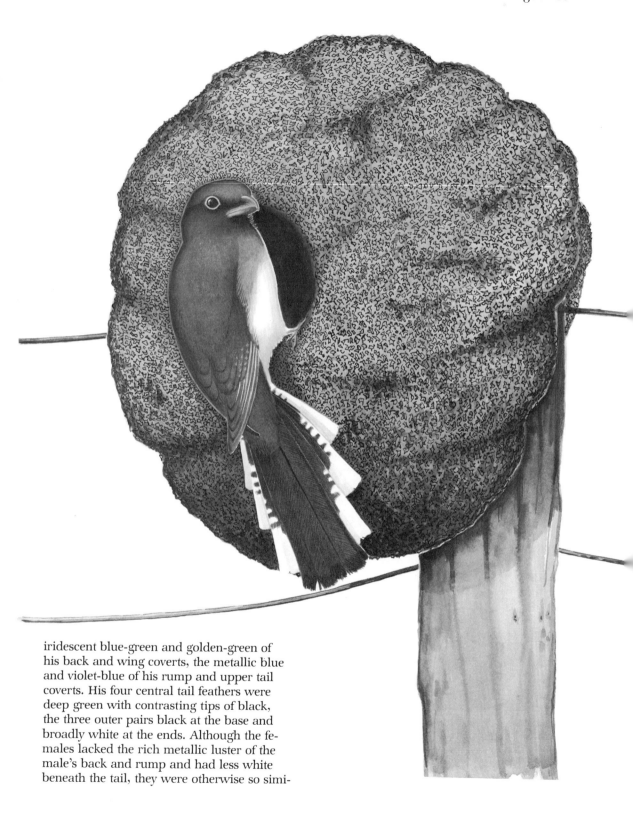

iridescent blue-green and golden-green of
his back and wing coverts, the metallic blue
and violet-blue of his rump and upper tail
coverts. His four central tail feathers were
deep green with contrasting tips of black,
the three outer pairs black at the base and
broadly white at the ends. Although the females lacked the rich metallic luster of the
male's back and rump and had less white
beneath the tail, they were otherwise so simi-

lar that, except in a favorable light, they were readily confused with the males. In both sexes, each brown eye was encircled by a ring of bare whitish skin, more or less tinged with blue. The male's bill was whitish or pale yellowish, that of the female darker.

One afternoon, I watched at least seven of these trogons, of both sexes, following each other through the understory, frequently pausing to call in new positions, close together. The usual call was an accelerated roll or rattle, in form much like that of the Vermilion-breasted Trogon but harsher and more nasal. The similar call of the female was weaker and drier. Although obviously competing for mates, these trogons chased but did not strike one another; indeed, I have never seen trogons of any kind grapple. They are such dignified, gentlemanly birds, always perching sedately erect, that to fight would be incongruous. Theirs is an ancient family, established in the tropics of the Old World as well as the New, that appears to have risen above vulgar scuffles.

These Black-headed Trogons in a Guanacastecan forest were near the southern limit of a species that, on the dry Pacific side of Middle America, ranges as far as El Salvador and, on the wetter eastern side ranges from northern Costa Rica to northeastern Mexico. Heat-loving birds, they barely ascend to 2,000 feet (600 meters) above sea level. Those that I studied most carefully lived in the humid lower reach of the Motagua Valley in Guatemala. Racially distinct from the birds whom I watched courting in Guanacaste, they had deeper black foreparts; their call was a low, throaty, unmelodious *cuk cuk cuk cuk*, the notes evenly spaced rather than accelerated, as far as I heard. While calling, the trogon jerked his tail up and down with rapid mincing strokes and shook his relaxed wings. While carving a nest cavity, a pair voiced low whining notes much like those of newborn puppies.

Like other members of their family, Black-headed Trogons eat both fruits and insects, which they pluck or catch while they hover momentarily on fluttering wings, at the end of a long upward or outward dart. I have seen them take the orange-colored pulp of the Central American Rubber Tree, the green fruiting spikes of the Cecropia tree, and various berries. Their animal prey includes dragonflies, mantises, grasshoppers, and other orthoptera; big caterpillars both hairy and hairless; and many smaller insects difficult to identify in their bills. Between swift darts to seize food, they rest motionless for prolonged intervals, with their long tails directed almost straight downward beneath upright bodies. Their flight is strongly undulatory.

The Nest
My first nest of any member of the family belonged to the Massena, or Slaty-tailed, Trogon, in a termitary high on a tree, beside a mountain torrent in the heavily forested foothills of northern Honduras (Skutch 1972, 1979). After losing this nest to a predator before the eggs hatched, I searched and searched but did not find another trogons' nest until I discovered one of Black-headed Trogons, in a situation surprisingly different. These trogons had chosen a great black termitary, atop a low wooden post which supported a barbed-wire fence that separated a weed-choked cattle pen from a small marsh, on the Alsacia banana plantation in Guatemala. The bulky termitary, only 3½ feet (107 centimeters) above the ground, was about 2 feet (60 centimeters) high and 16 inches (40 centimeters) thick. When, by rare good fortune, I found the pair of trogons digging into it, late in the afternoon of April 8, 1932, they had made a cylindrical opening that began near the bottom and struck obliquely upward into the heart of the termitary. The tube was already 7 inches (18 centimeters) long, and the termitary was still inhabited by many of the little white insects that had made it.

At dawn on the following morning, I hid in a tangle of vines in front of the termitary and waited until eleven o'clock. Although I repeatedly heard the distant notes of the trogons, they did not return to their work during my long vigil. As I passed by soon after noon on April 10, I noticed the female trogon perching on the fence near the termitary. Soon the male flew up from the direction of the nest to join her there, and both panted beneath the bright midday sun. After a minute or two, the female flew toward the termitary, which was screened from me by foliage. The birds were evidently at work; although I tried to reach my observation post amid the vines without disturbing them, by taking a circuitous course through dense bushy growth, I succeeded only in tearing my shirt and driving them away. They flew off in different directions but soon called to each other and reunited. After about a quarter of an hour, they returned to perch on the wire. The male was the first to resume work. I watched them for the next hour and for many hours during the following four days.

The two partners shared the strenuous task of carving into the hard black termitary, but the male was clearly the leader. Usually he arrived first on the wire where they rested during the operation, called his mate if she delayed, and, when she arrived, went first to work in the termitary. He always clung for many seconds or even minutes, back downward, beneath the entrance, carefully surveying the surroundings before he entered the boring. As he turned his head slowly from side to side, the broad ring of bluish white bare skin which separated each dark eye from his black face gave him an odd spectacled aspect. Sometimes, after looking around in this manner, he flew back to the wire, although I detected no cause for his mistrust. He was aware that, while working with his head hidden and much of his body exposed, he might be attacked by an unseen enemy. I thought he might have reposed more confidence in the vigilance of his mate, waiting on the wire a few yards away, and her readiness to warn him of approaching danger.

Satisfied at last that he was safe, the trogon climbed up into the hole until only his deep green, black-tipped tail was visible to me. From my hiding place in the vine tangle, I could hear the crunching of the hard material of the termitary and see black chips falling from the entrance. Whether he worked by pecking with his bill or by biting and twisting the thin, tough sheets of which the structure was composed I could not see, but from the sounds he made and the form of his

bill—not sharp like a woodpecker's but thick and blunt for crushing and tearing—I concluded that he followed the second method. When he dropped out after a spell of work, he went to perch close beside his mate on the fence; and she, after delaying beside him for an interval, flew over to take her turn at the task. Before entering, she, too, clung beneath the entrance, peering cautiously around with her oddly spectacled eyes, often for an interval much longer than she afterward worked. Thus the two shared the labor, turn and turn about; but, on my first afternoon of watching, their periods of work were very short, ranging from a fraction of a minute at the beginning to about three minutes at the end of the hour. Much of the time while the trogons toiled, they uttered a low, not unpleasant whine and called *cuk cuk cuk* in a voice so low that it was scarcely audible to me at a distance of 20 feet (6 meters).

In tropical lowlands, birds and people alike choose the cooler hours of early morning for most of their work. These trogons, however, did not arrive at the termitary until half past ten or eleven, and they worked, with short rest periods, through the warmest part of the day, sometimes until four or five o'clock in the afternoon. It must have been terribly hot inside the black termitary when the sun beat down upon it. When the birds emerged from a spell of work, they perched on the barbed wire to pant with open bills. On each successive return to the nest after an absence taken to rest or forage, the trogons' periods of uninterrupted labor gradually lengthened as they became more absorbed in the undertaking, but the male always worked longer than his mate. For example, from 12:50 to 2:50 P.M. on April 11 their intervals of labor, in minutes, were as follows: male, one; then female, one and a half; male, four and a half; female, eleven; male, twenty; female, twelve; male, twenty-four; female, five.

That the trogons actually worked while hidden from view in the termitary I could be sure, judging from the continuous crunching sound that issued from it and the constant falling of chips from the mouth of the boring. During the first of the female's longer shifts, her mate, becoming impatient of waiting on the fence wire, clung for a moment at the entrance while she was within, then flew back and forth in front of it several times. During the male's twenty-minute turn that followed, the female became even more restless; she flew to and fro in front of the termitary, calling in a low voice, and finally clung in the entrance, whereupon her mate at last emerged. During subsequent long shifts, both birds seemed more reconciled to separation.

By midafternoon on April 11, the tube was 12 inches (30 centimeters) long and had already begun to expand into the nest chamber at its upper end. On the following day, for the first time, the trogons emerged from the termitary headfirst, indicating that the nest cavity had become wide enough to turn around in. The male now assumed an increasingly large share of the task. Sometimes he would work a few minutes, drop down below the entrance to scrutinize his surroundings long and carefully, then enter to bite away more of the termitary, repeating this several times while his mate waited inactive on the wire. From the first, she sometimes clung below the entrance, peering around as though she intended to go in and work, but in the end she flew back beside her mate without having accomplished anything. He seemed to consider this as equivalent to a shift of work, and on her return to the wire he flew over for another spell of honest labor himself. As the task progressed, the female missed her turn with increasing frequency, while the male's periods of toil lengthened; once he worked for half an hour continuously.

On April 14, the final day of carving, the female was in the termitary less than two minutes during my five-hour watch. Even then, she apparently did no work, for I heard no crunching while she was within. Twice she grew impatient and flew beyond sight while her mate was in the cavity and could not see her go. When he emerged and found himself alone, he called in a low calm voice, waited, but received no reply. Again and again he called, becoming louder and more insistent, but his recalcitrant partner would not return. Finally, he went off to search for

her, and his voice became faint in the distance. He would never work unless the female remained perching near the termitary or, at least, unless she had been there when he last looked around. After a quarter of an hour they returned, and again the male entered the chamber for a long spell of work. Again the female absconded while he was busy inside. When he came out and found himself alone, he called entreatingly for fourteen minutes; his partner answered from the distance but refused to obey his summons. At last he flew away from the apparently finished nest cavity. By far the greater part of the task had been done in the six days after I found the pair at work.

Later, when this nest was no longer in use, I opened it for measurement. The chamber was 7½ inches high by 5½ in diameter (19 by 14 centimeters); the obliquely ascending entrance tube, which led into the top of this chamber, was about 6 inches long by 2½ in diameter (15 by 6.4 centimeters). The cavity was unlined.

The Eggs and Incubation
With the completion of the nest on the fence post, I found myself in a quandary. I wished to learn when the eggs were laid, how long they took to hatch, and what the hatchlings looked like. I wished to follow their development. For all this, it would be necessary to look frequently into the nest. But the ascending tube entered the top of the ellipsoidal black chamber and afforded no view of what rested on the floor. Moreover, it was too narrow to admit my hand. I thought first of cutting from the top of the termitary a segment which could be removed and replaced, but I doubted whether the trogons would accept so great an alteration—light would certainly enter through the joint. And I feared that ants, which destroy so many birds' nests, would find their way in. Then I considered enlisting the slender hand of a child to lift out the eggs, but upon reflection it appeared too likely that inexperienced fingers might break them.

Finally, it occurred to me to use a mirror. The few tools on this remote plantation were adequate to make what I needed. From a pocket mirror I cut a piece 1¼ inches (31 millimeters) square, the largest that would easily enter the nest, and attached it to a piece of wood that was pivoted by a screw to the end of a long wooden handle. It was so dark inside the chamber that I could see nothing without illuminating it with a flashlight bulb, pushed in on a cord that on the other end could be screwed into the socket of my flashlight. I found this simple apparatus so useful for studying not only trogons' nests but also those of woodpeckers and many other hole-nesting birds that I carried it constantly in my knapsack. With binocular, blind, and flashlight, it became an indispensable part of my field equipment.

To avoid too great disturbance of the trogons' nest at the critical period of egg laying, I at first looked into it at intervals of several days. Between April 20 and 23 two eggs were laid, the first apparently on April 21, a week after the nest chamber seemed finished. The third and last egg appeared on April 25. Accordingly, the interval between laying successive eggs was two days.

A nest beside a lagoon, of which I shall soon tell, likewise contained three eggs when found on May 6, and this was the number in the replacement nest of the first pair when discovered on July 9. In every instance, the eggs rested merely on some hard chips of the black material of the termitary, no softer lining having been taken in. As seen with artificial light and by reflection, they appeared pure white. Later, I opened a deserted nest and removed two old unhatched eggs, which measured 29.8 by 22.6 and 31 by 23 millimeters. A nest of the closely related Citreoline Trogon in a termitary above Tonalá, Chiapas, Mexico, contained, on July 17, 1934, two freshly laid eggs that were pure white.

By means of two long and several short vigils and many brief visits, I learned how the trogons incubated in the nest on the fence post. As with other species in the family, the male and female shared the task, the latter sitting through the night, the former taking charge of the nest through most of the day. Their hours in the nest were much the same as those of the pair of Massena Trogons that I had studied in Honduras. The female, continuing the long session begun the preceding evening, remained in the termitary until about an hour after sunrise. She flew off suddenly, without warning and without a signal from her mate, at about 7:00 A.M. Sometimes the male entered within a few minutes of her departure, but on other mornings he delayed more than an hour. Thus, on May 7 the female left at 6:59 and he did not enter until 8:15. If undisturbed, he then sat continuously through most of the day, about eight or ten hours in all. I marveled that he could endure the heat within his black nest when the morning sun shone fiercely upon it. Between three and five o'clock in the afternoon, he usually ended his long session. His method of emerging was very different from that of his mate, for he came out gradually. First, his whitish bill appeared in the entrance and remained there many seconds, while he hung looking downward. Next, his head and neck protruded, and he peered from side to side, surveying the world from which he had so long been isolated, before launching forth into it. Then, with a dart, he took off and undulated to a convenient perch, where he stood erect and called for his mate, who might be long in answering.

To make quite sure that the male trogon sat all day without intermission, I resolved to keep continuous watch. In order to avoid a vigil that would be long and tedious, I decided to divide my watch between two consecutive days, starting at one o'clock in the afternoon of May 8. The male, who was in the nest when I began, remained continuously until 3:12, when he left spontaneously. I waited until 4:00, but the female had not yet arrived. The following morning, I resumed my vigil before the termitary at sunrise. At 7:05 the female darted out and flew to perch near her mate, who was resting in a tree 50 feet (15 meters) away. If he had called to her, I failed to hear him, although he was nearer to me than to the termitary.

It turned out to be a beautiful day, such as one frequently enjoys in the Caribbean lowlands of Central America in the dry season, with bright sunshine and a clear sky but not oppressively warm. It was pleasant to stand in the shade of the vine-smothered bush, with sunbeams filtering through the foliage, and feel the slow passage of time. My eyes were fastened upon the termitary, which I dared not neglect for a second, lest the trogon dart away unseen. The morning slipped by without his so much as showing his head in the orifice. I had intended to end my watch at the hour when I began on the preceding day, but when one o'clock arrived I decided to continue until the trogon terminated his turn on the eggs. I had not much longer to wait, for in about fifteen minutes the children of the plantation laborers came noisily down the hillside behind the nest, and at the same time someone pushed a tramcar, which rolled with loud rumbling over the tracks 100 feet (30 meters) away. The combination of sounds brought the trogon to his doorway, where he hung head downward, peering out, undecided whether to go or stay. Just then the iron wheels of the car jolted noisily over an uneven joint in the light rails; he shot out and away and called in the distance.

An hour later, at 2:17, the female—after perching long on the wire, the very symbol of caution as she turned her head slowly from side to side to make sure that no enemy was in sight—flew directly into the nest, the earliest that I saw her enter. On May 7, she did not go in until 5:40 in the evening, although her mate had left at 5:02; and on May 3 she had not entered by 6:00, although the nest had been unattended since the male's exit at 3:58. Once within the termitary, the female usually remained until she relinquished her eggs to her mate the next morning.

While sitting in the nest, these trogons had become indifferent to the loud banging of a heavy wooden gate nearby and to the uncouth shouts of plantation laborers on the path that wound up the hillside behind the termitary. But let someone walk close behind the nest, swishing through the tall grass at the edge of the little marsh, or tap on the fence wire even a good distance away, and the birds darted out of their chamber in a flash.

Occasional visits to the nest beside the lagoon and short watches showed that the pattern of incubation was essentially the same as at the nest on the fence post: the male sitting through most of the day, the female by night. While incubating, the trogons regurgitated hard seeds of fruits. About a dozen, the size of cherrystones, accumulated on the floor of this chamber.

At the nest on the fence post, the last of the three eggs was laid on April 25, and a single one hatched on May 14, after at least nineteen days of incubation. The other two failed to hatch.

The Nestlings

The hatchling's pink skin was absolutely naked, its eyes tightly closed. At the age of a week, its eyes were still closed, but pinfeathers were sprouting through its skin. When it was eleven days old, these pins had become very long. Four days later, when its wing feathers were escaping from the tips of their sheaths, this young trogon lay dead in the termitary, headless and swarming with small brown ants. Apparently, a weasel had killed it. While I examined the ruined nest, the bereaved mother arrived with an insect for her lost nestling. Years later, I saw a male Collared Trogon bring food twice for a nestling that lay dead below the nest. Such persistence of parental attentiveness is widespread among birds.

After the loss of this nest, the one beside the lagoon claimed more of my time. This was in a massive black termitary, 33 inches long and 18 inches thick (84 by 46 centimeters), that was still full of termites, which had sealed off all the passageways that abutted on the cavity carved by the trogons. This structure was attached to the lower side of a fallen willow tree that leaned against bushes on the lagoon's steep bank, beside a banana plantation. The doorway on the underside of the termitary was only two feet (60 centimeters) from the bank's edge, so low that the birds often alighted on the weedy ground before flying up to enter it—surprising behavior for a trogon. Both parents fed the three nestlings with a variety of insects, including small mantises, green caterpillars, dragonflies, and others too small for identification, with rarely a berry. While delivering this food to the nestlings, they clung for several minutes in the entrance tube with only a few inches of tail showing; but, without being able to see inside, I could not learn what occupied them so long. To leave, they dropped backward from the nest and rose into the air, without touching the ground. When I approached their termitary, they did not scold or complain but flew off to a safe distance, if not beyond my view.

From the age of two or three days, the blind nestlings continually uttered little faraway peeps, faintly audible a few paces from the nest. I feared that such a telltale of their presence might defeat their parents' extreme caution in approaching them.

At the age of eleven days, the young trogons bristled with long pinfeathers and their eyes were open. Now they were quieter in the nest, making only a sort of hissing cry while their parents clung in the entrance tube to feed them. This was done much more quickly than while the nestlings were younger, which led me to believe that the parent with its head in the entrance had in some way prepared the big insect it had brought for them, and now that they were older this process was no longer necessary. Feedings were still infrequent, only three to five in an hour for the three nestlings. Now the parents no longer alighted on the ground

Black-headed Trogon: termitary at the edge of a banana plantation in which three nestlings were raised.

in front of the termitary since, with practice, they had learned to fly from the trees bordering the lagoon directly into the entrance tube. They became more excited when I visited their nest; although they made no hostile demonstration, they might perch above me, uttering at intervals a single low *cuk*, at the same time spreading and closing their tails fanwise, a movement which revealed momentary flashes of white. Sometimes, while I squatted in front of the termitary to look in with light and mirror, a parent arriving with food darted up very close before it appeared to become aware of me; once the male almost bumped into me. I never saw either parent remove waste from the nest chamber, which became so humid that the mirror I used for viewing the nestlings clouded with condensed moisture even on warm dry days, making a difficult observation doubly difficult.

When the nestlings were two weeks old, they bristled with amazingly long pins, from which hardly any plumage had escaped. During the next two days, in a marvelously rapid transformation, they became completely clothed with expanded feathers. Only in anis and antbirds have I seen the feathers burst from their horny envelopes as rapidly. Since the young trogons were ready to be photographed, on the following day I brought my camera and an Indian boy of ten as a helper. The lad's hand easily entered the tube, which was too narrow to admit mine. He drew forth one of the young birds and passed it to me.

Now, for the first time, I held and saw by direct vision a trogon nestling, for hitherto I had viewed them only by reflected light. It was a trogon in miniature, well feathered but only about a third of the adult size. It struggled to escape; but from my experience with kingfishers, motmots, and jacamars, which remain flightless for a few days after they are well covered with feathers, I doubted that it could fly. Holding it low in a clear space amid the banana plants, I opened my hand, ready for at most a short chase as the chick fluttered over the ground. But no sooner were my fingers opened than wings began to whir;

in an instant the nestling rose steeply into the air and flew over the tops of the banana plants, 20 or 25 feet (6 or 7.6 meters) high. The mother trogon, who had been watching us from a banana leaf with a long-horned grasshopper in her bill—uttering at intervals a staccato note—darted toward her chick; and both vanished among the giant leaves. Her plumage had become frayed, her belly discolored, in the performance of her parental tasks.

"Take out another, Macario," I requested.

Feeling in the nest, the boy reported that it was empty. Almost incredulous, I looked in with the mirror, only to find that he was right: the other two nestlings had gone, at the age of sixteen or seventeen days. Their ability to fly had come so suddenly that I had missed my opportunity to photograph them. I had not even observed their plumage carefully, for the one I held in my hand darted away before I could examine it. I did notice that its blackish wings, unlike those of its parents, were prominently marked with white, and its bill was shockingly dirty. The bottom of the nest was covered with accumulated droppings, among which maggots swarmed.

On a short visit to Alsacia plantation at the end of the same year, I examined all three of the termitaries in which the trogons had nested. The first, in which the single nestling had been killed, was still open on the side, as I had left it after enlarging the aperture. The termitary beside the lagoon had rolled down the bank when the willow log which supported it had decayed and crumbled; the trogons' nest chamber had not been closed. But the chamber in the second termitary on a fence post—the replacement nest of the trogons who had lost their first brood—had been completely closed by the termites of the thriving colony which still inhabited this structure. The only remaining indication of the birds' nest was a patch of slightly lighter brown on the surface, marking the spot where the doorway had been. A termitary in which Massena Trogons had nested was similarly repaired by the termites.

16. Vermilion-breasted Trogon

Trogon bairdii

In January, when the bright sun of the dry season glints from myriad glossy leaves in the rain forests of southwestern Costa Rica, a beautiful song floats down from lofty tree-tops. The mellow notes, at first distinctly separated, come faster as the song continues, until they form a prolonged roll, which often ends with a few more widely spaced notes. You may peer up into clouds of foliage until your neck aches without catching more than a fleeting glimpse of the author of this arresting song; fully to appreciate his loveliness, you must find him at lower levels or, best of all, watch him while he attends a low nest in sunshine. Then his blackish crown and hind-neck reflect violet-blue. The metallic green or blue-green of his dorsal plumage scintillates with iridescent blue and violet. His long central tail feathers are dark metallic bluish green or violet-blue, abruptly tipped with black. The exposed parts of the lateral feathers are pure white, so that the closed tail, seen from below, is almost wholly white. His throat and chest are black, tinted with violet-blue, and the remainder of his ventral plumage is vermilion or flame-scarlet. His short, thick, strongly serrated bill is almost white, and the ring of bare skin around each dark eye is pale blue to whitish.

The much duller-colored mate of this splendid bird is nearly everywhere dark slate-gray, with reddish orange abdomen and under tail coverts. Her wings are black, with narrow, widely spaced bars of white. Her four central tail feathers are dark slate color with still darker tips; the black lateral rectrices are crossed by narrow, widely spaced white bars. Her upper mandible is black, the lower grayish horn color. The bare rings around her yellowish brown eyes are pale blue. Her blackish legs and feet are darker than those of the male. Both sexes are 10 or 11 inches (25 or 28 centimeters) long.

This exceptionally handsome trogon is confined to the dwindling rain forests of the southern Pacific quarter of Costa Rica and the adjacent province of Chiriquí in Panama, from the lowlands up to about 4,000 feet (1,200 meters). From the forest, where it usually remains high, it occasionally enters neighboring shady clearings and may even nest in them. A solitary bird, it apparently does not live in pairs throughout the year, although I have seen a male and a female together, as though mated, in January. Larger groups, up to five or six individuals scattered through the trees, attract attention by much calling and occasional flying at one another, without fighting, as pairs form during the early months of the year. Like other trogons, Vermilion-breasts are dignified and sedate, perching upright with tails pointing straight downward or perhaps inclined slightly forward beneath the perch. They fly with strong undulations.

When alarmed or excited, the male Vermilion-breasted Trogon rhythmically spreads and folds his tail with a rapid movement, thereby sending brief flashes of white to an observer behind him. This tail movement, which is evidently related to his pure white lateral rectrices, is different from that of certain other trogons with less white on their tails. I was impressed with this difference one day when I watched some trogons and hummingbirds who, with a male Green Honeycreeper, had gathered around a Spectacled Owl that perched high in the forest. Protesting the presence of the great somnolent owl, a Violaceous Trogon uttered sharp rattling notes while he slowly raised his tail well above his back, thereby displaying the black-and-white bars on the outer feathers. The male Vermilion-breasted Trogon did not elevate his tail but fanned out the feathers laterally. None of the three trogons in the mobbing party approached nearly as close to the motionless owl as did the far smaller hummingbirds. The female Vermilion-breast sometimes fans her tail in the same manner as the male, although she has little white on her lateral feathers to display.

In foraging, this trogon hardly differs from the other American species. It perches quietly, looking around until it spies an insect amid the foliage, then darts suddenly upward or outward, seizes its prey in its serrated bill while hovering, then alights on a branch to devour it. The trogon's diet is diversified by fruits, often of considerable size, which it plucks from the trees while on the wing and swallows whole. A female who foraged among the Guava trees in the pasture in front of our house used procedures which one does not often see in the family. In addition to repeatedly fluttering against the foliage and sometimes against the bark, she thrice dropped to the ground and rested on the short grass for a minute or two. On one of her descents she caught a small dark lizard, which she held in her bill for a good while.

The accelerated roll distinguishes the Vermilion-breasted Trogon's song from that of associated species in the forests of southwestern Costa Rica—the Massena, Violaceous, Black-throated, and Collared—whose songs are usually shorter, less melodious, and at most only slightly accelerated. The Vermilion-breasted Trogon sings much from February to June, less frequently in the second half of the year, yet occasionally I have heard persistent singing in late September.

This accelerated song appears to be used chiefly to attract a mate and, probably, also to proclaim possession of territory. After he has won a partner, the male, who often seems more eager than she to prepare a nest, coaxes her to the site with utterances of a different character. His full, low, mellow notes, more evenly spaced and all at nearly the same pitch, form a melodious twitter or a liquid ripple of sound, soft and soothing, at times intensely pleading, and always most beautiful. While the members of a pair work alternately at their nest, the one not so engaged perches nearby, emitting a constant flow of these soft notes, as though to encourage its partner.

When approaching their nest with food, both parents sometimes repeat, too rapidly to count, a low soft *cow*. In the same circumstances, the male of another pair uttered clear staccato notes. When driven from his nest by my approach, this male delivered a soft throaty note, likewise accompanied by tail flashing. Arriving to replace her mate on the eggs, a female called with a low *tuck*, less melodious than the *cow* call, from which it differed also by the more distinct separation of the notes. These trogons have a fairly large vocabulary, with a variety of notes whose finer modulations I am unable to convey by means of the written word.

The Nest

In March, Vermilion-breasted Trogons start to carve their nest chambers, in the midst of the forest or in a neighboring shady pasture or coffee plantation. Although I have watched them digging at heights up to 50 feet (15 meters), the seven occupied nests that I have seen were 6 to 35 feet (1.8 to 10.6 meters) up, in massive decaying trunks. Four nests were carved in successive years, most probably by the same pair, in the trunk of an introduced Flame-of-the-Forest tree that stood at the edge of a pasture in front of our house, about 100 yards (92 meters) from the old forest where the trogons appeared to pass most of their free time. Each year this rotting stub was lower, forcing the birds to nest nearer the ground. Their successive doorways were 18, 17⅚, 9½, and 6½ feet (5.5, 5.4, 2.9, and 2 meters) up. The second of these openings was begun so close below the first that it broke into the old cavity, with the result that the trogons had an unusually tall chamber with two entrances.

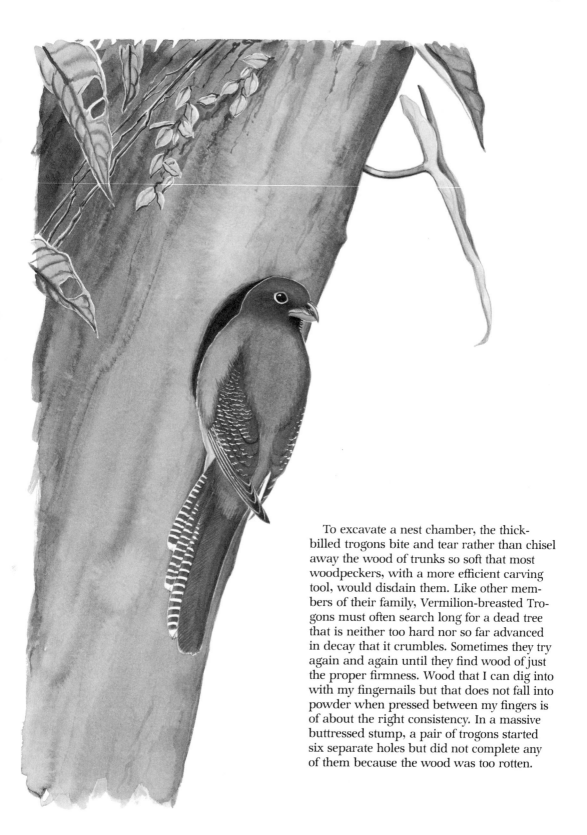

To excavate a nest chamber, the thick-billed trogons bite and tear rather than chisel away the wood of trunks so soft that most woodpeckers, with a more efficient carving tool, would disdain them. Like other members of their family, Vermilion-breasted Trogons must often search long for a dead tree that is neither too hard nor so far advanced in decay that it crumbles. Sometimes they try again and again until they find wood of just the proper firmness. Wood that I can dig into with my fingernails but that does not fall into powder when pressed between my fingers is of about the right consistency. In a massive buttressed stump, a pair of trogons started six separate holes but did not complete any of them because the wood was too rotten.

Like other trogons, the male Vermilion-breast chooses the nest site, sometimes before it is evident that he has won a mate, and tries to persuade a female to accept it and him. In early March, I watched a male who rested on a lower limb of a tall forest tree, tirelessly repeating his far-carrying song. He interrupted his singing to fly to the top of a neighboring barkless 50-foot (15-meter) stub, where, clinging upright, he bit into the rotting wood, dropping a few fragments to the ground. Then he returned to his former perch and continued to sing until past the middle of the morning. Prolonged watching failed to reveal that he had a partner. A fortnight later, in the same locality, I found a male, probably the same bird, whose courtship was farther advanced. After singing for a while, he flew to a nearby barkless trunk and dug into it with his bill. After a few seconds, he dropped down to a perch, and a female nibbled briefly at the same spot. Soon both flew, and I did not see them again.

To start a cavity, Vermilion-breasted Trogons dig obliquely upward into soft wood, carving the entrance tube of their deeply placed chamber. The male and female take turns, and while one works the other usually perches nearby, repeating the beautiful soft notes already mentioned. Between 11:10 A.M. and 12:07 P.M. on April 23, 1942, a pair carving a high nest in the forest worked as follows: male, five minutes; female, nine minutes; male, two minutes, after which he was frightened away by a falling branch; intermission, two minutes; male, ten minutes; female, ten minutes; intermission, two minutes; male, ten minutes; female, seven minutes. During an hour and a half, another pair, at a leaning rotten stump in a pasture, worked for similarly short spells of two to ten minutes. A male of still another pair carved continuously for fourteen minutes; and a female was inside, presumably working, for twenty-one minutes. Nearly always, as soon as one partner dropped, tailfirst, out of the ascending shaft, the other promptly went to work. The trogons made no special effort to remove the loosened particles of wood, which slipped down in front of them, to fall out beneath their tails. When, at the end of a

spell, the worker dropped out of the hole, a shower of fine wood particles was released; and many remained clinging to the bird's disheveled plumage. The first of these pairs made good progress. At the beginning of the hour, they carved with the head and back inside but the rump, ends of the wings, and tail exposed; at the end of the hour, only the tail remained outside.

Often, by murmuring pleading notes and working in her presence, a male tries to persuade his mate to continue with a hole they have started. Perhaps, after briefly entering the boring, she flies away, and all his coaxing fails to entice her back. Apparently, her surer judgment has found the trunk unsuitable, and in her absence he will not work.

The completed chamber is roughly ellipsoidal, with neatly rounded walls. Placed deep in the wood, it is entered by an obliquely ascending tube, about 7 inches long by 3¼ inches in diameter (18 by 8.3 centimeters). This shaft, which in some nests was wide enough to admit my hand but in one was too narrow, enters the chamber near the top; a ridge of wood separates it from the chamber's bottom and prevents the eggs from rolling out. In one instance, this ridge rose about 2 inches (5 centimeters) above the lowest part of the floor, which is covered only by coarse wood particles; no soft lining is carried in. A nest in a massive trunk smelled so strongly of iodoform that, when I stuck my nose in the doorway, it was easy to imagine that I was entering a surgery. Other nests lacked this peculiar scent, which is evidently a product of the decomposition of only certain kinds of wood. This trogon's chamber in a decaying trunk has the same form as those which Black-headed Trogons carve in termitaries and Massena Trogons make in either termitaries or wood. It is very different from the open niches which, as we shall see, Mountain, Black-throated, and Collared trogons carve in trunks.

The Eggs and Incubation

In a nest which was begun about July 17, 1957, and seemed to be finished in early August, I found the first egg on August 16. Probably this interval of about two weeks between the completion of the nest and the start of laying was exceptionally long. Two years later, another chamber in this same stub was finished about April 27, and the following day I found part of an eggshell in it, the remainder on the ground below. No more eggs were laid here. Higher in the mountains, a nest that seemed finished on March 23 received its first egg on April 1 or 2, my earliest date for laying. Four sets were laid in April, one each in May, June, and August. Eggs are laid at intervals of two or three days. Of my accessible nests, four contained two eggs and one had three. The slightly glossy white eggs may be either blunt or rather sharp at the narrower end. The measurements of seven eggs averaged 33.1 by 25 millimeters, with extremes of 31 to 34.9 by 24.2 to 25.4 millimeters.

At the exceptionally late nest in the Flame-of-the-Forest tree in August of 1957, the trogons were very dilatory. The first egg was laid about a month after they started to excavate the nest chamber; and, during the first four days after their set of two eggs was complete, they incubated most inconstantly. On most of my visits in this interval, the nest was unattended and the eggs cold. On the fifth day, however, the parents were more constantly present. The irregular lengths of the female's tail feathers suggested that she was molting, which perhaps retarded the nesting. After they have settled into their routine of incubation, Vermilion-breasted Trogons keep their eggs almost continuously covered, following the same simple schedule as the Black-headed Trogons.

At my first occupied nest, situated 16 feet (4.9 meters) up in a massive stub in the midst of the forest, the parents were so indifferent to my presence that I could watch them unconcealed. At 5:15 A.M. on June 2, 1942, I entered the dusky forest and sat beside a decaying log about 40 feet (12 meters) from the nest. From the trees above me came the soft, sweet notes of a Black-striped Woodcreeper. Off in the undergrowth, a Black-faced Antthrush repeated its mellow whistles. After a while, the sun rose above the high mountains in the east, and a few stray beams, filtering through the forest canopy,

fell upon the dark bulk of the rotting stump in which the female trogon sat warming her two eggs, surrounded by such thick walls that she could hardly have been aware of the sunshine. A male Gray-headed Tanager, who with his mate was building a nest in a low spiny palm not far off, sang sweetly in the underwood on the slope below, by the little brook whose liquid babble was a fit accompaniment to his soft childlike voice. Thus the morning wore on, with never a glimpse of the trogons whom I had come to watch.

Finally, at 9:03, the soft notes of the male trogon floated down from the treetops. With wings and white tail feathers spread, he fluttered down to a lower branch, nearer the nest, and repeated his subdued summons to his mate. He dropped yet lower and called again. Now she shot out of the round doorway in the stub's side and rose into a tree, where she called softly with rapidly repeated notes, like those of her mate. He descended to the doorway, before which he clung while he took a single lingering look around, then promptly climbed up the shaft and vanished. He seemed not to notice me sitting so near, unscreened by foliage.

For the next five hours, nothing noteworthy occurred in the silent forest around me. Soon after 2:00, rain began to fall and continued intermittently until midafternoon. At 2:59, the female reappeared and perched about 30 feet (9 meters) up in the tree in front of the nest. She called *tuck tuck tuck* over and over, slightly twitching her tail to beat time to her notes. Since her mate was slow to respond to her summons, she advanced to a bough nearer the nest and continued to call. Then she flew to the doorway and bumped into him as he was coming out. She retired to her last perch until he rose into the treetops. As soon as he had gone, she flew to the opening and entered in one continuous movement, not pausing at the doorway to look around, as trogons often do. It was then 3:03, exactly six hours after her partner had replaced her in the morning. I ended my long vigil, but on a number of other days I always found the female with the eggs after the middle of the afternoon. Once the male was incubating as early as 8:15 A.M.

These trogons, who lived in forest that had long been abandoned by the Indians and had only recently been invaded by Spanish-speaking settlers, were amazingly fearless. Usually no amount of hammering or scratching near the base of their trunk would make them emerge. Noises like clapping my hands and shouting, or chopping with my machete in the neighboring undergrowth, failed to bring them to their doorway. A disturbance nearer their own level, as when the top of my long ladder grated against the trunk, usually sent them forth. If this failed to move them, they left when I climbed up and shook a leafy branch in front of their doorway. But, on the day the eggs hatched, I ascended and saw the male's white-rimmed eyes looking down the entrance tube at me, his head a little over a foot above mine. When next I moved, he darted out.

When finally it flew from the chamber, the parent would rise to a low bough of a nearby tree and perch upright, its tail feathers strongly bent and crumpled by long confinement in a narrow space. On the morning when I found the nest, the male stayed there, a few yards from me, for nearly half an hour, while I measured and made notes. For a long time he complained loudly, flashing his white outer tail feathers, but before I finished he fell silent, staying in the same spot. Never had I known a trogon so steadfast in remaining in its nest, so loud and untiring in its complaints after it was driven out, so fearless in staying near the intruder. While I stood on the ladder to examine the nest, the female sometimes perched as close to me as her mate did, but, in contrast to him, she was always silent and immobile save for the occasional slow turning of her head. In the days immediately following my discovery of the nest, she was less strongly attached to it than was her partner. Before the eggs hatched, she became as steadfast and fearless as he was from the beginning.

After I finished my inspection of the nest, descended to the ground, removed the ladder, and retired a few paces, the parent who had been in charge of the eggs would soon return to them while I watched, without the long-drawn-out cautious survey at the doorway. Probably I would not have discovered this nest, as I passed through the forest tapping on trunks and stubs with holes, if I had not happened to encounter it at the critical time of the morning changeover. The female promptly flew out when I knocked, and her mate, who was nearby, entered while I stood directly below the doorway.

It is noteworthy that these trogons never darted toward me or threatened me or tried to lure me away by a distraction display. The male showed his concern for his nest only by calling, and the female never did even this while she watched me examine her eggs. Even after the nestlings hatched, the parents were equally undemonstrative, in this agreeing with all other trogons, of whatever species, that I have studied.

At the nests 18 and 17$\frac{5}{8}$ feet (5.5 and 5.4 meters) up in the Flame-of-the-Forest trunk in 1957 and 1958, the female was almost as confiding as the female of the first nest. Soon after she began to incubate, she would fly out when I tapped on the lower part of the stub. Later, however, she refused to leave when I did this; to make her emerge when I wished to examine her eggs, I had to scratch the stub near the nest with a long stick. Then she would fly out and perch nearby. Once, while she rested in front of the nest, she permitted me to touch her tail with the tip of my pole. In strong contrast to the male of the first nest, her mate was less confiding. At first he would leave the nest in response to a whistle or a handclap. As days passed, he became more wary and flew out whenever I walked in front, where he could see me by looking down the entrance tube. Then he rose to a higher perch than the female took in similar circumstances. Unlike the male of the first nest, he would not enter if he saw me watching, even from a distance.

Accordingly, to observe this more exposed nest, it was necessary to set up a blind, in which, on August 30, 1957, my wife, Pamela, and I watched alternately all day. At 5:37, long before sunrise, the male arrived and called softly from a tree near the nest. After ten minutes, he alighted on a branch in front of the doorway, the female emerged, and he entered. Throughout the sunny morning, no trogon was seen. At 1:04 the male darted out of the nest, where he had remained continuously for seven hours and seventeen minutes, rested in front, and called softly once. After six minutes, he reentered, as rain began with thunder. He stayed inside only a minute, then again perched in front and called. After another three minutes, he went to the doorway but did not enter, then flew to the forest beyond the shady pasture. Obviously, he was tired of incubating but hesitated to desert his post before relief arrived. At 1:23 the female appeared and perched silently in front of the nest, to enter at 1:27. Throughout the rest of the rainy afternoon, she stayed with her eggs without revealing herself, while her mate remained beyond my sight in the forest. At 6:15, I ended my vigil in the dusk. At this nest, the male's session was just over an hour and a quarter longer than that of the first male, and it came much earlier in the day.

On September 2, the male entered the nest in the Flame-of-the-Forest stub at 5:50 A.M. Two hours later, I heard him calling in a tree in front of the house, and while I watched he flew to the forest. Why was he not warming the eggs, as on all previous days at this hour? Suspecting that something had gone wrong, I promptly went to investigate. The nest was unattended. Soon the female arrived and went to the doorway. Evidently, she had met her mate in the forest, and this encounter had sent her back to her neglected eggs some four or five hours before her usual time to resume incubation. After hesitating, she entered. A moment later she shot out and alighted on a branch, shook herself vigorously all over, half lifting her wings, and pecked at her plumage. After a minute or so of this, she again went into her nest, only to come out as promptly as last time and shake herself as before. Then she flew silently back to the forest.

Bringing a ladder, I climbed to the nest and stuck in my mirror and electric bulb. The chamber swarmed with Fire Ants, which at this wet season were a terrible plague. I did not know how to get rid of them except by putting poison in and around the nest, which I hesitated to do for fear that it would harm the trogons. At half past ten

the male returned and called much by the nest, but I did not see him enter. That night the eggs were unattended; no female flew out when the male came to relieve her before sunrise the next morning. Through much of the morning he lingered near the nest, repeating his melodious calls.

During this day the Fire Ants withdrew, leaving the two eggs intact. After nightfall, I saw the female in the nest when I looked up into it by torchlight. The eggs had been left unwarmed for only a single night and parts of two days. I hoped that they had suffered no harm, but, to my great disappointment, they failed to hatch at the expected time. Throughout the remainder of September and the first eight days of October, the parents faithfully continued to attend these eggs; then they vanished without leaving a trace. From the laying of the second egg, incubation had continued for fifty-one days or about three times the normal period.

I did not again watch this nest throughout a whole day, but during the seven weeks that incubation continued I observed it many times. Only once, soon after incubation began, did I find the male taking two turns on the same day, one in the morning, another in the afternoon, separated by a short session by the female early in the afternoon. Thereafter, as far as I could learn, the pair followed the schedule widespread among lowland trogons, with only two changeovers each day. From August 25 to September 10, the male came early every morning; on twelve days in this interval, he arrived between 5:37 and 6:15 to call out his partner and begin his long session on the eggs.

For the next fortnight, I neglected to watch in the early morning. When I resumed observations, the male arrived much later; between September 25 and October 8, I often found the female in the nest between 7:00 and 8:00. If I put her out, even at this late hour, she returned rather promptly to await her mate's arrival. One morning at 7:35, I found a spider web spread over the doorway, suggesting that the female had stayed constantly within since the preceding evening. On September 28, the male did not arrive until 8:57 A.M. Now that he came later in the morning, he stayed later in the afternoon; he was sometimes on the eggs between 3:00 and 4:00. On the day when he came at 8:57 A.M., he was still present at 4:10. Sometimes he did not wait for the arrival of his mate, who now often came after 3:30, instead of between 1:00 and 2:00, as she frequently did before the invasion by the ants.

In the following year, when the trogons were again nesting in the same chamber, which they had provided with a second door-way and deepened, the male often began to incubate early in the morning, as he had done during much of the preceding nesting. Once his partner replaced him at the un-usually early hour of 12:24 P.M. Of the four years in which the trogons tried to raise a family in the Flame-of-the-Forest trunk, this was the only one in which they succeeded in hatching eggs. Sixteen days after their third egg was laid, two of them hatched. Because of the failure to hatch of one of the eggs, which may have been the last to be laid, this determination of the incubation period may be in error by a day or two. At a nest of a different pair, eggs were laid on April 2 and 4 and both hatched between April 20 and 21, after an incubation period of approximately seventeen days.

The Nestlings

Typical trogon hatchlings, the newborn Vermilion-breasts bore no trace of down on their pink skins. Their eyes were tightly closed. Their heel pads were rough with fine whitish projections; and on each pink foot the two inner toes were already turned backward, as in adults. They developed at about the same rate as the nestling Black-headed Trogons in their termitary. Their eyes opened when they were between nine and ten days old. They sprouted long feather sheaths, which remained closed until the nestlings were about thirteen days old, then raveled off so rapidly that two or three days later the chicks were fully clothed in dark plumage.

These nestlings used their voices freely. When newly hatched, they uttered hoarse little grunts. A two-day-old nestling, held in my hand, turned up its head and rhythmically repeated a low soft note that suggested the *cow cow* of the adults. It also made the same sizzling sound that it voiced while taking food from a parent. Week-old nestlings uttered soft, long-drawn-out notes in addition to the *cow cow*. When hungry, older nestlings repeated a deep mellow note that sounded melancholy. A three-week-old nestling uttered this note about thirty-four times per minute. While the nestling swallowed food, this note changed to a whining, sizzling cry. If the nestling was still hungry, the deep mellow note was resumed as soon as its throat was cleared.

In the five nests that I followed to the end, eleven eggs were laid and four hatched, but only a single young survived to fly. About the time its feathers began to expand, this chick was infested by no fewer than twelve *tór-salos*—larvae of a dipterous fly—each of which made a relatively huge swelling under its skin. Although the young trogon appeared to be otherwise in excellent condition and to suffer as little from its parasites as from the filthiness of its abode, this infestation may have been in part responsible for its long nestling period of twenty-five days—eight or nine days longer than that of the Black-headed Trogons, the most closely related species treated in this book.

Both parents brooded the nestlings, but after their first few days they were warmed little. When they were a week old, with only horny pinfeathers to cover their nakedness, they were no longer brooded by day. Their mother continued to protect the two in the Flame-of-the-Forest trunk at night until they were eleven days old, when they had become so big that she sat high, with much of her reddish orange abdomen visible when I directed my flashlight's beam up the entrance tube. Thereafter the young, whose plumage had not begun to expand, slept alone.

The nestlings' meals were large but infrequent. When the two in the Flame-of-the-Forest stub were five days old, each parent fed them only twice in the first six hours of the morning. When they were ten days old, their mother fed them twice in the same interval, but their father, who had become increasingly shy of my blind, failed to deliver the single item that he brought. The chicks became so hungry that their cries were plainly audible above the babble of the neighboring stream. When these nestlings were two weeks old, a predator tore through the very rotten wood above their chamber and took them.

Sixteen years earlier, at the massive trunk in the forest where the parents were so fearless of me, the female inexplicably vanished soon after the two nestlings hatched, and to the male fell the whole task of rearing the young. Possibly because he failed to take over the feminine office of brooding throughout the night—a point I did not check in the distant forest—one of the nestlings died when about a week old, but he faithfully attended the survivor until it flew when twenty-five days old. In my eleven hours of watching during the nestling period, four of them while both young were still present, he brought food only nine times. Sometimes a spider spun a web across the nest's entrance between his widely spaced visits.

The Vermilion-breasted Trogons' rate of feeding was much slower than that of Mountain Trogons, as discussed in the next chapter, but they brought much bigger items to nestlings that probably needed less food because they were in better-enclosed nests in a lower and warmer region. At both of the Vermilion-breasts' nests, large green winged insects formed the bulk of the nestlings' food. The kind that I most often recognized in a parent's bill had a huge swollen abdomen and relatively small wings that were partly or wholly pink. Sometimes the abdomen of such an insect was brought without the rest of the body. Some of the insects were either too large for a nestling to swallow or else were refused because the chick was already satiated. One day, when the surviving young trogon was becoming feathered, I removed from beside it a dead green orthopterous insect 3½ inches (9 centimeters) long. Its flattened, expanded thorax was 1½ inches (3.8 centimeters) wide; its massive abdomen was 1¼ inches long by ⅝ inch thick (3.1 by 1.6 centimeters). Other big insects that the nestling had failed to eat were decaying beneath it. Green caterpillars, often very long, were also given to it.

Early one morning, the male came to the Flame-of-the-Forest stub with a thick brown phasmid, or walkingstick, that seemed longer than his body, without the tail. Grasped by the middle, it hung down on each side of his thick whitish bill. Distrustful of my blind, he continued to hold the insect for the next hour and a half, while yellow-and-black Banded Wasps hovered around and even alighted upon it. The trogon rested inertly in the same spot, the insect hanging ever more limply in his bill, until the sneeze of a horse in the neighboring pasture frightened him away with it. During the next three hours, he failed to reappear.

The male trogon in the forest seemed to do most of his hunting high in the treetops, for his approach to the nest was always a descent. Usually I first became aware of his arrival when he flew down to perch at mid-height in the forest, where he repeated clear staccato notes while he rapidly spread and closed his tail feathers, fanwise, to send forth flashes of white. After delaying here for a brief interval, he would drop to a lower perch nearer the nest, then to one still closer and slightly below its level, on each of which he called and flashed his tail as before. As he drew nearer, the monotonous calls of the nestling within became louder and higher in pitch. Then the parent would dart to the doorway and cling there, with only his rump and tail outside, while he delivered the meal. While the nestling was very young, this might take five to ten minutes; but when it was older, the feeding was accomplished in a second or two, after which the trogon always flew up into the high canopy of the forest and vanished.

At this nest, as at the other that I watched, the parents never removed waste. This began to accumulate as soon as incubation started, for the sitting parents regurgitated the seeds of fruits that they had swallowed whole and left them in the chamber. In this nest were seeds of three kinds, the largest of which were half as big as the eggs beside which they lay. After the eggs hatched, the collection of seeds in the nest did not increase appreciably, thereby corroborating the conclusion that I drew from direct observation: the nestlings' food included few, if any, fruits. In this, the Vermilion-breasted Trogon differs greatly from the Resplendent Quetzal, which brings many large fruits to its nestlings.

The empty shells from which the nestlings had emerged were not removed but, broken into fragments, increased the litter on the nest's floor. Soon all this was buried by the young bird's excrement, in which maggots squirmed. Food that the young rejected swelled the putrefying mass, and even the dead nestling was left until I removed it. The antiseptic odor of iodoform which had pervaded this chamber before the eggs hatched was now replaced by the pungent fumes of ammonia, generated by decomposing nitrogenous matter. In what a strangely disordered nursery this young trogon grew up! Nevertheless, when twenty-five days old, it flew from the chamber with its plumage unsoiled. After it began to become feathered, I sometimes found it resting on the ridge separating the entrance tube from the chamber; this must have helped it to keep clean.

In early April, the only young male that I have seen in transitional plumage had green and violet dorsal feathers, much as in the adult. His breast was brown and his abdomen vermilion. The exposed parts of his right outer rectrices were pure white, but the corresponding feathers on the left were barred much as in the female, forming a queer contrast. This male was examining old woodpecker holes in a massive rotting stub and, as far as I could learn, he was alone.

Postscript

The devastating deforestation in the last half century throughout the limited range of this splendid bird, in southern Pacific Costa Rica and adjacent Panama, has drastically reduced its habitat and threatens it with extinction. Its best hope of survival lies in the Corcovado National Park on the peninsula of Osa, if this area can be preserved against rapidly increasing population pressure.

17. Mountain Trogon

Trogon mexicanus

In 1933, the year after I studied the Black-headed Trogon in the Motagua Valley, I passed the whole twelve months on the Sierra de Tecpán, a range rising above the town of the same name, at about 7,000 feet (2,150 meters) in west central Guatemala, to a summit 10,000 feet (3,000 meters) high. Of all the birds on the sierra, the Mountain Trogon did most to remind me that the cool forests of oaks, alders, and pines, the fields where violets, buttercups, dandelions, and speedwells grew, were in fact within the tropics. The brilliance of the male trogon's attire suggested the exuberant life of warm lowlands rather than that of those sterner, less prolific heights, where his neighbors were juncos, towhees, siskins, bluebirds, flickers, Hairy Woodpeckers, and other birds of northern types, as well as such distinctly Neotropical birds as motmots, toucanets, woodcreepers, antpittas, and honeycreepers. Even amid the towering cypress forests of the

mountaintop, where Golden-crowned King-
lets flocked, these trogons lived in fair numbers. Elsewhere in Guatemala, I occasionally
met them as low as 3,000 feet (910 meters).
They range widely through the mountains
from northwestern Mexico to Honduras.

The Mountain Trogon is a bird of medium
size, with a short, stout body, a long tail, and
a short, thick bill. The male is clad in shining metallic green, with a bright red belly,
separated from his green chest by a white
band. The female is mostly sober brown. The
red of her abdomen is neither so deep nor so
extensive as that of the male, for a belt of
brown crosses her breast below the white
band. Guatemalans call this trogon aurora,
apparently in allusion to the "rosy-fingered
dawn," which is rarely so intensely colored
as the male's under plumage.

By February, the auroras had begun their
mating calls. The full mellow *cow cow cow* of
the males, ringing through woods where

*View on the Sierra de Tecpán, Guatemala, home
of the Mountain Trogon, Blue-throated Green
Motmot, and Band-tailed Pigeon.*

oaks and alders were burgeoning, strengthened the impression of spring. When I came
too near a calling aurora, he ceased his
pleasant cowing and showed his annoyance
by uttering in its stead the low *cuk cuk cuk*
typical of trogons. As he delivered these
notes, he slowly raised and then depressed
his tail, at the same time slightly spreading it
to reveal the broad white tips of the black
outer feathers. If I continued my approach,
he retreated with undulating flight, uttering
a sort of frightened cackle. These indiscreet
habits, coupled with brilliant plumage, made
the auroras very conspicuous.

Like that of most of the birds of the sierra,
the breeding season of the Mountain Trogons
centered in the dry, frostless interval between
early April and mid May. They started to nest
somewhat earlier than many of the smaller
birds, a short while before the cessation of
nocturnal frosts, for on March 21 I found a
nest in which incubation was already well
advanced. Two more nests with eggs were
found in early April.

All three of these nests were carved into
the sides of low rotting stumps or stubs of
branches, the two lowest only 33 inches
above the ground, the highest 49 inches (84
to 124 centimeters). The nest chambers, of
rather irregular form, were from 8 to 11
inches (20 to 28 centimeters) high by 3¾ to
5½ inches (9.5 to 14 centimeters) wide. Their
unsymmetrical, vertically elongated entrances were high and broad, revealing
much of the birds who sat within. Like other
trogons, the auroras carried into the niche no
soft material to serve as a bed for their eggs,
which rested upon a shallow layer of fine
fragments of the decaying wood into which
the cavity was carved. I did not have the
good fortune to witness the excavation of
these nests; two at least were freshly carved,
as attested to by the abundance of newly removed wood particles on the ground below. I
have no doubt that the auroras made the cavities themselves, the male and female working alternately, as with other trogons.

As I roamed through the woods on the

Sierra de Tecpán in April, I noticed scores of places where auroras had recently tried their bills on decaying trunks, apparently in fruitless attempts to carve nesting holes. Usually the excavations were in low half-rotten stumps, but I found some as high as 12 feet (3.6 meters). Sometimes, after penetrating the soft outer layer of a stub, the birds had found the interior too hard for their bills and so had been forced to abandon the work. In other cases, the wood had been too rotten; or else the birds had carved so deeply that they broke through the side of the chamber and ruined it. Wood in which they were able to work was so soft that I could dig into it with my fingernails. When the wood reaches this advanced stage of decay, the trunk, unless it is very thick and has a more solid core, is so insecure that any slight pressure throws it over. While studying Mountain Trogons' nests, I had to be careful not to upset the stubs that contained them. I found several cavities that were apparently completed and seemed serviceable but were never used. Sometimes I pitied these splendid birds, whose bills seemed as ill adapted for carving into wood as for making a nest of stems or fibers yet who, on those cool heights, could find no large papery wasps' nests or termitaries composed of hard thin plates, which facilitate nest carving for some of the lowland trogons.

Mountain Trogon: nest cavity in an Arbutus tree.

The Eggs and Incubation

Each of my three nests contained two pure white, moderately glossy eggs that were quite blunt on both ends. The six eggs averaged 28.9 by 23.5 millimeters, with extremes of 26.6 to 30.6 by 22.6 to 24.2 millimeters.

The nest to which I devoted most attention was in the short half-decayed stub of a thick branch of a small Arbutus tree growing at the edge of an oak wood. It was not quite a yard above the ground and contained two eggs when found on March 21. A few days later I set my cloth blind among young pine trees 25 feet (7.6 meters) in front of it, while the incubating male watched me through his doorway.

On the following morning, I returned as the stars were fading and the three great

volcanoes, Agua, Fuego, and Acatenango, far across the plain, stood sharply outlined against dawn's first rosy glow. Entering the grove of young pine trees, I looked in vain for my little brown wigwam. After searching with a flashlight, I found it lying flat, overturned by the gale that had blown during the night. With the utmost caution to be noiseless, I reset it on its three poles and ensconced myself within. It was still too dark beneath the trees to distinguish aught but vague forms. The west-facing doorway of the auroras' nest was a hole of solid blackness in the side of the stub, into which I peered eagerly through my binocular without being able to detect anything that resembled a bird.

Was the trogon still on her eggs, or had the fall or perhaps the resetting of the blind frightened her from the nest?

As daylight slowly increased, I passed some anxious minutes. A Pink-headed Warbler sang sweetly just outside the blind. Finally I discerned, or imagined that I could discern, in the lowest part of the nest's doorway, something a trifle lighter in color than the utter blackness that prevailed in the remainder of the hole. Could this be the aurora still sleeping on her eggs? Then, as I continued to watch through my binocular, a head suddenly appeared from the indistinct form. She had just awakened and withdrawn it from beneath her right wing. In the obscurity, I could barely see the white crescents behind her eyes.

As daylight waxed, I could distinguish details of the female aurora's position in the nest. She always sat facing outward, usually with her short, thick, dark gray bill just visible above the doorsill. At times she sank so low that her bill was largely hidden by this rim, although I could still see her dark brown eyes. She held her tail sharply upward against the rear wall of the cavity, its end bent forward under the ceiling until it almost reached the upper edge of the entrance. The white crescent behind each eye gave her a startled expression, as though she were constantly on the point of darting out of her nest; but in reality she was quite at ease and apparently unaware that she was being watched. Her only movement was to turn her head slowly from side to side.

The aurora sat steadily during the early morning, while a strong wind soughed through the pine trees above us. The Pink-headed Warbler sang cheerily nearby. A White-eared Hummingbird poised at intervals before the few red salvia blossoms that remained after the long dry months, so near my blind that I could hear the hum of her wings. Rarely, a Brown-backed Solitaire sounded his wild woodland piping among the oaks down the mountainside. Periodically the aurora, becoming restless, shifted and squirmed about in her nest. To turn her eggs, she rotated sideways, since the chamber was wider from side to side than from front to back, and in this position she enjoyed more freedom to move. A dead branch crackled sharply in the wind. Alerted, she pushed forward into the doorway until the white bar across her breast was just outside and she enjoyed a wider outlook. She peered from side to side but saw nothing alarming. Reassured, she sank slowly back into her nest. This was the usual way of both the female and her partner when they heard certain sounds or when they saw me approach from directly in front: they did not dash madly away but moved forward until they could look around and carefully survey their surroundings. According to the results of this reconnaissance, they either resumed incubation or fled.

In spite of the monotony of her long, solitary session, the aurora never ceased to be alert. When a man's whistle sounded faintly in the distance, she raised her head, suspicious. Yet repeated blasting in a limestone quarry half a mile distant, a far louder sound as it reached us, caused not the slightest motion.

As the sun neared the zenith, the wind died away and birds ceased to sing. The male aurora had not appeared all morning, but, a few minutes after noon, I heard him call softly in the distance. Then he flew up and perched low in the bushes in front of the nest, very near my blind. Although evidently he had come to relieve his partner, she gave no sign of recognition, so after a few minutes he left. As the sun fell westward, its rays struck through a chink in the side of the chamber and illuminated the sitting trogon's tail. Finally, at 1:10, she spontaneously left her eggs, on which she had been sitting continuously, without food, since late on the preceding afternoon, nineteen or twenty hours. After fifteen minutes she returned, perched on a dead branch above the nest, and for several minutes turned her head slowly from side to side, carefully surveying her surroundings. Then she dropped down and clung upright in front of the entrance, where she continued her cautious spying. Satisfied at last that she was in no danger, she entered, about-faced at once, and settled down looking outward.

At 3:23 she left the nest again. In about ten minutes the male approached, perched on a low branch not far from the nest, and called many times in a low mellow voice, moving his tail slightly up and down as he emitted the notes. Then he clung upright at the entrance just as his mate had done. How splendidly his metallic green back and neck shone before my eyes, while bronzy reflections played over them as the slow turning of his head changed the angle of incidence of the light! Assured that all was well, he slipped in and turned around, revealing as he did so the bright red of his abdomen, and settled on the eggs facing outward. His whole head was visible above the sill; with his shining green crown, rings of deep red bare skin surrounding his dark brown eyes, and clear yellow bill contrasting with his black forehead, cheeks, and throat, he was far more conspicuous in the cavity than his mate had been.

As the sun sank lower, the thin mountain air lost its heat so rapidly that I became uncomfortably chilly sitting motionless in the tent. After the male aurora had been on the eggs for nearly two hours, his mate silently alighted on a dead limb near the nest. He pushed forward until the red of his belly showed beyond the sill, delayed a minute or so in this position, then very slowly came out and flew away. After the usual survey around and inside the nest, the female entered for the night. I expected to see her end her day by tucking her head among the feathers of her shoulder; but, as the cavity dimmed to a solid black in the twilight, she gradually faded out of sight until I could discern only the white crescent behind one eye. Soon this, too, was swallowed up by the blackness. I waited a few minutes longer, then cautiously stole from the blind and ended my day with the auroras.

Although at this nest the female did most of the incubating even by day, this was not wholly her partner's fault, for she did not always relinquish the eggs when he came to relieve her. On the following day he arrived earlier and incubated for nearly three hours (2:40 to 5:33) in the afternoon. On the next day I found him in the nest at 12:50 P.M., but I did not wait to learn how long he would

remain. I never found him in the nest before noon.

I spent a day watching the nest of another pair, breast-high in a slender oak stump in heavy broad-leaved forest. These auroras, who had been incubating for twelve days, arranged their times on the nest quite differently. Calling loudly, the male arrived at dawn, while it was still too dark to distinguish his mate in the cavity. For several minutes she sat motionless, seeming not to hear his call to come out. Although she appeared reluctant to go, she finally flew away to seek breakfast. Then the male, after the customary survey, settled on the eggs. After only forty minutes, he emerged and called, then flew off in the direction from which he had come. Ten minutes later, he returned and sat for forty minutes more, when he again left without apparent reason. Compared with other male trogons or with females of his own species, he was a most impatient sitter.

Soon after the male's second departure, the female returned to her eggs, at 8:07, and remained without any important incident until 12:30. About this time, the male began to call persistently in the distance, his clear voice coming gradually nearer and nearer, while his mate answered with a very low *cow cow* from the nest. She then flew off and continued to call from the woods, while he settled down to incubate. This time he remained in the nest for one hour and forty minutes, then departed abruptly, without waiting to be relieved. Twenty minutes later, at 2:30, the female returned to take charge of the nest until 5:15. As the sun sank low, the male came to replace her; but, after occupying the nest for just over half an hour, he left the eggs unguarded. While dusk deepened beneath the forest canopy, the female came to pass the night in the nest, and I hurried down the mountainside. In over twelve hours, the male aurora had sat for four intervals, ranging from 33 to 100 minutes and totaling 213 minutes. The female sat twice, for 263 and 165 minutes, a total of 428 minutes. The eggs were neglected for four intervals, ranging from 10 to 25 minutes and totaling 77 minutes. They were covered for 89 percent of the day.

The male of my third pair had the habit of taking a short turn on the two eggs in the early morning and a longer one occupying most of the afternoon. Yet at all three nests the female was chiefly responsible for keeping the eggs warm by day, as well as at night—which is very different from the habits of the lowland trogons that I have studied.

At one nest, the eggs hatched nineteen days after the last was laid; at another nest, where only one egg hatched, the incubation period was eighteen or nineteen days.

The Nestlings
Although the blind, pink-skinned hatchlings were quite naked, the sheaths of their flight feathers already protruded very slightly, and dark rudiments of body feathers were visible through the transparent skin. Their heels were covered with numerous prominent and sharp papillae to protect them from abrasion on their nursery's wooden floor. Two of their toes pointed backward, like those of the parents.

The two eggs in the Arbutus tree nest hatched on April 1 and 2. On the cool, cloudy morning of April 4, I watched the parents attend their nestlings in the rotting stub. Alternately, the male and female brooded almost continuously, but the latter, who was more eager to return after an outing, was in the nest for 174 minutes, the male for only 135 minutes. Returning with food in its bill, the parent who had been foraging called its mate from the nest. The male always called in his usual loud mellow voice, but the more prudent female announced her arrival in an undertone. The one leaving the nest always made a protracted survey, with its head projecting from the entrance, before it darted out.

These birds were aware that their sudden departure from the nest in the presence of a predator might betray its position, just as surely as their approach. Once while the male, in response to his mate's summons, was pausing halfway out of the cavity to look around, a squirrel climbed among low bushes about 20 feet (6 meters) from the nest, noisily rattling dry leaves as it searched for food. The aurora remained motionless for a minute or so, then gradually and stealthily backed into the cavity again. Here he remained until his partner, who had waited motionless for ten minutes, became impatient and called again in an undertone. Meanwhile, the squirrel had departed; and, after another survey with his head stuck forth, the male flew away. Then the mother entered to deliver her grub to the nestlings, who were crying for food. Excessive caution characterized every action of these birds in the vicinity of their nest; they neither approached nor left carelessly. Although the female was the more circumspect of the pair, the male was by no means lacking in caution.

The nestlings were given white and green larvae, moths, and other insects. On returning with food in its bill, the parent first settled down to brood, then, after an interval, it rose up and bent down its head to place the morsel in one of the opened mouths in front of it. At least, such was the female's behavior, but the male behaved most queerly. He first appeared that morning with a small insect and settled down in the nest with it. Neglecting to deliver this food, he sat holding it stupidly in his bill. When, after nearly an hour, his partner returned, he flew away still holding the insect! A quarter of an hour later, he came with a big gray moth and called his mate from the nest. While he clung before the entrance to look around before climbing in, his nestlings cried hungrily; but even these repeated pleas failed to stimulate him to deliver the food. Again he held the moth until his mate returned with a white grub. This was the occasion when the squirrel delayed his departure. When he started to leave the second time, he suddenly seemed to remember why he had brought the moth that he had held so long, backed up in the nest to permit the nestlings to rise in front of him, and gave it to one of them.

When the nestlings' father next appeared, he brought a large green caterpillar, which again he continued to hold until the female called him from the nest. After five minutes he returned to brood the nestlings, still bearing a green larva, apparently the same that he had carried away, sat holding it for ten minutes, and took it away a second time when his mate returned. In six hours of the morning, each parent brought food five times; the female gave the nestlings, now two and three days old, everything she brought, but the male only once delivered what he carried in his bill. If the female had been as inefficient, the nestlings might have starved.

The male aurora, who probably was attending his first nest, was not incapable of learning. When I next watched, two days later, he delivered fairly promptly everything that he brought. It would be interesting to know how he learned to feed the young, for his innate behavior was obviously inadequate. Whether he learned by watching his mate, or whether the cries and attitudes of the nestlings aroused the appropriate response, I could not decide. During these two days, the method of feeding had changed. Instead of entering the cavity with food in their bills, then rising to place it in the mouths of the nestlings beneath them, both parents now usually passed in their insects while clinging in front, even when they would enter to brood immediately after feeding. In six hours of the morning, the female fed the four- and five-day-old nestlings eight times, the male five times. She brooded for a total of 160 minutes, he for 110 minutes.

I tried to photograph the parents as they came to the nest with food, but they were too wary. It was of no avail to hide the camera behind leafy boughs and wait long hours; I could not cover the lens, and as long as that eye of Polyphemus remained staring even the cries of hungry nestlings could not draw the parents within its range. The female approached several times, but she always preserved a very safe distance from both nest and camera. The male appeared only once, noticed the camera's glassy eye while pausing for his usual survey well behind the nest, and fled immediately. Thereafter, he called beyond my view. What a contrast with the behavior of the much bigger Resplendent Quetzals, whom in Costa Rica I photographed at a low nest with both camera and photographer wholly exposed at close range! These quetzals lived in a wild, sparsely inhabited region where they had lit-

tle experience of humans; through centuries of persecution, the Mountain Trogons had learned caution.

The nestlings were a week old before their eyelids began to separate and their feathers to escape from the long sheaths. Two days later, for the first time they crouched at my approach, uttering a quavering hiss. The older could now just manage to hold itself erect on a perch. With their short, stout bills, stubby bodies, and queer alternation of lines of fluffy feathers and areas of bare skin, they were ugly mites. But, by their twelfth day, they had become as pretty as they had been homely a few days earlier. They were most winsome little creatures—but what nestlings are not when they acquire a decent covering of feathers and begin to look around with bright eyes? Now about 4 inches (10 centimeters) long, they preened themselves when at ease, called in small appealing voices when hungry, and uttered a rather nasal buzz when alarmed. In coloration, they resembled the adult female, with certain conspicuous differences, including the large buffy spots on their wing coverts (which adults lack), the bare yellow rings around their eyes, and, above all, their buffy instead of red abdomens.

Mountain Trogon: nestlings twelve days old.

These Mountain Trogons became feathered at a much earlier age than Black-headed Trogons. The feathers of the latter remained enclosed in their protective sheaths until the nestlings were two weeks old, when they bristled like little porcupines. Then the sheaths were so rapidly raveled off that in a day or two the nestlings underwent a marvelous transformation and became completely clothed with plumage. For these nestlings of warm lowlands, whose nursery was the interior of a termitary reeking with humid heat, this retarded feathering was an advantage, for the plumage was protected from the deleterious effects of excessive moisture until it was needed. But the auroras, raised in a drier and more open cavity in a much cooler climate, had an earlier need of feathers, which began to escape the sheaths when the nestlings were only a week old. As we shall see, Blue-throated Green Motmots, neighbors of the auroras in the high mountains, become feathered sooner than the Turquoise-browed Motmots of the lowlands.

The bottom of the auroras' nest became very dirty, for the parents gave not the slightest attention to its sanitation. They did not even remove the empty shells, as is done by a number of other birds that neglect nest sanitation. Despite the slovenly state of the nursery, its occupants remained as clean as the nestlings of any passerine bird, for, after their feathers sprouted, they always stood on their toes and padded heels and thus avoided soiling their plumage. Like other trogons, the parents neither threatened me nor tried to lure me away from their nest. They remained perching in the trees at a safe distance, uttering throaty notes of alarm, each accompanied by an upward twitch of the tail through a wide arc. At intervals they dashed, as though in panic, from branch to branch, rapidly repeating an indescribable high-pitched note.

On April 16, which proved to be the young auroras' last night in their nest, I went with a flashlight to visit them. Since diurnal brooding had long since ceased, I was surprised to find their mother in the nest or, more correctly, in the doorway. Her head protruded from the bottom and her tail from the top;

she appeared to be sleeping in a most uncomfortable position. The well-feathered nestlings were now too big to be easily covered, but their parent's body filled the doorway and kept out the cold night air. At this altitude, nestlings of many kinds appear to require protection from the cold even after they are completely feathered and too big to be brooded comfortably. I tried to steal away without frightening the parent from the nest, but the moment I removed the blinding electric beam from her eyes she flew out into the dark woods. It was then about nine o'clock on a chilly night, but the following morning the nestlings seemed not to have suffered from being left alone.

On the following morning, I watched the young trogons leave the cavity in the Arbutus tree. Although neither parent had hitherto paid much attention to the brown wigwam before which both had sat for many hours, today they were unusually excitable and wary. They hesitated long among the trees, clucking nervously and darting back and forth with undulating flight, before at last they gathered confidence to approach their young. The male went first. Clinging upright in front of the doorway, he gave a big white moth to the younger nestling, who accepted it with a sort of hissing sound and swallowed it whole, including the wings. The delivery of food, which earlier had been a protracted business, was now accomplished in a trice; and the parent flew away in less time than it had formerly spent clinging at the doorway, peering around, before it passed in what it held.

The older nestling, sixteen days of age, now claimed the center of the stage and pushed its sibling well to one side. It was restless and preened much. Hearing the calls of its parents returning with food, it climbed up on the sill and answered with a low *cup cup cup*. After another meal, it spread its wings and rose into the air, covering about 20 feet (6 meters) on this first flight and rising about 5 feet (1.5 meters) to perch in a shrub. Soon it vanished with its parents, who remained away for the next three hours.

Meanwhile, the younger chick was wholly neglected in the nest. At first it preened much and flapped its wings, but soon, becoming hungry, it started to call, uttering its soft little *cup* almost continuously, at intervals of a few seconds. After an hour or more of this, the calls changed in character and became more frequent. The voices of the parents sounded from such a distance that I was certain they could not hear the young aurora's weak cries. Finally, a few minutes before noon, its father's *cow cow* became louder, and it seemed to imitate him. It succeeded quite well with the tempo, but its voice was still far too weak to reproduce the tone.

At last, when noon had passed, the father returned in the greatest excitement. For ten minutes he called continuously, while swinging his tail vehemently. I could imagine that he urged "Come out, come out, come, come, come!" and that the fledgling's weak, monosyllabic reply was "No! No!" After a while, the father flew to the doorway and gave the chick a fat green larva—its first food in three hours. This meal appeared to satisfy it for the present; after swallowing the larva, it cried much less. I, too, was hungry after a long watch, so I stole away for lunch.

Before I returned late in the afternoon, the younger fledgling left, at the age of 15 days. None of the family was in sight, but I waited in the blind to learn whether the young would return to the nest chamber for the night and perhaps even be brooded again. But none of the auroras approached at nightfall. The nest—which had been a shrine before which I had passed many silent hours, in a spirit akin to worship, and had watched a miraculous transformation—was now only a dirty hollow in a decayed stub.

All the Mountain Trogons were not so fortunate as the pair whose history we have chiefly followed. Another pair hatched and raised only one nestling, which vanished from the nest, apparently spontaneously, when fourteen or fifteen days old. Revisiting a nest in a low pine stub, which had sheltered two nestlings a few days old, I found many downy gray feathers, some tipped with brown, others with pale red or vermilion, scattered over the ground, proof that the mother had been attacked if not killed by the predator that took her offspring. A week

later, in a different part of the woods, I noticed what had been an aurora's nest, only 20 inches (50 centimeters) above the ground in a rotting stump. The cavity contained fragments of eggshell, and so many of the female's feathers were scattered nearby that I was sure she had not come alive out of that encounter, whatever it was. Probably both of these female trogons, in their low nests, had fallen prey to some marauding mammal during the night. Apparently, the trogons were forced to use such perilous nest sites because higher decaying stubs were scarce in these woods, from which most of the dead trees were removed for firewood. In the Mexican state of Morelos, Rowley (1962) discovered a nest with two young 12 feet (3.6 meters) up in a rotting pine stub.

In early June, I witnessed a different disaster. For two days I had heard a half-grown aurora, still in fledgling plumage, call incessantly in pleading tones for food. It perched motionless in a pine or an alder tree and flew only when I came near. Doubtless, it had lost its parents. On the third day, I happened to see the outcome of its sad plight. It hung limply in the hand of an Indian boy, who assured me that he had not killed it; since, for a wonder, he was without a rubber catapult, I believed him. Apparently, the bird had become so exhausted that it fell dead while trying to escape the boy's pursuit. I told the lad that there was nothing to eat on the poor emaciated creature, but he seemed to think otherwise and carried it along for the pot.

The Mountain Trogons on the Sierra de Tecpán raised only a single brood in 1933. After the rains began in mid May, the males soon fell silent; but a fine clear day in the wet season might inspire them to utter their melodious *cow cow* a few times. The young birds soon began to acquire the adult plumage, the first conspicuous sign of which was the appearance of vermilion or pale red feathers on the belly, which I noticed on certain individuals as early as the first week of June. Molting, nearly full-grown juveniles continued to be fed by their parents. The young of both sexes acquired the plumage of their respective parents, at least in its main

features, by means of this first molt. The last obvious signs of immaturity were the buffy spots on the wing coverts; but after August I saw no auroras who bore even this distinguishing mark, and young birds seen on the wing looked exactly like adults. By this time, they had learned to fly against foliage or the bark of a tree and snatch off an insect or caterpillar without alighting, in the spectacular manner by which all trogons, highland and lowland, procure their food.

I am not sure whether the auroras preserved their pair bonds after their offspring achieved independence. The sexes certainly did not remain inseparable, like many tropical birds, nor, as far as I could discover, did they sleep together in the manner of Blue-throated Green Motmots. Through most of the year, I met auroras singly more often than with others of their kind. Nevertheless, a male and a female who have nested together may continue to occupy the same area of woodland and remain loosely associated until the following nesting season draws them more closely together.

18. Black-throated Trogon

Trogon rufus

In tropical rain forests, the most colorful birds wander through the sunlit treetops, while those in the deeply shaded lower levels are generally clad in sober browns, grays, and olives. An outstanding exception is the Black-throated Trogon, the most brilliant bird in the understory at Los Cusingos, as in many another forest in southern Central America, where I usually find it perching solitary, well above my head but far below the crowns of the great trees. From these high treetops come the calls of the three other resident trogons, the Violaceous, Massena, and Vermilion-breasted, which I hear far more often than I see.

The male Black-throated Trogon is bright metallic green over most of his upper surface and on his chest. Golden glints play over his glossy back. His cheeks and throat are black, his lower breast, abdomen, and under tail coverts yellow to orange-yellow. His central tail feathers are bluish green with black tips, the outer ones white with narrow black bars. The wing coverts, finely vermiculated with black and white, appear gray at a distance, and the longer wing feathers are largely black. Each large deep brown eye is encircled by pale blue naked skin. His bill, waxy yellow in sunshine, looks almost white in shade. On head and body the female is nearly everywhere brown, with yellow lower breast and abdomen. Her black-tipped central tail feathers are cinnamon-rufous, much brighter than her back, and the outer ones are white with black bars. A wide white crescent behind and a narrow one in front of each dark brown eye make her appear alert.

This lovely trogon is found from Honduras to eastern Peru, northern Argentina, Paraguay, and southern Brazil. It lives in the more humid ancient forests and older second-growth woods of the lowlands, up to about 2,500 feet (760 meters), rarely a little more, in southern Central America. Like other trogons, it perches erect, with its tail pointing almost straight downward. It sits long in one spot, then suddenly darts out, plucks an insect from a leaf while hovering, carries it to the same or another perch, and swallows it. This trogon sometimes catches berries or other small fruits in the same spectacular manner, but it eats fewer of them than some of the larger trogons do.

Black-throated Trogons perch so unobtrusively in deep shade that even the brilliant males would often be overlooked if they did not reveal their presence by their mellow *cow*, uttered slowly from two to four times—a soft, unassertive call, in keeping with the birds' gentle nature. The female's similar call is even weaker. These notes resemble those of the yellow-bellied Violaceous Trogon, which are delivered more rapidly in a longer series, usually from high in a treetop. They are more likely to be confused with the notes of the Black-throated Trogon's neighbor, the Chestnut-backed Antbird, which lives low in the undergrowth of the same forests.

When alarmed, or when cautiously approaching its nest, this trogon voices low churring and rattling notes: *krrrr* or *krr-ret* or *krr-re-ek*. As it utters these notes, the bird slowly raises its tail until it stands almost upright, then lowers it at about the same speed—a movement that makes the black-barred white undersurface of the tail flash out conspicuously. A less frequent utterance consists of low, clear, beautifully modulated notes, mingled with the subdued, melancholy *cow*'s grouped in twos and threes, which I heard once in June from a male who perched in sight of my blind.

The male Black-throated Trogon presents the unexpected contrast of glittering plumage, such as one associates with active, spirited birds like hummingbirds and jacamars, and calm, subdued demeanor, expressed by dignified upright carriage, long motionless perching, and low, shrinking, almost melancholy notes sparsely used.

The Nest

In the sunny month of January, as the dry season becomes well established in the Valley of El General, all the trogons in its forests call with increased frequency. Sometimes two male Black-throated Trogons call against each other, but even in rivalry their notes are subdued. Occasionally one dashes toward his opponent, who avoids contact by retreating. I have never seen them clash. As with nearly all the forest birds, I have not learned how territories are delimited and pairs formed.

The cavities used for nesting are carved into decaying wood by both sexes, often long before they will be occupied. I found a pair just starting to excavate a hole as early as February 11; but the work proceeded slowly, with long intervals of neglect—the nest was not finished until about the end of March, and it received its first egg on April 10. All the nests that I have seen were in slender upright stubs of dicotyledonous trees far advanced in decay or, in one instance, in the dead part of a trunk of a small living tree. Often the trunk was so weak that while studying the nest I had to be careful to avoid its collapse. I found two occupied nests on Barro Colorado Island in the Panama Canal Zone, two in the Caribbean lowlands of Costa Rica, and ten in the Valley of El General. Most were in old forest, a few in tall second-growth woods or at their edge, one in a weedy cacao plantation 100 feet (30 meters) from forest. The lowest of these nests was 30 inches (76 centimeters) above the ground, the highest about 20 feet (6 meters) up. Half were between 4 and 8 feet (1.2 and 2.4 meters) up, and the average height of thirteen nests was 8 feet. Black-throated Trogons probably do well to choose low sites, for the higher that a slender rotten stub is the more likely it is to topple over, as happened to the only one in which the cavity was over 12 feet (3.6 meters) high. Often they carve their niches well below the top of a low stub. Black-throated Trogons appear consistently to avoid massive dead trunks, such as are chosen by Vermilion-breasted and Massena trogons for their more deeply carved chambers.

The Black-throated Trogon's nest cavity is hardly more than a shallow niche, with most of the front open, like that of Mountain or Collared trogons. The entrance is usually roughly pear-shaped, widest near the bottom, although exceptionally it is widest at about midheight, and often its outline is rather irregular, with jagged edges. The eight doorways that I measured ranged from 4½ to 6½ inches in height by 2⅜ to 2¾ inches in greatest width (11.4 to 16.5 by 6 to 7 centimeters). The excavations extended from 1 to 3 inches (2.5 to 7.6 centimeters) below this opening, but most nests were more than 2 inches (5 centimeters) deep. This shallow depression where the eggs rested and the nestlings grew up was from 3 to 4 inches (7.6 to 10 centimeters) wide, usually about 3½ inches (9 centimeters). The back and sides of the cavity slope forward and inward to meet the narrow top of the doorway, so that the whole niche is 6½ to 8 inches (16.5 to 20 centimeters) high. This upward extension of the excavation lacks importance for the young occupants of the nest, but it contains the parents' long tails, which are turned upward and slightly forward above their backs while they incubate and brood. One exceptional nest, situated at the very top of a slender stump 12 feet (3.6 meters) high, had the usual entrance in the side, but this was confluent with an opening in the top of the stub, so that the eggs were exposed to the sky. Probably the top had broken off after the cavity had been carved. The trogons do not carry away the wood that they remove, as barbets do, but permit it to litter the ground at the foot of the stub.

The Eggs and Incubation

In this roughly carved chamber, the female lays her eggs upon the few loosened wood particles that remain on the bottom, as no lining is ever provided for them. Although I have found Black-throated Trogons continuing to incubate a single egg, another could have been lost, for the full set nearly always consists of two eggs; I have no knowledge of more. On both sides of Costa Rica I have found a few pairs incubating in March, but

throughout southern Central America these trogons lay chiefly in April. Three sets laid in El General in May probably replaced earlier layings that were lost. Although my latest set of eggs was laid at the end of May, near sea level in Costa Rica and Panama laying continues into June or July (Carriker 1910; Willis and Eisenmann 1979). The interval between the laying of the first and second eggs is about two days. One second egg was laid between 9:00 A.M. and 5:15 P.M. of the same day. Nine of the slightly glossy, white, bluntly ovate eggs averaged 28.1 by 22.2 millimeters, with extremes of 26.2 to 30.5 by 20.2 to 23.8 millimeters.

At noon on April 8, 1935, I entered my blind in front of my first Black-throated Trogons' nest on Barro Colorado Island, without disturbing the male trogon, who was then covering the two eggs. As we sat quietly throughout the afternoon, I could see his head rising just above the rounded bottom of the opening in the tottering stub, and sometimes the shining green feathers of his neck were ruffled over the rim. For hours he sat almost motionless; but the monotony of the long watch was broken when a Crowned Woodnymph and then a Dusky-capped Flycatcher basked in a patch of brilliant sunshine that sifted through the high canopy of the forest and fell upon a prostrate trunk just outside my right window. Both sunbathed in the same spot and attitude, lying flat with spread wings and fluffed-up plumage.

Later, when the sun was low, a band of seven Collared Peccaries walked in single file in front of the blind. Soon after their passage, the male trogon called in an undertone from the nest. After three minutes, I heard the soft reply of his mate, but probably his keener ears had detected her voice before he called. As he paused in the doorway before flying out, a pale ray of the declining sun illuminated his glossy green chest and soft yellow breast. After he vanished among the trees, the female clung upright in front of the doorway while she looked carefully around. In the mellow sunshine, the soft rich browns of her back, wings, and tail were hardly less beautiful than the male's iridescent green.

After a brief survey, she climbed inside, turned around, and settled on the eggs facing outward, at 5:26. At 6:45, I could no longer see her, and I walked away in the dusk.

At 6:00 the next morning, when the forest was still dim, I resumed my watch. As the light grew stronger, the female trogon's head became visible above the doorsill. Nothing noteworthy happened until 9:09, when the female called *cow cow cow* in a low voice and her mate answered with similar notes from among the trees. After they had exchanged a number of calls, the female moved forward to rest in the doorway, where she delayed for several minutes while she and her partner called to one another. Finally, at 9:13, she flew away, and six minutes later the male entered. He sat steadily until I ended my vigil at noon, and he was still present at 3:45 and 4:20 in the afternoon. Thus, in the course of twenty-four hours, the female took one long session, from 5:26 in the evening until 9:13 the next morning, and the male incubated all the rest of the time.

On April 15, 1958, with the help of my wife, Pamela, I made an all-day record at a nest with two eggs in the forest at Los Cusingos. At 5:35, I entered the blind in the dusky underwood, and as it grew light I detected the white crescents before and behind the eyes of the sitting female, then gradually the rest of her head. At a little before 7:00, the male arrived and called with churring and rattling notes, *krrr-rek* and *krrr-re-ek*, several times repeated. Then he changed to a low *cow cow cow* as his mate very slowly pushed forward into the doorway, looking around as she did so. At 7:01 she darted off, and two minutes later the male entered. Although he stayed continuously throughout the morning and early afternoon, he was restless, frequently rising up to lower his head into the bottom of the cavity. He did this just as I had seen at the earlier nest, turning sideways in the niche or even completely around, until his yellow belly filled the lower part of the doorway, while his black-barred white outer tail feathers occupied its upper part or sometimes projected slightly outside—he almost seemed to stand upon his

head. This reversed position made it easier for him to reach the eggs in the narrow niche, but whether he turned them or merely examined them I could not see.

At 2:34 P.M., when the sky was darkly overcast, a Violaceous Trogon called *cow cow cow cow cow* loudly overhead, and this apparently stimulated the Black-throated Trogon to call with his lower notes from the nest where he had been sitting all day. After more calling while he rested on the doorsill, he flew to a neighboring branch and repeated his *cow cow cow*. From 2:38 to 3:23 the eggs remained unattended, while rain fell. Then, after repeating a long low rattle over and over, raising her tail over her back each time she did so, the female entered to resume incubation.

Soon after 4:00, the shower stopped and the sun penetrated the clouds. I was certain that the female, sitting quietly, had settled down for the night; but to my great surprise the male returned at 5:03, called her out, and after five minutes went to the doorway, lowered his head as though to feed nestlings, then entered to incubate. He was permitted to stay only until 5:25, when the female replaced him, to remain visible until she faded into the darkness of the cavity. The male had sat continuously for seven hours and thirty-five minutes and again for seventeen minutes in the late afternoon. Not counting the few minutes when the eggs were left uncovered at the changeovers, they were unattended for only one interval of forty-five minutes during the whole day. The female sat all the rest of the day and throughout the night.

Since the male's short evening session seemed pointless in a bird who incubates continuously for hours, I resolved to watch again to learn whether it was habitual. My first opportunity came two days later, when I entered the blind late on a darkly clouded afternoon, while the female was sitting. I did not have to wait long for the male, who arrived at 4:42 and, after seven minutes of krrring and cowing, persuaded his reluctant partner to make way for him. Then he promptly went to the nest, holding in his bill a small object that I could barely discern in the dim light which filtered through the dark clouds and masses of foliage. Clinging in front of the doorway, he lowered his head into the hollow as though feeding nestlings. After a while he entered, still holding the particle, but presently he rose up, turned around until his yellow belly was in the doorway and his tail stuck up into the air, and appeared to offer the food again. Soon he settled down in his usual incubating posture, still with food in his bill.

After fourteen minutes the female returned and continued her rattling call until he relinquished the nest to her. I could detect nothing in her bill, nor did she lower her head into the nest as though offering food to nestlings. To make sure the eggs had not hatched, I put her off the nest and looked in with my mirror, which reflected only two intact eggs. By the middle of the following morning, however, one had hatched, an event which the male had anticipated. Possibly he had sat so restlessly three days earlier, and had so often stood on his head to inspect the eggs, because he had heard the imprisoned chicks' first weak efforts to break out of their shells. His return in the late afternoon, clearly with food, on the second occasion that I witnessed it was evidently due to a desire to feed the still unhatched nestlings rather than to incubate when it was the female's time to occupy the nest. Such anticipatory food bringing has frequently been recorded for male birds, less often for females (Skutch 1953, 1976).

In addition to the 2 long watches, I have records of 124 visits, at various times of the day, to nests with eggs. The latest hour of the morning at which I saw a female incubating was 11:25, at one of the nests on Barro Colorado; but it was unusual to find her present after 9:00. The earliest hour at which I found a male in the nest was 7:00. My latest record of the presence of a male is 5:26 P.M., and my earliest record of the female's afternoon return is 3:00. Between 11:25 A.M. and 3:00 P.M. I have never seen a female attending eggs. When the female continues to incubate as late as 11:00, this may be because, if her partner came to replace her unusually early in

the morning and she would not relinquish the nest to him, he went off and stayed away a long while, as I have seen at nests of Mountain and Collared trogons.

Black-throated Trogons sit closely and have remained on their eggs watching me set a blind 8 or 10 yards (7.3 or 9 meters) in front of them, an operation which often involves much movement and some noisy chopping of undergrowth. Frequently, too, I have been able to enter or leave a blind, or to remove it, without chasing away the incubating male or female. But because they sit steadfastly while I set up a blind does not mean that they would enter the nest if I watched without concealment. They remain firm in the presence of an intruder because their departure might betray the nest's location if it had not already been noticed; for the same reason, they hesitate to approach the nest if a person or some other animal capable of harming it is in view.

At a newly begun nest that I discovered on February 11, I did not see an egg until April 10. Since I had not visited the nest on the preceding day, it could have been laid earlier. The second egg was deposited on April 11. One egg vanished in the course of incubation. The surviving egg was pipped on the afternoon of April 27 but did not hatch until two days later, on April 29. Thus, the incubation period was at least eighteen days, possibly a little longer if the surviving egg was the first rather than the second of the set.

The Nestlings

The hatchling has pink skin devoid of down or visible rudiments of feathers, and its eyes are tightly closed. Just behind the tip of the upper mandible is a prominent white egg tooth. The interior of the mouth is pinkish, and on its roof, at the rear, are inwardly directed bristles, which help keep food moving in the proper direction. At the corners of the mouth are prominent white oral flanges, as in passerine nestlings. The heel pads as well as the whole lower surfaces of the foot and toes are thickly covered with low, rather sharp projections, whose function appears to be not only to prevent abrasion but also to help the nestling cling to the sloping base of the chamber's side wall, above the filth that soon accumulates on the floor. Newly hatched young hold their heads bent sharply upward, even when held in a hand. After a few days, they appear more relaxed as they rest with their breasts against the wall, which they continue to do until they fly. I could never make these nestlings stretch up with gaping mouths, as still sightless passerine nestlings do so readily in response to a hand moved above them, a slight sound, or a gentle shaking of their nest.

When six days old, the nestlings bristle with rapidly sprouting pinfeathers. At ten days, these pins have become so long that they almost cover the nestlings' upper parts; but, except for a few feather tips, the plumage is still tightly enclosed in them. But the horny sheaths are now so rapidly shed that twenty-four hours later, or at the age of eleven days, the nestlings are fairly well clothed with freshly expanded plumage. The tail feathers, however, are still wholly enclosed in their sheaths, and this is also true of many of the feathers of the crown. A day later, the plumage of the crown has expanded and the rectrices are escaping their sheaths. When thirteen days old, the young trogons are completely feathered on head, upper parts, and breast. Except for the large roundish buffy spots on the wing coverts and the buffy-brown rather than yellow of the abdomen, they rather closely resemble their mother in their rich brown attire. Like her, they have prominent white crescents behind and in front of each eye, but these are joined by a narrower rim of white above and below the orbit, while on her the crescents are not confluent. Their bills are dark gray, with lighter base and tip. A day or two later, at the age of fourteen or fifteen days, the young trogons leave the nest.

On April 19, 1958, I watched from 6:30 to 11:30 A.M. at a nest with two day-old chicks. They were brooded constantly by both parents, except for brief intervals occupied by changeovers and the delivery of their meals. Their father, who was in the nest when I arrived, sat for three periods of over 49, 79, and 120 minutes, a total of over 248 minutes.

Their mother brooded only twice, for 17 and 7 minutes. Undoubtedly, she would have covered the nestlings longer if her partner had not always returned so soon to replace her. But she, who controlled the length of his sessions of brooding, as he did of hers, stayed away much longer, once for two hours.

Arriving to replace its mate on the nestlings, each parent behaved much as it did when it came for its turn at incubation: it called with soft notes or churrs and rattles, or a combination of the two, until the brooding partner slowly left the nest, sometimes after calling softly in answer. Each time that a parent returned it brought an insect or some unrecognized item, usually small and green, although once the female came with a winged insect surprisingly large for a day-old nestling. After the departure of its mate, the newly arrived parent clung upright in front of the doorway, its tail pressed against the trunk, while, with head lowered into the cavity, it patiently delivered the insect, usually taking about two to four minutes, although the female needed eight minutes to give the very large morsel to a nestling. The meal over, the parent climbed in and turned around to brood facing outward, just as it had incubated. In five hours, the two nestlings were fed as many times, twice by their father and thrice by their mother. Since, as far as I could see, a parent brought only one article at a time, the most equitable division would have given no more than three insects to one nestling and two to the other.

On April 24, when the two nestlings were six days old, I again watched from 6:30 to 11:30 A.M. Although the morning was cloudy and cool, the still featherless young were left exposed nearly as much as they were covered. Their mother brooded twice, for thirty-five and then for thirty-two minutes, their father only once, for a long session that had lasted ninety-six minutes when I went away and left him sitting. The female brought two green insects, well mashed but so big that the nestlings, who were probably torpid from long exposure, could not swallow them. Finally, she ate them herself, twisting her neck from side to side to force the larger one down. The male brought three items, all of which the nestlings appeared to take. The parents evidently did most of their hunting well up in the trees, for when they approached I first heard their voices floating down from above me. After a while, they dropped down to perch in sight of the blind.

I next watched this nest from 6:30 to 11:30 A.M. on April 29, when the nestlings were eleven days old and their plumage was rapidly expanding. On this sunny morning, they were not brooded. Their father came seven times with as many insects, most of which were very large and green, although one was brown. As formerly, to deliver a meal he clung upright before the doorway, his tail pressed against the side of the trunk and usually spread just wide enough to reveal the barred outer feathers. But now he did not need to bend his head into the cavity, for, with loud sizzling, the nestlings reached up well above the sill to take their meals. One of them spent about two minutes forcing down the large insect that it had received.

Not having glimpsed the nestlings' mother once during the morning, I watched for her again in the evening. The young trogons now rested with their heads visible in the doorway. Their father brought them two more meals between 4:30 and 5:30, making nine feedings in six hours that day. Their mother did not arrive until 5:45, when daylight was failing beneath the great trees. Although she clung in front of the nest before she entered to brood, I was not sure that she fed her young. She sat very high in the cavity, with much of her yellow ventral plumage visible in the doorway—not only her head, as while she incubated the eggs. Here I left her in the dusk. This was the last time that I saw her. If I had not watched her come to brood the nestlings throughout the night, I would have concluded from her failure to feed them on that and later days that some mishap had befallen her. Now it was evident that she was merely losing interest in her family.

When I entered the blind at 12:20 P.M. on May 1, both nestlings, now well feathered, were looking through their doorway. Their white eye-rings made them appear bright and alert. In the next four hours, their father came eleven times, bringing eleven insects,

some so big that the nestlings had difficulty forcing them down. For half an hour rain fell rather hard, but neither parent brooded. Neither came to cover the young at nightfall.

The next morning, May 2, I resumed my watch as it grew light. The father first brought food at 5:43, and by 6:00 he had given the nestlings four meals, after which he came more seldom. At about half past six, a nestling rested with its breast against the doorsill. Soon it grew restless, preened, and stretched its wings. Then for a while it drowsed with closed eyes, to be aroused when its father arrived with more food. After this meal, it jumped up to perch on the sill, which it grasped with pinkish toes—the first time I saw it there. Now it began to utter rhythmically a low soft note, hardly audible above the voices of the cicadas that buzzed stridently in the forest. It preened, then drowsed. After a while, the other nestling tried to push its head through the doorway beside it.

In midmorning, the father came with an insect, alighted on a low branch about 20 feet (6 meters) from the nest, and churred as usual. Thereupon, the nestling flew from the doorway toward him, going well for a few yards but falling when it tried to alight on a twig. Its father darted toward it as it fluttered to the ground, close in front of the blind. Here it rested behind a fallen palm frond and continued to utter the low soft note at intervals of a few seconds, while its father, perching low and still holding the insect, alternately voiced churrs and soft *cow*'s. Soon the fledgling flew again, rising a few feet but dropping to the ground about 5 yards (4.5 meters) from its starting point. Presently it was out of sight, and, although I heard its low notes for nearly half an hour more, I never saw it again. Only fourteen days old, it seemed too small and weak to face the perils of the tropical rain forest.

The young trogon in the nest, not the one who had just flown out, received the insect which its father held when that event occurred. The stay-at-home also received the next meal, an insect so large that the chick took six minutes to gulp it down. The parent perched low and called many times, as though encouraging the first fledgling to rise from the ground. After this feeding at 9:40, he remained away from the nest for the next four hours, no doubt attending the older fledgling, who had now wandered beyond hearing as well as sight of the watcher in the blind.

Late that afternoon, I found the second nestling in the niche, with its father close by. Soon the young trogon began to repeat the same soft monosyllables that the other had voiced just before it flew, and until it left it uttered these notes much of the time, now louder, now softer, at a rather constant rate of twenty-four to twenty-eight per minute. As it delivered each note with closed bill, its throat swelled out conspicuously, so that often it was easier to count the movements of its throat than the low notes themselves. At its loudest, however, the nestling's call resembled the soft *cow* of the adults and was not difficult to hear. When taking food, it made the usual sizzling sound, but it might resume the rhythmic monosyllables even with a partly swallowed insect protruding from a corner of its mouth. In a little over an hour that afternoon (4:40 to 5:44), the father brought seven meals to the nestling, who, after its long interval of neglect, jumped up high as it eagerly seized its food.

The next morning, we watched from daybreak to past noon, hoping to see the other young trogon depart. Before sunrise it began its monotonous calling, but it was wary and fell silent while a squirrel passed close by the nest, to resume after the rodent vanished. When a great dry frond of a Chonta palm crashed down loudly nearby, the young trogon crouched in the bottom of its nest and remained silent for about twenty minutes. But it was calling loudly and persistently when its father arrived with its first meal of the day two hours after daybreak. By midmorning it had been fed four times and was feeling strong enough to flap its wings and preen vigorously. Then followed a long interval of fasting and persistent calling, until at 11:49 its father brought an insect, then another nine minutes later. The spacing of these meals suggested that the male trogon was attending his offspring alternately, first feed-

ing the one off in the forest until it was satisfied, then bringing a number of insects in fairly rapid succession to the one in the nest. I doubted that the fledgling who had gone out of sight was receiving food from its mother, who had so long been neglecting the nest.

When I left the blind at midday, the second young trogon had not once stood in the doorway and was resting so quietly in its niche that I thought it would stay through the night. But, when I returned late in the afternoon, the nest was empty. If, as is probable, the young trogons abandoned their nest in the order of their hatching, the first was about fourteen days old, the second close to fifteen days, at the time of their departure. Although the first flew from the doorsill just after its father alighted on a neighboring branch with food, the parent did nothing which I could interpret as an attempt to produce this result. Nor did he, as far as I could see, make the least effort to lure the laggard fledgling from the nest during the more than a day that it remained alone. As has nearly always happened at nests that I have watched, the departure of the first fledgling was spontaneous, that of the second probably so.

Of the twelve Black-throated Trogons' nests of which I know the outcome, only this and two others survived long enough for the young to fly. Eggs disappeared from seven of them, a callow nestling from one, and one nest fell before the eggs hatched. Such poor nesting success is usual in tropical rain forests.

After the nestlings' departure, a heavy deposit of waste covered the bottom of the niche, for the parents had never cleaned it, at least not in my presence. The only recognizable objects in the dark, disintegrating mass were a number of yellowish maggots and a few hard parts of insects, including a beetle's elytron, a leg resembling that of a grasshopper, and a long antenna. Some days before the nestlings flew, I had removed from beside them a large green insect from which all the internal organs had somehow been extracted, leaving the empty exoskeleton, which from the head to the tip of the long ovipositor measured 4¾ inches (12 centimeters), from the head to the tips of the wings 2¾ inches (7 centimeters). The stout body was about 2 inches (5 centimeters) long. A number of insects that I saw the parents carry to the nest appeared as big as this, and some were even longer. Their size explains the infrequency of the feedings through most of the nestling period. I never detected a fruit in a parent's bill when it came to the nest, and I searched in vain for a regurgitated seed among the debris in the bottom. All the evidence pointed to the conclusion that the nestlings' diet consisted wholly of insects, which are also the chief food of the adults.

Although at the nest chiefly studied the mother stopped bringing food at some time between the nestlings' sixth and eleventh days, all female Black-throated Trogons are not so neglectful. At an earlier nest, the single nestling vanished when ten or eleven days old. Late in the afternoon of the eleventh day after it hatched, both parents were near the devastated nest, the male with a long-winged green insect in his bill, the female with some smaller item. Later, I saw her cling in front of the empty niche, as though offering a meal to a nestling. Black-headed and Collared trogons also bring food for dead or vanished nestlings, and such persisting solicitude for the young is not uncommon in other families of birds.

Although the female Black-throated Trogon's premature neglect of her nestlings is certainly not invariable and may not even be usual, it is, nevertheless, true that in the trogon family as a whole the females' attachment to the nest is weaker than that of the males, as is evident from our histories of several species, including the Resplendent Quetzal and, possibly, the Vermilion-breasted Trogon.

Although young Mountain Trogons acquire adult plumage when a few months old, Black-throated Trogons, at least males, appear to take longer. I have seen them in transitional plumage in January as well as in April, when they were evidently about a year old. A male that I saw in January was largely green on his upper parts; but his cheeks, the front and sides of his neck, and his breast were mostly brown, with some green feathers appearing in the center of his breast. His wing and tail feathers resembled those of the adult female, but his bluish eye-rings and greenish yellow bill were similar to those of the adult male. In April the green on head and breast was greater, and remiges and rectrices of the adult plumage had replaced those of juveniles. On these males in transitional plumage, a conspicuous whitish bar, similar to that on adults of the related Mountain and Collared trogons, separated the brown on the breast from the yellow abdomen, although this feature becomes inconspicuous in the adult plumage of the Black-throated Trogon. After April, I have seen no males changing into adult plumage. I have never, as in certain other birds, found a trogon of any species breeding in transitional plumage. Since yearling males still wear such plumage at the height of the nesting season, I infer that these birds do not reproduce until about two years old. At Los Cusingos, trogons have survived, better than other birds such as toucans and jacamars, the changes that inevitably occur in a small forest sanctuary surrounded by farmlands. But, because they mature slowly and have such poor nesting success, the adults must live a long time, and try repeatedly to raise young, in order to maintain the population.

19. Collared Trogon

Trogon collaris

Some birds, like the Black-headed, Black-throated, and Vermilion-breasted trogons, range from lowlands up to varying elevations in the mountains. Others, including the Mountain Trogon and the Resplendent Quetzal, first appear well above sea level and extend up to tree line or at least as high as they find flourishing forests with abundant food. A third group of birds avoid extremes and are found only or chiefly at middle altitudes. Among these is the Collared Trogon through much of its immense range from southern Mexico to Peru, Bolivia, and southern Brazil. Although at the northern extremity of its distribution, as far south as Honduras, it is occasionally seen in the lowlands, even here it is found chiefly from 2,000 to 6,500 feet (600 to 1,980 meters). In Costa Rica, I have met it as low as 2,000 feet on the windward Caribbean slope. On the Pacific side, where the dry season is more pronounced, I have never seen it at Los Cusingos, around 2,500 feet (760 meters), although I found it nesting only 500 feet (150 meters) higher. In this country and in Panama, it is most abundant between 3,500 and 6,500 feet (1,050 and 1,980 meters) and rarely ascends as high as 8,000 feet (2,440 meters), which is also its upper limit in northern Venezuela (Meyer de Schauensee and Phelps 1978). The Collared Trogon's home is the humid rain and cloud forests,

forest edges, and older second-growth woods. It also frequents tree-shaded coffee plantations, which have replaced vast areas of mid-level forests over much of tropical America.

Both male and female Collared Trogons closely resemble the corresponding sexes of the Mountain Trogon. The male is shining green on head, back, central tail feathers, and chest. A prominent white band or collar separates the green of his chest from the bright red of his more posterior ventral plumage. His bill is bright yellow, and the bare skin around his dark brown eyes is of nearly the same dark color, so that it does not stand out like the bare orbital rings of certain other trogons. His chief difference from the Mountain Trogon is seen on the underside of his tail, which is black, closely and narrowly barred with white, earning him the alternative name of Bar-tailed Trogon. The female is brown above, brightest on her rump and tail coverts; and the brown of her chest is separated from the red of her abdomen by a white band, as in the male. The white crescent behind each brown eye is conspicuous in her dusky face. Her bill, paler yellow than the male's, has a broad black stripe along the ridge.

Like its relatives, the Collared Trogon is a quiet, retiring, dignified bird. Except in the nesting season, I have nearly always met solitary individuals, perching nearly erect, well up in forest trees. These birds catch insects and pluck berries during swift aerial sallies, as do other trogons. The male's call is a low clear *cow cow* or, less commonly, *cow cow cow*, a soft restrained utterance in keeping with the whole manner of the bird. The female's call is similar but weaker. In both its quality and its usual limitation to two or three notes, the call of the Collared closely resembles that of the Black-throated Trogon. Related species with similar notes rarely occur together: on the Pacific slope of southern Costa Rica these two trogons inhabit different altitudinal belts, the highest individuals of the heat-loving Black-throated Trogons hardly ranging as high as the lowest of the Collared Trogons.

When alarmed or suspicious, the Collared Trogon has a very different utterance, a low, long-drawn-out *churr-r-r-r*, which is sometimes almost a rattle. While delivering this complaining call, the bird executes a characteristic tail movement. First it slightly spreads its tail fanwise and at once closes it, all very rapidly. The spreading is not pronounced, but it is enough to reveal to anyone behind the bird the white on its outer tail feathers, which flashes out momentarily, perhaps as a warning signal to its mate. No sooner is the tail closed than it is slowly elevated, with a deliberation that contrasts sharply with the preceding lateral spreading.

The Nest and Eggs

Between 4,200 and 6,000 feet (1,280 and 1,800 meters) in the cloud forest on the Sierra Madre del Sur, in the Mexican state of Oaxaca, Rowley (1966) found five nests in dead stubs or dead limbs of living trees. The cavities, all between 4 and 12 feet (1.2 and 3.6 meters) above the ground, "seemed unusually small for birds with such large, flow-

ing tails . . . a tail feather of a brooding female protruding from the cavity . . . betrayed her nest site." Between May 13 and June 11, each of these nests held two slightly glossy, unmarked white eggs, of which the largest measured 31.7 by 23.5 millimeters, the smallest 27.3 by 22.9 millimeters. Much farther south, in Darién, Panama, Wetmore (1968) discovered a nest 6½ feet (2 meters) up in a shallow hole in a stub amid the forest. At the end of February, it contained two white eggs, which measured 28.8 by 22.1 and 28.5 by 23 millimeters.

My only occupied nest of the Collared Trogon was found on January 24, 1937, in the foothills of the Cordillera de Talamanca, on the northern side of the Valley of El General, at an altitude of about 3,000 feet (910 meters). The nest cavity was 12 feet (3.6 meters) up, near the top of a slender barkless stub of the soft-wooded Burío. This stood in a clearing, amid tall grasses, rank weeds, and tangled vines, but only 25 yards (23 meters) from tall heavy forest. The open niche had evidently been carved into the decaying wood by the trogons themselves, for the marks of their short, stout bills were clearly impressed on the margins of the aperture. This was irregularly pyriform in outline, much higher than wide, and broadest near the lower end. The cavity itself extended only a few inches below the doorway, so that the sitting trogons were visible from in front. A split in the wood passed through the rear wall of the niche as a wide gap, through which I could see the sky.

The Burío stub was so weak and tottering that I did not dare to set a ladder against it or even to clear away some of the tangled vegetation which surrounded and apparently helped support it, in order to make space for a stepladder. But with a mirror attached to a long stick I could see two white eggs, resting on fragments of wood in the unlined cavity.

On February 5, while I was studying this nest, a boy led me to a nest which had been found during the felling of heavy forest on the slopes higher up the valley, at an altitude of about 3,300 feet (1,000 meters). It was in a barkless decaying stump, 7 feet (2.1 meters) high, which had escaped being crushed by the great fallen trees amid which it stood. The two eggs, which, I was told, had been present on the preceding day, had vanished. The niche so closely resembled my occupied nest that I had no doubt that it belonged to the same species. This conclusion received a measure of confirmation when a male Collared Trogon alighted in a tree a little higher on the steep mountainside and repeated over and over a low full-voiced *cow cow*, which, at the devastated nest amid the chaos of newly destroyed forest, impressed me as most melancholy. Although I hesitate to describe nests that I have not seen birds build or attend, I thought that I could safely make notes on this. It was 5 feet (1.5 meters) above the ground. The entrance, rounded at the bottom and pointed at the top, was 6 inches high by 2⅞ inches in extreme width (15 by 7.3 centimeters). The cavity, extending 2½ inches (6.4 centimeters) below the sill or lower edge of the doorway, measured 4½ inches from front to back and 4 inches from side to side (11.4 by 10 centimeters). It appeared to be freshly carved and closely resembled the nest cavities of Mountain and Black-throated trogons.

Incubation

When I found my first nest in midafternoon of January 24, the male trogon was covering the completed set of two eggs. It was his glittering green head and bright yellow bill, framed in the wide doorway, that first caught my eye and led to the discovery of the nest. Unperturbed, he returned my gaze while I examined through my binocular what was to be seen of him in the cavity. Reluctant to leave, which I desired so that I could see all of him for certain identification and also examine the contents of his nest, he did not fly out until I started to cut my way through the vegetation that separated me from his stub. Then he shot out and did not pause until he had vanished among the tall trees of the nearby forest.

After completing my inspection of the nest by means of my mirror, I left. Returning at 4:20 P.M., I found the female in the nest, sitting even more steadfastly than her mate. It required much handclapping and whistling to make her raise her head and look over her doorsill. She watched my advance to the base of her stub; and when I shook and tapped upon it as hard as I dared, in view of its infirm state, she merely leaned out far enough to look down at me. Only after I had tossed up my cap a few times did she fly out and perch nearby, where I saw her well and confirmed my identification. On subsequent visits, I found her equally steadfast in my presence. Sometimes, when I tapped on the stub to make her leave the eggs so that I could see whether they had hatched, she would rise to a bough almost over my head, where she would churr and move her tail as already described. Her utterances might draw her mate from the forest, to call and perform with his tail just as she did. Sometimes, appearing to be more concerned than the female for the safety of the eggs, he would remain near me and the nest, churring, after she had tired of complaining and flown beyond my view.

Although both partners were so strongly attached to their nest, to learn how they incubated I deemed it advisable to conceal myself in a blind. In an old potato patch at the forest's edge, I found a spot where, taking advantage of the steep slope, I could set my brown wigwam and watch from above the level of the nest. When I began at 1:00 P.M. on January 30, the male was incubating, with his yellow bill resting on the doorsill. In the drowsy hours of the afternoon he sank lower in the nest, until I could see only the top of his head and his bright green tail, held upright against the rear of the niche and easily visible from outside.

At 4:48 the female emerged from the forest to alight on a branch beside the potato patch. Twice she called *cow cow* in a subdued voice. Her mate promptly left the nest and flew past her into the forest. Three minutes after her appearance, she settled down to incubate. For a short while, she continued to look over the doorsill; then her head slowly sank until her bill and eyes were hidden behind the rim and only her bright brown tail, held upward against the cavity's rear wall, stood out clearly. Without interruption, she sat until she faded out in the dusk.

When I resumed my vigil at 5:40 the next morning, the female trogon was still in her nest. As daylight increased, I heard her mate call *cow cow* and *cow cow cow* in a low voice, off in the forest. At 7:00 he emerged at the upper edge of the clearing and from an exposed perch repeated the same notes many times, apparently calling his partner from the nest so that he could incubate; but she did not even raise her eyes above the sill and look out. After delaying within hearing for many minutes, he wandered farther back into the forest, where his pleasant voice no longer reached me.

At about 8:40 the female, who had steadily continued to sit, began to look out more often. Soon the sun's rays fell upon her through the doorway, which faced east. Finally, at 11:27, she slowly moved forward to stand on the sill, from which she flew across the clearing and well up into the forest, where she continued to call at intervals for several minutes before she vanished. Just at noon she returned from the opposite direction, flying up over the bushy growth on the deforested slope below the nest, which she entered after churring many times. Now, beneath the hot midday sun, she sat high, her whole head visible in the doorway, her bill open, panting. At 1:00 I left her so. I saw nothing more of the male trogon until I returned at 3:10 in the afternoon and found him incubating.

My long vigil at the Collared Trogons' nest had not fallen on a typical day. On other mornings I found the male sitting at 9:10, 9:05, 10:10, and, when the eggs were on the point of hatching, 8:34. When I came earlier, at 8:33 on one morning and at 8:08 on another, the female was covering the eggs. When I watched from the blind on the morning of January 31, the male arrived so unusually early that his partner was not ready to leave. Then, when she ignored him, he went away and, as though piqued by her failure to respond, stayed away until past one o'clock. So great was the female's attachment to her eggs that she remained covering them, without food, until long after her usual hour of going for breakfast. Finally, at half past eleven, hunger overcame her; she emerged

from the nest and called her mate, but without response. Since he failed to appear, she returned to the nest after an absence of about thirty minutes to sit, apparently, until his belated arrival. This whole sequence was very similar to one I had earlier seen at a Mountain Trogons' nest.

On afternoon visits, I once found the female Collared Trogon in the nest at 4:20, once at 4:15, never earlier. Thus, the male appeared to be usually responsible for the nest from between 8:30 and 9:00 A.M. until between 4:00 and 5:00 P.M., while the female was in charge for the remainder of the twenty-four hours—the typical trogon pattern, which closely resembles that of pigeons.

The Nestlings

When I arrived early in the morning of February 4, the male trogon was in the nest. He flew out when I raised the mirror, which revealed that one egg had been pierced by its occupant. The next morning at 8:35, he was covering two nestlings, pink, naked, and sightless, like other trogon hatchlings. The empty shells were visible in the nest for at least five days, after which they were apparently covered by the growing accumulation of waste, which the parents never removed.

On the afternoon of February 8, the brooding male watched me set the blind once more, closer to the nest, in the old potato patch. The following morning, while the dawn light was still so dim that I could barely discern their brooding mother, I began to watch the trogons attend the two four-day-old nestlings. At 6:15 the male's low *cow cow* called the female from the nest. He rested in a tree at the edge of the clearing, holding a big brown insect with very long antennae. He delayed in the same spot, moving his head slowly from side to side, while the rising sun, which at his arrival caressed only the highest summits of the mountains across the valley to the west, drove the shadows quite to their feet. Then he flew to another perch nearer the nest and continued to look around, repeating at intervals his low *cow cow*. At 6:44 his partner returned with an insect slightly smaller than his, clung upright in front of the entrance with her feet on the sill, placed the insect in a nestling's mouth, and departed. Then, at last, the male delivered in the same manner the insect that he had held for half an hour. He did not stay to brood.

At 7:02 the female returned with an unrecognized object in her bill, rested on a dead branch near the nest for twenty-seven minutes, then darted away, still bearing the object. At 7:55 she returned and again perched on the dead branch holding food. After another delay of twelve minutes, she advanced to the nest and offered the article to the nestlings while she clung in front. During an exposure of nearly two hours, they had become too cold and numb to respond. She entered, settled in the nest, then rose to present the food to the young beneath her—with no better success than before. She turned sideways, then backward, bent down to the nestlings with her red belly resting in the doorway and her long tail rising into the outer air, and in this posture tried persistently to feed her chilled offspring. Soon the food vanished, and the parent continued to brood more reposefully.

It appeared that these trogons were behaving abnormally because they were still shy of the blind or because, made overconfident by their earlier acceptance of my presence, I had at first watched with the little windows too widely open. Accordingly, I cut short my vigil on February 9, to resume it on the following morning, after giving the birds another day to become accustomed to the blind being only half as far from the nest as while I watched them incubate. This time I opened the front window barely wide enough to use my binocular, which was indispensable for the recognition of the food brought by the parents. Nevertheless, they behaved much as on the preceding morning, with some interesting minor variations.

The female was again brooding when I arrived at daybreak on February 10. At 6:20 she flew from the nest, alighted on a high bough at the forest's edge, and repeated her low churr many times over before she flew up into the woods. Returning at 6:47, she bore what appeared to be a green tree cricket with long antennae. For the next hour she

delayed in sight of the nest with this insect in her bill. At 7:45 I saw the male for the first time that morning as he alighted in front of the nest with food. As soon as she saw him coming, the female broke her long period of inactivity by flying toward the nest with him. Arriving at about the same time, she knocked him away with his contribution undelivered. The mother placed the green insect, which she had held for a whole hour, into the upturned mouth of a nestling, then left, whereupon the father went again to deliver his insect at the nest. Clinging upright at the doorway, his glittering golden-green back toward me and the morning sunshine, his tail slightly spread to reveal the fine black-and-white barring of the outer feathers, with a patch of red showing beneath his left wing among the green upper plumage, he was magnificent. For five minutes I enjoyed his loveliness, while he delayed at the doorway, looking from side to side; then he flew back to the forest.

At 8:08 the father returned with a big green insect that resembled a grasshopper with exceedingly long antennae. After only four minutes, he delivered it while clinging in front of the niche, then entered to brood the nestlings, sitting much higher than while he incubated. After covering the young for eight minutes, he emerged as his partner arrived with food. She delivered this promptly, went off, and soon returned with another big green insect, which she gave to a nestling at 8:53. Then she brooded until, at 10:43, her partner appeared at the forest's edge with an insect. In the next 36 minutes he made four successive advances, which brought him to within 30 feet (9 meters) of the nest. Then, suddenly and inexplicably, he darted back into the woodland with the green insect that he had so patiently held.

The direct, confident manner in which the parents sometimes advanced to their nest with food contrasted strangely with their long hesitation at other times. Perhaps their keen eyes now and then detected mine through the narrow slit in the blind by which I watched. But, whether or not mistrust of the blind was responsible for their long periods of almost immobile perching with food in their bills, this patient stolidity was wholly consistent with the trogons' reposeful nature and their long sessions on the eggs. A more restless bird, a wren or a wood warbler, kept from its nest by suspicion of danger nearby, would never have rested in the same spot, holding the same insect for an hour, as these trogons did. The prolonged, immobile waiting of one parent was sometimes broken by its partner's approach to the nest, which seemed to fillip the procrastinating one out of its lethargy or perhaps gave it greater confidence.

In seven and a half hours on the mornings of February 9 and 10, the two nestlings, four and five days old, were fed three times by their father and five times by their mother, a total of eight meals or one insect for each nestling about every two hours. In addition to the food actually delivered, each parent brought an insect once and carried it away. The large size of the insects compensated for these infrequent meals. Despite the parents' erratic behavior, their rate of feeding was not remarkably low for trogons. On the cloudy morning of February 10, during the five hours between the female's first departure at 6:20 and the end of my watch at 11:20, the still naked nestlings were brooded once for 8 minutes by their father and once for 110 minutes by their mother.

When the nestling trogons were five days old, I distinguished their sprouting pinfeathers in the mirror. When they were nine days old, their plumage began to shed the horny sheaths and expand, and at eleven days they were well covered with brown feathers. The whitish spots on their wing coverts were conspicuous in the mirror. Thirteen days after the nestlings hatched, I found one of them lying dead below the nest, its head chewed or torn open and covered with ants. The other remained in the nest, apparently unhurt. But three days later, when the survivor was sixteen days old and seemed ready to fly, it, too, lay dead below the nest. Fully feathered, it resembled the adult female, the most conspicuous differences being the light spots on the wing coverts and the tawny instead of red abdomen, with no white bar across the breast. The chick's tail was

still very short. I detected no lesions other than those which might be attributed to the ants that were devouring the corpse. On the preceding day the trogon had appeared to be in good condition, and I could not imagine what calamity had befallen it.

The dead nestling appeared to have been well fed; and that it had not perished from parental neglect was proved by the arrival, while I made notes on its plumage, of its father with a fat green insect in his bill. He rested on a low perch at the opposite side of the clearing and complained with a subdued churr, spreading his tail and swinging it up and down while he repeated his notes of distress. After a while, he returned to the forest with the insect, but soon he reappeared with a hairy caterpillar and perched a long while at the lower edge of the clearing, sometimes complaining and sometimes silent. His mate did not arrive while I remained in view of the nest. Similar behavior is related in our accounts of the Black-headed and Black-throated trogons.

The Orange-bellied Trogon

In the mountains of Costa Rica and western Panama lives a trogon—called the Orange-bellied Trogon—that differs from the Collared only in having an orange or orange-red instead of a red abdomen. Older taxonomists inclined toward regarding this bird as only a color variety of the more widespread Collared Trogon. In recent books (as in Wetmore 1968, which reviews the evidence) it is listed as a distinct species, *Trogon aurantiiventris*, but not with full confidence in the soundness of this treatment. During three months in extreme southern Costa Rica in 1964, I looked hard for these trogons in forests between 3,500 and 4,000 feet (1,050 and 1,200 meters). In March, all the trogons that resembled the Collared had abdomens so red that I did not hesitate to ascribe them to this species. Not until early April did I see one with an abdomen so light that I took it to be an Orange-bellied Trogon. In June, however, I saw no trogon of this type with a really red belly; all of both sexes that I met had abdomens ranging from vermilion to yellow. It is well known that in museum cabinets the red of trogons fades, and I strongly suspected that the same had occurred with wear during the breeding season. Moreover, I detected no difference in the notes of the red-bellied and the orange-bellied birds; both uttered the low quiet *cow* two or three times, rarely more, in a series. When two species very similar in plumage breed in the same area, their voices are nearly always quite different, which helps prevent hybridization. Although further studies of these two forms where they occur together are desirable, I doubt that they are different species.

Classification and Nest Forms of Trogons

Currently, all Central and South American trogons, except the Resplendent Quetzal and its four South American relatives of the genus *Pharomachrus*, are classified in the single genus *Trogon*. Older systematists, however, recognized four genera that are now lumped in *Trogon* (Ridgway 1911). In addition to the morphological characteristics on which they were originally based, these genera differ in the forms of their nests. *Trogonurus* contains species, including the Mountain, Black-throated, and Collared trogons, which carve shallow niches in decaying wood that permit much of the sitting bird to be seen from in front. The species of *Trogon* (in the restricted sense), including the Black-headed, Citreoline, and Vermilion-breasted, excavate in either termitaries or wood well-enclosed chambers, entered through an ascending tube, that completely conceal the incubating or brooding parent. *Curucujus*, exemplified by the Massena, or Slaty-tailed, Trogon, carves in either trunks or termitaries chambers hardly different from those of *Trogon* (Skutch 1972). *Chrysotrogon*, represented by the Violaceous Trogon, digs a nest chamber in the heart of a large, top-shaped, papery wasp's nest hanging high in a tree, from which it has previously removed most of the wasps; or sometimes it excavates a cavity among the compactly massed roots of an epi-

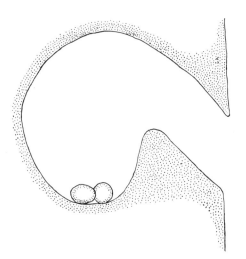
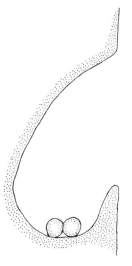

Diagrams of trogons' nests. Left: nest chamber carved by Black-headed, Citreoline, Vermilion-breasted, and Massena trogons in termitaries or decaying trunks that are usually massive. Right: niche carved by Mountain, Black-throated, and Collared trogons in decaying stubs that are usually slender.

phytic fern or some other plant—both sites not known to be used by any other species (Skutch 1972, 1981). A puzzling exception to the rule that closely related species make nests of the same type is the northernmost of the American trogons, the Coppery-tailed, which differs from other species of *Trogonurus*, at least at its northern limit in Arizona, by nesting in a deep hole, supposedly made by a woodpecker or by decay, in form not unlike that of the Resplendent Quetzal.

Associated with the migratory habit of the Coppery-tailed Trogons who nest in Arizona are aspects of behavior that appear never to have been witnessed among the permanently resident trogons of tropical America. Males engage in territorial encounters, on a broad low limb or even on the ground, puffing out their scarlet breast feathers and snapping their bills. One pair, boldly attacking a large snake that was climbing toward their nest, continued to menace and even to strike it with their wings until it fell to the ground (Taylor 1980). Probably because they have less time to establish territories, build nests, and raise their young, migratory birds often behave more aggressively than their permanently resident relatives of the tropics.

20. Resplendent Quetzal

Pharomachrus mocinno

Nearly half a century ago, while northern Guatemala was still a remote region with scarcely any highways, I struggled across an abrupt, forested mountain called Cerro Putul, leading my horse because the steep, narrow trail, strewn with rocks where not deep in mud, was too rough for riding. As I descended through tall, broad-leaved forest where Slate-colored Solitaires sang enchantingly, a large bird shot out from the treetops high above me and flew across the deep ravine below the trail, to disappear in the leafy crowns of trees on the farther side. His pigeon-sized body appeared black against the sky; his abdomen was deep crimson; the underside of his tail was white; and behind him two yard-long plumes rippled like slender pennants in the rhythm of his undulating flight.

Before the surprise and delight of this unexpected encounter had faded, a second bird, equally splendid, followed the first across the ravine. Instead of diving into the foliage, he obligingly alighted on an exposed branch, where, through my binocular, I enjoyed a fleeting glimpse of his crested head and the wonderfully iridescent green plumage that covered most of his body. My first view of a living quetzal, the most splendid member of the magnificent trogon family, by general acclaim the most gorgeous bird in the western hemisphere, and certainly one of the most elegant in the whole world!

Before this meeting with quetzals in the northern part of the department of El Quiché, I had already spent two years in Guatemala, much of the time in the highlands, to which these birds are restricted.

During these years I had averted my eyes from many a stuffed skin in homes and shops—this was not the way I wished to see quetzals. The abundance of these lifeless specimens, along with the extensive destruction of the highland forests, helped me understand why it had taken me so long to see a living quetzal. At the date of my sojourn, during President Jorge Ubico's administration, Guatemala's national bird was protected by laws that were apparently well enforced; but, as too often happens, the species was not given legal protection until hunters seeking its glittering plumage had made it rare.

In addition to stuffed quetzals, I saw countless images of the graceful birds: on the medallion in the center of Guatemala's blue-and-white banner, on its postage stamps, on the walls of its public buildings, and, in more stylized form, on the lovely fabrics woven by Indian women at home and in textile factories. Guatemala has chosen as its national emblem a peaceful creature that not only contrasts refreshingly with the fiercely predatory animals and fire-breathing monsters that other countries have selected to symbolize their national spirit but, moreover, lends itself exceptionally well to decorative design; and Guatemalan decorators have made good use of it. Guatemala has named its monetary unit for its national bird, as other nations have named theirs for famous men, including Columbus (the colón), Balboa, Bolívar, and Sucre. On my travels about the country, I had carried many monetary quetzals in my pocket, to pay hotels, fares, and porters, before I set eyes upon a living quetzal. Some of these quetzals were spent in Quezaltenango—the "place of quetzals"—the attractively quaint metropolis of the western highlands. But I failed to see a single flying quetzal in the neighborhood of Guatemala's second-largest city.

Before Europeans arrived, the quetzal figured prominently in the myths, symbolism, and decorations of the Indians. The great god Quetzalcoatl, rain deity of the Toltecs, is an intriguing image. On his back waved long plumes from the quetzal's train; in his hand he bore a peculiarly shaped staff, sometimes in the form of a serpent; and his name is often translated as Feathered Serpent, although more literally it is Quetzal Serpent. In all nature no strife is more widespread and relentless than that between birds, many of the larger of which eat snakes, and snakes, the chief predators on the eggs and nestlings of birds. Why this union of creatures so antagonistic as bird and serpent—as though one were to make a single deity of God and Satan or of the old Persian Ormuzd and his opposite, Ahriman? Could it be that, as the prophetic vision of Isaiah saw the lamb dwelling safely with its enemy the wolf and the baby playing unharmed on the asp's hole, the old Toltecs symbolized by this puzzling combination both an end to the strife of nature and the peaceful coexistence of all creatures? In any case, Quetzalcoatl, who gave the people maize, was a god of peace and plenty. Until his expulsion by the martial Aztec deity Tezcatlipoca, the ancient inhabitants of the Mexican plateau enjoyed a golden age worthy of the pacific quetzal (Spence 1945).

The quetzal plumes that reached Montezuma's capital, now the site of Mexico City, must have come from the southern parts of his dominions, for in Mexico the bird is now found only in the states of Oaxaca and, chiefly, Chiapas. The use of these plumes was restricted to royalty and the nobility, who wore them in elaborate headdresses, as one can see on pre-Columbian carvings and representations of ancient scenes by modern artists.

To obtain these long plumes from the male quetzals, who alone produce them, hunters are said to have caught the birds, deprived them of their coveted feathers, then released them to grow new ones. Thus, the aborigines showed more concern for conservation than did their conquerors, who before long began to exploit the quetzal mercilessly. Apparently because it had already become so rare as to be regarded as mythological, this bird was neglected by Linnaeus when, in the mid eighteenth century, he gave scientific names to the plants and animals known to him. It did not receive such a name until the year 1825, when Temminck published a painting

of it with the designation *Trogon pavoninus.* Seven years later, the French ornithologist De la Llave gave it the name by which it is now known, *Pharomachrus mocinno.* The publicity which the quetzal received by this scientific recognition did it no good, for museums and private virtuosos now desired this spectacular bird for their exhibits and cabinets. To meet the demand, hunters ransacked remote mountain forests, especially in the Alta Verapaz of Guatemala, sending to Europe a stream of dry "skins" that further depleted the remaining populations of living quetzals.

While I traveled about their country, Guatemalans proudly told me that their national bird, symbol of liberty as well as of peace, invariably wasted away when deprived of its freedom. The myth was too beautiful to be shattered; but, unfortunately, the quetzals died in captivity only because they were not properly nourished. With greater knowledge of the birds' nutritional needs, modern zoological gardens exhibit them for long periods, far from their native forests.

As often as Guatemalans told me that the quetzals would not live in captivity, they volunteered the information that it nested in a hole in a trunk, with two openings, so that the male, who helped incubate the eggs, could enter by one doorway and, when his turn of sitting ended, leave by the other, without turning around in the cavity, to the detriment of his plumes. On the other hand, the only account of the quetzal's nesting by an ornithologist that I could find told of a nest in what appeared to be an old woodpecker hole. It had a single entrance, and its discoverer, Osbert Salvin (1861), opined that only the female incubated. To further complicate the picture, a Costa Rican *campesino* told me that the male sits in the nest, presumably with head inward, with his long plumes projecting through the single doorway. Accordingly, when I left Guatemala in 1935, much myth and misinformation had gathered around the famous quetzal, but scarcely any accurate information was available about its life as a bird that breathes, eats, lays eggs, and rears young.

The subject of this chapter is now known as the Resplendent Quetzal, to distinguish it from the four related species, beautiful birds but less magnificent, that inhabit South America—three in Andean cloud forests, the fourth in warm Amazonian rain forests. From southern Mexico, the Resplendent Quetzal ranges through the mountains to western Panama. Altitudinally, it is found from about 4,000 to 10,000 feet (1,200 to 3,000 meters), rarely lower or higher. Like many highland birds with this distribution, the populations separated by the belt of lowlands across southern Nicaragua and northern Costa Rica have, over the ages, diverged so much that they are now considered to be different races or subspecies. The quetzals to the south of the Nicaraguan Gap differ from the northern race chiefly in that the plumes of the male's train are substantially shorter and narrower. Nevertheless, they are hardly less lovely than their northern cousins. Not only do the Costa Rican quetzals continue to be more abundant than their relatives in Guatemala, but their prospects of survival are better, for they are protected in national parks and reservations that preserve much mid-level and high-altitude forest, especially Chirripó National Park in the Cordillera de Talamanca.

The forests in which quetzals dwell are composed of crowded lofty trees, those that form the canopy ranging from 100 to 150 feet (30 to 45 meters) or more in height. Oaks of a number of species grow throughout the quetzals' altitudinal range but are more abundant toward its upper limit, where, with huge boles and spreading crowns, they dominate the forest. Alders are abundant in many places, becoming nearly as tall, although not so massive, as the oaks. But more important for the quetzals are the numerous members of the laurel family (Lauraceae), including wild relatives of the avocado (*Persea* spp.) and species of *Nectandra* and *Ocotea*—variously called *ira* and *quizarrá* in Costa Rica, *tepeaguacate* in Guatemala—whose exceptionally nourishing fruits enter largely into the diet of these birds. These forests are watered by abundant rainfall, and at all seasons they are bathed in cloud-mist much of the time. The constant moisture favors the devel-

Subtropical forest at the headwaters of the Río Sarapiquí, Costa Rica, home of the Resplendent Quetzal, Prong-billed Barbet, and Emerald Toucanet.

opment of an epiphytic vegetation whose luxuriance is hardly imaginable by those who know only the woods of the north temperate zone or even those of the lowland tropics. Each larger tree upholds a mass of encumbering vegetation which must be estimated, not in pounds or in hundredweights, but in tons. In the dense covering of mosses and liverworts are rooted ferns, herbs, shrubs, and even trees of fair size. Especially noteworthy are the myriad orchids, the Cavendishias and related ericaceous shrubs, with glossy leaves and heads of pink-and-white blossoms. The undergrowth is often dense, with tangles of slender-stemmed bamboos, ferns in bewildering variety, and no lack of shrubs and herbs, including many elegant members of the acanthus and gesneria families.

Montane forest of this type appears indispensable to the quetzal. While it often ventures beyond the forest to forage and nest in adjacent clearings with scattered trees, it is absent from districts from which all the heavy woodland has been shorn. The almost total destruction of the original forest over the central valley of Costa Rica and nearly all the *altos* or central highlands of Guatemala, no less than direct persecution by humans, is responsible for the disappearance of the quetzal from these regions.

By 1937, when I was living in Costa Rica, I had found nests of seven other species of trogons, and I was eager to include in my studies the most celebrated member of the family, especially since I could not believe much that I had heard about it. At that date, forests still covered most of Costa Rica, but they could be reached only by trails that much of the time were forbiddingly muddy; and to find a place to live in or near them, and study the quetzal, was far from easy. After much searching, I had the good fortune to rent an unexpectedly comfortable little cottage that stood on a ridge overlooking a vast expanse of primeval forest at Montaña Azul, on the northern slope of the Cordillera Central between active Volcán Poás and quiescent Barba, at an altitude of about 5,500 feet (1,675 meters).

In the year that I dwelt there, high above a profound gorge through which a mountain torrent rushed with many a lofty cascade, not only did I learn much about the quetzal and other birds of the mountain forests but, equally important for a proper understanding of their lives, I felt in my own flesh the climate in which they lived. Through much of the year the northeast trade winds, sweeping in from the Caribbean Sea across the forested lowlands to the north, drove the clouds over our mountain, for weeks continuously obscuring the sun and bathing everything in a cold mist. Although at this altitude frost did not form, the saturated atmosphere was so penetratingly chilly that I repeatedly consulted the thermometer to convince myself that the temperature was well above the freezing point. During the stormy months late in the year, when I rarely saw a quetzal, it was difficult to avoid depression and preserve hope that in due course I would find them nesting. But when at last the welcome sun rose into the bluest of skies, illuminating the bright colors of the stupendous wealth of orchids and other epiphytes that burdened all the trees and stumps, cold and mist were forgotten in the joy of living in a land as unimaginably fair. In this region of alternate gloom and delight I studied the quetzal, the Prong-billed Barbet, the Emerald Toucanet, and their neighbors amid the dripping forest.

The loveliest inhabitant of these forests was the quetzal. The frowzy mounted specimens that one too often sees convey no conception of the magnificence of the living, vibrant bird. It is difficult to find a photograph or painting that does full justice to it. Accordingly, I shall give here, with only slight verbal changes, a word picture that I wrote in my journal on April 28, 1938, when I had the living birds daily before me: "The male is a supremely lovely bird, the most beautiful, all things considered, that I have ever seen. He owes his beauty to the intensity and arresting contrasts of his coloration, the resplendent sheen and glitter of his plumage, the elegance of his ornamentation, the symmetry of his form, and the noble dignity of his carriage. In the simplicity and restraint of his ornamental plumes is a chaste and classic elegance, which contrasts pleasingly with the oriental or arabesque profusion and superabundance of decoration of some of the more ornate birds of paradise. His whole head and upper plumage are an intense and glittering green. His lower breast, belly, and under tail coverts are the richest crimson. The green of his chest meets the red of his breast in a line that is convex downward. His head is adorned by upstanding bristly feathers that form a narrow, sharply ridged crest extending from the forehead to the hindhead. His bill is bright yellow, rather smaller than those of other large trogons. His glittering eye, nearly black, is set directly among the green feathers of his face, without the white or bluish or golden orbital ring of many trogons.

"His remiges are largely concealed by the long, loose-barbed, golden-green, plumelike coverts, whose separated ends, passing beyond the wings onto the sides of the bird, stand out beautifully against the crimson that glows between them. The ends of the black remiges, extending beyond the covert plumes, contrast with the green rump, upon the sides of which they rest when folded. The dark central feathers of his tail are wholly concealed by the greatly elongated tail coverts, which are golden-green with blue or violet iridescence and have loose soft barbs. The two middle and longest of these covert feathers are longer than his body and stretch far beyond the tip of his tail, which is of normal length. Slender and flexible, they cross each other above the end of the tail and, thence diverging gradually, form a long, gracefully curving train which hangs below the bird while he perches proudly upright on a branch and ripples lightly behind him as he flies. His white outer tail feathers contrast with his crimson belly when he is viewed from in front or as he flies overhead. To complete the splendor of his attire, reflections of blue and violet play over the glittering metallic plumage of back and head, when viewed in a favorable light.

"The female quetzal is far less beautiful than her exquisite mate. She is one of the few female trogons whose upper plumage is green like the male's, instead of brown or slate-colored. Her head is dark smoky gray, more or less tinged with green, and bears no trace of the male's crest. Her bill and large eyes are black. The green of her back and rump is less intense than that of her mate. The upper coverts of her wings and tail are green and elongated like his, but not nearly as much. The tips of her wing coverts scarcely extend beyond the margins of her folded wings, and her longest tail coverts only slightly exceed her tail in length. Her chest is green, but her breast and much of her belly are dark gray; only the lower abdomen and under tail coverts are red, of a shade paler than that on the male. Her outer tail feathers, instead of being pure white, are narrowly barred with black."

From the cottage on the ridge, I often watched quetzals emerge from the forest in the ravine to eat the large green one-seeded fruits of a huge Ira Rosa tree. They plucked the fruits in the usual manner of trogons: darting up, seizing one in the bill, and pulling it off without alighting. (Most of my information about the quetzals' extremely varied diet was gathered while I watched them feed their nestlings; this will be given when I tell of their care.) Such fruit catching, spectacular in any trogon, was especially delightful to watch when practiced by a male quetzal with a long rippling train. I noticed that, when a male left his perch, he did not fly forward, as most birds do, but dropped off backward. Thereby he avoided dragging his long plumes over rough bark, which would soon have frayed them. Females, without plumes that would be damaged, sometimes took off in the same way. Between flights, the quetzals perched very upright, with their tails directed downward or even inclined slightly forward beneath the branch, as is usual with trogons. When alarmed, both sexes rapidly spread their tails fanwise, sending forth evanescent flashes of white from the outer feathers.

From my arrival at Montaña Azul in July until the last days of February, I attributed only a single kind of call to the quetzal. This was a loud, startled-sounding *wac-wac, wac-wac* that was often voiced in flight. The call somewhat resembled the alarm notes of the smaller trogons, which have a startled, cackling character but are less powerful than this utterance of the quetzal. In late February, as the nesting season approached, I began to hear very different notes. In March, the quetzals called much, revealing a varied vocabulary, including notes of rare beauty. They were most vocal in calm, cloud-veiled dawns and late on misty afternoons; in bright weather they called less, and on windy days they rarely broke the silence. Their notes reminded me of the utterances of the clearer-voiced of the small trogons, including the Mountain, Collared, Violaceous, and Black-throated, yet they were different from any of these. At its best, the quetzal's voice is softer yet deeper, fuller, and more powerful than that of any other trogon I have heard. The notes are not distinctly separated but are slurred and fused, producing a flow of mellow sound that is indescribably beautiful as it floats out of the misty forest. Even as the quetzal surpasses his kindred trogons in splendor of plumage, so he excels them in richness of voice. Rarely, I heard a female give a clear call, resembling that of the male but in much weaker, more subdued tones.

At times, especially at the outset of the nesting season, the quetzals voiced notes of a whining, complaining character, which seemed to be mating calls. I could not then ascertain whether both sexes made this sound or only one, nor which it was, but sometimes I heard it when they were together at the forest's edge. Later, when they were incubating, both the male and the female often delivered rather similar nasal or whining notes, as each came to replace the other in the nest. In May, I became aware of an utterance very different from all of the foregoing calls—a high, soprano, sliding *whooo*, not especially loud—a surprising performance which, when I first heard it, I was inclined to attribute to a mammal rather than to a bird.

The flight display of the male quetzal is accompanied by an utterance all its own, obviously a modification of the flight note already described. From March to July, the male occasionally flies up well above the treetops, circles around in the air, then descends into sheltering foliage. His flight on these sallies is strong, swift, and direct, often with little of the usual undulatory motion; but, if he rises very high, it may at the end become strongly wavy and jerky, suggesting that he has reached his limit. As he soars up into the air, he shouts loudly a phrase which at various times I wrote as *wac-wac, wac-wac, wac-wac* but often as *very-good, very-good, very-good*. These spectacular ascents spring from pure exuberance; they appear not to be used in courtship and are certainly not for the purpose of finding food.

At times I saw the male, when relieved of his long turn on the eggs by his mate's arrival, set forth directly from his doorway on one of these high flights, calling loudly as he rose. He seemed to be exulting in his new freedom from the confining nest chamber, exerting his strength for the sheer joy of flight. Such aerial sallies are not rare among birds of open fields and low thickets, including the Skylark and Bobolink or, to take closer neighbors of the quetzal, the Olive-crowned Yellowthroat, Streaked Saltator, and Lesser Elaenia; but they are uncommon among inhabitants of heavy forest. I know of no other trogon, or any bird of dense tropical forest at whatever altitude, which indulges in similar exercises. The gliding flights of Crested and Black guans, in the midst of which they drum loudly with their wings, are different. The high flights of quetzals are another expression of the abounding vitality that has produced their elegant plumes, the approach to male coloration in females, although this is unusual among trogons, and the long breeding season extending into inclement months.

One afternoon in early March, I stood in a narrow clearing in the forest, in the midst of which was a tall decaying trunk, where a pair of quetzals were interested in a possible nest site. As the sun sank low, I heard mellow calls mingled with whining notes

float out of the bordering woodland. Presently a male rushed out into the clearing—in a wild, dashing, irregular flight, his long, loose wing covert and tail covert plumes lashing about—shouting *wac-wac-wac-wac way-ho way-ho*. This appeared to be a different kind of flight display, accompanied by a slightly different call.

Although I have been told of flocks of quetzals in the Costa Rican mountains, I have never seen them. When I arrived at Montaña Azul in early July, the quetzals were probably still nesting, although I found no nest until the following year. I saw a number, mostly solitary individuals, in July; but during August and early September I met none and began to suspect that they had left the region. However, in the second half of September I noticed two. Nevertheless, from August to February, they were rarely seen, and the few that I encountered were mostly silent and alone. Not until late February or early March did quetzals appear to become abundant in the neighborhood. Possibly they had arrived from elsewhere; but their apparent increase may have been caused by their greater activity and, above all, the more frequent use of their voices. By early March, they seemed quite generally to have paired. Once four flew through the shady pasture together, but they appeared to be rivals rather than members of a flock. Possibly at times quetzals congregate in numbers at a tree with abundant fruits; and, in the mating season, several competing males may call together, as do other trogons; but I doubt that they form true flocks, which appear not to occur among the American members of the family.

The Nest and Eggs

The quetzal nests in a hole in a decaying trunk, upright or slightly leaning, which may be situated in the forest or in an adjoining clearing, sometimes as much as 100 yards (92 meters) from woodland. The six nests that I found in 1938 ranged from 14 to about 90 feet (4.3 to 27 meters) above the ground. In size and form, the cavities closely resembled those of the larger woodpeckers. The single entrance at the top was irregularly round, about 4 or 4½ inches (10 or 11.4 centimeters) in diameter. A hole that appeared to be freshly carved (the man who showed it to me said that he had seen the quetzals at work) extended only 4½ inches (11.4 centimeters) below the doorway and contained broken eggs. Another nest, old and weathered when the quetzals began to use it, was 11 inches deep by 6 inches wide (28 by 15 centimeters). Although the other nests were inaccessible, it appeared, from the positions of the birds when incubating or feeding nestlings in them, that most were much deeper than the shallow one with the broken eggs. In form, the quetzal's nest differs as much from the chambers that Black-headed and Vermilion-breasted trogons excavate deep in termitaries or trunks as from the shallow niches of Mountain and Black-throated trogons.

The trunk in which quetzals nest is sometimes in the last stages of decay. One nest cavity was 30 feet (9 meters) up, in the top of a massive but very rotten stub standing in a pasture. Since I had not, at the time of finding this, seen a lower nest, I tried hard to glimpse its contents by standing on the next-to-highest rung of a tall ladder and holding a mirror at the doorway, still above my head, while the interior was illuminated by an electric bulb. While I was engaged in this foolhardy venture, a visiting naturalist prophesied disaster. I could see nothing in the hole, yet I dared not step upon the top-most rung and depend for support on the trunk alone. Later, after the nestlings had flown, we put a rope around this trunk, cut some of the supporting prop-roots, and pulled it over in order to examine and measure the cavity. When it struck the ground, the upper part fell into a formless heap of rotten wood. We could not even find the place where the nest had been. We had a similar experience with a trunk containing an empty 18-foot-high (5.5-meter) nest, which we pushed over in the forest for examination: after it struck the ground, nothing was left to examine. Not infrequently, a woodpecker hole remains intact and sound after falling from twice or thrice the height of these quetzals' nests. The low nest chamber,

to which I gave much attention in July and August, was covered in front only by the bark of the decaying stump, a large sheet of which seemed on the point of falling away and exposing the eggs. I deemed it prudent to hold it in place by tying a cord around the trunk.

I did not in any instance see quetzals actually carve their nest chamber. The three nests in which first broods were raised appeared old and weathered when I found them. But the shallow cavity already mentioned had been freshly carved, in decaying wood still considerably sounder than that which collapsed into a heap when it fell. Moisés Larra, in front of whose cabin this trunk stood, told me that he had seen the male and female quetzals taking turns carving it. This is the way that most, if not all, species of trogons make their nests.

Early in March, a pair were interested in a tall, branchless, decaying trunk that stood in a pasture near the forest's edge. The female clung upright in front of an old, long-abandoned woodpecker hole near the top of the stub. She braced her spread tail against the trunk, revealing the white outer feathers narrowly barred with black, and bit at the decaying wood around the doorway, tearing off fairly large flakes and dropping them, while her mate rested nearby. She continued this occupation for a minute or less; then both returned to the forest. This pair finally nested in an old hole in the top of a neighboring dead trunk.

Over most of the quetzal's altitudinal range, only smaller woodpeckers breed. Before it could occupy one of their nest holes, the quetzal would need to enlarge it, especially the doorway. I believe that this is what the pair which I watched had started to do, but they abandoned the undertaking when they found something that could be made to serve with less effort. Whenever an old hole of their own remains from a former year, still sound enough to hold their eggs even if in a precarious state of decay, they appear to use it again; and, when still available, the cavity in which the first brood was raised is occupied for the second, after the parents clean it out. When they can find nothing ready-made, the quetzals appear to carve their cavity from the beginning, in soft decaying wood, as do other trogons. At lower elevations, where their range overlaps that of Pale-billed and Lineated woodpeckers, quetzals may find cavities of adequate size all ready for them; but, over most of their range, they can hardly avoid a certain amount of hole carving.

The female lays her eggs upon loose fragments of wood on the unlined bottom of the cavity. I saw only two sets, one in May and the other in June. The eggs in the May nest had been broken before I was taken to see them; feathers scattered around revealed the work of a predator. There had been at least two light blue eggs. The one still whole enough to be measured was 38.9 by 30.2 millimeters. The June nest also contained two light blue eggs, which I did not deem it prudent to remove from their deep, rather dilapidated cavity, the most convenient for study of all that I found. In a high, inaccessible nest, at least two fledglings were reared. In Guatemala, LaBastille, Allen, and Durrell (1972) examined three nests, each with two eggs or nestlings. Four light blue eggs averaged 38.9 by 32.4 millimeters, with extremes of 37 to 41.5 by 31 to 34 millimeters. Here laying occurred from late March to late May.

Incubation

On April 5, I was elated to find a male quetzal sitting in a cavity high in a massive trunk beside the forest. I had passed this badly decayed trunk so often that I could hardly have missed seeing the birds at work if they had carved here recently. I wrote in my journal: "He sat facing outward, with his head and shoulders projecting through the aperture. His tail was at the back of the cavity, but one of the long feathers of his train was bent double and projected through the entrance, above the bird's left shoulder. Where, then, is the Guatemalan story of the nesting cavity with two entrances, so that the male quetzal's tail can project through one? Or the Costa Rican version that the bird sits in the nest with head inside and tail dangling through the single doorway? . . . For years I have dreamed of studying the nest life of the quetzal. Is this the substance of my dream, still above any possibility of laying hands upon it but not above the range of my field glass?"

Three days later, I first found the male quetzal apparently incubating, as his body was wholly invisible. I approached very quietly, so that he did not hear me and look out. All that I could see of him was the projecting ends of the two longest plumes of his train. Had the trunk been covered with epiphytes, as it would have been if it had not been too rotten and crumbly to afford a roothold, these feathers might have been mistaken for the green fronds of a fern.

On subsequent visits to this and two other nests, I learned that I could always detect from a distance the presence of the male by the ends of these long central tail coverts, which projected from 6 to 12 inches (15 to 30 centimeters) into the outer air. Although all the rest of the bird was hidden in the deep cavity, the visible parts of these plumes indicated that he sat facing forward, with his tail held upright against the rear wall. This is the incubating posture of Mountain, Collared, and Black-throated trogons, which are easily seen in their shallow niches. The male quetzal's long train, continuing upward, then bending outward, pressed against the top of the doorway, which held the flexed ends almost horizontally. These plumes made a good barometer. When the weather was fair and calm, they pointed straight outward and were motionless. When a breeze blew, they fluttered gracefully. When raindrops burdened the loose barbs, they drooped forlornly. In this wet year of 1938, I saw them all too often in this dejected attitude.

It was early evident that both sexes took substantial shares in incubating the eggs. In order to learn in more detail how they divided the day between them, I watched the nests for about fifty-eight hours during this period. I made records covering all hours of the day while my first pair incubated both their first and second sets of eggs and while my second pair incubated their second set. Usually I made continuous vigils of from five to seven hours, beginning in the middle of the day, watching until nightfall, and, when the weather was not too unfavorable, resuming my watch the following dawn and continuing until midday. In addition to these long records, I made a number of briefer observations to time the morning and evening changeovers. Although the first nest was high, I watched from a blind. But the pair at the low second nest gradually became so accustomed to me that they were not disturbed when I sat beneath a tree in view of them.

The records for all three nestings showed substantial similarity in the division of the day between the male and the female. She incubated every night and during the middle of the day. The male took a long turn on the eggs in the morning and again in the afternoon. Thus each sex was in charge of the nest twice in every cycle of twenty-four hours. Their turns were not always continuous but might be interrupted by short absences, during which the eggs were unattended. The female most probably slept in the nest continuously throughout the night, for quetzals, like other trogons, appear to be strictly diurnal. Although the basic pattern was the same for all the nests, I noticed minor variations both from nest to nest and on different days at the same nest, which we shall now consider.

The male quetzal began his morning session at times ranging from 5:52 to 7:27, but he inclined toward the earlier hour as the eggs neared the point of hatching. If he arrived very early, the female might continue her long nocturnal session until he came to replace her. Usually, however, she flew out still earlier, from 5:35 to 6:00; if the male did not appear fairly promptly, she returned in from five to fourteen minutes to wait for him on the eggs. The male's period in charge of the eggs during the morning ranged from two hours and thirteen minutes to four hours and thirty minutes. This longest turn was interrupted by one spontaneous absence of two minutes; another of twenty-one minutes occurred when he was frightened from the nest by a passerby. One male took charge of the nest for three hours and fifteen minutes, with three short absences totaling thirty-eight minutes.

The female's midday session began at times varying from 8:21 to after 11:10. Since I usually watched from midday to nightfall and from dawn to midday, I timed in full only two periods. One began at 9:35 and continued until 1:14, three hours and thirty-nine minutes, broken by a single recess of seven minutes, from 11:03 to 11:10. The second, at the same nest, began at 8:21 and continued until 12:49, four hours and twenty-eight minutes, interrupted only by an absence of eleven minutes, from 12:23 to 12:34.

The male's afternoon session began at times varying from 12:53 to 4:36. Four sessions that I timed lasted fifty-two minutes, one hour and nine minutes, two hours, and three hours and three minutes. All were uninterrupted. Each of the males is to be credited with one long and one short session. The noon-to-noon record of the first nest shows that the male incubated a total of seven hours; that of the second nest credits him with six hours and seven minutes, out of the quetzals' approximately thirteen hours of daily activity.

On a wet, mist-shrouded afternoon soon after her eggs were laid, the female of the first nest resumed incubation at 2:14 and remained in sole charge until the following morning, with brief absences from 4:18 to 4:27 and from 5:48 to 5:58. This was unusual. As a rule, the male sat until about 5:30, then left the eggs uncovered until the female returned for the night, from five to forty-one minutes later. The female at the first nest arrived consistently earlier than her neighbor at the second nest. The two evening returns that I witnessed occurred at 5:30 and 5:53. On three evenings, the other female entered at 6:09, 6:01, and 6:07, when daylight was fading.

Why do quetzals incubate for much shorter intervals than smaller trogons? Except for the Mountain Trogon, the latter nest in lower, warmer regions, where they need less food to maintain their body temperature. On the other hand, the quetzals' eggs should chill more quickly when left exposed. Temperament also appears to influence constancy of incubation—a matter to which we shall return in the chapters on toucans. The quetzals' exuberant spirits seem to make it difficult for them to take such long sessions on the eggs as some of the smaller trogons do. Larger birds of other families often incubate less patiently than their smaller relatives.

Arriving to replace the mate on the nest, both male and female quetzals often, but by no means always, called with whining or nasal notes while they perched nearby, at the same time flashing their white outer tail feathers by momentarily spreading the tail fanwise, then twitching it upward—a typical trogon gesture. Sometimes the partner in the nest emerged when it heard the notes, but at other times it disregarded this summons. If the bird in the nest did not come out, the other might fly up in front of the doorway, but it always veered aside and went to a perch when it saw that the hole was occupied. This move usually caused the other to quit the eggs. At times, the new arrival would fly up to the doorway in this fashion, with no previous announcement of its presence. Each of the males, but especially that of the second pair, was sometimes guilty of calling his mate from the eggs, then flying off with her as she departed, leaving the nest unattended until either he or she returned to take charge of it. The female more rarely did this. Thus, there was no set nest-relief ceremony. Less closely synchronized than mated birds of certain other kinds, one member of the pair might come before its mate was ready to go; or one would go before the other came. Nevertheless, in spite of these inconsistencies, they managed to get through their three-shift day without leaving the eggs exposed for many minutes. After incubation was well started, the nest was rarely left unattended for more than half an hour at a stretch, although once both members of the pair were absent for sixty-seven minutes, on another occasion for fifty-one minutes.

For many trogons, the entry into the nest is a protracted procedure. They cling before the doorway, peering cautiously from side to side, often for several minutes, before they slip in. If they notice something that excites their suspicion, they dart away, to return later and repeat the time-consuming performance. The quetzals entered with less hesitation, often hardly delaying in front of the doorway or at most making only a brief survey from this position. In this, as in other things, they seemed to feel more secure than their smaller cousins.

On quitting the nest, the male, as already related, sometimes soared high into the air on a flight display, shouting as he went. I saw one male do this six times, the other thrice. These spectacular flights were made at any hour of the day; one male left his nest in this fashion when his mate relieved him at sunset. Even when frightened from the nest, the reckless bird might soar up and make himself conspicuous to all the neighborhood. Or at times he would call loudly as he flew off, without rising above the treetops.

While I watched them, the quetzals did not often need to drive intruders from near their nests. Soon after they began to incubate, the male and female of my first pair joined to chase a trespassing female of their kind. Later, I saw this male pursue an Emerald Toucanet, who might have eaten his eggs, and he twice chased a Masked Tityra, who seemed to be prospecting for a nest cavity in the same trunk. Another pair of quetzals were worried by a pair of Sulphur-bellied Flycatchers who were building a nest near their own. Once, while the male quetzal was brooding nestlings, a strange female flew to his doorway, with no food visible in her bill. One of the flycatchers chased her; and the quetzal, emerging from the nest, also darted at her but did not touch her. She flew directly away, and I saw her no more.

Only at the second nest of the second pair of quetzals could I see the eggs and learn the length of the incubation period. I was extremely eager not to lose this nest, which was in a low rotting stub in a shady pasture, by an ill-considered move, and through an excess of caution I did not set up a ladder and look in with a mirror until I was certain that incubation had begun. At this late nest, the parents started to incubate on June 23 or 24, and the nestlings hatched on July 11, after an incubation period of seventeen or eighteen days, which agrees closely with the periods of other trogons.

The Nestlings

Like other trogon hatchlings, those of the quetzal bore no vestige of down on their pink skins. Their eyes were tightly closed. Each had a prominent white egg tooth near the tip of its upper mandible, which was slightly shorter than the lower. Their heels were studded with the short protuberances typical of birds that grow up in nurseries with unlined wooden floors. When I first saw the two newly hatched young, only a few fragments of blue eggshell remained in the nest.

During their first few days, the young quetzals were brooded much of the time. They were nourished almost if not quite exclusively with small insects; not until later did fruits become abundant in their diet. The parents at first kept the nest clean, removing all droppings, which they must have swallowed, for I saw none carried away in their bills. On the nestlings' fourth morning, I heard their mother scraping and scratching in the nest, doubtless to clean it out. This attention to sanitation was eventually relaxed. Nevertheless, quetzals do more to keep their nests clean than the other trogons that I have studied, who did not even remove empty shells.

When the nestlings were two days old, the sheaths of both body and flight feathers were emerging from their pink skins. At four days, the chicks showed slight change, except that they were bigger and their pinfeathers were longer. When they were five days old, their eyelids began to separate. At eight days, they could open their eyes, although much of the time they rested with their eyelids closed. On the seventh day after hatching, the feathers of their bodies were escaping from the ends of their sheaths, but not those of their heads. The nestlings were ten days old before the remiges and rectrices began to expand, a day after the wing coverts had reached the same stage. Their bills and feet were now becoming blackish.

At this stage, the young quetzals always rested side by side on the bottom of the chamber, with their heads supported against the wall and their bills pointed almost straight upward. They did not appear to be comfortable unless their heads were in this position; even when removed from the nest and placed where they lacked a chin support, they held them turned abruptly upward. From time to time, when they appeared to be hungry, they stretched up their necks, opened their mouths, then sharply closed them with a snap. Evidently, like young woodpeckers and motmots, they took food from their parents in this abrupt fashion, instead of holding their mouths passively open, in the manner of passerine nestlings.

Until their tenth day, the young quetzals seemed to be nourished wholly with animal food; I had not yet seen a parent bring a fruit. On their eighth morning, their mother came with a Golden Beetle about 1 inch (2.5 centimeters) long. Everywhere a lustrous, shining golden color, it was the most splendid coleopteron that I had ever seen, among beetles what the quetzal is among birds, appropriate food for nestlings that would develop golden glints in their plumage.

Resplendent Quetzal: female about to deliver a Golden Beetle to her nestlings.

When the nestlings were eleven days old, buffy spots appeared on their wing coverts. At two weeks, their bodies were well covered with feathers, at least when their wings were folded; but the feathers of their heads had only on the preceding day begun to escape their horny sheaths. The contrast between the well-clothed body and the naked head was striking and gave the young quetzals a slightly vulturine aspect. On their fourteenth day, they were photographed for the first time.

From this age onward, fruits, especially those from trees of the laurel family, became increasingly prominent in the nestlings' diet; and the large regurgitated seeds began to accumulate in the bottom of the nest, where the parents could not easily reach them for removal. Nevertheless, the adults had kept the nest clean almost as long as Black-throated and Mountain trogons remain in their uncleaned nurseries.

When the nestling quetzals were sixteen days old, their mother began to behave most unaccountably. She ceased to brood them by night, although they seemed too young to be left uncovered in that inclement climate, and by day she fed them less and less. She delayed nearly an hour, holding a green fruit, until her mate's arrival prompted her to take it into the nest. In nearly five hours on the following day, she came only thrice with food. Twice she waited dully in a nearby tree, holding the article in her bill, until the male fed the nestlings, and only then, as though stimulated by his example, did she go to the nest and deliver what she had brought. After this, I did not see her in the vicinity. Such early cessation of feeding by the female may be rather frequent among trogons, as I have noticed it in two other species, the Vermilion-breasted and the Black-throated.

To the male quetzal, then, fell the whole task of attending the two nestlings during their last five or six days in the low hole. With his plumage showing unmistakable signs of his strenuous activities and the long feathers of his train broken off short, he was an Apollo in the service of King Admetus. He no longer brooded, but the young birds'

cloak of feathers made this unnecessary now. Nor did he clean the nest, with the result that the growing accumulation of big regurgitated seeds and other waste slowly raised the level of the floor, and the young stood each day higher in their nursery, nearer the doorway, where it was easier for them to reach up for their meals.

From the first, the male had been a faithful provider of food at this nest, although I saw him bring nothing so spectacular as the Golden Beetle delivered by the female. Like other trogons, he fed the nestlings infrequently, bringing only seven meals to the two of them in four and three-quarters hours of the morning when they were seventeen days old. Sometimes he brought one article in his bill, passed this to a nestling, then returned to a convenient perch and regurgitated a fruit, which he took to the nest. On the preceding day I first saw the parents pass food to the nestlings through the doorway, without themselves entering. Now the male regularly delivered meals while he clung in front of the entrance; he did not pass through it unless the young were sluggish. When hungry, they jumped or climbed to the doorway, where I glimpsed them momentarily when they were fed. Their higher floor, as well as their increasing size and strength, made this feat possible. Now they uttered low soft whistles while they awaited their meals.

I watched again from six to nine o'clock on the morning when the nestlings were nineteen days old. Their mother failed to appear, but their father came seven times. On three of his visits he regurgitated a second item, making ten feedings in three hours. This was not many, but he brought such substantial items, including lizards and big fruits, that the young appetites were soon satisfied. By half past seven, the nestlings took their meals sluggishly. When hungry, they would appear in the doorway and snatch the food in a trice; but when satiated they remained in the bottom of the chamber, making a low sizzling sound as nourishment was presented to them. Then their father would enter and coax them to swallow what he had brought. Even when he went inside, he was not always successful in delivering the meal. Then he would emerge, fly to a nearby tree, and rest there, patiently holding the article in his bill for many minutes, while the nestlings' digestive juices acted upon earlier contributions. After a while, he would go again to the nest with the same piece of food, and at length, when a nestling had room for it, one would swallow it.

Perhaps it will be of interest to record here the food of the two nineteen-day-old quetzals. From six to nine o'clock on the morning of July 30, 1938, their father gave them the following, in this order: a big green fruit brought in his bill and another in his throat; a small lizard; a small lizard; a big green fruit from his bill and another from his throat; an unrecognized object, which the nestlings were slow to take; a lizard; and a larva. After delivering this last item, he regurgitated a fruit, which he offered repeatedly over an interval of twenty minutes, before a nestling accepted it.

The diet of the young quetzals, which reflected that of their parents, was surprisingly varied, including insects of many kinds, often green and of fair size, the most easily recognized of which were the Golden Beetle and the even more numerous Greenish-gold Beetles of slightly larger size; green larvae; small green and yellow frogs; small lizards; small land snails, whose regurgitated shells remained in the nest; and hard, large-seeded, green-skinned fruits of the Ira Rosa and other lauraceous trees. Other trogons that I have studied brought few or no fruits to the nest, although the adults of some of these species ate them.

The course of feathering of the nestling quetzals, and their partial change in color during their final week in the nest, was most interesting. When we last glimpsed them, they were two weeks old and fairly well clothed, except on their heads, as long as they kept their wings folded, and at this age they nearly always did. Their upper plumage was then generally dull blackish relieved only by the buffy spots on the wing coverts, which had become evident a few days earlier. But, from the age of two weeks onward,

green became increasingly prominent in their plumage. This change was accomplished as the dull early plumage was covered by brighter feathers that expanded later.

The feathers of the anterior part of the dorsal tract lagged far behind those of the posterior part of the same tract. Long after the latter had escaped their sheaths and spread over the surrounding bare skin, the anterior feathers remained tightly enclosed. Only when the nestlings were sixteen days old did the tips of these feathers of tardy development begin to peep out from the ends of their sheaths. They were golden green, in striking contrast to the dusky plumage that surrounded them. Two days later, green-tipped feathers became visible among the scapulars, long after blackish feathers in the same region had expanded. Green tips then began to push forth from the sheaths on the sides of the neck. A little later, the two green central tail coverts became visible. Only on the nestlings' twenty-third day did I notice that green

Resplendent Quetzal: nestling twenty-one days old.

feather tips were emerging from the lateral sheaths of the posterior half of the middorsal tract, a full two weeks after the neighboring, centrally situated, blackish feathers had begun to expand. Green feathers were also just beginning to appear on the foreneck. Although the blackish body feathers that developed early were loose and fluffy, the green-tipped feathers of tardy appearance had firmer, more cohesive webs. The exposed ends of the new feathers on the center of the back were a beautiful golden-green; their concealed bases were blackish, like the whole lengths of the early downy feathers.

Thus, when they left the nest, the young quetzals wore a motley garb, blackish, brown, buff, and green, with the last-named color promising soon to overshadow all the others. The crown was dark brown, the hindhead a lighter shade of brown. Around the eyes were dull green feathers. The sides of the neck and the upper back were golden-green, the lower back and the rump dull black, with green feathers appearing. The two central tail coverts were green, with black tips and brown subterminal spots. The remaining upper tail coverts were dull black, with a brown subterminal spot on each of the next-to-middle coverts. The tail feathers were still very short, but, as far as was visible, the six central rectrices were dull black, while the outer three on each side had white vanes and black shafts. The wing plumes likewise were dull black, with buffy outer margins on all but the outermost, these becoming increasingly prominent on the inner secondaries. The wing coverts were black, variously margined with buff, except on the lesser coverts and the greater coverts of the primaries.

Turning now to the underparts, the chin and throat were tawny-buff, with some green feathers just sprouting on the foreneck. The breast was buff with scattered green-tipped feathers, the flanks paler buff, and the center of the abdomen nearly white. The bill was black, the irises brown, and the feet plumbeous.

These two young quetzals, of unknown sex, appeared very much the same as others that I saw at greater distances. Although they resembled neither parent, they were most like the female, from whom they differed most conspicuously in the smaller amount of visible green, the lighter color of the breast and upper abdomen, the absence of red on the belly and under tail coverts, and in many other less noticeable particulars.

Like the Mountain Trogon, the quetzal acquires a warm coat of feathers earlier than lowland trogons, just as the highland Blue-throated Green Motmot, as we shall see, expands its plumage earlier than lowland motmots. Like the quetzal, this motmot undergoes a striking change in coloration while in the nest. Since coloration hardly affects the safety of a motmot in its nursery at the end of a long dark tunnel or of a quetzal in a deep cavity in a trunk, one wonders why the nestlings do not more promptly array themselves in the bright hues that they will soon wear. Because their parents brood them little after the first few days, these highland nestlings early acquire a downy vesture to protect them in their cold nurseries. It is equally important for them to guard their feathers of firmer texture from wear, by keeping them enclosed in horny sheaths, until the day when they will be needed—for, on quitting the nest, both the quetzal and the Blue-throated Green Motmot enter a world of chilling rains. These firmer-textured body feathers are those that bear the green color. Thus, the change of coloration while in the nest appears to be incidental to more important alterations.

The Fledglings' Departure

On the morning of August 1, when the nestlings were three weeks old, I first saw one stand on the doorsill, looking out, for a few minutes after its father had fed it. Two days later, I removed one of the young from the cavity and placed it on a mossy log beside me, while I wrote a description of its plumage. Neither of the nestlings had ever tried to use its wings when taken from the nest in the past, and at first this one made no attempt to fly. But, after standing quietly beside me for a while, it suddenly spread its wings and flew about 25 feet (7.6 meters) on a horizontal course, to alight upon another fallen log. Its father, who had been watching us from a tree in front of the nest, followed immediately and alighted close beside it on the log. After remaining there for a minute, he moved to a low perch a short distance beyond the nestling. When I approached to retrieve the young quetzal, it did not try to escape me.

When, after completing the description of its plumage, I took the fledgling to its nest, the other was in the doorway, looking out. As I mounted the ladder toward it, this bird took wing and flew down the slope in front of the nest, covering about 150 feet (45 meters) on a slightly descending course, to alight about 25 feet (7.6 meters) up in a small Yos tree. Its first flight was direct but slow. Its father, who meanwhile had returned to the tree in front of the nest, darted after the fledgling and followed it closely, in the manner of parent birds of many kinds when their young first fly. For an hour, the young quetzal rested on the branch where it first alighted and received food from its father. While perching near the fledgling, the parent called many times in a clear but subdued voice, no louder than that of the Collared Trogon. Meanwhile, the other fledgling, whom I had replaced on the bottom of the hole, had climbed up to stand in the doorway, looking out. At eleven o'clock, I left them in these positions.

When I returned early in the afternoon, the second fledgling was resting in the tree in front of the nest, where it repeated over and over a beautiful low and soft whistle. The other, who had flown first, had moved farther down the slope to perch high in a tree at the edge of the woods. Here its father brought it food and rested close to it when not off foraging. While this fledgling received as much as it could eat, the other called and called in vain for attention, although its soft whistles were faintly audible at the edge of the woods where its father perched. All afternoon it lingered in the same tree in front of the nest, and the parent did not come near it.

At five o'clock, finally despairing of attracting attention in front of the nest, the second fledgling flew down the slope, in the direction where it had last seen or heard its parent. Alighting in a small tree, it continued to call tirelessly. Now it varied its whistles, uttering some that were longer and slightly sharper than those I had previously heard and others that sounded pleading and mournful. Still nothing was brought to appease its hunger.

At a quarter past five, the neglected fledgling continued down the slope to the edge of the woods and perched in a Cecropia tree covered with a dense tapestry of climbing bamboo. But the other fledgling, accompanied by its father, had long since gone farther into the woods, and neither was now in view. The young quetzal continued to call ceaselessly, until at half past five its father at last brought it the big green fruit of an ira, which quieted its pleas. For the next half hour the parent, doubtless tired after a long day devoted to hunting food for his young, rested quietly on a nearby branch, without bringing another meal to the fledgling. As night fell, he flew into the woods, leaving the young bird alone on the Cecropia branch, where it still perched quietly when I departed in the rainy dusk. Here it passed its first night in the open. After my arrival at a quarter of two, it had received no food except the single fruit brought to it nearly four hours later. Just as happened with broods of the Mountain Trogon and the Black-throated Trogon, the fledgling who remained behind was for hours neglected while the male parent attended the one who flew first. At dawn, I found the second young quetzal on the Cecropia bough where it had passed the night. Soon its faithful father fed it, then led it deeper into the woods, thus ending my long association with the quetzals of Montaña Azul.

Going to examine the deserted nest chamber, I found that during the last nine or ten days of occupancy, when the parents no longer cleaned it, waste had accumulated to the depth of 3½ inches (9 centimeters). The chief components of this debris were the seeds of the lauraceous fruits which the parents had brought in such great numbers. Ellipsoidal in shape, they measured 1⅜ by ¾ inches (35 by 19 millimeters). Mixed with them were the regurgitated shards of beetles and other hard parts of insects, a few snail shells, a few smaller seeds, and much excrement.

These fledgling quetzals, who left the nest at the age of twenty-three days, probably flew prematurely because they had been removed for photography and examination. The lowness of their nest, with trees conveniently situated in front, may also have encouraged their early departure. At the first nest, high and inaccessible, the parents were seen to carry in food on April 21. On May 14, I saw a nestling in the doorway. Two days later, I glimpsed both nestlings in the entrance at the same time. They departed between May 19 and 20, when at least twenty-nine days old. At the higher first nest of the pair whose second brood flew when only twenty-three days old, food was carried in as early as April 19, and the last nestling left on May 20, indicating a nestling period of thirty-one days.

The Second Brood
Each of the three pairs of quetzals to which I devoted most attention raised, or attempted to raise, a second brood. Incubation of the first set of eggs began in early April, and the nestlings departed about May 20. At least two of these pairs, and probably all three, were successful with their early broods. In June, all three were incubating again. The two pairs whose 60-foot-high (18-meter) holes were still available laid their second set of eggs in the same cavity as the first. I watched one of these pairs clean out the old nest, but I could not learn how thoroughly they performed this task. The pair whose 30-foot-high (9-meter) nest we pulled over, fortunately after the brood left, laid again in a lower hole, 50 yards (45 meters) from the first, where at last I could see the eggs and follow the care and development of the nestlings, as already told.

While he incubated the eggs and attended the nestlings, the male quetzal's ornamental plumes suffered severely from constant flexing and from friction against the rough edges of the nest's single entrance, on his innumerable passages in and out, in addition to the hard usage they received while he hunted food. It would undoubtedly be to the advantage of his ornaments, if not to the perpetuation of his kind, were the quetzal to occupy the legendary nest with two doorways. The wear and tear began to tell on the male's long tail coverts even before the nestlings from the first clutch were old enough to be left unbrooded. As early as the end of April, I noticed my second male sitting in his nest with only the short length of a single plume projecting from the doorway to show that he was within, instead of the two long graceful pennants that had proclaimed his presence before the eggs hatched. Even the visible part of the stub was badly frayed. Most of the males, I believe, suffered similar losses by the time their first broods were awing. The point where the plumes broke off was often a little beyond the tip of the tail. But at least one male proudly displayed both his banners before his doorway while he incubated the second set of eggs. Possibly he was a new mate of the female who had attempted to rear a first brood in the same hole.

Postscript
In no other region have I found birds of nearly all kinds so fearless of me as in Costa Rica's more remote highland forests. In this respect, they differed greatly from those that I had studied in the Guatemalan highlands, where the human population was much denser. The quetzals were not the most confiding of the birds, yet I never ceased to marvel that such large and brilliant wild creatures should at all times be so bold in my presence. No matter how close I came to their nests, they never darted threateningly at me or tried to lure me away by simulating injury; they merely perched nearby to watch me, nervously twitching their tails, or at most flew excitedly from branch to branch. In contrast to the behavior of certain other birds that I have studied, the quetzals' tolerance of their watcher increased rather than diminished while they attended nestlings. With the exception of one pair of Vermilion-breasted Trogons, I have found the smaller members of the family far more wary.

The quetzals would usually feed their nestlings while I stood conspicuously nearby; one female did so while, to test her confidence, I stood directly below her nest, 30 feet (9 meters) up in a rotting trunk. Both of the males that I knew best were at first less trustful than their mates, but they grew more confiding as we became better acquainted. Without concealing either myself or my old-fashioned 4-by-5-inch camera, set on a tripod at close range, I photographed both the male and the female at the low nest. The first nest of the birds whose young I studied was in the same trunk as that of a pair of Southern House-Wrens—the tiny dull brown wrens were far more wary than the great, glittering quetzals! Their race had wider experience of the ways of human intruders.

In August, when I took leave of the quetzals, after more than a year in their beautiful but uncomfortably wet and stormy forests, they had become as silent as they were when I arrived. They wore only the tattered remnants of their splendor, but soon they would molt and renew the adornments that make them the western hemisphere's most magnificent birds.

21. Amazon Kingfisher

Chloroceryle amazona

In contrast to the great and varied assemblage of kingfishers in the Old World, only six species in two genera inhabit the New World. Although many of the eastern hemisphere's kingfishers are forest dwellers of varied diets that seem to be misnamed, all the American species are primarily fishers that only occasionally take other foods or nest at a distance from water if no suitable riverbank is available. The largest of the New World kingfishers is the Ringed, of which I have told in another book (1972). Next in size is the Amazon, a stout bird about 11 inches (28 centimeters) long, with a big crested head and a short tail. The male's upper plumage is deep metallic bronze-green; he has a broad white collar across his hindneck, white spots on his tail, and white ventral plumage with a chestnut breast. The female is similar but lacks chestnut; the white of her breast is invaded by intrusions of green from both sides, which sometimes approach or even meet in the center. (In this respect the coloration of the Amazon is just the reverse of that of the migratory Belted Kingfisher, in which the female, not the male, wears the chestnut.) The Amazon Kingfisher's long, straight, stout bill is black, its eyes brown, its short legs and feet black.

This attractive kingfisher is distributed across continental tropical and subtropical America from southern Mexico to Argentina, in both humid and arid regions, but it is absent from the Antilles. It prefers the broader, quieter, more open waterways, although it establishes itself along broken, rushing mountain torrents if they are rather wide and contain scattered deep pools. Hence this bird is largely an inhabitant of the lowlands, where rivers flow broad and deep, with winding lagoons and oxbows on the coastal plains. Although it is rarely seen

above 3,000 or 4,000 feet (910 or 1,200 meters), along the Río San Juan at Aguacatán in the department of Huehuetenango, Guatemala, I met a single individual at 5,700 feet (1,750 meters) above sea level, on November 13, 1934. In Venezuela it has been recorded as high as 8,200 feet (2,500 meters) (Meyer de Schauensee and Phelps 1978). Like the other tropical American kingfishers, the Amazon never flocks and is usually seen singly except in the breeding season. However, it is not unlikely that a male and a female will stay together on their territory throughout the year.

As long as it can procure them, the Amazon Kingfisher appears to subsist exclusively on fishes. Sometimes, from a perch on a pro-jecting bough, it plunges directly into the water; at other times it hovers on vibrating wings while it sights its prey beneath it. So rapidly do its wings beat while it poises in midair that, to one standing directly in front or behind, its body appears to be suspended between two misty spheres of some imponderable substance which buoys it up in the atmosphere. Suddenly the wings close, the hazy circles vanish, the kingfisher plunges swiftly downward, head foremost, breaks the surface with a splash, and often wholly submerges itself. If its plunge has been successful, it promptly emerges with a fish in its strong black bill, flies to some convenient perch by the shore, shakes the drops from its plumage, and proceeds to beat its prey against a branch until all struggle ceases, when the victim is swallowed headfirst.

Although a specialist whose life is devoted to cultivating the art of fishing, the kingfisher does not find this an easy way to earn a livelihood. It appears to miss more fishes than it catches, and it is only because repeated failures do not discourage it that it finally procures a meal. Often it waits long and patiently for a minnow to appear in a suitable position beneath itself, only to have the prospective victim dart away as it plunges toward the water; the bird then planes off before striking the surface and, with a loud *kleck kleck kleck*, returns to a perch for another attempt. Often, too, it disappears beneath the surface, only to reappear with an empty bill. Once I watched an adult male plunge unsuccessfully four times in succession in a stream which abounded in small fishes.

Often, sitting on the bank of a clear, smoothly flowing tropical river, I have watched the little silvery-scaled fishes flash in the current. As each at intervals turned on its side, its presence was revealed by a bright, momentary gleam of silver, which vanished as soon as the fish righted itself and became almost invisible against the sandy bottom with which it so well blended. Now here, now there, from a score of points, but only for an instant from each, came the glints from as many different fishes—as fireflies flash at a hundred spots scattered over a meadow on a summer night, but rarely twice in the same place. Are these the telltale gleams for which the kingfisher waits while it perches motionless on a streamside bough or hangs between its two hazy circles of beating wings? If so, it must indeed be quick to seize its prey, for the silvery gleam from the minnow is as fleeting as the firefly's spark.

Sometimes the male kingfisher hunts in the dusk, well after sunset, and then, especially, the reflection of light from the scales of fishes as they turn on their sides must help him. This late supper puzzled me, until I learned how the sexes arrange their turns on the nest while they incubate.

In addition to the hard rattle and reiterated sharp *kleck* typical of its tribe, the Amazon Kingfisher has a quite different utterance, which is apparently what Hudson (1920), who knew the bird in La Plata at the other extremity of its vast range, referred to as "*warbling* long clear notes, somewhat flute-like in quality." This is a pleasing performance, consisting of a clear "singing" note, repeated at first in ascending pitch and with increasing tempo, until at last it falls rapidly in both pitch and speed. I represented it as follows:

$$joy \; joy \; joy \; joy \; joy \; joy \; joy \; joy \; joy \; joy \; joy \; joy \; joy \; joy$$

Almost any soft monosyllable might be used to paraphrase the song, for it is above all the tone quality that is distinctive. The kingfishers sometimes use this refrain to greet their mates and to express alarm when their young appear to be in peril.

On a warm afternoon in early April, I walked along the bank of the Río Corubicí, a large, gently flowing stream shaded by great spreading Espavel, Saman, Guanacaste, and other trees, in northwestern Costa Rica. A pair of Amazon Kingfishers rested on a fallen branch in the shallows by the shore. As I approached, the female passed a small fish to her mate, who ate it. Possibly he had earlier given it to her, and she was not hungry. For a long while they perched inactive, not far apart. Then the male flew off and soon returned with a fairly large minnow, which he gave to his companion. After a few minutes, he brought her another fish, which she eagerly accepted. Evidently, she was preparing to lay her eggs. For many minutes, a male Green Kingfisher rested close to the bigger Amazons, who seemed to ignore him.

The Burrow

In Central America, Amazon Kingfishers breed in the drier months, when there is less danger that their low burrows in riverbanks will be inundated or washed out by high water, when the earth around the brood chamber is drier and more readily absorbs the nestlings' excreta, and when the clear water favors fishing, which seems to become more difficult in the strong, muddy currents of periods of heavy rain. At Los Cusingos, these kingfishers incubate in February and feed nestlings in March, the months when the swiftly flowing mountain torrent that borders the farm is lowest. Late broods are still fed in the burrow in April, when light rains have returned and the stream gradually rises. In the Caribbean lowlands of Honduras and Guatemala, where I discovered four burrows in 1930 and 1932, digging began in February, if not earlier, and one pair had nestlings a few days old by March 23. A replacement brood, however, did not hatch until early June, when the streams had become swollen and turbid.

All the burrows that I have seen were in riverbanks, with water flowing beneath or close in front of their doorways. In rocky banks where digging is difficult, the kingfishers may use the same tunnel for more than one year. Along the Río Peñas Blancas in front of our house, in a high bank composed of rounded waterworn boulders and pebbles of all sizes, closely packed together with the interspaces filled with blackish sandy loam, a burrow dug into one of the few available pockets of soil was occupied for nesting in three consecutive years, 1943, 1944, and 1945. In 1946 this pair of kingfishers bred in a new burrow about 10 feet (3 meters) downstream from their old one. These tunnels were so crooked that I could not see what they contained by looking in at the mouth, and they were too deeply embedded in the rocks to be opened. I marveled that the kingfishers could dig such long tunnels in this soil so full of closely compacted rocks that we find it difficult to make a hole big enough to set a post or plant a fruit tree.

More favorable for study were the burrows in low sandy banks of lowland streams in northern Central America. Here, where digging was relatively easy and where tunnels in the friable soil did not often last through the wet season, kingfishers of several kinds appeared to excavate fresh burrows each year. The point where Amazon Kingfishers began to dig was from 17 to 38 inches (43 to 97 centimeters) below the tops of the vertical banks which they selected. A burrow beside the Río Morjá, a tributary of the Río Motagua

in Guatemala, was already 36 inches (90 centimeters) long when found on February 22. By February 29 it was 44½ inches (113 centimeters) long, and by March 9 it measured 58 inches (147 centimeters), after which it ceased to lengthen. The excavation was extended 22 inches (56 centimeters) in sixteen days, at the rate of 1⅖ inches (3.5 centimeters) per day. If the kingfishers worked at the same rate from the beginning, they must have started their burrow in late January and spread their leisurely task over five or six weeks. After the tunnel ceased to lengthen, I made a small opening at the inner end and closed it with a board, so that I could look in daily and time the laying of the eggs. After this, the kingfishers continued for a few days to enlarge the chamber at the end of the tunnel, but finally they abandoned their work and dug another burrow upstream. The latter, as is usual with replacement nests, progressed far more rapidly than the first, and eggs were laid in it about the beginning of April. The abandoned tunnel was promptly claimed by Rough-winged Swallows.

Although I spent many hours in sight of the earlier of these burrows beside the Río Morjá, the kingfishers worked in such a desultory fashion that I did not witness any sustained digging. Both male and female entered for intervals of one to three minutes, suggesting that they shared the labor of digging, as was plainly evident when a neighboring pair of Ringed Kingfishers dug far more actively in my presence. The male of this pair of Amazon Kingfishers also gave his partner a fish. When the female flew up and alighted beside her perching mate, or when he settled beside her, he raised his wings above his back and held them so for a few seconds in greeting.

In length and diameter, the burrows of the Amazon Kingfisher are intermediate between those of the smaller Green Kingfisher and the larger Ringed Kingfisher, which are often dug in the same banks. Four burrows which I measured were 47, 56, 58, and 63½ inches (119, 142, 147, and 161 centimeters) long. All curved gradually to the right or left, making it impossible to see into the nest chamber when looking in at the entrance with a flash-light. The burrows also sloped slightly upward, so that the space where the eggs lay was higher than the doorway, a provision that helped keep the chamber dry. This enlargement at the inner end of the burrow was in one instance 10 inches wide, about 18 inches long, and 6½ inches high at the center (25 by 46 by 16.5 centimeters). The tunnel which led to this chamber was 3¾ inches wide by 3¼ inches high (9.5 by 8.3 centimeters).

In an occupied nest, this tunnel is furrowed by two well-marked parallel grooves made by the kingfishers' short legs as they shuffle in and out. Each side is also scored by a rather deep groove made by the bills of the excavating birds. When burrows deserted by kingfishers are occupied by nesting Rough-winged Swallows, a multitude of irregular scratches replace the parallel ruts made by the original owners. Neither Amazon, Green, nor Ringed kingfishers take any lining into their nests—they lay their eggs on the earthen floor, which soon becomes covered by a hard pavement composed of scales and bones of fishes regurgitated by the incubating birds and compacted by their feet.

The Eggs and Incubation

Each of three burrows that I opened in Guatemala and Honduras contained four eggs or naked nestlings. From one of these burrows, the contents disappeared as the eggs were hatching, and about three weeks later the female completed a replacement set of three eggs. In Trinidad, Belcher and Smooker (1936) found a set of four eggs in a burrow only 3 feet (90 centimeters) long. The eggs are short ovate, pure white or sometimes slightly tinged with buff. Seven eggs, all laid by the same female in Guatemala, averaged 31.5 by 27.1 millimeters, with extremes of 30.2 to 32.1 by 26.6 to 27.8 millimeters.

I studied the kingfishers' incubation schedule at a nest beside the Río Morjá which contained four eggs within a few days of hatching. To assure myself that no kingfisher entered or left the burrow while my attention wavered during long watches, I set a twig

upright in the entrance, in such a manner that no kingfisher could pass without pushing it over. The female sat throughout the night, and by day the two partners took turns on the eggs. On April 19, the male incubated for at least seven hours and seventeen minutes, including a morning session of three hours and twenty-five minutes and an afternoon session of three hours and fifty-two minutes. On the following day, the male incubated for a total of about eight and a half hours, including a long afternoon session of six hours and five minutes. The female's urge to incubate by day was weak; if disturbed as she was about to return to her eggs, she might stay away a long while or omit her session entirely.

The Ringed Kingfishers that I watched on the Río Morjá entered the burrow before the sitting partner emerged, but the Amazon Kingfisher announced, by calling *ket ket* or *keck keck* in a low voice at measured intervals, that it had arrived to take charge of the eggs. Although this sound was not loud, it evidently reached the mate at the end of the burrow, who flew out almost at once. Then the other entered. The Amazon Kingfisher's pattern of incubation resembles that of its relative, the Green Kingfisher, as will be told in the following chapter. In Africa, male and female Half-collared Kingfishers also alternated on the eggs, sitting from one to two hours at a stretch and keeping them almost constantly covered. Because the sexes of this small kingfisher look alike, Moreau (1944) could not learn which incubated at night. The Ringed Kingfishers followed a schedule, quite different from that of these smaller species, which involved much longer sessions. Each sex was in charge of the nest for alternate periods of twenty-four hours, so that the male sat throughout one night, the female throughout the next. The single daily changeover occurred between seven and ten o'clock in the morning, and thenceforth the oncoming partner was solely responsible for the eggs until the next morning. The Ringed broke its long period of duty by a single outing in the afternoon, when the nest was unattended for from half an hour to an hour.

After studying how the Amazon Kingfishers incubated, I understood why the male sometimes fished in the dusk, after other diurnal birds had retired to roost. His mate relieved him from incubation late in the evening, and, after fasting all afternoon, he probably needed several fishes to satisfy his hunger.

Like other members of their family, Amazon Kingfishers are strongly attached to their nests and remain at their posts in spite of danger. This was very evident at the burrows that I prepared for study by making a small opening at the rear of the chamber, which after each visit was closed with a stone and covered with tightly packed earth. At first, when the stone was removed and light suddenly appeared at the wrong end of the burrow, the parent would fly out by the front entrance, klecking wildly. A few days later, it only retreated into the tube, where it stayed until the chamber was again closed. Toward the end of the period of incubation, however, it sometimes remained on the eggs and permitted me to touch it gently. But the kingfishers never, at any stage of the nesting, simulated injury or made hostile demonstrations when I visited their burrows. Birds rarely feign injury unless they have a suitable stage for the act, and the water that flowed in front of the burrows would hardly have served for the broken-wing display.

The single burrow that I prepared for observation before eggs were laid was deserted, and it was only through a fortunate accident that I learned the length of the incubation period. At a neighboring burrow, apparently made by the pair of kingfishers who deserted the first burrow, I made a small opening at the back of the chamber a few days before the eggs were pipped. The eggs or nestlings vanished at about the time of hatching; I never saw the latter or learned what befell them. But I continued to look into this burrow from time to time, expecting it to be occupied by the Rough-winged Swallows who had long been waiting for the kingfishers and motmots along this stream to abandon their burrows so that they might begin their own belated nesting. Great was my surprise when, nineteen days after the eggs of the ill-fated first brood were hatching,

I looked into this burrow to find that the kingfishers had slightly lengthened and deepened their old nest chamber and the female had already laid two eggs. On the following day, May 14, the third and last egg of this replacement set was laid. All three of these eggs were pipped at 9:00 A.M. on June 3. One had hatched by 10:30 A.M. on June 4, and at 9:30 A.M. on June 5 I found three nestlings. Thus, the incubation period was twenty-two days. This may be compared with the period of twenty-three or twenty-four days of the Belted Kingfisher (Bent 1940) and that of nineteen to twenty-one days for the much smaller European Kingfisher (Kendeigh 1952). It is also close to the incubation periods of the related motmots, which in the case of the Blue-throated Green Motmot is twenty-one or twenty-two days.

The Nestlings

The method of emergence from the shell of kingfishers and motmots was different from that of the other small birds that I have watched hatch, as exemplified by the Groove-billed Ani. Kingfisher and motmot chicks cracked the shell in a number of spots scattered irregularly over an entire quadrant, between the greatest circumference and the thicker end, and the cap that they finally pushed off was highly asymmetrical, separated from the rest of the shell by an oblique rather than a transverse line. The young kingfishers took from one to two days to break their way out of their shells.

To follow the development of the young, let us return to my first nest, which early in May 1930 I found in a low sandy bank of the Río Tela in northern Honduras. To explore the interior of such a burrow was a novel experience; as I dug down to the nest chamber from the level ground at the top of the bank, I felt all the excitement that archaeologists must know as they start to excavate an ancient temple or palace. After I had removed a little earth, the female kingfisher, disturbed by the noise above her, shot out from the front of the tunnel and protested with a little rattle as she flew down the river, doubtless to search for her mate. Her voice was not raised above the tone she ordinarily used when

A quiet stretch of the Río Tela in northern Honduras, where Amazon Kingfishers and Turquoisebrowed Motmots nested.

cruising above the stream. A pair of Vermilion-crowned Flycatchers, feeding three newly hatched nestlings in a roofed nest among the branches of a dead tree that had fallen into the river in front of the burrow, seemed far more perturbed by my activities than the kingfisher herself.

After removing a few more shovelfuls, I broke into the burrow. The widening aperture revealed four naked and squirming nestlings, who barely escaped the rain of loosened sand that I vainly tried to stem. They had apparently just hatched, and two of the empty shells lay on the floor of the chamber beside them. Not the slightest trace of down shaded their pink, peculiarly transparent

skins. They could not by any standard be called pretty, least of all when viewed in profile. Two black knobs, rising above the forehead, indicated the points where their eyes were buried beneath the skin. They were decidedly prognathous, the lower mandible projecting about 2 millimeters beyond the upper. They could already stand upright and even walk unsteadily, supporting themselves on the abdomen and the entire foot. Each heel was covered with a thick pad of skin roughened by numerous small tubercles, which protected them from abrasion through the long days when the young kingfishers groped around on the sandy floor of their dark nursery. They uttered a little high-pitched buzzing or sizzling sound when I touched them.

After carefully uncovering the nest chamber, I roofed it with a pane of glass, above which I fitted a wooden lid to exclude the light. Then I covered the excavation with boards laid across it at ground level and strewed concealing leaves and litter over the boards. Only because kingfishers cling so tenaciously to their young did this pair continue to attend their brood in the elaborately remodeled nest. The much simpler procedure of making a small opening at the rear of the chamber and closing it with a stone is the only one that the birds are likely to tolerate before their eggs hatch, and it exposes the nest to less risk of discovery by predatory animals and prying humans. But, if one wishes to follow the development of the young, this method of opening the burrow has the disadvantage that—when the stone at the back is removed and light suddenly enters the aperture—the young kingfishers, even when newly hatched with tightly closed eyes, retreat forward into the tunnel, where it is difficult if not impossible to reach them. When the entire chamber is uncovered, it is easier to catch the nestlings before they can escape into the tunnel.

Sometimes, when I lifted the lid over the kingfishers' nest, I found one of the parents brooding the nestlings. It flew up against the glass before retreating toward the burrow's mouth. Never until I had this close view from above did I appreciate how intensely green the adult's upper plumage is.

The two parents shared rather equally in the care of their progeny. As far as I saw, they brought them nothing but fishes, which were delivered and apparently swallowed whole. They showed a nice discrimination in adjusting the size of the minnows to the capacity of their nestlings. When the latter were only a few days old, the parents brought minnows so small and slender that, when carried lengthwise, they were almost concealed by the bills. However, the parents often held such tiny fishes athwart their bills. They gradually increased the average size of the fishes until, when the nestlings were

feathered, they brought many that were longer than their bills and quite thick. These larger fishes were always carried lengthwise, with the head inward. If I happened to be in sight when a parent arrived with food, it delayed on a branch overhanging the stream, repeatedly elevating its head and tail simultaneously with a jerky motion, as though the two were hinged together like a mechanical toy and could not move independently. Each time its head and tail went up, the kingfisher emitted a nasal click.

When the nestlings were about five days old, their eyes began to open, and the black rudiments of pinfeathers were visible through their transparent skins. Two days later, their eyes were fully open. They were at least eleven days old before the upper mandible caught up with the lower in length. At the age of twelve or thirteen days, their body feathers started to escape from the horny sheaths, which had grown very long. Now for the first time they tried to bite my fingers when I picked them up. When about nineteen days old, they were well clothed with plumage and even had rather prominent crests. They had wholly outgrown their infantine ugliness, and they had already acquired the parental habit of jerking up head and tail simultaneously as they stood on the ground. I believed that I could distinguish their sexes. All four young closely resembled their mother, with broad peninsulas of dark green projecting from their sides onto the white of their breasts; but the white pectoral feathers of two of them were perceptibly tinged with chestnut in the position of the band across their father's breast, and these were probably males. Their upper mandibles were now longer than the lower ones. They did not try to fly until they were about twenty-four days old, and even then they could do no more than flutter. Now they defended themselves with spirit, biting my fingers whenever I gave them an opportunity.

Kingfishers, like motmots and jacamars, do little to keep their burrows clean. The indigestible bones and scales of fishes regurgitated by the nestlings add to the accumulation of such material already begun by the incubating parents. Maggots crawl in this debris on the floor of the nursery, and green flies buzz out when the burrow is opened. The decomposition of nitrogenous wastes generates enough ammonia to make my eyes smart when close to the opening. However, the light sandy soil in which king-fishers often dig their burrows absorbs much of the offensive matter and prevents the chamber from becoming unbearably foul. I noticed that one chamber was somehow en-larged while it sheltered nestlings, and the earth dug or worn from the walls covered some of the filth on the floor. In dry, porous soil, the burrow remains surprisingly clean throughout the long period of occupancy. The young kingfishers themselves, except their bills and feet, are usually as neat and clean as though they had just been washed and brushed. They rise superior to their environment.

Amazon Kingfisher: nestling nine days old.

Amazon Kingfisher: nestlings twenty-four days old.

Twenty-eight days after I found the newly hatched nestlings, I opened their burrow and placed a female on the ground beside me, while I held one of her pretty brothers. Their mother was flying over the river nearby, and the fledgling answered her loud calls in a much weaker voice. Finally, I noticed that I had set the young female down in a spot where Fire Ants swarmed. I tried to pick her up, but she would no longer submit to handling. Beating her wings, she rose from the ground, traversed the river without difficulty, and alighted in a Willow tree on the opposite shore. I started to cross the channel on a fallen log to retrieve and return her to the burrow; but, now that she had tasted freedom in the sunlight, she would not permit herself to be caught and replaced in her subterranean nursery. Before I was halfway across, she took wing for a much longer flight and rose into a tall Willow tree, where her mother joined her. She had been long in discovering the use of her wings, delaying a week after her feathers seemed sufficiently expanded to support her in the air, but, finally, flight came to her all at once. The importance of both the long nestling period and the sudden acquisition of the power of flight after the young are well grown is apparent in a bird whose burrow frequently opens onto a wide expanse of river or lake—a weakly fluttering departure from the nest, such as many fledglings make, might bring a young kingfisher to a premature and watery grave.

When I approached the river the next morning, the parent kingfishers' alarmed cries forewarned me that the rest of the brood was on the wing. Uncovering the burrow, I found it empty—only a single silvery-scaled minnow lay dead on the sandy floor. The young had remained in the burrow twenty-nine or thirty days, several days less than young of the larger Ringed Kingfisher, whose nestling period is thirty-five days or more. In Africa, Half-collared Kingfishers leave the burrow when about twenty-seven days old (Moreau 1944). Twelve days after it flew from the nest, I watched one of the young Amazon Kingfishers dive for a fish—unsuccessfully.

The brood whose incubation period I determined was exceptionally late. Because the parents had deserted their first burrow after I opened it, and lost their first brood as soon as it hatched in the new burrow, their replacement brood did not hatch until early June, when most other young kingfishers were already flying. The rainy season now set in, and the muddy floodwaters of the Río Morjá rose to within a foot of the tunnel's mouth. Fishing must have been difficult in the swift, turbid current; but the parents somehow managed to catch enough minnows, and in July they were feeding at least two of their young in the trees along the bank.

I found no indication of a second brood in either the Amazon, Green, or Ringed kingfishers, and Bent (1940) believed that the Belted rears only one brood in a season. Although New World kingfishers do appear to be single-brooded, the Half-collared Kingfisher of Africa raises two broods between September and March, during the short rains and subsequent hot dry season.

Bathing

Although the kingfishers' burrows in the high stony bank of the Río Peñas Blancas in front of our house were much less favorably situated for study than those that I had earlier found in the almost stoneless banks of lowland streams in northern Central America, I saw here a phase of behavior that I had not previously noticed. After entering the burrow with large fishes for older nestlings, the parents regularly bathed in the river. Sometimes, emerging from the tunnel, the female would plunge directly into the water. Then she would fly to a rock projecting in midchannel above the shallow dry-season current and take additional baths. More often, the parents of both sexes went first to the boulder, from which they dipped into the stream. I never saw them omit these ablutions after emerging from the burrow. The number of dips they took after a visit to the nest varied from two to five. They did not completely immerse themselves in the shallow water. After the last plunge in a series, they sometimes preened their plumage as well as they could with their great bills and shook their wings and tails. Then they flew downstream or up for more fishing. Since the water where they most often bathed flowed shallowly over a rocky bottom, it is not likely that these plunges were for the purpose of catching fishes; I never saw them capture one on these occasions.

Lockley (1953) observed that Common Puffins regularly went to bathe in the ocean after a spell in a burrow with an egg. Moreau (1944) wrote of the Half-collared Kingfisher in Tanzania: "About the middle of the fledging period the tunnel must have got into extremely foul condition, because liquid faeces were constantly oozing from its entrance. The old birds evidently disliked this: it became their invariable custom when they emerged to plunge repeatedly into the water to clean themselves. Usually they did this four or five times, but once eighteen plunges were recorded. A similar observation on the European Kingfisher . . . has been recorded by Ris."

I never examined a burrow of kingfishers, motmots, jacamars, or puffbirds in such a foul condition as Moreau described. As already remarked, the burrows of Amazon Kingfishers that I studied in northern Central America were, despite their ammoniated atmosphere, surprisingly clean, considering the parents' inattention to sanitation. Perhaps for this reason the adult birds were never seen to bathe after emerging from them. Although I could not open the burrows beside the Río Peñas Blancas for examination, doubtless in this rocky ground waste did not drain off as well as it did in the sandy loam along northern rivers. Possibly a large rock, impervious to liquids, formed the chamber's floor. Hence these kingfishers' greater need to bathe. Probably only their feet and ventral plumage were soiled as they shuffled in and out of the burrow, since these were the parts which the kingfishers seemed to wash by their partial immersions in the stream.

22. Green Kingfisher
Chloroceryle americana

In daintiness and grace of form and movement, the slender-billed Green Kingfisher surpasses all its New World relatives, not excepting the Pygmy Kingfisher, which is more richly colored but not so well proportioned. This is the fairy bird that patrols tropical American streams. The bright green of its back and white-spotted wings and tail contrasts with the pure white of its underparts. The male's breast is crossed by a broad

chestnut band; his mate wears one or two bands of green spots across hers.

While toiling over the rocky bed of a narrow torrent rushing down a mountain valley, where huge trees arch overhead and shut out the sky, I have often heard a pleasant cheep and turned to watch a solitary Green Kingfisher fly swiftly past, low above the water and following all the curves of the channel, until lost in the depths of the forest. In the

highlands of Guatemala, I met it up to 7,000 feet (2,150 meters), where it was less common than on lowland waters. Whereas its larger relatives need deeper water and a longer drop, this kingfisher often plunges from a boulder projecting only a foot or so above a shallow channel. It rarely hovers above the water in the manner of the larger kingfishers. Although it fishes on the smaller streams from which they are absent, it joins them on the broader, more sluggish waterways. More widely distributed, latitudinally as well as altitudinally, than any other New World kingfisher, the Green ranges from the southwestern United States to northern Chile and central Argentina.

The Burrow, Eggs, and Incubation
Although burrows of the larger kingfishers and the Turquoise-browed Motmot, situated in plain sight in bare, exposed banks, were readily found, those of the Green Kingfisher that I have seen were hidden either behind a fringe of vines and dead vegetation draping the top of a bank or behind exposed roots, so that I discovered them only by seeing a bird enter or leave. Accordingly, theirs were the last of the nests of the three kingfishers that I encountered in the Motagua Valley. I found only two, late in the season, although Green Kingfishers were no less abundant than Amazon Kingfishers. As befits the smaller bird, its burrows were much shorter than those of the larger species; the two that I found were only 22 and 25 inches (56 and 64 centimeters) long.

On a morning in late April, I sat eating breakfast on a fallen log beside the Quebrada de Arena, a brook so narrow that I could easily jump across it, which flowed through a pasture overgrown with low bushes and thorny tangles of vines. Presently a male Green Kingfisher flew downstream, perched on a branch before me, ticked a great deal, and seemed annoyed by my presence. Since early in the month, when I saw a kingfisher fly from under the steep bank to my right, I had suspected that it had a nest there; but the only burrow that I could discover was an incomplete one of Turquoise-browed Motmots, which, in my ignorance of the kingfishers' tunnel, I took to be theirs and thus waited vainly for eggs to appear. The little kingfisher's persistence in remaining along that stretch of the brook renewed my conviction that his burrow was near. Removing my shoes, I waded up and down, examining every promising bit of bank, while the kingfisher flew back and forth to avoid me. I discovered only old burrows, whose lack of fresh foot furrows showed clearly that they were no longer used. Baffled, I paused beneath overhanging bushes to watch the kingfisher, who in a few minutes, after again calling *tick tick tick*, flew up beneath the exposed roots of a half-washed-out dead stump and vanished.

The male flew out as I started to open the burrow with my machete. The tunnel sloped so sharply upward that the nest chamber was less than 3 inches (7.6 centimeters) below the surface of the ground; I broke into the rear of it before I supposed that I had well started to dig. Here lay three white eggs, which measured 26.2 by 20.6, 25.8 by 19.8, and 25.4 by 19.8 millimeters. They were well advanced in incubation, to judge by their opacity. The male fluttered several times in front of the burrow, eager to enter even before I closed it. I fitted a stone over the small aperture that I had made, covered it with earth, and laid logs across the roof of the nest chamber to prevent the mules who were pastured here from stepping upon it and breaking through. The kingfishers continued to incubate.

The pair of Green Kingfishers arranged their turns on the eggs much as the Amazon Kingfishers did. The female passed each night on the nest. Soon after six o'clock in the morning, the male flew downstream, low above the water, uttering at intervals the high-pitched cheep that was his flight call. Perching on one of the roots of the old stump projecting in front of the tunnel, he called *tick tick tick* in a low voice, which his mate heard in the burrow. She shot out, greeting

him with a single cheep as she flew swiftly past, and turned downstream to fish.

Her behavior was unpredictable. One morning she could not await his arrival, although he was hardly late. She popped out of the nest without warning and flew off, but a minute later she returned with her partner. He alighted on the root in front of the tunnel and ticked just as much as he was accustomed to do to call out the female, although he could certainly see that she was not inside; then he entered the burrow. The next day the female acted very differently. Just after six o'clock on a cloudy morning after a night of hard rain, the male flew downstream, perched in front of the entrance, and ticked for her to come forth. She ignored his repeated calls. He flew a short distance downstream, then returned to call *tick tick tick* again. Still no response, so he flew beyond my sight. Ten minutes later he reappeared and rested again on the root in front of the burrow, where he called at intervals for two minutes before his mate emerged. Then he entered.

The male incubated until the female returned from breakfast to relieve him. One morning she left him on the nest less than two hours, but the next morning she was absent nearly three. She covered the eggs for the remainder of the morning. The male was chiefly responsible for keeping them warm during the afternoon, until his mate called him from the nest and entered for the night between five and six o'clock.

One morning I reached the brook before sunrise, just in time to see the female kingfisher fly from her burrow. Five minutes later the male entered, only to emerge almost immediately and fly beyond my view around the bend upstream. I suspected trouble. When I opened the burrow, it was swarming with myriad small amber Fire Ants, a scourge to humans and birds alike. Invading the nest, they had worried the birds until they fidgeted on their eggs and cracked them; then the intruders had pushed through the cracks to eat the embryos. I had cleaned the ants out on the preceding evening, but to no avail. The nest was ruined.

That same morning, Fire Ants had attacked and killed three young Golden-fronted Woodpeckers in their nest in a dead stub standing a few paces from the kingfishers' burrow. This low sandy pasture was so badly plagued by these creatures that I could not leave a knapsack, or any other article that had touched a perspiring body, on the ground for five minutes without finding it infested with ants, which attacked relentlessly and inflicted stings that made blisters. In humid coastal regions, ants are one of the chief enemies of nesting birds. I found more eggs and nestlings destroyed by them than by all other known agents combined; but this is in part because, having entered a nest, they remain for many hours to devour its contents, while larger predators such as snakes consume or carry off the eggs or young and promptly depart, rarely leaving a clue to their identity. Whether a bird nests among high leafy boughs, in a cavity in a trunk, on the surface of the ground, or in a burrow underground, it is not safe from ants.

The Young

Before this tragedy terminated a promising study, I had seen a Green Kingfisher with a tiny minnow in his bill disappear behind a curtain of dead vegetation at the top of a bank of the Río Morjá, beside a banana plantation—thereby disclosing the location of his burrow, which was concealed no less effectively than the first one. Digging with a machete and my hands, I soon broke into the nest chamber. When I reached into the dark burrow, my fingers encountered something soft and feathery. I lifted out a dainty little bird clad in green and white, who struggled weakly in my grasp and tried to bite with its sharp, slender black bill. Thinking that I held a fully fledged young kingfisher in my hand, I promptly placed it in my knapsack and tried to secure its nest mates before they could escape. I groped in the darkness again, but instead of another feathered bird I brought out a handful of pink-skinned, totally naked, blind nestlings, five in all. Then the truth dawned on me. I removed the first bird from my knapsack and found her white breast crossed by two broad bands of green speckles. She was the mother, who would not

desert her young through all my probing and digging and permitted herself to be caught rather than abandon them. Meanwhile, their chestnut-breasted father circled around in front of the burrow with a small fish in his bill, uttering little impatient *tick*'s, his equivalent of the loud *kleck* of the larger kingfishers.

The nestlings, like those of the larger species, had thickened, papillate heel pads and lower mandibles that projected beyond the upper ones. After I found a stone to block the opening I had made, I replaced them in the burrow, then gently laid their mother over them. Here she stayed while I closed the back of the chamber and covered the stone first with earth, then with banana trash. Throughout these lengthy proceedings, she uttered not a syllable.

Whenever I visited this burrow, the parents flew around over the water or perched on brushwood stranded near the shore, ticking softly while they jerked up their heads and tails. But, despite their great devotion to their young, they never tried to drive or lure me away, in this agreeing with all the other burrow-nesting birds that I know, including motmots, jacamars, puffbirds, and Rough-winged Swallows.

When the five nestlings were well feathered, the chest of each was crossed by a band of white feathers marked with green, giving a spotted appearance. The lower breastband, which in their mother was complete, was represented only by areas of spotted feathers on the sides, interrupted in the middle by the continuous white of the underparts. On one nestling the white of the upper band, as well as the breast immediately below this, was strongly tinged with chestnut, suggesting that this was a male. On the breasts of his sisters was no tint of chestnut.

Eighteen days after I found these nestlings, when they were probably not more than twenty-five days old, they could flutter only a few feet. One flew into the river, where she spread her wings on the surface and headed for the shore. I threw her into the shallow water, and again she turned unerringly toward the marginal rocks, beating her wings on the surface until she gained a footing.

Green Kingfisher: nestlings nearly ready to fly.

After this, I returned her to the burrow. The following morning, when I placed the young kingfishers on the shore for a photograph, two found their wings and easily crossed the 50-foot (15-meter) channel, flying low. The power of flight had come to them almost overnight.

One evening in early June, after the sun had fallen behind the bordering fringe of Willow trees, I was resting on a log stranded on the floodplain of the river, when a young Green Kingfisher flew upstream, calling cheep at intervals, and perched on a pile of brushwood almost in front of the burrow where it had grown up. Presently its father came flying downstream, with a small fish in his bill, and alighted on the same pile of brushwood, not far from the other. The

young bird approached him, as though to receive the fish, but the adult raised his wings above his back. The young kingfisher, taking this as a warning to remain aloof, perched a short distance away. Not satisfied with the interval that separated them, the male darted at the young bird, who retreated a few feet. Several times it tried to approach its father, but each time it was warned to stay away by the spread wings, a picturesque attitude. Several times, too, the bird with the fish dashed at the supplicant for it, and finally, still holding the fish in his bill, he chased the young bird down the river and out of sight. The young kingfisher had been out of the nest twenty-nine days and must now learn to dive for its own fish.

23. Turquoise-browed Motmot

Eumomota superciliosa

The small family of motmots is best represented in Middle America, where eight of the nine species occur. During my early years in Central America, few birds so attracted and delighted me. It happened that the first motmot that I saw was the most beautiful of all. In 1930, I spent six months at the Lancetilla Experiment Station in northern Honduras, where Wilson Popenoe, a leading authority on tropical fruits, had gathered a large variety of fruit trees and shrubs from the tropics of both hemispheres. From the banana-shipping port of Tela, a light tramline ran along the valley of the Río Tela for several miles, mostly through neglected pastures and rank second-growth thickets, to the station back in the hills. As the little open motorcar chugged along the rails, I often saw a Turquoise-browed Motmot perching on the telephone wire beside the tracks. As the car approached, the bird would fly swiftly down toward the Willow-shaded river where it nested. Two years later, I found these motmots amid banana plantations and similarly lush thickets in the humid lower reach of the Motagua Valley in Guatemala.

These motmots that lived in clearings in rain-forested regions were hardly typical of a species more widely distributed in drier country, although they had been in these rainy lands long enough to have evolved distinct, more richly colored races. Higher in the Motagua Valley, in the arid stretch between Zacapa and Progreso, I found them exceedingly abundant among cacti, prickly pears, and low, thorny, scattered trees. With Russet-crowned Motmots, they were among the most conspicuous feathered inhabitants of the region. The sandy walls of barrancas and the rises of the terraces on barren hillsides were penetrated by innumerable burrows, most of which had apparently been dug by these two motmots. I also found Turquoise-browed Motmots abundant in the light, largely deciduous woods of northwestern Costa Rica, where the dry season is long and severe. From here they extend up the Pacific coast to Chiapas and Oaxaca in Mexico, and they are also common on the arid Yucatán Peninsula and in Veracruz. From the lowlands they range upward to about 4,500 feet (1,370 meters). Although in northern Central America they inhabit clearings in rain forest, I never found them inside the forest itself.

It is a paradox that one of the most beautiful birds is hatched and reared in a foul hole in a bank, only to emerge at last with its lovely plumage undefiled. It is still more strange that the Turquoise-browed Motmot acquires its colors in the earth, for they are not brightly glittering like gems and metals but as soft and delicately blended as the rainbow and the sunset sky. Central America has numerous birds more brightly colored— many tanagers, orioles, trogons, jacamars, and hummingbirds are more brilliant—but the subdued beauty of the motmot is of a different, and perhaps higher, order. While these others might be painted in enamels, pastels are more appropriate for the motmot. Its most arresting color is the broad band of turquoise above each eye, margined below by a black line extending from the bill to the ear. Elsewhere the motmot is largely shades of green and chestnut, delicately blended. In the center of its throat is a heavy black streak, bordered with blue. The wing coverts

are olive-green and the remiges blue, broadly
tipped with black. The feature of the motmot
which most attracts attention is its tail. The
two central feathers extend far beyond the
lateral ones, and their shafts are partly denuded of vanes. At the end of each naked
stalk is a roundish disk of blue vane, tipped
with black. No other motmot has so great a
length of naked shaft, which imparts to its
tail an airy grace that the others lack. The
sexes are alike in plumage, even to the racquet-shaped tail feathers.

The elegance of the motmots' plumage is matched by the grace of their bearing and movements. They perch long in one spot, often in a Willow tree overhanging a stream, where with a good binocular one can admire at leisure their blended tints. Far from conspicuous against a background of foliage, on dull days they are often difficult to detect until they move. At intervals, as they rest quietly as though sunk in meditation, they turn their heads from side to side or swing their racquet-shaped tail feathers sideward, like a pendulum that has almost lost its impulse. The motmot's movements, following a long period of inactivity, are so sudden and unexpected that they take the watcher by surprise and are difficult to follow. It is amusing to watch the bird's quick about-face while it perches on a twig. It whisks its long tail up and over the perch with an elegant flourish, like a skillful flag bearer handling a banner to avoid furling it around the pole. The motmot's flight, rapid and undulatory, is rarely long-continued.

Because of its sedentary habits, Guatemalans sometimes call the motmot *pájaro bobo* ("stupid bird"); but as too often happens a placid disposition has been mistaken for dullness. As they perch in seeming abstraction, the motmots keep their eyes open for suitable food, upon which they dart with astonishing swiftness. They eat insects of many kinds, including beetles, caterpillars, and butterflies, also spiders, worms, and lizards. The motmot's keen eyes detect a green larva against a green leaf at a surprising distance. The birds make a swift sally, pluck their prey from the foliage without alighting, and return in a trice to their original perch, against which they beat their victim. The loud rhythmic clacking of the heavy bill striking against a limb sometimes calls attention to a motmot hiding in a thicket. At times they dart out to catch an insect flying past. Motmots and jacamars are the birds I have most often seen capture the larger, more colorful butterflies.

In northern Central America, motmots in general are sometimes known by the name *toro voz* ("bull voice"), which fits this species better than the others. Although usually silent birds, in the mating season, which begins in March, Turquoise-browed Motmots frequently call *cawak cawak* or sometimes a single long-drawn-out *cawaaalk* in a deep throaty voice, as though they talked with a full mouth. In scrubby thickets, male and female call with their thick lusterless voices, perch motionless side by side, and at intervals fly down to examine the bare banks where they will soon dig their burrows.

The Burrow
Where there are enough sites for burrows, each pair of Turquoise-browed Motmots prefer to nest alone; but, where banks are rare in the midst of territory otherwise favorable to them, a number may dig their burrows close together. I recall a railroad cut in the middle of a large area of scrubby second growth, poor in nest sites, where seven pairs of motmots excavated their tunnels only a few yards apart, despite interruptions by the passage of numerous pedestrians and an occasional train. On the Yucatán Peninsula, Orejuela (1977) found up to thirty pairs in a single nesting colony, although colonies of ten to twenty pairs were more usual. Some burrows were only 12 inches (30 centimeters) apart, but a separation of 20 to 80 inches (50 to 203 centimeters) was more frequent.

The Río Tela of Honduras, emerging from the deep shadows of the primeval forest that covered the precipitous mountain slopes among which it was born, flows for 4 or 5 miles (6.4 or 8 kilometers) through a narrow flat valley to the Caribbean Sea. The bottomlands of the valley had once been covered by banana plantations, but, after these were ravaged by disease and abandoned, they were overgrown with low tangled thickets, amid which Turquoise-broweds flourished. At the end of April, I found one of their burrows in a low sandy bank, beside a delightful reach of the stream, where the clear water flowed over a clean sandy bottom between Willows and Riverwood trees. The owners of this burrow sat motionless in the Willows for seemingly interminable periods. Once the one that I took to be the male flew up beside his mate and solemnly gave her an insect, all without a sound or any display. One member of the pair drove away a Great Kiskadee who had dropped down to forage on the bank below the burrow.

Since the motmots no longer dug in the tunnel, I surmised that they had started to lay in it, and, eager to follow all the details of their nesting, I promptly set about uncovering the nest. I dug into the soft sandy loam with my hands, not daring to use a shovel for fear of breaking the eggs, and soon made an opening in the side of the chamber, where four pure white eggs lay on the bare earth. Carefully replacing them, I covered the chamber with a glass plate and a wooden lid, just as I did at the Amazon Kingfishers' nest. The motmots' eggs were fresh, while the kingfishers had newly hatched young; the former promptly deserted, although the latter clung tenaciously to their offspring.

I was not altogether sorry that the motmots deserted their burrow, for three days after I opened it they started to dig a new one a few feet from the first, thereby providing an opportunity to study their nesting from the beginning. One of the motmots clung repeatedly to the bank at the point where the new tunnel would begin; then both set to work with such zeal that they drove their shaft horizontally into the light soil for 20 inches (50 centimeters) in little more than a day. With leafy boughs of the Riverwood tree, I built a blind at a spot where I could observe both their favorite perch—a dead branch of a Willow tree—and the bank where they dug. Here I spent many hours watching the pair at work.

Both sexes toiled in the burrow, but it was soon evident that they did not take equal shares. Although I could not distinguish the sexes by their plumage, I concluded that the one who occasionally presented an insect or a spider to his partner was the male. By a disarranged feather or a dust spot, I could avoid confusing the two for short periods. The supposed female did by far the greater part of the work but was rewarded only rarely by her mate's offerings of food. Flying down to the entrance, she paused a minute, then went in, throwing out a shower of sand or, to be more exact, two parallel intermittent jets, as she kicked vigorously backward with her feet, alternately. This stream followed the digger inward, probably until she reached the head of the excavation, with the result that each time she entered some of the earth that had been loosened on earlier visits was shifted outward. She remained in the burrow for intervals of one to eighteen minutes, and she always backed out of the tunnel, tailfirst.

Emerging, the female motmot usually flew up beside her mate in the Willow tree. After lingering beside her for a few minutes, he in turn flew to the tunnel. Sometimes he entered, throwing out earth as he went in, just as she did, and came out tail foremost after from one to four minutes. It was impossible to see what he did while hidden in the bank, but I believe that he must be credited for doing a little work. On other occasions, after the female alighted beside him, he dropped down to the tunnel's mouth, then promptly returned to the Willow perch. Once he gave his partner a caterpillar, flew to a point on the bank near the burrow, where he clung a moment, then returned to his perch. As soon as he regained his place beside the female, she entered the tunnel and worked for five minutes. It appeared that, by his offerings and visits to the burrow, the male was trying to induce his mate to continue her task.

At other times, the male stood in the entrance of the burrow, scratched a little with his feet, looked around at his mate, scratched out a little more earth, looked around again, and finally flew back to perch beside her, without having accomplished anything. On his return, the female usually resumed digging. Such behavior strengthened my impression that the male motmot was coaxing his mate to increase her exertions, with a fair degree of success. On the second afternoon that I watched, the female emerged after eighteen minutes in the tunnel and went to the Willow tree to preen. Her mate then flew to the bank, where he clung for a few minutes, then moved over to the entrance, where he alternately scratched and pecked with his bill at the sand, at intervals looking around at the female, who appeared to pay no attention to him. Rested at length from her long spell in the tunnel, she flew to its mouth and the male made way for her, but instead of entering she went to perch on a neighboring stem. Again the male returned to the entrance and repeated his wiles, scratching and pecking as before. At last the female seemed to heed him: she entered the burrow and worked for seven minutes. While she toiled, the male sometimes stood in the doorway and sometimes pretended to dig with his bill at a nearby part of the riverbank.

On the first afternoon when I watched, the motmots worked until five o'clock and drove their tunnel 15 inches (38 centimeters) farther into the bank. The following day, they again worked until five o'clock, adding another 15 inches to their burrow. On the next day I did not watch them; but by the following morning they regularly emerged from the burrow headfirst, indicating that they had already made the chamber at the inner end wide enough to permit them to turn around. The tunnel was now 62 inches (157 centimeters) long and had been dug in somewhat less than five days. The diggers' plumage, still remarkably fresh, appeared to have suffered little from their strenuous labor underground. Some people manage to keep themselves neat and clean at whatever task they are engaged in, and birds possess this innate tidiness to a high degree.

Expecting that birds who dug their burrow in such haste would promptly lay in it, on the day after they emerged headfirst I opened it, so that I could date the appearance of the eggs and learn the incubation period. This time I proceeded with greater caution, making a hole at the rear barely wide enough to admit a hand and closing it with a board. I felt confident that the motmots would not be upset by so slight an alteration of their burrow. Unfortunately, the nest chamber had not yet reached full size. When the motmots proceeded to enlarge it, they were evidently annoyed by my board, for they promptly abandoned their work. The *pájaros bobos* were not so obtuse as this name implies! Three days later, they had started a third burrow, midway between the two that they had deserted because of my interference and lower in the bank, where it

would be more difficult to open. Before they finished this, I found the nest of another pair of motmots much nearer my residence and uncovered their eggs without causing desertion. Accordingly, I decided to permit the much persecuted first pair to finish their nesting without molesting them more.

Sometimes Turquoise-browed Motmots display considerable adaptability in digging their burrows, but at other times they lack foresight. Along the Río Morjá in Guatemala, I found a burrow in a low bank beneath a canebrake. This bank was composed almost wholly of coarse gravel, into which the birds could not have dug, overlaid by a shallow stratum of sandy soil only 4 inches (10 centimeters) deep where it was exposed. The motmots started their tunnel at the bottom of this sandy layer, nearer the top of the bank than any other burrow that I have seen. Fortunately for them, the workable layer became deeper as they followed it inward from the bank; and they inclined their tunnel downward, with the result that the chamber at its end was 1 foot (30 centimeters) below the surface, about the usual depth for burrows in low riverbanks. It is not probable that the motmots could have foreseen the dip of the sandy soil, but they were sufficiently adaptable to take advantage of it when they discovered how it went, whereas most motmots extend their tunnels in a more horizontal plane.

Another pair, less clever, began to dig only 10 inches (25 centimeters) below the top of the riverbank, from the edge of which the ground sloped downward on the landward side. When they had nearly completed their tunneling, they suddenly found themselves digging into the light and air—two surprised motmots! Promptly they started another burrow nearby, at the end of May when it was late for their nesting. Evidently, the female's need to lay her eggs became so pressing that she lacked time to give the burrow its full length, for the pair widened the nest chamber when it was only 40 inches (102 centimeters) long and so straight that with a flashlight I could look from its mouth to its end.

Burrows of Turquoise-browed Motmots closely resemble those of their neighbors, the

Amazon Kingfishers, but are distinguishable by their slightly inferior diameter. Six that I measured were 40, 51, 55, 55½, 60, and 61½ inches (102, 130, 140, 141, 152, and 156 centimeters) in length. In Baja Verapaz, Guatemala, Owen (in Salvin and Godman 1879–1904) found burrows up to 8 feet (244 centimeters) long, and those examined by Orejuela (1977) on the peninsula of Yucatán ranged from 39 to 118 inches (99 to 300 centimeters). Most burrows curve gently to the right or left, making it impossible to look into the nest chamber from the front. This enlargement at the end of the tunnel is 8 or 9 inches (20 or 23 centimeters) wide and about 4 inches (10 centimeters) high at the center. Here the eggs are laid on the bare ground, and the nestlings remain until they fly. At the entrance, the tunnel is about 3½ inches (9 centimeters) wide by 3 to 4 inches (7.6 to 10 centimeters) high. As with kingfishers, it is easy to distinguish occupied from deserted burrows by the presence or absence of deep parallel ruts.

Where banks into which Turquoise-browed Motmots can dig burrows are lacking or infrequent, the birds may nest in quite different situations. Martin and Martin (1980) found them feeding nestlings in deep recesses, rectangular or circular in cross section, in walls and ceilings of both outer and inner rooms of Mayan edifices at archaeological sites in Yucatán. Some rooms sheltered more than one pair of the birds. A pair attended eggs as late as the first week of July.

The Eggs and Incubation

The earliest eggs that I have seen were found in a burrow beside the Río Morjá on April 22, when they appeared to have been newly laid. Another set, also apparently freshly laid, was uncovered in the same locality on May 1. Beside the Río Tela, I found one set of eggs on May 6 and another, far advanced in incubation, on May 19. The earliest of these four sets contained three eggs; each of the other three sets had four eggs. According to Owen, Turquoise-browed Motmots in Baja Verapaz usually laid four eggs, and this is the number found in fifteen nests by Orejuela, who also noticed one set of five and

one set of two. The short ovate eggs, pure white when newly laid, resemble those of kingfishers. The fifteen eggs in my four sets averaged 26.5 by 22.5 millimeters, with extremes of 24.6 to 27.8 by 21.8 to 23 millimeters.

The male and female incubate by turns, often sitting for several hours at a stretch. On the Yucatán Peninsula, Orejuela found males incubating for one-third of the daytime, females for two-thirds and usually throughout the night. When one member of the pair comes to relieve its mate, it perches above the burrow's entrance and calls in a low voice for the other to come out. In my experience, these motmots are more easily driven from their burrows than the three species of kingfishers that are often their neighbors, and they desert their eggs with less provocation. While incubating, they regurgitate the shards of beetles and other indigestible parts of their food, until a mass of such material accumulates on the floor and forms a bed beneath the eggs.

The curvature of the longer tunnels made it impossible to see the motmots sitting on their eggs, but the exceptionally short burrow already mentioned was straight enough to permit a view of the lovely birds while they incubated. I went at night to visit this nest in the bank of the Río Morjá, passing through a silent grove of tall banana plants, whose polished stems glinted in the beam of my flashlight. Emerging on the riverbank, I disturbed a Boat-billed Heron, who flew downstream with a weird *quok, quok, quok, quok, oo-wa-ee*. On the sandbar across the river, a raccoon eating at the water's edge looked into the flashlight's beam with two brilliant orbs, then turned and walked deliberately away.

Approaching cautiously along the sandy shore at the foot of the low bank, I threw the beam into the motmots' burrow, only to behold a creature strange to me. Some gray furry animal, with a large patch of chestnut in the middle of its back, had stolen into the burrow, devoured the motmot and her eggs, and now slumbered curled up in her place. But no! there was turquoise on the animal's head and blue on its sides; it must surely be the motmot, sleeping peacefully on her eggs but so transformed in the yellow light of the electric torch that I did not immediately recognize her. Her back and all the regions which by day are a soft green appeared yellowish gray, for they were compounded of wavelengths inadequately represented in the rays from the incandescent filament. The bird's soft, loose plumage was fluffed out and resembled fur. But the blue on the wings and especially the turquoise on the brow shone with such a bright and radiant luster that I switched off the light, half expecting to find them self-luminous—but all remained dark in the burrow.

The motmot's tail ran outward toward the mouth of the tunnel, where the blue-and-black racquets rested so far behind the inward-facing bird's body that they appeared to be isolated, unconnected disks caught up on the ceiling. I returned several times and always found the motmots incubating with head inward and tail running outward into the tunnel, where alone it found ample space without becoming bent. This was the secret of how the motmots preserved their long racquet feathers clean and unbroken while they incubated.

At one of my nests, the eggs which appeared to have been freshly laid when I first saw them hatched seventeen days later. This falls within the range of fifteen to nineteen days given as the incubation period by Orejuela.

The Nestlings

The first Turquoise-browed Motmots' burrow that I succeeded in opening without causing desertion was situated beside the narrow-gauge tramline that ran along the Lancetilla Valley in Honduras. As I dug down behind the nest chamber, the owners perched in a tree across the tracks and complained with low guttural notes, but otherwise they showed no excitement. Making a small opening at the back of the chamber, I found four partly incubated eggs lying among beetle shards. Then I closed the aperture with a board and filled the pit with earth. Happily, these motmots accepted my slight alteration and continued to incubate.

Eight days later, on May 27, I first noticed that the eggs were pipped. For more than twenty-four hours the chicks tapped at their white prison walls, at times peeping weakly, before they broke through and escaped. Instead of fleeing from the burrow when I removed the board at the rear, the parents, bolder now, only retreated into the entrance tunnel, where they voiced low frightened grunts. The four pink-skinned, blind nestlings, with no trace of down or feathers, resembled the equally homely newborn kingfishers. The most conspicuous difference was in their bills. The upper mandible of the hatchling motmot was slightly longer than the lower and strongly hooked at the tip, whereas the young kingfisher's upper mandible was straight and shorter than the lower. The nestlings peeped in weak hoarse voices; they could already stand; and, sensitive to light although sightless, they shuffled into the tunnel when their nursery was opened at the back.

To study the care of these nestlings, I made a little wigwam of green coconut fronds, across the tramline from the burrow. Seated within this leafy retreat, I could watch the motmots without being seen by them. Both parents fed the nestlings with an extremely varied fare, including moths, large and brilliantly colored butterflies, small green mantises, green caterpillars, many insects too small to be identified in the motmots' bills, and lizards up to about 6 inches (15 centimeters) long. The prey was nearly always dead when the parents arrived with it in the tree in front of their burrow, but if it still struggled they knocked it vigorously against the perch until it ceased to move, before they took it to their offspring. Before they gave the lizards to their young, the adults apparently pecked or bit off the reptiles' heads, then pressed out the viscera and other soft parts through the neck, for I found several empty skins lying almost entire on the chamber's floor. The rate of feeding varied greatly from day to day. When a week old, the four nestlings received ten items in one hour and forty-five minutes. On the preceding morning, they were fed only five times in two hours.

Although while watching I was well hidden by palm leaves, the parents went to the burrow with the utmost caution. They never made a direct approach, but, emerging from the thicket where they hunted, they alighted in a small tree on the opposite side of the tramline, where they surveyed their surroundings with great deliberation. Advancing from this point, they sometimes delayed again on a banana leaf close above the burrow's entrance; and many minutes were lost between the first appearance of a parent with food and its delivery to the nestlings. Often the two flew up together with food and perched in the low tree across the tramline. Here one delayed, sometimes uttering a subdued *wha wha*, while its mate entered the burrow. When the latter emerged tailfirst, as happened almost invariably when they fed the nestlings, it flew up beside the waiting partner, who now in turn carried its offering to the hungry young. Sometimes one member of the pair, holding food in its bill, procrastinated in front of the burrow while the other came and went, feeding the nestlings several times in the interval. Thus, one morning a motmot held a lizard for twenty-five minutes, during which the other fed the nestlings three times. Sometimes a parent delayed so long, holding food evidently intended for its progeny, that it grew hungry and swallowed the article itself, then flew away to hunt for more.

When the nestlings were a week old, their eyes began to open, and the sheaths of their body feathers started to push through the skin. When the burrow was opened at the back, the young motmots retreated down the tunnel more quickly than at first, but they could be driven back into the chamber if we directed the flashlight's beam into the burrow's entrance. When twelve days old, the young bristled with long pinfeathers, from the ends of which the true feathers were just emerging. When the nestlings were twenty days old, we removed them from the burrow for another photograph, not without some difficulty in extracting one from the tunnel, beyond reach from either end. Now well feathered, the young screamed and tried to bite when handled. The nest was becoming

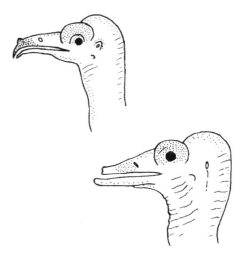

Profiles of day-old Turquoise-browed Motmot (left) and Ringed Kingfisher nestlings. From author's field sketches, not drawn to scale.

Turquoise-browed Motmot: nestling twelve or thirteen days old.

Turquoise-browed Motmot: nestlings twenty days old.

disgustingly foul and swarmed with maggots, for motmots are as careless of sanitation as the related kingfishers, so that it was necessary to wash the young birds' bills and feet to make them presentable for their portraits. Their docility, when we arranged them in a row on a perch, was in marked contrast to the restlessness of Amazon Kingfishers at the same age. Already they seemed to be developing a taste for a life devoted largely to motionless watching.

When we removed the twenty-five-day-old young from the burrow for their final photograph, they resembled their parents in coloration but were stubby-tailed and lacked the black throat patch. We marveled that such loveliness could have developed amid such

foul surroundings. The chicks' body feathers had long, pliant, free barbs, making their plumage very soft and downy. We noticed that both mandibles of their broad, heavy black bills were finely serrated along the apical third of their length, for a firmer grasp upon their food, and that, like flycatchers and other birds who catch insects in flight, they had long stiff bristles at the base of the bill. Their two outer toes were united for the greater part of their length, and only a single toe was directed backward, as in their relatives the kingfishers.

One of the twenty-five-day-old motmots, removed from the burrow, slipped from our hands and flew into the dense thicket behind the nest, where it could not be recovered.

The remaining three were posed for a photograph, but two escaped and flew strongly for about 30 feet (9 meters). They alighted at the edge of a thicket, slowly swayed their short tails from side to side, in the manner of their elders, and made queer throaty sounds somewhat like the calls of their parents. With difficulty we caught them and replaced one in the burrow, which it left, apparently spontaneously, three days later, when twenty-eight or twenty-nine days old. Along the Río Morjá, I studied a burrow with three nestlings. One of these slipped through my hands and flew too well to be retrieved when twenty-five days old; the other two left the burrow when between twenty-five and twenty-seven days of age. Unfortunately, all these young motmots had been handled; if quite undisturbed, they might have remained in their burrows a few days longer. Sixteen nestlings watched by Orejuela on the Yucatán Peninsula left at ages ranging from twenty-four to twenty-nine days, with a mean of twenty-six days.

We kept two fledglings from the earlier nest to follow their subsequent development, especially to watch the denudation of the shafts of the central tail feathers. But, when I beheld through the meshes of a cage a bird that I had hitherto known only wild and free, I regretted what I had done. If I reared these fledglings as dull, spiritless captives, motmots could never be the same to me as they had been: shy, lovely creatures that brightened a solitary walk. I decided to return the young birds to their parents, if it were not too late, and to take my chances as a field naturalist of seeing motmots trim their tail feathers in their natural environment. I carried the fledglings back to the vicinity of their burrow, where they heard the loud *cawak cawak* of their parents and answered with weaker voices. They flew from my opened hands into the thicket, whither their two nest mates had preceded them; and the parents led the united family farther into the impenetrable tangle. What I might have lost in knowledge I gained in contentment, for the motmots' nesting had ended as I wish every nesting over which I watch to end—with the parents leading their brood to food and safety.

Postscript

Years have sped by, and still I have failed to surprise a motmot trimming its tail feathers. Gaumer (1881–1882) reported that, in the dry limestone country of Yucatán, Turquoise-browed Motmots nest and pass much of their time in caverns and crevices of the porous rocks and in the pitted walls of wells, in the seclusion of which alone they alter their tails. The regions where I have known this species are devoid of such subterranean retreats, yet the motmots seem equally careful not to trim their tail feathers in public. I never saw a Turquoise-browed with a fully grown central tail feather which did not have its shaft denuded. In early July, I found a young motmot, still attended by its parents, whose central rectrices protruded only an inch beyond the others; nevertheless, the shafts were already naked for a short distance above the terminal racquets. At the beginning of the breeding season, I saw an adult motmot, evidently just finished molting, whose central tail feathers did not project at all beyond the lateral ones, yet the shafts had already lost some of their vanes. The bare shafts were not noticeable against the background of the other tail feathers; only when wind blew the tail sideward, or when I looked carefully through my binocular at close range, could I distinguish them.

The central rectrices of other kinds of motmots, including the Broad-billed, are nearly or quite full-grown before the vanes fall from the subterminal part of the shafts, as I shall tell in the following chapter. The earlier denudation of Turquoise-browed Motmots' central rectrices appears to be somehow related to the greater length of naked shaft that eventually develops.

24. Broad-billed Motmot

Electron platyrhynchum

In April and May, as dawn's first feeble rays seep into the lofty Caribbean rain forest of Costa Rica, hoarse croaks shatter the stillness. The deep *cwaa cwaa* sounds from every side, perplexing the newcomer, who—vainly peering up into the masses of foliage for a glimpse of the sound's source—cannot decide whether this is a frog or a bird. Less frequent repetitions of the unbirdlike notes, later in the day, may guide keen eyes to a small motmot perching immobile well up among the great trees. The foreparts of its short body, including the head, neck, and chest, are mainly cinnamon-rufous, with a large black patch on either side covering the cheeks and auricular region, a smaller patch of black in the center of the foreneck, and greenish blue on the chin and upper throat. The more posterior parts of the body, including the back, rump, and abdomen, are green, more olivaceous above, more bluish below. The wings are blue, tinged with green on the primaries. Each of the two central feathers of the blue-green graduated tail, much longer than the others, is terminated by a roundish black-tipped disk, connected with the basal part by a short length of naked shaft. The bill, black with a light tip, is broad and flat, with finely serrated cutting edges. The upper mandible has a low keel along the center.

The Broad-billed Motmot ranges through rain forests from northern Honduras to Ecuador, Peru, Bolivia, and Brazil. An inhabitant of warm lowlands, it is rarely found above 3,000 feet (910 meters), although it has been recorded as high as 4,750 feet (1,450 meters) on the Caribbean slope of Volcán de Chiriquí in western Panama (Wetmore 1968). Except when attending its nests, it generally perches well above the ground in forest trees. Often it swings its tail, pendulumlike, from side to side, in the typical motmot gesture.

This small motmot subsists largely on insects and their larvae, with an admixture of spiders, centipedes, small frogs, and lizards. Among insects, cicadas supply a substantial part of the motmot's food in the season of their abundance. Large butterflies and dragonflies are occasionally captured. I have never seen this motmot eat fruit, and, during my many hours of watching at three nests, none was given to the nestlings. Turquoise-browed and Blue-throated Green motmots likewise eat little or no fruit, but the larger Rufous and Blue-diademed motmots include much fruit in their varied diets.

Like other motmots, Broadbills forage in a manner that avoids wasted movement. They perch quietly, scrutinizing their surroundings, until they spy some suitable item, which they then snatch from a leaf, a twig, a trunk, or the air by means of a sudden dart. Without alighting at the moment of seizure, they carry the object to some convenient perch, against which, if their victim be large, they beat it noisily while holding it firmly in their broad serrated bills. At times, from a low lookout, they fly downward to capture some small creature in the ground cover. Occasionally they join the crowd of birds that gather to catch fugitives from the army ants, a habit which they share with Blue-diademed and Rufous motmots.

In addition to the far-carrying wooden *cwaa cwaa*, which in April and May was often the very first call of a diurnal bird that I heard in the rain forest at daybreak, these motmots sometimes utter similar but shorter notes in rapid succession, *ca ca ca ca ca ca.*

Rarely, I have heard from them a low rattle or clicking, *k-e-e-e*. A parent motmot hesitating to take food into its burrow, while I stood near, continued to repeat a sharp *keck keck keck*. Low throaty notes express excitement or distrust.

The voices of fledglings, of which I shall have more to say later, are amazingly different from those of adults. The young utter soft mellow notes of a sort rather frequent among birds; sometimes they might be mistaken for those of the Black-throated Trogon, at other times for the notes of the Chestnut-backed Antbird, both of which live in the same forest. Possibly the ancestors of present-day Broad-billed Motmots had soft voices that were confusingly similar to those of some of their avian neighbors, but through the ages natural selection favored individuals whose notes were more distinctive, until today these motmots have far-carrying calls that can hardly be confused with any other sound in the forests where they dwell.

It is well known that, when the central rectrices of racquet-tailed motmots first grow out, their vanes are continuous to the tips, although they are commonly constricted in the subterminal region, where the shafts will finally be denuded. My best opportunity to follow the course of racquet formation occurred on Barro Colorado Island in the Panama Canal Zone. One evening in late December of 1930, just as we were finishing supper, a Broad-billed Motmot perched on the petiole of a papaya tree close beside the main building and startled us with a loud *cwaa cwaa*. For the next three weeks, this bird, whom we took to be a male, entered the clearing from the surrounding forest almost every evening after sunset, to continue to eat when it was growing too dark in the woodland. Sometimes he was accompanied by another motmot, easily distinguished by the condition of her tail, who was apparently his mate. They had certain favorite low perches on which they rested while they looked for insects, which they caught on aerial sallies or flew down into the grass to seize. Their eyesight was truly amazing: in the gathering dusk, they could detect and capture a small insect amid the grass 20 feet

(6 meters) away. Often they did not return to the forest until it became too dark for us to see them clearly.

These motmots were far from shy. By setting our heavy, old-fashioned, ground-glass-plate cameras on tripods and focusing them on the birds' habitual perches, with a thread attached to the shutter release so that we could trip it from a distance, Frank M. Chapman and I obtained a series of photographs showing the progress of denudation of the central tail feathers. The motmots rested so quietly in one spot that a three-second exposure in the fading light often revealed no movement.

At the beginning of January, the motmot who was our most regular visitor had central rectrices of unequal length. The left was the longer of the two and appeared to be full-grown, but the shaft above the terminal racquet had been denuded for only a very short distance. The right central rectrix was about an inch shorter and had not been trimmed at all. By January 7, the full-grown left central rectrix appeared to have the shaft denuded for the usual distance. When I last saw this bird, on January 20, the right central rectrix, now nearly as long as the left, still showed no sign of denudation.

On another Broadbill that I saw about this time, the condition of the central tail feathers was just the reverse: the right one was longer, with the subterminal part of the shaft denuded, whereas the left feather reached only a little way beyond the beginning of the racquet on the other and had uninterrupted vanes. In mid January some Broadbills had their tails fully trimmed, while on others the two central rectrices were apparently full-grown with no trace of denudation. From these observations, we may conclude that in this species the process of racquet formation does not begin until, or at some time after, the central tail feathers have stopped growing. This contrasts with the situation in the Turquoise-browed Motmot, whose much greater length of naked shaft loses its vanes while the central rectrices are no longer than the lateral ones and far from attaining their full length. In no motmot have I actually witnessed the removal of the vanes. Loosely at-

Broad-billed Motmot: adult with one central tail feather trimmed (from a time exposure in twilight on Barro Colorado Island).

tached to the part of the feather shaft that will become naked, they may fall away of themselves, or as the bird preens, or by striking against twigs and foliage—a point that remains to be settled. Apparently, the motmot does not deliberately try to improve its appearance.

On Barro Colorado Island, one morning in mid January, I followed the calls of Broad-bills until I came in view of two of them resting, about 6 feet (1.8 meters) apart, on a branch somewhat below midheight of the forest, apparently engaged in courtship. At short intervals, each uttered a deep *cwaa cwaa*, sometimes simultaneously, sometimes

one following or answering the other, but neither obviously acting as leader. As they continued this monotonous conversation, they sat serenely still, as is their fashion. From time to time, one darted out to pluck an insect from a neighboring branch or twig and carry it to a different perch, after which they resumed their courtship, if such it was, in altered positions. Once the motmot with unequal central tail feathers, whom I took to be the male, snatched a beetle from a large limb and was knocking it resoundingly against his perch when the other flew straight toward him, as though to claim the insect. But the male, far from gallantly presenting the food to the female, as I saw the Turquoise-browed Motmot do, churlishly withheld it. Appearing to become angry, he repeated several times a loud *ca-a-wak, ca-a-wak* and switched his tail vehemently upward, while the other motmot, rebuffed, flew to another perch. Presently the monotonous *cwaa cwaa* was resumed; but after about an hour the responses of the supposed female became less and less ready, until she ceased to reply and soon thereafter departed. Then the male's calls became weaker, until he tired of uttering them unanswered and continued to perch in silence, motionless except for an occasional plunge after a passing insect. A stolid courtship, surely, but in keeping with the motmot's impassive nature!

The Burrow and Eggs

At La Selva, a nature reservation in northeastern Costa Rica, on May 14, 1967, I discovered my first Broad-billed Motmots' burrow. In a high wooded bluff rising steeply above the Río Puerto Viejo was a small bay or recess, about 20 yards (18 meters) across, probably formed by a landslip long before but now overgrown with ferns, palms, saplings, and small trees. At the head of this natural amphitheater rose the vertical bank of earth into which the burrow had been dug. It was screened by trees and vines from the broad expanse of river, and behind was a great tract of heavy forest. The exposed entrance to the burrow was 3½ feet (107 centimeters) below the top of the bank. The tunnel curved to the right, so that I could not see to the end when I directed in the beam of a flashlight; but the motmot in charge of the eggs moved outward far enough to reveal its head and shoulders and stayed there gazing into the light. Since I could not examine the eggs without an excavation so extensive that it would have jeopardized the nest, I did not attempt to do so. When we left La Selva on June 11, the parents were feeding nestlings in this burrow.

When next I visited this embayment in the bluff, on March 12 of the following year, I found a new burrow about 4 yards (3.6 meters) from the old one. Although it was still unoccupied, parallel furrows along its bot-

tom, made by the motmots' short legs as they passed in and out, showed that it had been recently entered. No pile of freshly dug earth below its mouth revealed that it was newly excavated; perhaps, like Blue-diademed Motmots, Broadbills dig their burrows months before they lay in them. This new burrow ran straight into the bank; the enlargement at its inner end was offset slightly to the left. Looking in at the front, I needed a mirror to see all the eggs that were later laid, but much of the sitting bird would be visible with no other aid than a flashlight. This burrow was 33 inches (84 centimeters) long. Near its mouth, it was 3 inches wide by 2⅞ inches high (7.6 by 7.3 centimeters).

My third burrow was, like the first two, in the nearly vertical wall of an indentation in a high bank above a stream, in this instance a small tributary of the Río Puerto Viejo. The landslide that had left this nick in the bank had occurred years before, and it was now overgrown with vegetation. Several large clumps of plumelike fern fronds grew on the bank above the mouth of the burrow, which was 39 inches (99 centimeters) long and quite straight, so that a light was all that I needed to see what it contained. The bore of this tunnel was also wider than high, 3¼ inches in horizontal diameter by 2¼ in height (8.3 by 5.7 centimeters).

During the week following my first visit to the second burrow on March 12, a twig set in its mouth showed that it was seldom entered, and no bird slept in it. Then followed three very rainy weeks, during which the bank became too soft and slippery to be safely climbed. When, after two dry days, I revisited the burrow on April 13, it contained three eggs, their pure white shells already slightly soiled from contact with the earthen floor of the unlined nest chamber. As with other motmots, no soft material had been carried in to form a bed for them. These eggs hatched on April 29; they had been laid in the second week of April. The third nest, more advanced, contained two nestlings with sprouting pinfeathers when discovered on April 30, 1968. The eggs from which they hatched had been laid at the beginning of the month.

Broad-billed Motmot: mouths of two burrows used in consecutive years, in a bluff above the Río Puerto Viejo, Costa Rica.

Incubation

Of the parents who attended the first burrow in 1967, one had an intact but somewhat worn tail; the other, who passed the nights in the nest, had lost both racquets. The following year, the motmots at the new burrow close by, evidently the same pair, showed the same differences—one had two whole racquets, but the other, who slept in the burrow, had none; indeed, by the time the nestlings flew, it had only a short stub of a tail. Apparently, the long hours it spent in the burrow in earth soaked by daily rains damaged its tail feathers. To distinguish these motmots, we called one Racquets and the other Diskless. Probably the latter, who regularly attended the eggs and nestlings by night, was the female.

At the third nest, also, one parent had two whole racquets while the other had none, although its tail was otherwise in good condition, by no means so worn as that of Diskless. I found this burrow too late to learn which parent occupied it by night, but the more frequent calling of the one with both racquets suggested that this was the male.

In sharp contrast to Blue-diademed Motmots, which when nesting in cultivated districts are sometimes so wary that they can hardly be watched even from a blind, these forest-dwelling Broadbills were all amazingly fearless in our presence. Often they would enter their burrows while we stood at the edge of the bank directly above the doorway, our feet not 2 yards (1.8 meters) from their heads. Once, while I looked into the burrow, a parent arriving with food almost bumped into me, then alighted so near that I came within an inch of touching it. Although their tolerance of an observer varied with the individual motmot and with time, in some cases decreasing if they had not been watched for a week or so, they would soon become reconciled to our presence. Sitting unconcealed only 3 or 4 yards (2.7 or 3.6 meters) from their burrows, we could watch these motmots carry on all their usual activities.

As in other motmots, both sexes incubated. To learn the pattern of incubation, we watched directly at the critical times of the changeovers and set a little stick upright in the burrow's mouth to indicate whether any bird had come in or out during the long hours when no movement was expected. The least touch by a passing motmot would push over this small sentinel. The ease with which the two partners could be distinguished by their tails greatly facilitated our study. In 1968, when the burrow was straight, we could look right in and see who was present, without disturbing the birds.

Observations made on twenty-six days in the two years showed that these motmots followed a simple schedule. In each twenty-four-hour period, the male and the female almost always replaced each other only twice, at dawn and in the middle of the day. Diskless incubated from around noon until the following dawn, Racquets throughout the morning. Diskless usually flew silently from the burrow before 5:00 A.M., when the loud calls of Broadbills were sounding through the forest but the light of approaching day was still so dim that I could hardly see her go. Sometimes I was apprised of her departure only by the swaying of the dusky foliage in front of the tunnel. The earliest hour at which I recorded her exit was before 4:40; the latest was 5:14. The eggs then remained unattended until Racquets arrived from sixteen to forty-five minutes later, before sunrise, at times varying from 5:15 to 5:46.

After sitting for from five and three-quarters to eight and three-quarters hours, Racquets left the burrow at times ranging from before 11:00 A.M. to 2:03 P.M., but on most days he emerged between 11:45 and 1:30. Sometimes he deserted the eggs before his relief arrived, and once they remained unattended for more than 130 minutes; but often he stayed at his post until his partner came. Sometimes, hearing her low croaking notes as she alighted on a slender palm stem leaning in front of the burrow, he would fly out before she entered; on other days, she entered first and he emerged a minute later.

The stick set in the mouth of the burrow after Diskless entered nearly always remained upright until nightfall, and this was true even on the morning when she came before 11:15. But on April 16, when Diskless was found on the eggs at 12:10, she was absent that afternoon at 5:10. A minute later, she reentered while I stood above the burrow. This was the only time when the sentinel indicated a departure from the usual routine of one entry and one exit by each partner every twenty-four hours.

Only minor differences in the schedule of this pair were noticed in the two years. In 1967, when these motmots incubated in May, the morning departure of Diskless and the arrival of Racquets tended to be earlier than those in the following year, when they incubated in April and day dawned somewhat later. When I looked into the straight burrow in 1968, I nearly always saw the motmots sitting on their eggs with head inward and tail projecting straight outward into the entrance tunnel, just as I had earlier found at a nest of the Turquoise-browed Motmot in Guatemala.

The Nestlings

In the straight burrow where I could see the three eggs, the young hatched on April 29, and the empty shells promptly vanished. The hatchlings were blind, pink, and devoid of down. They could already stand and move around, keeping their abdomens above the floor and supporting their weight on their heels, which, as in other motmots, were doubtless protected by smooth callose pads, although I did not notice this detail in these nestlings beyond my reach. When they were a week old, their pinfeathers were pushing through the skin, which had become a darker pink. At nine days, some of the body feathers were escaping from the ends of their long sheaths. When they were eleven days old, the motmots were partly feathered.

I still had not seen the nestlings with their eyes open, but perhaps they closed them in the beam of the flashlight. While I was looking into the burrow two days later, however, a parent arrived with food and called, whereupon one of the thirteen-day-old nestlings, after pushing another aside, ran down the tunnel toward the entrance, with open eyes. I stood aside, so that it could not see me, and the nestling came about two-thirds of the way to the burrow's mouth. When I looked again, necessarily with the light, it ran back to join its nest mates at the inner end. At fifteen days, the young were taking their meals at the burrow's mouth, making it unnecessary for their parents to enter. When sixteen days old, the nestlings were nearly covered with plumage. Nevertheless, they remained safely in their burrow for another eight or nine days.

When the thirteen-day-old nestlings heard the voice of an approaching parent, they trilled softly, and the parent answered with a throaty rattle. Thereafter, the young motmots became increasingly noisy; their trills, which grew louder and clearer, were often given when no parent was near. On their last day in the nest, the choruses of trills were punctuated by loud, full, almost soprano notes, such as I had never before heard from a Broadbilled Motmot.

On June 1, 1967, when the nestlings in the first burrow were a day or two old, Racquets entered with food at 5:20 A.M. (about the time he entered while he incubated) and remained brooding for 138 minutes. Twenty-two minutes after his departure, Diskless entered to feed and brood; she was still inside when I left 80 minutes later. On June 5, we watched from 5:25 until noon. Racquets fed the nestlings, but Diskless was not seen. Unless she remained in the burrow all this time—which was unlikely—the nestlings were not brooded on this wet morning. On the following afternoon, from 1:30 until 6:00, the naked nestlings were certainly not brooded, for both parents were bringing food and neither delayed in the nest longer than was necessary to deliver each morsel. Likewise, a pair of Blue-diademed Motmots did not brood week-old nestlings in the course of a morning. They even discontinued nocturnal brooding when their nestlings were about five days old. Evidently, nestling motmots stay warm enough in their deep burrows without a parental coverlet; and the early cessation of brooding reduces the risk

that a predatory animal, blocking the only avenue of escape, will capture a parent along with its young.

The newly hatched Broadbills were given small insects so thoroughly mashed that it was hardly possible to recognize their kinds. But, when only five or six days old, the nestlings received objects as large as cicadas, which had doubtless been prepared by some beating against a branch but were only slightly mutilated. Thereafter, cicadas, which were abundant in the forest at this season, became a prominent item in the nestlings' diet. In a total of nineteen hours of watching, when the nestlings in the first burrow, of unknown number, were five to ten days of age, they were fed forty-three times, one object on each parental visit. These meals included twenty cicadas, two green mantises, fifteen other insects, one spider, one tiny frog, one small lizard, and three unrecognized objects.

On May 23 of the following year, when the three nestlings in the second burrow were 24 days old, we watched throughout the day. The first feeding occurred at 5:10 A.M., the last at 5:55 P.M. In this interval of twelve and three-quarters hours, fifty-four meals were taken to the burrow. These included sixteen cicadas, four beetles, three caterpillars, two grasshoppers, one butterfly, one walking-stick, and two centipedes. Most of the remaining meals consisted of insects of undetermined kinds. The cicadas were brought chiefly during the middle of the day, when they were most active and noisy. Between 9:00 A.M. and 2:00 P.M., they accounted for half of the nestlings' meals. On this day, one young motmot left the burrow at 2:03, and thereafter we could not see how often it was fed. During the nine hours when all three nestlings were within, they were fed forty-two times, at the rate of 1.6 meals per hour for each of them.

While watching these motmots carry cicadas to their nests, I was struck by the similarity of their broad heavy bills to those of Boat-billed Flycatchers, which also eat many cicadas in their season. Such bills appear well fitted to deal with these large hard-bodied insects. However, White-fronted Nunbirds, with bills of a quite different shape, also take many cicadas. Although in both years Racquets and Diskless gave many cicadas to their young, this was not true of other pairs of Broadbills. At the end of April, I spent nine hours watching the third nest, which then contained two blind nestlings with sprouting pinfeathers. They were fed thirty-nine times, at the rate of 2.2 times per hour for each nestling. Their meals included at least thirty-one insects, of which one was a dragonfly, one a damselfly, one a butterfly, one a beetle, and three were larvae. There were two spiders and six unrecognized items, but no cicadas. Nine meals were brought between 7:00 and 8:00 A.M., eight between 10:00 and 11:00.

At this nest, the parent with a complete tail brought food twenty-three times and the other, whose disks were lacking, fourteen times. At the first nest in 1967, we saw Racquets bring food twenty-five times and Diskless eighteen times; but if we exclude the morning of June 5, when Racquets brought food seven times and Diskless was not seen, each parent fed the nestlings eighteen times while we watched. During the first nine hours of May 23, 1968, Racquets brought food nineteen times, Diskless twenty-three times, to the three nestlings who were about to leave. Thus the two sexes take nearly equal shares in feeding the young.

Arriving with food for their nestlings, the parent motmots usually alighted on a branch in front of the burrow and uttered low throaty notes while twitching their tails sideways. Sometimes they beat against their perch the insect that they held conspicuously in their bills, nearly always with its wings still attached; but, as a rule, such preparation as the food received was done before they came into view. After more or less delay, with perhaps an advance to an intermediate perch, the parent darted into the burrow. Soon it shot out headfirst and flew away. When the nestlings were eight or nine days old, however, the parents began to emerge tailfirst, after a visit lasting only a few seconds. Evidently the nestlings were now advancing part of the way up the tunnel to take their food, making it superfluous for the parents to go inward as far as the chamber,

where alone they could comfortably turn around. During the second half of the nestling period, the young motmots trilled and purred when the parents came to feed them. On their last day or so in the burrow, they stood visibly in its mouth to take their meals, which they did the moment a parent alighted in front of them, to leave an instant later. Now the adults did not enter the burrow at all.

We did not see the parents carry any waste from the burrow. After they ceased to go in far enough to turn around when delivering meals, they probably never entered the brood chamber to clean it. Soon the filthy floor swarmed with white maggots, which probably helped break down the waste. Even before they were feathered, the nestlings, standing on their heels, could hold their bodies out of contact with the floor, so that they emerged in clean, fresh plumage.

The first arrival of Diskless with food for the feathered nestlings in the second burrow, in the dim light at 5:10 A.M. on May 23, set off a chorus of loud, clear trills and duller churrs, mixed with the full, soft, mellow notes already mentioned. For the next hour, the trilling and churring in the burrow continued with little interruption, finally to die away as the nestlings' hunger was satisfied. Throughout the day, the approach of a parent with food usually released a fresh outburst of churring, purring, or trilling, which varied in intensity and duration with the young motmots' appetites. As we could see when one stood in the burrow's mouth, their throats swelled out strongly as they produced these sounds.

The full mellow notes, heard increasingly as the day advanced, were most surprising. Usually they were delivered in pairs, sometimes three together. Even those of the same pair might differ in pitch and tone, so that they sometimes reminded me of the Chestnut-backed Antbird's plaintive whistles, sometimes of the Black-throated Trogon's subdued *cow cow cow*. We were often to hear these soft notes from young who had left the burrow.

As the hours passed, the nestlings, after receiving food from their parents, delayed more and more in the entrance, looking out. After receiving a cicada at 2:03 P.M., the young motmot who had been resting in the doorway with its foreparts exposed took wing. It flew about 60 feet (18 meters) on a slightly descending course, to alight in the thick crotch of a riverside tree. The parent who had just fed it escorted it closely on this first flight. Resting in the fork, the fledgling preened its fresh plumage, which resembled that of the adults, except that its tail was very short and it lacked the black patches on face and foreneck. Another nestling promptly stationed itself in the burrow's mouth.

After three more meals had been delivered to the young in the burrow, another flew out, at 3:45, two minutes after it was fed. It appeared to leave spontaneously rather than in obedience to any parental urging. Flying obliquely upward for about 20 feet (6 meters), it tried to alight on the tip of a palm frond; but, finding itself unable to cling there, it reversed its course and descended to the ground at the edge of the bank, just above its burrow. After remaining there for a quarter of an hour, it flew back into the forest beyond my view.

The nestling still in the burrow continued from time to time to give the mellow call, and often it was answered by the one who had emerged first. During the last hour of the day, this chick received six meals, all from Racquets. Diskless, who alone had been present when the first young departed, was evidently giving all her attention to the fledglings in the open; we saw little of her.

After the departure of the second fledgling, the parents apparently divided the brood be-

tween them, as do many other birds. The next morning Racquets started to feed the nestling in the burrow at 5:20. By 6:30 this young motmot had received five winged insects and one larva. When the seventh meal was offered, the satiated nestling refused it. For ten minutes, Racquets continued to hold this insect, instead of taking it to one of the fledglings whose trogonlike calls sounded plainly among the neighboring trees. Finally, he swallowed what he had been holding and flew away. By 7:00, when I left, Diskless had not been seen. She seemed to be wholly occupied with the two fledglings, as Racquets was with the one still in the burrow.

By noon of that day the last young motmot had flown, leaving a dying cicada in the tunnel. The young had remained in the burrow for twenty-four or twenty-five days, a short nestling period for a motmot. During the day after the young Broadbills flew, their soft calls sounded at intervals from the forest behind the burrow, where they perched so inconspicuously amid the foliage that I succeeded in glimpsing only one, who swung its short tail from side to side, just as the adults did with their long tails. It was alert and flew off as I approached. After two or three days in the open, the young motmots became much quieter, and I rarely heard the soft calls which revealed that they were still nearby.

The stick that I set upright in the burrow's entrance after the last young Broadbill flew testified that it was not entered during the following week. As far as I know, none of the lowland motmots uses its burrow as a dormitory.

25. Rufous Motmot

Baryphthengus martii

In coloration, the Rufous Motmot closely resembles the Broad-billed Motmot, but it is much bigger, from 17 to 20 inches (43 to 50 centimeters) long instead of 12 or 13 inches (30 or 33 centimeters). Well over half the length of this largest of motmots—sometimes called the Great Rufous Motmot—is occupied by its racquet-tipped tail. These two so similar species live together in rain forests from Nicaragua to western Ecuador and western Amazonia. (I follow Wetmore 1968 in regarding the form of eastern Brazil, Paraguay, and northwestern Argentina, with racquetless tails, as a distinct species, *B. ruficapillus*.) Since to judge the size of a bird perching high in a tree is often difficult, the two motmots may be hard to identify when silent but are readily distinguished by their voices. Like the Broad-billed, the Rufous prefers warm lowland forests and has rarely been found as high as 4,000 feet (1,200 meters) in Panama (Wetmore 1968).

From the tall wet forests where they dwell, Rufous Motmots sometimes venture into adjoining shady plantations, such as those of cacao and bananas, to hunt for food. In the forests they seem generally to remain high, where when silent they escape detection, but they often forage in the undergrowth, especially when accompanying army ants. Mostly they are found alone or in pairs; but at La Selva in northeastern Costa Rica, where they were abundant, thirteen gathered before sunrise on a morning in late April in a fringe of forest between the house and the river. They were highly excited, moved around and called much, but were not seen to fight. One held in its bill something green that was apparently a fragment of leaf, reminding me of the similar puzzling habit of Blue-diademed Motmots in their courtship gatherings. One of these thirteen Rufous Motmots lacked racquets on its tail. To see so many of these handsome birds together was a memorable experience.

The Rufous Motmot's diet is varied, including large quantities of both vegetable and animal foods. On Barro Colorado Island, Chapman (1929) watched them eating the yellow plum-sized fruits of the Nutmeg tree, which they plucked while fluttering—although, as he remarked, there seemed to be no reason why these birds with fairly strong feet and bills should not detach the fruits while perching near them. At La Selva, I watched a Rufous Motmot gather, while perching, a number of the little orange fruits of a small palm. To their nestlings they carried fruits of various sizes, as well as white objects that appeared to be seeds of *Inga* or *Protium* species, enclosed in soft, sweetish white coats. They eat many insects, which they catch in the usual way of motmots: perching motionless until they sight their victim, then swiftly seizing it by a sudden sally. When foraging with army ants, as they frequently do, these motmots commonly perch somewhat more than head-high and pluck fugitive insects and other small creatures chiefly from foliage and trunks, but occasionally they descend briefly to the ground to capture them. Once, in a cacao plantation, I saw a motmot pick a large, pale red, cylindrical millipede from among fallen leaves. Still standing on the ground, the bird beat its prey until it broke, then swallowed it piecemeal. According to Wetmore, this motmot eats caterpillars, wasps, beetles, large orthoptera, spiders, lizards, small fishes, small crabs, and large scorpions, as well as fruits.

In the wet Caribbean forests of southern
Central America, the hollow hooting of
Rufous Motmots, starting soon after the
Broadbills' lusterless croaking, is one of the
characteristic dawn sounds. Until they have
been traced to their source—which may take
a long time—the deep, soft, scarcely birdlike
notes create an atmosphere of unfathomable
mystery. It is easy to imagine that the ghosts
of vanished aborigines are calling to each
other through the dripping woodland. The
notes come in pairs or triplets—*hoo hoo* or
hoo hoo hoo—or sometimes four or more
come together, often with strong contrasts in
pitch. One morning I heard three low *hoo*'s
followed by three higher ones, then three distinctly lower. This series of nine notes was
repeated several times; but in the feeble
dawn light I could not learn whether a single
motmot was hooting or whether a male and
a female were calling antiphonally, with
voices differing in pitch. On another morning, while standing near a nest in the earliest
dawn, I listened to two motmots, on opposite
sides of me, calling alternately with phrases
of two notes. I took this to be a mated pair
answering each other: *hoo hoo—hoo hoo—
hoo hoo* . . . If so, there was little difference
in the voices of the two sexes. But soon a
third Rufous Motmot, farther to my left,
joined in with similar notes and complicated
the situation, so that I could reach no definite
conclusion.

Nesting
While I watched the nest of the Broad-billed
Motmots on the wooded bluff above the Río
Puerto Viejo at La Selva, a pair of Rufous
Motmots carrying food betrayed the location
of a nest which otherwise I would never have
found. About 50 feet (15 meters) from the
Broadbill's burrow was a small opening in
the canopy made by the fall of a tree. Amid
the clutter of trunks and branches below this
opening was a cavelike den or burrow,
which seemed to have been dug by some
middle-sized mammal. This cavity in the
steeply sloping ground was roughly semicir-
cular, about 1 yard (90 centimeters) wide
and high; but the entrance was too narrow to
admit my shoulders, and access to it was

impeded by a large log lying in front. Illumination of the den by flashlight failed to dis-
close just where the nest was. Probably the
nestlings rested at the end of a long tunnel
which the motmots had dug, starting from
the side of the little cave. Blue-diademed
Motmots often choose similar situations for
their burrows, making them exceedingly difficult to find.

Early in the morning of May 16, these
Rufous Motmots were carrying fruits and
white arillate seeds into the cave, but later in
the day they chiefly brought well-mangled insects and other small invertebrates, always
one at a time, held in the tips of their serrated bills. To enter the den, they alighted on
the mound of excavated earth in front and
hopped down the declivity until they vanished underground. Soon they came hopping
up the mound, from the top of which they
took wing. These motmots and the Broadbills
nesting nearby never seemed to notice one
another.

On the morning of May 20, a Rufous Motmot carried a white seed into the den, only to
emerge after a short interval still holding it.
Then the bird swallowed the seed and flew
away. Perhaps the young had just flown, but
I could not find them in the vicinity. Could
they have succumbed—possibly drowned—
during the heavy rains two days earlier?

My conjecture that some mishap had befallen the nestlings was strengthened when,
on June 6, the parents were discovered preparing to nest again in the same den, for
motmots are not known to rear two broods in
a season. The two sexes alternated in the task
of digging a new tunnel from the side of the
den or lengthening the old one—I could not
tell which. Arriving with clean bills, they
perched side by side on a low horizontal
branch in front of the cave, into which one
presently vanished. While it was underground, the mate on the branch tirelessly repeated a low *coot* at measured intervals.
After a quarter of an hour, the digger reappeared, its black bill caked with brown
earth. While they rested close together between spells of work, both kept up this
sound, as I could assure myself by watching
their throats swell slightly as each note was

uttered, with closed bill. The muddy-billed bird returned for another spell of work. After it emerged, the partner with a clean bill went underground, to reappear seven minutes later with its bill muddy, too. Then the first motmot went in for another turn of digging. While waiting in front of the den, the motmots preened their lovely plumage with clay-encrusted bills, which seemed to me a foolish thing to do. After about forty minutes, one of the pair flew away, and its mate soon followed. Neither would work unless the other were nearby.

These motmots worked at various times from late morning to early afternoon. As they descended into the cave from the mound of excavated earth in front, they kicked the loose soil backward with alternate strokes of their feet, as all motmots do when they enter a burrow that they are digging. Doubtless, they continued this activity after they passed from view, thus gradually shifting outward the earth that they removed from their tunnel and preventing the cave from filling up. Sometimes, too, a motmot emerged from a spell of work with a lump of clay in its bill, to drop it after perching. Probably only a

minor portion of the excavated earth was removed in this second manner.

We did not remain at La Selva to learn the outcome of this second nesting of the Rufous Motmots in 1967. In May of the following year, they were again incubating somewhere in the side of the same den in the bluff above the Río Puerto Viejo. Again they were close neighbors of the Broad-billed Motmots; but, whereas in the former year their eggs had hatched more than two weeks earlier than those of the Broadbills, this year they hatched a whole month later. A few observations indicated that the incubation pattern of the Rufous Motmots was the same as that of Broadbilled and Blue-diademed motmots. One partner left the burrow at daybreak and the other entered soon after, to remain until the middle of the day. A changeover occurred in the early afternoon. Apparently, the parent then entering remained uninterruptedly until the following dawn; but, since the gaping mouth of the cave gave doubtful value to the use of sentinel sticks to indicate whether a bird had passed in or out, I did not prove this. By June 1, these motmots were feeding nestlings in the cave.

26. Blue-diademed Motmot

Momotus momota

The most widespread, adaptable, and familiar of the motmots is a handsome bird about 16 inches (40 centimeters) long. Its black crown is encircled with blue, as by a diadem that is widest on the forehead. A black mask, narrowly bordered below with turquoise, crosses its cheeks from the base of its bill to its ears. Its back, rump, and upper tail

coverts are, according to the race and the individual, varying soft shades of green. The wings are brighter green, with bluish green or blue primaries. The two central tail feathers, much longer than the others, greenish basally and bluer toward the ends, have short lengths of naked shaft, like slender stalks, that support spatulate expanded tips,

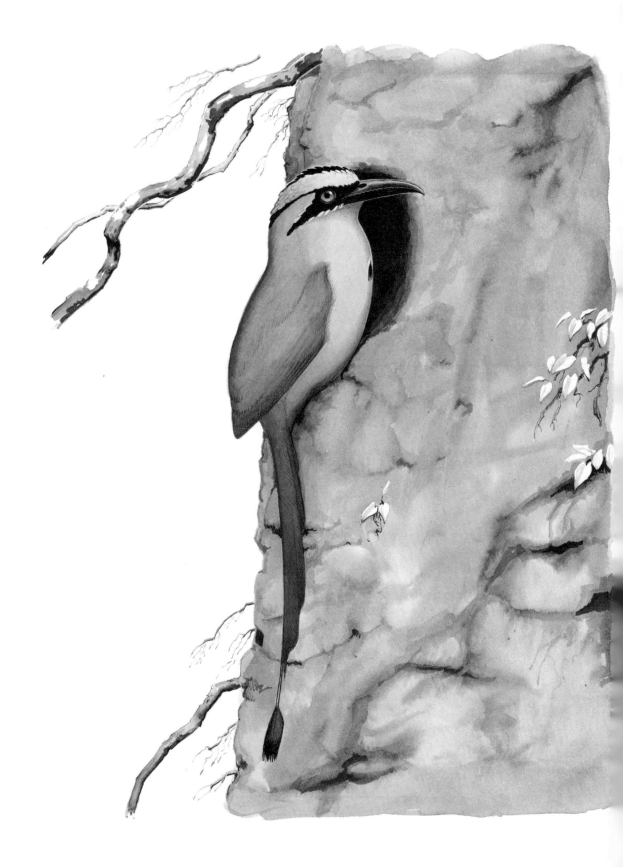

blue with black ends. The throat of some races is light bluish green. The foreneck and chest vary, on different individuals, from light olive-green to tawny and rufous, which color becomes paler on the abdomen. The center of the chest bears a small but conspicuous patch of black, edged with blue. The motmot's black bill is broad and heavy, with coarse serrations along the edge of the upper mandible in its middle half. The large eyes are dull red, and the short legs and feet are gray. Only the northernmost race of this motmot, confined to northeastern and central Mexico, has a wholly blue crown. It is unfortunate that the name Blue-crowned Motmot has been applied to the whole species, of which far more widespread, more often illustrated races have prominent black crowns.

The Blue-diademed Motmot ranges from northeastern Mexico to northwestern Peru, Bolivia, northern Argentina, and Trinidad and Tobago. From the lowlands it extends, in various parts of this wide range, up to 4,000 or 5,000 feet (1,200 or 1,500 meters), and in Costa Rica I have found it sparingly as high as 7,000 feet (2,150 meters). It inhabits not only very rainy regions but also some with a long and severe dry season, such as the Pacific coast of Middle America north of the Gulf of Nicoya. However, I did not find it in the more severely arid middle stretch of the Motagua Valley, where Turquoise-browed and Russet-crowned motmots abounded among cacti and thorny scrub. In northern Honduras, where Turquoise-browed Motmots were numerous in the second-growth thickets of the Lancetilla Valley, the Blue-diademed was largely confined to the tall rain forest on the hills. At La Selva, where I studied the abundant Rufous and Broad-billed motmots, I did not find this species, which is rare or absent over much of the Caribbean lowlands of Costa Rica. In the central highlands and the southern Pacific slope of this country it is common, inhabiting coffee plantations with low shade trees, light secondary woods, thickets, hedgerows, shady gardens and pastures, wooded ravines, and the remaining stands of ancient forest, especially their margins. Most surprisingly, this conspicuous bird manages to persist and

even to nest in populous suburbs, including those of San José, amid cats, dogs, and boys with rubber catapults—proof of its wariness and adaptability.

Blue-diademed Motmots often perch quietly in the shade, at no great height, scanning the ground, where they find much of their food. When in an excited or inquisitive mood, they swing their long racquet-tipped tails slowly from side to side or sometimes twitch them more rapidly sideward. Often a motmot holds its tail stiffly to the right or left. When more strongly excited, it may elevate its tail. To turn around on a perch, it lifts this member over the branch with a flourish, thereby avoiding abrasion. The motmot's flights are swift and direct but rarely long-continued; it passes from tree to tree like a flash of green and blue.

These motmots never flock but live in pairs at all seasons. During the day, the members of a pair often forage separately, and it is not always obvious that they are mated; but in the evening, as they go to roost, they associate more closely. In the central valley of Costa Rica in late October, I repeatedly saw a pair of motmots resting about 6 inches (15 centimeters) apart in a low tree near the edge of a small coffee plantation, into which they soon flew to pass the night; and one evening I noticed a second pair perching equally close together. (I have never seen them actually in contact.) I have often heard two motmots calling softly to each other, in the thickets where they roost, in the evening or the morning twilight. The fact that in the fall the motmots dig the burrows in which they will nest in the following spring is additional evidence that they are mated through most, if not all, of the year. Neither when they are competing for a mate, nor on any other occasion, have I ever seen motmots of any species fight.

I have investigated the possibility that Blue-diademed Motmots sleep in these burrows which they excavate long before the nesting season, as Blue-throated Green Motmots do, but always with negative results. Although they are so elusive and retire into such dense vegetation that I have never succeeded in glimpsing them on their roosts, all the evidence points to the conclusion that these birds sleep amid foliage. In the Valley of El General, I have heard their calls issuing at nightfall, and again at daybreak, from dense thickets at the forest's edge. While I resided in the central valley, I often heard, at the first sign of day, the voices of a pair coming from the coffee plantation outside my window. I searched carefully for a burrow in which they might have slept but found none. Active in the twilight, motmots go to rest later than most birds.

Blue-diademed Motmots eat large amounts of both insects and fruits. In a shady pasture where dung beetles were active, I often saw a motmot perching on a low limb, intently watching the ground, to which it suddenly descended to capture one of these burly scavengers. Other insects that I have noticed in motmots' bills include large cicadas, phasmids or walkingsticks nearly as long as the motmot without its tail, large green orthoptera, and larvae of various kinds. Occasionally they capture spiders, small lizards, and snails, but rarely the large conspicuous butterflies that Turquoise-browed Motmots often eat. Sometimes a motmot stands on the ground and assiduously pushes fallen leaves aside with regular sweeps of its bill, alternately right and left, searching for an insect that it has spied, or perhaps dropped. The motmot beats its prey against a perch until it becomes quiescent, often until it is badly mangled, before it is swallowed or carried to young. Once I watched a motmot struggling with a large winged insect in forest shade. The bird picked up its victim, beat it against the ground, dropped it, and picked it up again, repeating this until the wings fell off.

Occasionally a motmot accompanies a swarm of army ants, along with a variety of smaller birds, to catch the insects, spiders, lizards, and other creatures that the ants drive from concealment in the ground litter and make readily available to the birds. I have most often seen motmots with army ants in the margins of the forest.

I have seen Blue-diademed Motmots eat the orange pulp of the Central American Rubber Tree; the green drupes, like small olives, of the Olivo; the fragrant white Rose Apple; the globose fruits of a wild ginger (*Renealmia exaltata*), filled with small arillate seeds; and the larger arillate seeds of *Dipterodendron elegans* and species of *Protium*. I have seen them fly up to bunches of fruits of the spiny Pejibaye palm, apparently to pluck off pieces of the hard flesh, of which many tanagers, woodpeckers, and other birds eat freely; and I have found the regurgitated seeds of other kinds of palms in their burrows. The motmots swallow whole the large seeds of trees of the nutmeg family, including *Compsoneura sprucei*, to digest the thin bright red aril that embraces the seed and cast up the latter intact. Occasionally I have found these motmots resting in pairs on a bare roadway in the twilight, apparently to pick up food, although possibly it was gravel that they sought. Blue-throated Green Motmots have a similar habit.

From time to time, a Blue-diademed Motmot eats pieces of banana on our feeder in front of the house, while tanagers, honeycreepers, finches, and thrushes stand aside, awaiting its departure. On the island of Tobago, where many birds appear to be much more fearless of humans than on the mainland, motmots enter buildings for food. "One bird in particular would regularly take a cherry from the palm of a guest. Furthermore, these birds would appear at the breakfast table of guests, perch on the back of a chair, or the table itself, and take bits of papaya and watermelon. A guest awoke one morning to find a motmot sitting on the bedrail waiting patiently for a breakfast snack" (Hundley and Mason 1965). At the Grafton Estate, I watched a motmot take cheese from a porch rail, close beside a delighted tourist. On Tobago the motmot also eats soaked bread (ffrench 1973).

The literature contains scattered references to Blue-diademed Motmots preying upon smaller birds, but it is not always clear whether this behavior was observed in free or caged motmots. I have never seen a motmot take eggs or nestlings, but one apparently tried to capture Variable Seedeater fledglings, who flew from their nest. The anxiety of parent birds of a number of small species when a motmot approaches makes me suspect that it is indeed a nest robber. Even large Garden Thrushes repeat their plaintive cries incessantly when a motmot comes in view of their nest. Nevertheless, this persecution of smaller birds appears to be infrequent. In the many years that I have lived among them, I have only once seen one of them with an avian victim: a small, mangled, apparently adult, unidentifiable gray bird that a parent motmot carried to its nest.

Blue-diademed Motmots dust bathe, often in twilight. One evening, as I hurried home along an unpaved road, I stopped to watch a motmot ahead of me. Lying flat in the road, it stirred up dust with its wings, raising little clouds that floated away in the light breeze. The motmot lowered its head until its bill rested flat against the road, stirring up more dust with it and at times seeming to swallow something, probably grit. Soon its mate flew out from a nearby thicket, alighted in the road close beside it, and dusted itself in the same fashion. Then, one by one, they flew into the coffee plantation on the other side of the road, evidently to roost. Although not often seen, dusting appears to be widespread among motmots. In Brazil, Mitchell (1957) watched a pair of Great Motmots "dust-bathing like a couple of old hens under a car-port." I have seen no record of any motmot bathing in water.

In Honduras, I transcribed as *kut kut* the deep, resonant, far-carrying call of the Blue-diademed Motmot. The corresponding note of the motmots here in southern Costa Rica seems to me softer, and I have generally written it as *coot coot*. This call, which mated birds use to answer each other, is frequently repeated in the dim light of dawn and again as the day fades; it is heard far less often while the light is strong. Sometimes, especially near their burrows, the motmots produce a low hollow sound, *whoo-whoo-hoot*, whispering and ghostly, such as may be crudely imitated by blowing across the mouth of a large empty bottle or, better, an aluminum canteen. When approaching their nests, the motmots may voice an even lower *whoo-whoo-o-o-o-o-o*, uttering these sounds with a distinctly undulatory or rippling effect, apparently to express caution or slight anx-

iety. When alarmed or when concerned for the safety of its offspring, the motmot gives voice to a dry nasal *wac wac* or to a clacking sound such as may be at least suggested by tapping sharply with a pencil upon a thin board of hardwood. Sometimes these wooden notes follow the ghostly *whoo-whoo-hoot*. A motmot perching several yards above a large Mica, a snake that preys insatiably upon the eggs and young of birds, protested with surprisingly loud, sharp, staccato barks or cackles—notes which seemed indicative of the highest pitch of alarm. When they detect smaller snakes, motmots complain with dry notes that sound like pebbles striking together. With keen-eyed motmots and equally vigilant Scarlet-rumped Tanagers to sound the alarm, few snakes can enter our garden undetected in daytime.

Early in February, the soft *coot coot* of Blue-diademed Motmots, repeated over and over, drew my attention to three of these birds perching close together in the top of a Guava tree behind our house. One held in its bill a green Guava leaf over 1 inch (2.5 centimeters) long. For several minutes, the trio rested motionless, except for abrupt sideward or up-and-down movements of their long tails. Presently they shifted positions, until two, including the holder of the leaf, sat close side by side, while the third perched a yard or so away from them. This bird now plucked a small dead twig, hardly larger than a matchstick, held it in its bill for a moment, then dropped it. The other motmots remained side by side for a number of minutes, the one with the leaf repeating a soft *coot* over and over. Meanwhile, the lone bird called *coot coot* again and again. Then the motmot who thus far had taken nothing in its bill moved to a neighboring twig and plucked a fragment of bark or dead leaf, which it promptly dropped. Soon after this, the three flew off through the trees, and the motmot with the green leaf carried it up to a high bough. One now vanished, but the other two followed each other from tree to tree, in each of which they rested for a while to call *coot* and *coot coot*. One seemed always to use the single and the other the double note, but I could not tell the sex of either.

From time to time in the following years, I again noticed motmots holding leaves or other inedible objects, sometimes moss or liverworts plucked from trees. Before sunrise in early September, I watched two motmots high in an *Inga* tree. One had in its bill a small piece of green leaf which it held for a good while. The other held a smaller object that I did not recognize. On an evening in early September of a later year, I was watching two motmots resting in a tree, when a third approached with some rather large dead leaves hanging limply from its bill. Soon all flew into a neighboring thicket, where I could not follow. These motmots carrying inedible objects seemed to be courting or pairing and, in some instances, to be trying to win a mate by disrupting an established pair. The dates of these episodes suggest that pairs are formed in autumn (when nest excavation begins) as well as early in the year. Nest material is sometimes held by courting birds of other families; but it is most surprising to find motmots doing so, for they make no use of such material but breed in burrows quite devoid of lining. Can we infer from this behavior that their remote ancestors built nests or lined their burrows? Or do the inedible objects substitute for the courtship feeding of the Turquoise-browed Motmot?

The Burrow

The nests of birds who breed in burrows are often easy to find, for the tunnels are dug in bare vertical banks where the opening is visible at a glance, as is true of some kinds of kingfishers and motmots. But, at least in Central America, the secretive Blue-diademed Motmots often choose far less obvious sites, so that their burrows are difficult to discover even when, by watching the birds, one learns their approximate location. Instead of beginning its tunnel in an exposed soil surface, this motmot prefers to start from the side of some pit or hollow in the ground, such as the den of a burrowing animal or a hole dug by man. The mouth of the burrow may then be invisible until the searcher peers into the larger excavation, which may be so dark that artificial illumination is needed to reveal the entrance. Five of the fourteen nests which I have discovered in over forty years were so situated; I passed by some of them repeatedly without ever suspecting their presence until I saw the parents nearby with food in their bills.

The first of these nests was found in Guatemala, at the foot of the Sierra de Merendón, beside the level valley of the Río Motagua. It was close by a burrow of the Rufous-tailed Jacamar that I had been watching. I had often seen the motmots in the vicinity and had walked over their burrow many times, before one of them revealed its presence by flying out of the earth. They were already bringing food, and I decided to open the chamber to see the nestlings.

The motmots had started their tunnel 6 inches (15 centimeters) below ground level, in the side of what appeared to be the old den of some burrowing animal, now nearly filled with loose earth and vegetable debris. When I inserted a vine into the motmots' shaft, it entered for a distance of 3 feet (90 centimeters). Measuring this distance back from the edge of the pit in the ground, I began to dig, expecting to make contact with the rear of the nest chamber. After much digging in hard stony soil penetrated by many roots, I broke into the burrow, but, to my surprise, I had struck the entrance shaft rather than the nest chamber. At this point the tunnel turned sharply about forty-five degrees to the left, and this bend had stopped the probe that I had used to measure the burrow's length. After uncovering the tunnel for 2 more feet (60 centimeters), I finally reached the chamber, where, by stretching my arm to its utmost limit, I managed to extract three nestlings, whose plumage was just expanding. The roof of their nursery was 29 inches (74 centimeters) below the surface of the hillside. The whole burrow, from its mouth to the back of the chamber, was 65 inches (165 centimeters) long. Although not the longest bird's burrow that I have opened, this was probably the most difficult for the birds to dig, because of the hardness of the soil and the many stones and roots that it contained.

After admiring the three nestlings, I re-

Blue-diademed Motmot: nestlings nearly ready to fly.

placed them in their deep chamber. Then I split a log to form a ceiling over the length of the tunnel that I had uncovered, and above the slabs of wood I filled in the earth to ground level. While I was engaged in these laborious operations, the parents made not the slightest protest, although they saw me at work. After my withdrawal, they continued to attend their young in the altered burrow, creeping beneath 2 feet (60 centimeters) of wooden planks each time they carried food to them. Without much doubt, they would have abandoned their nest if so great a change had been made before the eggs hatched.

I have not again tried to prepare a Blue-diademed Motmots' burrow so that I could study the incubation and nestling periods and follow the development of the young, because the risk of causing desertion appeared too great; but, some years ago, I dug out a burrow after the fledglings left. This was situated in level stony ground, in an open spot amid light second-growth woods, beside a cattle path. Like my first burrow, it led from the side of a hole or den which had apparently been dug by a mammal but was no longer used by it. The entrance of the motmots' tunnel was beneath overhanging sod, so that I could not see it until I lowered my head into the larger hole. This burrow, 86 inches (218 centimeters) in total length, was nearly straight except for a gentle bend to the left near the inner end. Apparently, the motmots would have made their burrow even longer if they had not encountered rocks, as I inferred from the presence of a short spur leading up between them. The top of the chamber was 12 inches (30 centimeters) beneath the surface of the ground; I could not learn its dimensions because its walls were destroyed by my digging. In the top of the entrance tunnel were two holes—apparently made when horses or cattle walked over the burrow and their hooves broke through—which communicated with the surface and admitted daylight.

An unexpected site of a motmot's burrow was in the vertical side of a pit about 5 feet (1.5 meters) deep, left by treasure hunters who had opened an old Indian grave. Vegetation draping over the pit's rim concealed the mouth of the burrow until I jumped down into the grave. Another burrow was begun in the great mass of clay that clung to the roots of a tall Campana tree that had been laid flat by a violent wind. What had been the lower side of this mass now formed a vertical wall about 8 feet (2.4 meters) high, and in the center of this uneven bulk of bare red clay the tunnel was begun, but it was never used for breeding.

Occasionally, perhaps only when a less obvious site is not available, Blue-diademed Motmots dig or acquire a tunnel in an exposed bank. Once I found a pair feeding nestlings in a bank only 2 feet (60 centimeters) high, situated at the top of a steep slope at the forest's edge. This burrow went in so far that I could not see its contents. Over an interval of fourteen years, a pair of motmots, possibly always the same individuals, have nested at least eight times in the high bank of the road cut into the hillside behind our house at Los Cusingos. Above the bank is a pasture with scattered trees; below the little-used roadway are tall second-growth woods which these motmots frequent. With one exception, these tunnels penetrated so far into the steep slope that to reach the nest chamber it would have been necessary to dig a deep pit; and they curved so much that I could not look into the chamber from in front. The exceptional burrow, so short and straight that I could see the chamber from the entrance, offered unusual advantages for study, as will presently be told.

As already mentioned, these motmots start to dig their burrows long before they will nest in them. In the Valley of El General they often begin toward the end of August or in early September and continue to excavate at a leisurely rate until the end of October or even past the middle of November. If they suffer setbacks and have to make fresh starts, as happened when men removed clay from the bank in which they were digging, they may work at their burrow well into December. I have never found them digging after December, when the dry season begins and the soil hardens. Apparently, if they lose a recently dug burrow early in the year, they do not hastily prepare a new one for their eggs but find an old one, perhaps made by some other kind of bird, which they may lengthen a little before they lay. Usually, however, these motmots dig a new burrow for each nesting, even when their burrow of the preceding season remains nearby, apparently intact. Contrary to my experience in Costa Rica, on the Yucatán Peninsula a banded pair occupied the same hole in successive years (Orejuela 1977).

The burrow for the 1963 nesting season was first noticed by me on September 1, 1962, when it was 4 inches (10 centimeters) long. After the motmots had been working at this tunnel for at least three weeks, I set, in the roadway 50 feet (15 meters) from its mouth, the same blind from which I had watched them incubate and attend their young the preceding year. Then, although obviously suspicious of the unobtrusive little brown tent, they had gone about their parental chores in front of it; now, doubtless because their motivation was much weaker, it upset them more. In the five days that I left the blind in view of the nest, they lengthened their tunnel only 1¾ inches (4.5 centimeters)—less than they sometimes did in a single day. Attempts to watch the birds at work always failed, doubtless because their sharp eyes detected mine through the narrow slit that I left open for observation. Indeed, they were so easily disturbed that even the twig, no larger than a matchstick, which I set in the burrow's mouth to tell me if they had entered deterred them from digging, though never from attending eggs or young. However, by frequently measuring the tunnel's length and by catching the earth that the birds removed, I learned that they worked chiefly in the late morning and early afternoon, between 9:00 A.M. and 1:00 P.M., rather than early in the morning, when many birds prefer to build their nests. Now, at the height of the wet season, heavy rain fell on most afternoons and often into the night. Mornings, although often cloudy, were seldom rainy, and frequently they were sunny. By delaying their work until late in the morning, the motmots gave yesterday afternoon's rain a few more hours to drain from the ground, thus they dug in soil as dry as they could find at this season.

In a few hours in the middle of the day, the motmots, working alternately, sometimes lengthened their shaft by 2 or even 2½ inches (5 or 6.4 centimeters). On most days, however, they accomplished less than this, and the tunnel grew very slowly. In the whole month of September, its length increased from 4 to 38 inches (10 to 97 centimeters), at the rate of slightly over 1 inch (2.5 centimeters) per day. It continued to be extended at about the same average rate through the following month, and on October 29 it was 70½ inches (179 centimeters) long. By November 9 it was 80 inches (203 centimeters) long, and after this it ceased to lengthen, although a little more earth was removed, doubtless in expanding the terminal chamber, during the next four days, after which work stopped. These motmots had devoted about two and a half months to digging their burrow. In the preceding year, 1961, when evidently they started somewhat later, they worked slightly harder and reached the final length of 80 inches (203 centimeters) by November 5. This pair of motmots dug at nearly the same time every year. In 1963, I first noticed their new burrow on August 30, when it was 5½ inches (14 centimeters) long. When completed about October 30, it was 75 inches (191 centimeters) long.

By preparing their burrow in the rainy season, far in advance of its use, the motmots gain two advantages. First, they find the soil soft and easily worked, although it is often muddy enough to cake on their bills, whereas if they excavated just before they lay their eggs in March or April they would, in many parts of their range, be obliged to dig in earth which had become dry and hard during the more or less severe dry season that

prevails in the early part of the year. Second, in the long interval between the excavation of their burrow and its occupancy, the loose soil, which at first lies conspicuously beneath the tunnel's mouth and draws attention to it (unless the tunnel is dug from the side of a pit or mammal's den), is compacted by rain and more or less covered by fallen leaves. When laying begins, the burrow already looks old and perhaps is less likely to arouse the interest of predators.

After the completion of their burrows late in the year, the motmots neglected them for months. Between November and March, a twig set upright in a tunnel's mouth remained upright for days together. From time to time it would be knocked over, but whether by a motmot, a Rough-winged Swallow prospecting for a nest site, or some other creature I could not tell. As has already been said, the motmots did not sleep in their burrows when not breeding. Finally, at one burrow at the beginning of March, the twig was more frequently upset. A few days later, a motmot spent the night in the burrow, and incubation began.

Of Blue-diademed Motmots of a different race in Trinidad, Belcher and Smooker (1936) wrote: "Excavation of the nesting-tunnels, which are usually in fairly high banks, but not more than a few feet above ground-level, begins long before the eggs are laid. Trial holes are made only to be abandoned. The tunnel with eggs may be from five to fourteen feet long, and not all in one line. Probably holes are used more than once, and excavated farther each time. May is the laying month . . ."

Like other motmots, the Blue-diademed lays its eggs on the earthen bottom of the nest chamber, for no lining is carried in. As incubation proceeds, the shards of beetles and other indigestible parts of insects, regurgitated by the parents, accumulate and are compacted into a hard floor.

The Eggs and Incubation

The nest that I opened in the Motagua Valley of Guatemala on May 17, 1932, held nestlings beginning to become feathered. The eggs from which they hatched had evidently been laid early in April. In the Valley of El General, one pair laid about March 8, and the latest brood flew from the burrow about May 17. Here eggs are laid chiefly in March and April, as the dry season passes into the wet season.

I have seen the contents of only two burrows, one of which held three nestlings and the other three white eggs. In Trinidad, Belcher and Smooker found two sets of three eggs, which they described as "broad, roundish ovals, of a pure glossy white, smooth and hard-shelled." The measurements of their six eggs averaged 33.4 by 27.4 millimeters. Farther north, in Mexico, Orejuela examined two sets of four eggs, one of five eggs, and one of three eggs.

Both sexes incubate. At the nest in the roadside bank behind our house in 1961, I studied the pattern of incubation throughout the last ten days before the eggs hatched. Each day I stood quietly beside the burrow, where the motmot could not see me until it was already outside, to watch it emerge in the dim early light. On a number of days I watched, from a blind, the other partner enter a little later, and on several days I witnessed the changeover soon after noon, likewise from concealment. During most of this ten-day interval, the sentinel sticks in the burrow's mouth remained undisturbed for hours continuously.

At this burrow, I could distinguish the partners. One of them had completely lost the racquet from one of its tail feathers and retained only a fragment of the other racquet, whereas both racquets of the other partner were still present, although badly frayed and disheveled. The latter sat throughout the night and was probably the female.

These two motmots replaced each other on the eggs according to a simple schedule, which reduced movement at the burrow to a minimum, at the price of very long and patient sittings. Like the Broad-billed Motmots, they relieved each other only twice each day. In the dim light of dawn, when other birds were beginning to sing, the motmot who slept in the burrow flew out silently, without warning. On ten mornings, its time of departure varied from 5:21 to 5:34. At the earliest, it was colorless in the dim light; at the latest, I could barely distinguish its colors. After an interval of thirteen to twenty-four minutes, at times ranging from 5:44 to 6:00, the mate entered the burrow, nearly always before sunrise. There it stayed continuously for the next seven hours or a little more, rarely less. On the three days when I determined most exactly the length of this morning session, it lasted for seven hours and ten minutes, seven hours and nine minutes, and seven hours and thirty-two minutes. On one day the motmot, who had entered before 5:53, left before noon. On other days it flew out at times ranging from 12:30 to 1:45, rarely later. The signal for its departure seemed usually to be the notes of its mate approaching through the woods in front of the burrow. Once, when I heard no call from the approaching motmot, it alighted on the bank about ten yards (9 meters) from the burrow, evidently to pick up food; a minute later its mate flew from the tunnel, perhaps having heard the wingbeats of its partner. After a careful survey of the surroundings, the newcomer entered in a few minutes, to stay with the eggs until the following dawn or for about sixteen hours.

Approaching their burrow, these motmots were extremely wary. I had set my blind 50 or 60 feet (15 or 18 meters) from its mouth, and I could not move it much nearer without upsetting them. Even after they had had several days to become accustomed to it, I could watch them only through a narrow slit; they became alarmed if I looked through a wider aperture. Only after the nestlings hatched could I open the window wide enough to accommodate my binocular without keeping the parents away. After they entered their burrow, the motmots invariably remained within when disturbed, even when I threw a beam of light on them and looked down the tunnel. If I happened to approach when one was near the mouth, preparing to leave, it would back deeper into the burrow instead of flying out, thereby reducing the probability of betraying the nest's position at the price of increasing the risk of being trapped by an enemy. One morning the motmot was about to leave just as I arrived at 5:23. When I surprised it at the burrow's mouth, it retreated backward and stayed inside thirteen minutes longer. What a contrast between the wariness of these motmots that manage to survive close to humanity and the confidence of Broad-billed Motmots in their wild forests!

In the following year, 1962, when the burrow of this pair (or their successors) went deep into the neighboring hillside, I did not see the eggs or watch long from a blind; but, by setting twigs in the doorway and visiting the nest often, I followed the course of events. A motmot first slept in the burrow on the night of March 7 to 8, and incubation evidently began about this time. After the first few days, the incubating pair followed much the same schedule as in the preceding year. On March 30, the twig was pushed over so often that I had no doubt that the parents were feeding nestlings, which hatched after about three weeks of incubation—a period which corresponds closely with that more accurately determined at nests of the Blue-throated Green Motmot.

The Nestlings

The exceptionally short burrow, so favorable for study, in the roadside bank behind our house was only 40 inches (102 centimeters) long, without a lateral curve but higher in the middle than at either end. This rise in the floor permitted me to see only the head of the incubating parent when I looked into the entrance with a flashlight. To see the eggs and newly hatched young, I needed to insert a mirror on the end of a stick and a small bulb attached by a cord to a flashlight. This burrow had been dug or at least enlarged by a pair of Buff-throated Automoluses in 1956, when they raised a brood in it, as they did again in the following year. Then for about four years no bird nested in it. When occupied by the automoluses, the burrow was only 29 inches (74 centimeters) long, and the entrance was considerably narrower than when I found the motmots using it. Whether the motmots themselves, or some other creature, added eleven inches (28 centimeters) to the burrow's length and widened the tunnel I do not know. The motmots took possession of it with the utmost secrecy. When, in March of 1961, I noticed that the old burrow had been

cleared of cobwebs and was being entered by a bird, I looked into it periodically, expecting that the automoluses had returned and would build a nest. Days passed, and no nest material was carried in; then, when I threw in the beam of my torch one morning, I saw at the far end of the burrow a motmot, already incubating three eggs.

In this short burrow, all three eggs hatched within twenty-four hours, and I first saw the nestlings when the parent left at dawn on April 16. They had downless pink skins and tightly closed eyes, as in other hatchling motmots. For the first four or five nights after they hatched, they were brooded by a parent, who continued its old habit of flying from the burrow at daybreak. Thereafter, although still quite naked, they passed the night alone. Diurnal brooding decreased very rapidly. On April 18, when just over two days old, the chicks were brooded for a total of about 116 minutes during the first five hours of the morning. One spell of brooding lasted at least 54 minutes, another at least 42 minutes. On April 23, the week-old nestlings, with sprouting pinfeathers, were not brooded at all in the first five hours of the morning. This early cessation of brooding reduces the risk that the parent will be captured along with its offspring by a predator that crawls into the mouth of the burrow.

I watched this burrow during the first five hours of the mornings of April 18, 23, and 29 as well as May 5 and 11. The number of meals that the parents brought in each hour is given in the accompanying table. Occa-. sionally, the nestlings did not accept food that was taken into the burrow, probably because they were not then hungry, and the parent emerged still holding it, to eat it in my presence or to carry it beyond my view. Thus, toward the end of the first hour on their nineteenth day, the nestlings refused three of the eleven items that were taken to them. But such refusals were exceptional. The rate of feeding steadily increased until the nestlings were nineteen days old and fairly well clothed in feathers; but, when they were twenty-five days old, they received fewer meals than when they were thirteen days old. Evidently their need for food de-

Feeding Frequency of Three Nestling Blue-diademed Motmots at Various Ages

Hour (A.M.)	2 Days	7 Days	13 Days	19 Days	25 Days
5:45 to 6:45	4	8	4	11	7
6:45 to 7:45	3	3	2	6	6
7:45 to 8:45	1	2	7	4	3
8:45 to 9:45	1	5	8	8	3
9:45 to 10:45	7	3	5	6	5
Total	16	21	26	35	24

creased after their feathers expanded. A similar decrease in the rate of feeding occurs in other birds with long nestling periods.

One parent seemed to bring food more often than the other. On the last four of the five mornings when I watched, I credited the parent with both racquets on its tail with bringing fifty-three meals, the parent with part of one racquet with forty-four meals; but on nine occasions the food bringer darted into the burrow without being identified. When the nestlings were nineteen days old, the parent with both racquets brought at least twenty meals, the other at least thirteen meals, and only two other meals were delivered. On the morning when the young were twenty-five days old, the parent with both racquets brought fourteen of the twenty-four meals that were delivered. This was the parent who took charge of the nest throughout the night. Each meal, as far as I saw, consisted of a single article.

The food given to the nestlings consisted largely of winged insects, which were often badly mangled, and caterpillars. Of the former, those which I recognized were chiefly beetles, with a few cicadas, dragonflies, and grasshoppers. When the young motmots were only two days old, a parent took into the burrow what appeared to be a dark-colored snake at least 6 inches (15 centimeters) long; since it was not brought out again, I assumed that a nestling had eaten this object much longer than itself. Other elongate objects taken to the young were flat and might have been slugs. When the nestlings

were a week old, a parent entered the burrow with a large white downy feather, apparently from a domestic chicken, but this was still in its bill when it emerged a few minutes later. When the nestlings were thirteen days old, they were given the only avian victim of a motmot that I have seen: the small gray bird already mentioned. Other animal food that I recognized in the parents' bills included a few spiders, a millipede, and a small lizard. At a Blue-diademed Motmots' nest in Guatemala, several lizards were given to the young.

Beginning when they were thirteen days old, the nestlings received, in increasing quantities, large seeds, each enclosed in a bright red aril rich in oil and starch, which I traced to a slender tree of *Compsoneura sprucei* that grew just within the edge of the forest, separated from the burrow by a pasture about 200 yards (180 meters) wide. In its sleevelike aril, the seed of this tree measures about 1⅛ by ⅞ inches (29 by 22 millimeters), which seemed to be a very large mouthful for a nestling. Even the adults appeared to open their bills as widely as they could to grasp a seed between the tips of their mandibles. Rarely, instead of bringing a whole seed, a parent came with a detached aril or a piece of one. When the nestlings were nineteen days old, eight of the thirty-five meals given to them in the course of the morning were these seeds or pieces of their red arils. These brilliant seeds were certainly not the nestlings' favorite food, for I frequently found one of them lying in the burrow in front of the young. Once a parent took in an insect and emerged with a red seed, which it had apparently picked up from the floor. It returned to the burrow with the seed, which was evidently accepted, for when the adult again flew out its bill was empty. Only the thin arils of these seeds were digested, the seeds themselves being regurgitated.

I never saw a parent remove waste or excreta from the burrow; yet, even after a month's occupancy by the nestlings, scarcely any odor emanated from its mouth. Although hard rains soaked the earth around the young while they were growing up, their fresh new plumage remained remarkably clean; but their bills and doubtless also their feet, which I could not see, became caked with mud.

Since I did not take these nestlings in hand, I could not follow their development closely. When they were five days old, I first noticed feather rudiments pushing through their pink downless skins. At thirteen days, they bristled with long pinfeathers. At sixteen days, the feathers began to escape these horny sheaths on their backs, shoulders, and heads. The expansion of the plumage was so rapid that three or four days later, at the age of about twenty days, the young motmots were well covered on all those parts of their bodies that I could see; but they remained in the burrow for another ten days.

Contrary to what one would expect in view of the parents' extreme caution in approaching the burrow, the nestlings who inhabited it were far from silent. When they were a week old, they made a rapid, low, throaty rattle or trill when I directed a beam of light upon them at dawn. At this time, one ran forward toward me, opening and closing its mouth with a grasping motion, as though to take food; but, before it had come halfway down the tunnel, it discovered its error and rejoined its siblings in the nest chamber. They did not again mistake me for a parent. After they were feathered, the nestlings frequently uttered a soft rippling *who-o-o-o*, which seemed to have developed from the trilling or purring sound they had made while they were younger. If I stood quietly to one side of the burrow's mouth, I sometimes heard sharp *wac*'s and other harsh notes, which suggested that the chicks might be squabbling.

On a nocturnal visit to the nest when the nestlings were a week old, I found, at the entrance to a hole in the bank about 2 feet (60 centimeters) from their burrow's mouth, a huge brown hairy spider of the kind reputed to kill birds and to bite horses and cows, causing great swellings that suppurate for days. I marveled that the spider had not already attacked the nestlings, who now slept alone, and I dispatched it to protect them and the horses in the adjoining pasture.

After the nestlings were well feathered, I could rarely see more than two when I looked into their burrow. The third seemed to be hidden behind them. On May 15, twenty-nine days after hatching, the two that I could see were farther back in the chamber, whence I inferred that one had left. These two were still present on the following day. At 6:00 on the morning of May 17, only one remained in the burrow, facing the rear wall instead of looking outward, as I had nearly always found the young motmots in the past. An hour later it was in the same position, but by 9:30 this last fledgling had flown. Two of the young had remained in the nest for thirty-one to thirty-two days, and apparently one had left at the age of twenty-nine to thirty days.

On the day of its exit, I found one of the young motmots in the road in front of the burrow. It was alert; as I came in view it flew into the neighboring thicket, where I saw the parents, one with food in its bill. These fledglings resembled their parents in plumage; but their eyes were brown instead of red, and their tails were very short. Neither the parents nor the young returned to sleep in the burrow, which is in accord with my earlier conclusion that the burrows are not used as dormitories.

In the following year, when the parents had begun to carry food into a different burrow by March 30, the last nestling did not leave until May 7, when it could not have been much less than thirty-eight days old. When I found it in the roadway opposite the burrow on May 7, it was wary and flapped

over the ground ahead of me until it reached the safety of the neighboring thicket, but it could not fly. Its plumage, especially on the top of its head and hindneck, was caked with mud, as was its bill; its short tail was frayed. This fledgling's retarded development, compared with that of the brood of the preceding year, may have been caused by the very wet weather, which kept the ground soaked during its last fortnight in the burrow. Possibly, also, food was scarcer in 1962 than in 1961.

Neither in these burrows nor in others

where the parents had apparently nested successfully was a second brood attempted. I am fairly certain that in El General Blue-diademed Motmots raise a single brood each year. After the young are fledged, the adults molt, dropping their badly worn tail feathers. Since it requires weeks for the long central rectrices to grow out and lose their vanes from the subterminal part where they are narrowest and loosely attached, at this season one rarely sees a motmot with racquet-tipped tail feathers.

27. Blue-throated Green Motmot
Aspatha gularis

The morning dawned dark and cheerless, with a strong west wind driving chilling mist across the Sierra de Tecpán in Guatemala, where the Mountain Trogons lived. I fled before the wind and clouds down a long, steep, south-facing slope through a close stand of oak trees, a coppice growth from stumps left at an earlier cutting, among which stood an occasional pine, alder, or Arbutus. The ground was thickly covered with oak leaves and pine needles, which rustled beneath my tread and made the descent excitingly slippery. Near the foot of the long slope I reached a region where the more open stand of trees permitted shrubs and herbs to flower. The sun shone from a blue sky, which appeared to be reflected by the pretty blue flower heads of a shrubby ageratum. On this leeward slope, wind and cloud-mist seemed remote.

A green bird shot across a clear space and vanished among the close-set branches of an oak tree. It retreated as I approached but finally remained stationary on a low perch, in full view. I was delighted with my find. The bird was about 10 inches (25 centimeters) long, clad in a beautiful soft shade of green, except for its pale buffy cheeks, black ear coverts, azure throat, yellowish under tail coverts, and the blue ends of its two long central tail feathers. Turning its big head toward me, it calmly returned my gaze with large brown eyes. The deliberate way it swung its tail from side to side, with an occasional abrupt jerk up and down, betrayed its affinity to the motmots; but the long central tail feathers were entire, without the racquet tips of all the members of this family that I already knew. When the bird about-faced on its perch, lifting its tail over the branch with a graceful flourish, I no longer doubted its classification, despite the untrimmed tail feathers. The broad heavy bill, hooked at the tip, with stiff bristles springing around its base, was added proof that my new bird was a motmot. After a few minutes it darted away, without having voiced a single note. I have used the neuter pronoun because I afterward learned that the sexes of the Blue-throated Green Motmot are alike. This small motmot is confined to the highlands of Chiapas, Guatemala, El Salvador, and Honduras, chiefly from 4,500 to 9,500 feet (1,370 to 2,900 meters) above sea level, rarely higher or lower.

The Burrows and Their Occupants

My first meeting with the green motmot occurred on my first visit to the Sierra de Tecpán in November 1930. When I returned early in 1933, I found a number of burrows in roadside banks. The absence of cobwebs in the tunnels, plus the freshness and sharpness of the two parallel grooves or ruts that ran along the bottom, left no doubt that they were used by birds; but I doubted that they contained eggs or young so early in the year. Aside from the Black-capped Swallows, whose tunnels would be marked by many fine scratches instead of deep furrows, the motmots were the only burrow-nesting birds that I had found on this high mountain; but my conjecture that the burrows belonged to them needed confirmation.

By setting sentinel twigs in a burrow's mouth, I learned that it was entered only at the day's end. Before sunset on the following evening, I hid among bushes on the opposite side of the road. After an hour, Whip-poor-wills began to call and the earliest fireflies to flash, but still no bird came to enter the tunnel. Just as I was about to end this fruitless watch, a form dimly seen flew out of the dusk, uttering a laughterlike call, and darted into the burrow. I did not see the vapory figure clearly enough to identify it. It was already too dark to write in my notebook, and most diurnal birds had fallen silent. Only the Rufous-collared Thrushes continued their twilight caroling from their roosts among the pine trees.

The next morning, long before dawn, I went out into the mist and cold drizzle to try again to solve the mystery of the burrows. Dawn had scarcely begun to augment the wan gray light that filtered through thin clouds from the waning moon, when an obscure form shot out, uttering the same queer note I had heard as it entered, and was immediately lost in the fog. Although this note was sharper, it resembled one of the Blue-diademed Motmot's calls enough to strengthen my belief that its author belonged to the same family. Before leaving, I reset my twig in the burrow's entrance. When I returned half an hour later, it had been pushed outward. Evidently a second bird had left the burrow.

The following morning, as dawn's earliest glow brightened the eastern sky, I waited quietly beside a different burrow. Before the brighter stars and waning moon had lost their brilliance in the growing daylight, low musical murmurs emerged from the bank beside me. A minute later, a long-tailed bird flew out, uttering a low throaty note which again faintly resembled the call of an excited Blue-diademed Motmot. After another minute, a second bird flew out and alighted in the road directly in front of the burrow. By taking a single step forward, I might have bent down and touched it or, at least, the spot where it stood. It was still too dark to distinguish colors, but the bird's graceful form was sharply outlined against the gray roadway. It must have lingered in this motionless attitude a full minute before it flew up. A moment later, a clear, mellow, almost soprano call sounded from among the oak trees.

By this time I was fairly certain that the roadside burrows belonged to the green motmots, but I needed a better view of the birds to dispel all doubt. It was useless to stand beside the burrows in the dawn—the occupants always emerged before the light was bright enough to reveal colors—so I decided to delay their departure until an hour more convenient to myself. Toward the night's end, I stopped the mouths of several burrows with handkerchiefs. I waited until it was quite light before removing the obstructions, then stepped aside to watch the birds emerge. At first, I only managed to alarm them, and they would not abandon their deep retreats while I waited. But my failures taught me what precautions I must take; and finally one morning, a few minutes after I had stealthily pulled the handkerchief from a tunnel, two Blue-throated Green Motmots darted out and were clearly seen. These, then, were the tenants of the baffling burrows.

On my rambles over the mountain, I had discovered more than a dozen similar burrows, chiefly in roadside banks among the forests of oak, alder, and pine between 8,000 and 9,000 feet (2,440 and 2,750 meters); but a few were in the sides of washouts on steep slopes. I decided to make a census and learn how many occupants each contained. After a few more unsatisfactory trials, I abandoned the attempt to count the motmots as they entered for the night. They never retired into their dormitories until the light had grown so dim that it was difficult to follow their swift movements. For a variety of reasons, it was not practicable to watch the majority of these burrows from a blind. Although it was difficult for me to see the birds in the dusk, their keener eyes always picked me out from my partial concealment amid shrubbery. They flew back and forth, hesitating to enter in my presence, sometimes fluttering before the doorway without going in, and confusing my count because I could not clearly see what they did. At times they flew away to pass the night elsewhere.

The best time to count the motmots was as they left their burrows in the dawn. On many a frosty morning of February and March, I arose before the east began to brighten, dressed hurriedly and warmly, and walked briskly through the cold air to watch at a distant burrow. At the earliest glow of dawn, I stationed myself in the roadway, a few feet to one side of the entrance, where the motmots could not see me until they were already outside the burrow. I soon discovered that, if I leaned against the bank, slight sounds or vibrations through the earth would warn the shy occupants that some animal was nearby, and they hesitated to come forth. Then, before the brightest stars had been

quenched by the flood of day, while the Rufous-collared Thrushes and Brown-backed Solitaires welcomed the dawn from the dark woods, the motmots' low musical murmurs emerged from the bank at my side. Sometimes they were repeated again and again; but usually, upon hearing them, I had not long to wait until a motmot—dim, shadowy, and colorless in the faint light—darted from the burrow so close beside me that I heard the rustle of its beating wings, crossed the road voicing low, rapidly repeated, guttural notes, and vanished among the bushes on the opposite side. Sometimes a second unsubstantial figure followed almost immediately; sometimes it delayed a few minutes before it joined the first in the thicket below the road. Then, from amid the dark foliage came a deliciously mellow piping, full, round, and clear, an undulatory sound that carried far across the dim woods and frost-whitened meadows. At times the first to emerge raised its clear voice while its mate delayed in the burrow, and the answer came as a liquid murmur from within the earth; but usually the earlier riser waited for its partner, and the two sang in unison to greet the newborn day with a single fluid harmony. When the two motmots were so far apart that I could distinguish their separate voices, I noticed that the tones of one, probably the male, were deeper and fuller than those of his mate.

This dawn song, which is rarely repeated during the hours of full daylight, and then almost exclusively in the mating season, is so clear and melodious that its author must be ranked with the tinamous as one of the most gifted vocalists among families which are not true songbirds. It is incomparably more musical than the call of any other motmot that I have heard. How different from the dull wooden *cawak cawak* of the lovely Turquoise-browed Motmot, or the deep lusterless *cwaa cwaa* of the Broad-billed Motmot, or the froglike *coot coot* of the Blue-diademed Motmot; how different again from the hollow *hoo hoo* with which the Rufous Motmot greets the day! In addition to the rapid, undulatory piping just described, the Blue-throated Green Motmot sometimes delivers a series of single liquid notes, which follow rapidly with rising inflection—an utterance no less pleasing than the other.

The green motmots' burrows were scattered along roadside banks, always close to woods and usually at least 50 yards (45 meters) apart. A 3-foot (90-centimeter) bank was high enough for a burrow if it was nearly vertical. Rarely, two occupied burrows were close together. At the top of a narrow washout on the slope of a deep ravine, covered with cypress trees, I found two burrows only 7 feet (2.1 meters) apart, which was exceptional. Of thirteen burrows that I visited at dawn in February and March, eleven were occupied by one pair in each. One burrow, from which a single motmot emerged, was found the next morning to be deserted, and so it remained throughout the year. Three motmots slept together in one of the closely spaced burrows in the washout, two in the other. At this season, the burrows were rarely if ever entered during the day, as my sentinel twigs always testified—the burrows were dormitories in which the motmots avoided the nocturnal chill of high mountains. Motmots of low altitudes, as far as I can learn, occupy their burrows only while they hatch their eggs and rear their young.

Among the oak forests below 9,000 feet (2,750 meters), I found seven pairs sleeping along a mile (1.6 kilometers) of winding mountain road, in burrows that were easy to find in bare earthen banks. Although this indicated a fairly dense population of green motmots, they were so elusive that I rarely saw one unless I watched at a burrow. I was told of an experienced bird collector who, a few years before my arrival, had worked for a month on the same property without finding a single individual, although the *pájaro verde* had been described to him and he searched for it. Basing my estimate on the number of nests of each species that I found, and allowing for the greater ease of discovering nests concentrated in banks instead of scattered throughout woodland, I concluded that the green motmot was no less abundant than the Mountain Trogon, which, while wandering over the mountain, I saw a score

of times for every once that I glimpsed a motmot. The trogon's red abdomen and foolish habit of flying with a noisy cackling when approached made it conspicuous, whereas the green motmot lurked so discreetly amid green foliage and stole so silently away that it was extremely difficult to detect.

Among the cypress forests near the summit of the Sierra de Tecpán, the motmots were less abundant. Indeed, I never suspected their presence until I found a burrow, and I never saw one of the birds except when I stood at the entrance of the burrow to watch its occupants emerge at daybreak. By searching the banks along several miles of logging roads, I found one more burrow. These two burrows were at an altitude of about 9,600 feet (2,925 meters), and a single pair of motmots slept in each.

As March advanced, I waited for the motmots to dig new burrows for their eggs. When they failed to do so, I decided to prepare the old ones, in order to time laying. I intended to use the method that I had found most successful at burrows of kingfishers and lowland motmots—this involved locating the end by probing with a flexible vine, then digging a hole that connected with the back of the brood chamber, which I closed with wood or a stone. But the green motmots' tunnels were often so tortuous that I could not even guess where they ended. Some made one or two sharp turns, which stopped the vine that I pushed in to measure their lengths. One burrow went straight into the bank for 22 inches (56 centimeters), turned ninety degrees to the right, and continued for 18 inches (46 centimeters) more. Then it turned abruptly more than ninety degrees to the left and extended 24 inches (60 centimeters) more to the end. To locate the end, I found it necessary to uncover much of the tunnel at the first bend, whence, by feeling with a stick and groping with my hands, I determined the approximate location of the sleeping chamber. Here I dug a second shaft which, fortunately, touched the side of the chamber. I roofed the uncovered part of the tunnel with pieces of wood, then filled in the earth, above which I spread leaves and other litter. The aperture in the side of the sleeping chamber, through which I intended to look inside from time to time, was closed with a stone, and the hole was filled and concealed in the same manner.

These twists and turns in the tunnels were apparently made when the motmots struck roots and stones which forced them to change the direction in which they dug. The end of another burrow, almost directly beneath a small oak tree, was even more troublesome to locate, requiring several attempts on different days, including the sinking of two shafts, before I finally reached it. Later, while trying to reach a third nest after the eggs had been laid, I erred in my calculations and dug directly into the top of the nest chamber, where, unfortunately, I broke a fresh egg. It was necessary to roof this chamber with a plank of oak wood before I could refill the hole. The remarkable outcome of my excavations and remodelings was that not one of the four burrows that I opened was deserted, undoubtedly because the owners had become strongly attached to them during the long months of occupancy. What a contrast with the kingfishers and motmots that I had studied in the lowlands, who nearly always abandoned their recently dug burrows if I made the slightest alteration before incubation was well advanced! Yet these lowland kingfishers and motmots were much less shy than the green motmot of the highlands, where the human population was denser and far from friendly to birds.

The four burrows that I prepared ranged from 56 to 70 inches (142 to 178 centimeters) in total length and were exceedingly diverse in shape. At the inner end, each widened into an oval chamber, with a low vaulted roof, in which the motmots slept and afterward reared their young. The chambers ranged from 10 to 14 inches in length and from 7½ to 8½ inches in width, and they were from 4 to 5 inches high in the center (25 to 36 by 19 to 22 by 10 to 13 centimeters). No bedding of any kind had been carried in; but the floor of each chamber was covered with a great mass of fragments of the indigestible parts of insects, especially beetles,

mixed with loose earth. These fragments, regurgitated by the motmots during many nights, revealed what they had eaten. The paucity of seeds showed that they ate few fruits. The volume of regurgitated shards and exoskeletons indicated that the burrows had been occupied for a long while, for below the loose debris they had consolidated to form a hard floor of considerable depth. Aside from these, the dormitories were clean, with no traces of excrement and little odor.

The Eggs and Incubation

I had now prepared four burrows into which I could peep whenever I wished. After each inspection of a chamber, I was careful to close with wood or stone the aperture I had made, then to fill in and tamp down the earth above it, and finally to conceal the whole with leaves and other litter. Largely as a result of these precautions, I did not lose a single egg or nestling (except the egg I broke while preparing a burrow for study).

All four female Blue-throated Green Motmots laid three white eggs during the first ten days of April, just after the last of the nocturnal frosts at this altitude. They were deposited on alternate days, at intervals of about forty-eight hours. The presence of eggs in the burrows did not change the sleeping habits of the tenants, who continued to enter in the late dusk and pass the nights in their customary chambers. Whether the eggs were incubated by night before the set was completed I had no way of learning, but by day I frequently found them warm; and sometimes, even in the late afternoon, a motmot flew out when I opened a chamber.

One afternoon, both motmots flew from a burrow, after I had been digging for many minutes above their heads. When finally I uncovered the opening I had made in the side of this chamber, I could feel two warm eggs within. The following afternoon, when there were still only two eggs, the attendant bird permitted itself to be touched with my fingertips. I prudently repressed a desire to lift it out for a closer acquaintance with one of these retiring birds; a better opportunity would come later. This motmot was unusually steadfast; all the others left their eggs before I could uncover the side entrances to their chambers.

The measurements of the eleven eggs in the four burrows averaged 28.8 by 22.8 millimeters, with extremes of 27.8 to 30.6 by 21.8 to 23.8 millimeters. These eggs were almost equally blunt at the two ends and scarcely ovate. The pure white shells had little gloss.

During the whole period of incubation, both parents continued to sleep in the burrow at night. I regretted that I could not learn whether one or both warmed the eggs. They continued their old habit of emerging at the first light, at about half past five. Now I failed to hear the soft murmurs that had preluded their departure during the colder months; the motmots were either silent or uttered only one or two low notes. The exits of the two parents were sometimes separated by only a minute or two, sometimes by as much as ten. After emerging, they continued to duet in their soft melodious voices, but no more, and often less, than on the frosty mornings of February and March. Although not more inclined to sing, they called much more, especially before sunrise, when each member of the pair sounded its flutelike monosyllable over and over at intervals of a few seconds, answering each other from various parts of the wood. While they breakfasted, their eggs remained fairly warm for half an hour or more in the snug niche in the dry earth. While both parents were absent, I opened the burrows to see whether the eggs were hatching.

This much I was able to learn by standing beside the burrows in the dawn, as I had done for the past two months; but to discover how the green motmots arranged their turns on the nest during the remainder of the day it was necessary to use a blind. The motmots were so wary that the presence of my wigwam of brown cloth, 25 or 30 feet (7.6 or 9 meters) from the burrows, would keep them away if the blind itself were not at least partly screened by the abundant Raijón bushes. By spending the better part of three days in my tent, and by using green twig sentinels at other burrows as subsidiary evidence, this is what I learned.

After both parents flew from the burrow at dawn, the eggs were left unattended for from three-quarters of an hour to an hour. Then, usually between 6:15 and 6:30, one partner (whom, to my regret, I can only designate as A, since I do not know its sex) reentered the burrow. Here it remained, warming the eggs, until about 10:00 or 10:30, roughly four hours. Then the other (B) returned, relieved A, and sat for about four hours longer, until, between 2:00 and 3:00 in the afternoon, A returned for another spell of incubation. At about 6:00 in the evening, the latter flew from the burrow, leaving the eggs unattended while it went for supper. In about half an hour, one member of the pair (now impossible to tell whether A or B) returned to the nest; and, when the evening twilight had become very dim, its mate joined it for the night.

These were the approximate times that I found at one burrow; but I noticed considerable variation in the hours of changeovers of different pairs, although I believe that the general pattern of incubation was the same for all. On the first day that I watched from a blind, when I did not know that it would be so objectionable to the motmots, one remained with the eggs, faithfully awaiting its long-delayed relief, for more than seven hours and probably for a full nine, from some time before nine o'clock in the morning (when I began to watch) until after four in the afternoon (when I removed the offending blind). This, however, was a session exceptionally long, caused by exceptional circumstances. On another day, this same motmot sat for six hours, as I learned by setting a twig in the entrance without delaying relief by my presence. Sometimes, especially at the start of incubation, I found the eggs cold as early as half past four or five o'clock in the afternoon, indicating that the motmot who had been in charge of the nest had gone early for supper.

Sometimes the bird arriving to relieve its mate flew directly into the burrow, without any warning except the whir of approaching wings, and the partner who had been sitting darted out a minute later. At other times, the oncoming partner perched near the burrow and called with the peculiar low sound that I had often heard earlier in the season, as the motmots prepared to enter their burrows in the evening twilight. This call was so low that it was barely audible to me in the blind, but it did not fail to register on the keen ears of the mate in the burrow, who promptly yielded the eggs to the newcomer.

Although in the lowlands I had repeatedly tried to learn the incubation periods of kingfishers and motmots, the birds' readiness to desert if I altered their burrows before incubation began nearly always frustrated my efforts—except in the unusual case, already told, of the Amazon Kingfisher. I had better success with the green motmots, whose eggs in the four burrows hatched twenty-one or twenty-two days after the last in each set had been laid. In two of the burrows, all the eggs hatched within twenty-four hours; in each of the other burrows the first two nestlings were born on the same day, the third on the following day. Yet in each nest the first egg had been laid five days before the last, and in this interval the parents not only passed every night in the burrow but were sometimes found within during the day as well. It appears that during the period of laying they did not incubate the eggs by night but slept beside them.

The Nestlings

For three or four days the motmot chicks pressed upon the white shells that enclosed them, before they made a gap that extended most of the way around the egg and could push off the large end and wriggle out. The pink-skinned hatchlings bore no trace of feathers. Their eyes were represented by a prominent black lump on each side of the head. Before they were a day old, they could stand erect on each full foot, with the swollen abdomen as the third point of the tripod, and even walk a trifle in a halting, tottering fashion. The empty shells from which they had escaped promptly disappeared from the burrows.

On the day when the nestlings hatched, their parents' devotion reached its highest, most ardent pitch; and they remained covering their infants throughout all the noise of

opening the burrows. I reached into a dark chamber and took hold of the guardian bird—mother or father, I could not tell which—who struggled ever so gently to escape. Slowly and carefully, I drew it forth into the light and beheld a creature whose feathers were as fair to the eye as I had already found them soft to the touch—and I have never placed hands upon a bird with softer, finer, looser plumage than these motmots. Silently, resignedly, the parent looked up at me with large deep brown eyes, as soft in cast as its plumage was soft in texture. When I placed it on its back for a few seconds, it seemed to fall into a waking sleep and lay quite passive in my hand, as other birds do when similarly held. After I had replaced the nestlings, I lowered the parent carefully over them, where it remained while I closed the hole, packed the earth upon it, and went away.

From only one of the four burrows did the parent motmot fly out while I opened the chamber on the day the eggs hatched. But, after the nestlings were two days old, the parents invariably retreated into an inaccessible part of the tunnel or else flew out and away, before I could uncover the aperture in the side of the chamber and reach in. Only once while it incubated the eggs had I been permitted to touch a motmot on the nest.

The pinfeathers of nestling kingfishers and motmots usually grow long and conspicuous before the horny sheaths start to ravel off and release the enclosed feathers. The feathering of the green motmots was quite different. At the age of ten days, when Turquoise-browed and Blue-diademed motmots bristle with long horny pins and bear no trace of downy feathers, the Blue-throated Green Motmots were nearly covered with long, soft, ample down. Their backs were almost hidden beneath abundant dark gray down, while the down on their sides and flanks was more or less tawny. These downy feathers sprang from certain limited regions of the body; but the long soft filaments billowed over and concealed the bare skin of the extensive featherless regions, so that the nestlings already appeared fully and warmly clad. This difference in the feathering of the Blue-throated Greens and their lowland cousins corresponded to their different needs. The former, resident in cold highlands, required early protection, so that their parents could cease to brood them by day and devote more time to finding their food; the latter, in their burrows in warm lowland soil, had no immediate need of feathers. The earlier appearance of downy feathers on the green motmots was not an indication of a generally more rapid development; on the contrary, they matured more slowly than Turquoise-browed Motmots and remained in their burrows several days longer. We noticed a similar acceleration in the feathering of the Resplendent Quetzal in relation to lowland trogons.

The nestling green motmots were twelve days old before their eyelids began to separate. Since sight could be of little use in their dark burrows and, moreover, particles of the earthen ceiling might fall into their eyes, this lengthened sightlessness was advantageous. The flight feathers did not begin to shed their long sheaths until the nestlings were sixteen days old. At this age they could hardly perch but walked clumsily about, supporting themselves upon the whole foot, the heel of which was protected by a prominent thick callosity, smooth like that of jacamars rather than roughened with tubercles or little spikes, as on kingfishers, toucans, trogons, and woodpeckers. Whenever I opened a burrow to examine the nestlings, they were at first silent; but, if I waited quietly for a minute or two, they started to call and trill in soft pleasant voices.

Both parents brought food to the nestlings, chiefly big hairless caterpillars and other insect larvae, with an admixture of winged insects. On the morning when the three nestlings in my second burrow were fifteen days old, they were fed nineteen times in four hours. Exceedingly cautious in approaching the nest, the parents alighted low in the Raijón bushes across the road, whence they carefully surveyed their surroundings from comparative concealment. Assured that they were safe, they flew rapidly across the road and into the burrow, silently or with a queer little throaty sound. The food delivered, they shot forth headfirst from the burrow, one to five minutes later.

Like other motmots and most birds that nest underground, the parents never made any demonstration or feint of attack when I removed their nestlings from the burrow, and they never tried to lure me away. They remained at a safe distance, either silent or repeating low throaty notes.

By night, both parents continued to sleep in the burrow with their young, even after the latter were well feathered and seemed too big to be brooded. A habit of such long duration was not easily broken. Both emerged at daybreak, as they had long done. During the nestlings' final ten days in the burrows, however, some adults changed their routine. The pair with only two nestlings continued to sleep with them as long as they remained underground. At another burrow, only a single parent stayed with the young during their last few nights in their nursery. A third pair behaved still differently. First one, then the other parent ceased to sleep in the burrow, leaving the nestlings alone during the last four nights before they flew.

Parents who slept in the open must have found the change from their snug underground quarters most uncomfortable, for the rainy season had by this time returned with full force and the nights were wet and cold. But the grown motmots who continued to sleep in their nests also had troubles. In the morning before they flew out, the nestlings made a terrible din, importuning to be fed with many loud trills and mellow-voiced calls, which might have been pleasant enough to hear if the young had not all clamored at once, with no attempt to keep time, in so confined a space. After continuing for many minutes, this din ended abruptly when the besieged parents fled into the open. They lost no time in bringing breakfast to their hungry offspring—sometimes they returned with insects in their bills before the light was strong enough to reveal their colors.

Meanwhile the nestlings, who when last glimpsed were clumsy little balls of gray down, scarcely able to see or to perch, had been rapidly acquiring plumage and strength. It was interesting to watch their transformation from gray to green. A bird may change its colors in several ways. The most usual is by molting, when the old feathers are shed, a few at a time, and replaced by new ones of different colors. Another method of transformation that is not uncommon is known as plumage wear; the dull tips that terminate the newly sprouted feathers gradually drop off, revealing brighter hues that were overlaid and concealed by them. The young motmots followed neither of these methods. They could ill afford to shed their warm gray down—they needed every plume of it to get through the ordeal that lay just ahead—so they retained it all but covered it with green feathers of subsequent growth.

Blue-throated Green Motmot: downy nestling eleven days old. Compare this with the photograph of the twelve- or thirteen-day-old Turquoise-browed Motmot.

Blue-throated Green Motmot: nestlings twenty-four days old.

While the development of certain feather rudiments was accelerated to give the naked hatchlings a protective garment of fluffy down, other feathers continued to grow more slowly. This was especially true of those along the very center of the back, which showed only their green tips when the marginal feathers of the same tract had become fluffy tufts of down. These green feathers continued slowly to grow out of their sheaths and, spreading sideward, pushed down and concealed their loose gray neighbors, which a short while before had been so prominent. Spreading still more broadly, the green feathers of the central row finally overlaid the gray down on the shoulders. Meanwhile the wings, which were gradually becoming green, hid the loose gray and tawny feathers of the sides and flanks. Blue feathers appeared on the throat, tawny ones on the cheeks, and black ones over the ears. When this process of overlaying and concealing the infantine down was completed, the young motmots, now about four weeks old, closely resembled their parents, except for their shorter wings and tails. They had gained a coat of green and lost nothing. They had lost even less than young passerine birds lose, for the natal down of the latter, pushed out on the tips of the body feathers, must drop off before the fledglings appear grown-up. (Compare this with the color transformation of the Resplendent Quetzal, as described previously.)

On the morning of June 3 I arose early, for I had a number of visits to make before daybreak. I climbed down a bushy slope to see whether a Pink-headed Warbler slept with her nestlings, then entered the heavy forest to peep into a Slate-throated Redstart's nest, and finally ended my journey beside a green motmots' burrow in the roadside bank a mile from my abode. As the cloud-mist that shrouded the mountain paled from black to gray, soft musical murmurs issued from the earth. Soon one of the parent motmots flew out, followed by its mate five minutes later. In the pine trees across the road the pair dueted briefly, in spite of the unpromising dawn. The sounds from within the burrow continued after their departure, for the last of the nestlings had not yet left. Soon its notes became louder and quite different in quality from any that I had heard from a young motmot who had not yet flown. They continued intermittently for many minutes, sounding as though they came from a point near the entrance; then the fledgling launched forth on its first flight. Its course was somewhat wavering; but it used its hitherto untried wings surprisingly well, rising steadily to a high branch of a pine tree down the slope. As it emerged from the burrow, one of its parents greeted it with loud excited calls. Its graduation from the nest marked also a turning point in my own activities, for it was the last to leave the burrow of the eleven young motmots over whose infancy and childhood I had watched. All flew from their nests when from twenty-nine to thirty-one days old.

The New Burrows and Their Tenants
Now I confidently looked forward to seeing the whole family reunited in their burrow in the evening, for the wet season was firmly established, and a cold rain fell almost every night. But predictions about the behavior of animals, feathered or otherwise, are hazardous. At the close of the night following the departure of the last young motmot, I again stood beside the burrow that it had left. As day broke, a single motmot silently flew out, not the four, parents and young, that I had expected to emerge. Two mornings later, both parents flew from this burrow, which they continued to occupy nightly until the year's end. Meanwhile, their fledglings were apparently left to weather the rainy and misty nights amid foliage.

Other pairs followed a different course. The parents who had left their nestlings quite alone during their final nights in the burrow never returned to it but apparently shared their offspring's fortunes in the open. After the young left the burrow in which a single parent had accompanied them during their last few nights in it, the other parent resumed sleeping there; and the united couple continued to occupy it until their new burrow was ready. Another pair of motmots, who also continued to sleep in the burrow after their fledglings left, abandoned it when, a few days later, a pair of Black-capped Swallows carried in leaves and pine needles for a nest.

Like kingfishers and jacamars, the Blue-throated Greens had failed to clean their burrows, which became foul during the long tenancy of the nestlings. Those who continued to lodge in the old burrows after the young departed awaited a favorable opportunity to dig new ones for themselves. At first, they were too busy feeding their fledglings to undertake this laborious task, and the weather was so continuously wet that the excavation of a burrow in the sodden ground would have been a most unpleasant undertaking. But, in the last week of June, a lull in the rains gave the motmots better conditions for digging new burrows. The soil was now right for working, neither wet and muddy nor dry and powdery, as it was toward the end of the long dry season when they started to breed. Most of the young birds had now been awing for a month and were doubtless able to find much food for themselves, relieving the parents of this burden and freeing them for the new undertaking. No young motmot came within my view while I watched a pair, parents of three, dig their burrow. Yet the excavation of new dormitories seemed to be a seasonal activity, not directly controlled by the circumstance that the young could now feed themselves. A pair whose offspring were still in the nest more than two weeks after most nestlings had flown dug their new home at the same time as all their neighbors.

The site chosen for the new burrow was usually in the same bank, close by the old. One pair started their new tunnel only 20 inches (50 centimeters) from the one they had occupied during the previous year; another pair dug their new home 28 feet (8.5 meters) from their old one. These were the extreme distances among the five pairs that I watched. One other pair, already mentioned, continued to occupy their old burrow, in which they had raised two nestlings, until at least the end of the year. The chamber at the end of this burrow was the one to which I had given a wooden ceiling, which was evidently not distasteful to the occupants.

At the beginning of July, I spent many hours in the blind, watching a pair of green motmots at work. Their plumage was worn and faded, for they had not yet replaced the feathers frayed by their arduous labors of the past three months. They had two periods of work daily: one in the morning, from about seven o'clock to about nine or ten, the other in the afternoon between three and six. As far as I saw, they worked longer and more steadily in the afternoon. The male and female shared the task, laboring in alternate shifts of from three to twelve minutes. They always arrived together, and one remained perching nearby while its mate dug. As with jacamars, puffbirds, kingfishers, and other motmots, I doubt that either partner would have entered the excavation to work unless the other were nearby to keep guard. Entering the tunnel, the motmot kicked vigorously backward, throwing out two parallel, intermittent jets of loose earth, which followed the digger inward, until they fell short of the entrance and finally disappeared in the darkness of the burrow. On leaving, the motmots never pushed or kicked the loose soil before them.

While one of the motmots worked inside, its mate, resting in nearby bushes, almost incessantly repeated a low soft monosyllable, and at intervals it swung its tail slowly from side to side. Usually the partner who had been waiting entered the burrow promptly after the other emerged, most often alighting in the road before rising to the mouth of the tunnel. Rarely, it became impatient and entered while the mate was still inside, but then one or the other always came out very quickly.

As soon as the new burrows were ready, their makers slept in them. No eggs were laid in them that year, for the motmots, like most of the birds on the Sierra de Tecpán, raised a single brood. They were used as dormitories only, and all were still occupied when I left the sierra early in the following January. The events in the motmots' lives from now onward were not so exciting as those that I had witnessed during the breeding season; but I continued to make occasional visits to each burrow in the dawn; and so, in the dim light of the fog-drenched mornings of the wet season or the frosty dawns of November and December, I received vague intimations of the vicissitudes in the lives of the tenants. During the second half of the year, they were far more silent than they had been in February and March. Now, standing beside a burrow in the dawn, I seldom heard the low confidential murmurs which then had preluded their departure. Sometimes they sang a little after emerging, but seldom as much as early in the year; on many a blustery November morning, they were quite silent.

In August, one burrow was abandoned. Illuminating the interior with a flashlight, I could barely glimpse the dead body of one of its tenants, seeming to gaze with lusterless eyes upon the outer daylight to which it could never return. I lost interest in this burrow, supposing that it would remain deserted. The survivor called much in the vicinity of the abandoned dormitory. Then, in early November, I noticed the dead motmot's skull lying in the road below the tunnel. Looking in, I saw that the ruts made by the feet of motmots passing in and out were again sharp and fresh, proof that the burrow had been reoccupied. The following morning, two birds flew out into the cold, dark, windy dawn. The persistent calls of the survivor had been answered, and he or she had won a new mate. Then the pair, possibly after nights passed elsewhere, had cleaned the burrow, making it fit for continued occupancy. But, when I last visited this burrow in mid December, only one motmot slept in it.

The pair that I watched dig their burrow in early July continued to lodge there every night (as far as I saw) until mid November, when I discovered that one of them was absent. For two weeks the remaining bird slept alone, but after that it found another mate—or possibly the same one returned after an absence. My imperfect glimpses into the motmots' lives did not enable me to give definite answers to these important questions. Not long afterward, at a different burrow, I found three full-grown motmots sleeping together, for the second time in a year. This arrangement was only temporary, for a week later the third individual was no longer present.

These fluctuations in the number of occupants suggest that, when nights are longest, the motmots may occasionally visit burrows of other pairs, leaving their mates to sleep alone for a while.

Despite these temporary departures, if such they were, the green motmots nearly always lived in pairs throughout the long months when they were not engaged in reproduction. Because most of the burrows were so crooked, I could not peer in from the front and see how the occupants slept. But, one evening in November, darkness overtook me as I passed along a road through the forest, still far from my abode. As I approached a burrow that I had seen many times by day, it occurred to me that I had never tried to look into it by night. I directed in the beam of my flashlight and, to my great surprise and delight, found that this exceptional burrow was so straight that I could look right into the dormitory at its end.

The ray revealed a formless mass of light green in the center of the chamber. I could not distinguish either head or tail of a bird or decide whether one motmot or several were present. The only definite objects that I could discern among the mass of fluffy feathers were some wing plumes—and these but poorly. The sleepers were not awakened by the unaccustomed glare; but, when I clucked softly with my mouth at the entrance, one unburied its head from among the green downy feathers. More clucking and some whistling were needed to rouse the second bird, who faced directly into the light and started to preen its feathers. The two were pressed so closely together that, until they raised their heads, they appeared as one. I turned out the light, waited a minute, then peeped in once more, to find that the motmots had already fallen asleep again, with their heads lost among their feathers. They must have felt very secure in their deep chamber, not to have been greatly alarmed by the unprecedented intrusion.

The Behavior of Captive Juveniles
Now that we have followed the adult Blue-throated Green Motmots through the cycle of a year, an additional question remains to be

answered: when do the young birds mate and dig their own burrows? To this question I can, unfortunately, give no definite answer. I waited for the appearance of more burrows along the mile or more of roadway that I kept under constant surveillance. Six families of motmots had been raised along this stretch of roadway, probably about seventeen young birds in all; yet by the year's end not a single new burrow had been dug there, except those which the parents had excavated close beside their old ones. This was not because the banks were overcrowded; long stretches remained unoccupied, including a considerable length which had sheltered a seventh pair earlier in the year but which had been abandoned in March.

This hardly helps answer our question, but I made some suggestive observations. At the end of June, an Indian boy brought me two young motmots who had hatched late and could not yet fly. When we went to the spot beside a stream where he said he had picked them up, we found no burrow from which they could have come; their origin remained a mystery. I decided to try to raise the two foundlings until they could take care of themselves, then release them.

The first evening, it was necessary forcibly to open their mouths and drop in food; but already by the next day they took particles from forceps. One showed greater skill at this than the other. We gave them chiefly hard-boiled eggs, elderberries, and blackberries. When hungry they called loudly, repeating a note that sounded like *cry cry cry*, and snapped avidly for food. They did not direct their grasp precisely toward the food but only toward the feeder, who had deftly to drop the item into an open mouth. They tried to swallow everything that their gaping bills contacted, including one another, which was of course impossible. I inferred from this behavior that in the burrow mealtime would present a very disorderly scene, were anyone able to watch it. Probably in such crooked burrows, even more than in the straighter tunnels of many other birds that nest underground, the light is too dim for the parents to see their nestlings clearly, and the latter must grope wildly about with snapping bills until

one of them hits the food and swallows it—which is all very different from the well-mannered behavior of nestlings reared in the open, who merely stretch up gaping mouths and wait for the parent to drop in nourishment.

When not interested in food, the two foundlings rested standing in contact with each other. At first, they kept their eyes closed even in daylight, as nestlings probably do in the burrow. By night, they slept pressed close together, each with its head turned back among the fluffed-out feathers of a shoulder. The young motmot who took its food poorly from the first soon succumbed. The other lived several weeks, until it died of a respiratory infection apparently contracted from the domestic chickens.

Before the second motmot died, it could perch, fly across a room, and pick up food for itself. When it had acquired these accomplishments and was probably over a month old, I surprised it behaving queerly one afternoon. It dropped to the bottom of its box, pecked at the paper covering or at the wall in front, then kicked back rapidly with both feet, sounding a tattoo against the board. At the same time, it half spread its wings and voiced low little murmurs. Now pecking and kicking are the chief activities when digging a burrow; can it be that at this early age the impulse to dig a burrow for sleeping was arising in the juvenile motmot? If this be so, it is probable that the young birds, after dispersing from the parental territory, mate and dig their own dormitories at the same time as the adults do, at the end of June or in early July, when they are between two and three months old and hardly to be distinguished from their parents. This is the only period in the whole year when I found burrows being excavated, except once in March, when somebody maliciously plugged the entrance of a dormitory and the evicted tenants needed to dig a new one.

This, at least, is my present belief, which needs confirmation by additional studies. But, with the destruction of the highland forests throughout the Blue-throated Green Motmots' range, opportunities to learn about these unique birds steadily diminish.

28. Rufous-tailed Jacamar

Galbula ruficauda

At Birichichi beside the Río Ulúa in Honduras stood a grove of stately Cohune palms, whose tall, massive, columnar trunks bore spreading crowns of gigantic pinnate leaves. High as they grew, they were overshadowed by the noble Silk-cotton trees and a few other giants of the forest. Scattered among the palms were many strangler fig trees, most of which had probably started life on the trunks of palms that had vanished long before. Here lived a large troupe of black Howling Monkeys, protected by the owner of the banana plantation in which the grove stood. Their voices reverberated through the still air at dawn and answered the rumble of passing trains. Their grove was situated between the railroad and the river, with plantations of bananas on the other two sides. Reluctant to descend to the ground, the Howlers had remained here and multiplied since the emigration of their ancestors had been precluded by the felling of the surrounding forest more than twenty-five years earlier—they were isolated almost as effectively as though their grove were an island in the sea.

Here, among many interesting birds, I saw one cloudy afternoon a slender, graceful creature—scarcely larger than a Starling—with a long sharp black bill held with a jaunty upward tilt. I watched it trace wide loops and figures of eight as it caught insects on the wing, usually returning to the same perch after each sally, to sit quietly awaiting its next victim. Since the bird was of a kind new to me, I tried to write a description as it rested there, to help me identify it when I returned to my books. But I had undertaken a task more difficult than I anticipated. The dark metallic plumage was so wonderfully variable, in the dim light that filtered through the clouds and the palm fronds, that I could not decide what color it was. After I wrote "green" for the color of the bird's crown, he moved his head and I substituted "blue"; and, after I had described the broad band across his breast as blue, he shifted his position and it appeared green. At first his wings looked dusky, but when next I glimpsed them, in a more favorable light, they were also green. Finally, I gave up in despair and wrote: "Plumage wonderfully iridescent."

The next time I saw a Rufous-tailed Jacamar, it was on the bushy floodplain of the Río Tela. Under a clear sky, I was certain that the bird's principal color was bright metallic green; but over the feathers of the back and wings flickered glints of gold and burnished copper and bronze. A broad green band across his breast separated his white throat from his chestnut belly. His outer tail feathers, of the same shade of chestnut, contrasted prettily with the green central feathers when his tail was spread in flight. The female differed from her mate chiefly in the color of her throat, which was faintly tinged with buff instead of pure white, and in the paler chestnut of her abdomen.

Jacamars are among the most attractive birds that I know. They have all the physical features that win so much admiration for hummingbirds—metallic brilliance of plumage, richness and variety of color, abundant vitality, gracefully dashing movements—yet they are much larger than hummingbirds with no detriment to their delicacy of form. Accordingly, they are easier to watch and more companionable because they are nearer our own size. And, when we consider their family life, we find close nup-

tial bonds which contrast strongly with the aloofness of most male hummingbirds.

The jacamar's voice, freely used, is in keeping with its appearance: it helps create the impression of a bird keyed up to the highest pitch of excitement. The note that I most often heard in Honduras and Guatemala was a little squeak or squeal, an appealing, endearing sound that reminded me of the squeal made by a loved childhood toy when I squeezed it and that prompted a fleeting desire to caress this aery, gemlike bird with bright brown eyes and rapier bill. When mated birds were together, this simple

squeak underwent a number of surprising modifications. In one of the most characteristic of these, the notes were at first delivered slowly, but gradually they came faster and finally again came more slowly, with a higher pitch:

be be be be be be be be be be be be be be

Both sexes also utter a high-pitched, very rapid trill, which at best is almost silver-toned but at other times is duller and resembles the rattle of a small kingfisher delivered at high speed. This trill is ordinarily voiced with the bill widely opened and the lower mandible rapidly vibrating; but even with its bill closed on an insect the jacamar can produce a lower, less clear trill. The male sometimes sings a pretty song that begins with little squeals, which become more animated and melodious as the lay proceeds, to merge into rapid trills and high-pitched whistles.

Although the slender, finely pointed bills of jacamars seem poorly fitted for catching insects on the wing, the birds obtain nearly all their food in this manner. They dart from a perch with a whir of wings and seize an insect with a resounding snap as the bill closes upon it; but the clack is loudest when they miss their intended prey and the mandibles strike together. Although their movements are precise enough to seize even small insects in such slender bills, they prefer bigger ones. Jacamars and motmots are the only birds that I have seen catch many large brilliant butterflies. When a glittering jacamar overtakes a great blue Morpho or a magnificent yellow-and-black swallowtail butterfly, it returns to its perch with the hapless creature fluttering in its bill, beats its victim against a branch until the lovely wings, vibrating rapidly until the end, fall away one by one and go twirling slowly to the ground, then swallows the wingless body. The splendor of this display distracts attention from its harshness and makes one forget for a while the great tragedy of evolution, which has created many animals that are unable to live without destroying others that likewise cling to life and may be equally beautiful. All the jacamar's prey, except soft-bodied flies, is beaten long and loudly against a perch before it is swallowed.

One who admires Charles Kingsley's *At Last* can hardly refrain from quoting a fine passage which touches upon this very point. He describes his first meeting with a Rufous-tailed Jacamar in the forest of Trinidad: "Or are our eyes, accustomed to the blaze outside, unable to expand rapidly enough, and so liable to mistake for darkness air really full of light reflected downward, again and again, at every angle, from the glossy surfaces of a million leaves? At least we may be excused; for a bat has made the same mistake, and flits past us at noonday. And there

is another—No; as it turns, a blaze of metallic azure off the upper side of the wings proves this to be no bat, but a Morpho, a moth [!] as big as a bat. And what was that second larger flash of golden green, which dashed at the moth, and back to yonder branch not ten feet off? A Jacamar—kingfisher, as they miscall her here, sitting fearless of man, with the moth in her long beak. Her throat is snowy white, her underparts rich red brown. Her breast, and all her upper plumage and long tail, glitter with golden green. There is light enough in this darkness, it seems."

Rufous-tailed Jacamars live chiefly in the heavier second-growth of humid lowlands, among tangled vegetation where they are more easily heard than seen, although they show little fear of humans. Frequently they forage above a stream which flows through scarcely penetrable thickets or along a trail through the riotous growth that has covered an abandoned plantation, where the clear space above the waterway or pathway favors their aerial pursuits. They also inhabit forest that has been thinned by lumbering, an operation which increases the amount of light that reaches the ground and augments the bushy undergrowth. More rarely, I have found them in the dark shade of tall primeval woodland.

Digging the Burrow

On the afternoon of April 22, 1932, while sliding and slipping down a steep hillside sparsely covered with small trees, vines, and bushes, at the base of the Sierra de Merendón on the boundary between Guatemala and Honduras, I frightened up a pair of jacamars. Searching the area whence they arose, I found a small depression, about 1 inch (2.5 centimeters) deep and freshly dug, which seemed to be the beginning of a nesting burrow. It was situated beneath the roots of a small tuft of grass on a nearly bare part of the slope. When I returned on the following afternoon, I found, just below this, a new excavation that had been started within the last twenty-four hours and was already 9 inches (23 centimeters) long. I dug into the steep slope a shelf wide enough to hold my campstool, set an umbrella blind above it, and within its shelter passed two days watching the jacamars at work.

The members of the pair approached the burrow together, but the buff-throated female was clearly the leader in the undertaking. As she entered the tunnel, she kicked earth backward with her feet, throwing out twin jets which became shorter as they followed the digger inward. She kicked out loosened soil just as kingfishers and motmots do. When, after a few minutes in the burrow, she emerged tailfirst, her mate caught a large filmy-winged dragonfly and started to beat it against the limb where he habitually perched. When it slipped from his grasp, he darted out and easily overtook it. When it was sufficiently lifeless, he gave it to the female, who had been waiting expectantly close beside him. Then she entered again, while the male waited on a dead limb in front of the burrow, incessantly uttering little squeals that sounded far away. When she came out after working for two minutes, the male flew to the entrance, only to stick his head into the tunnel and promptly leave.

So two hours passed, the female alone digging the burrow while her mate waited nearby, squealing and sometimes trilling, as though to encourage her to work harder. When he perched on a large fern that grew beside the burrow, I noticed that his chestnut belly was nearly the same color as the scales that covered the heavy "fiddlestick" of an expanding frond. When the female emerged from a spell of work, her partner often rewarded her with a dragonfly, a large butterfly from which he had removed the satiny wings, a small beetle with splendidly metallic green shards, or some other insect. Often he flew to the burrow but did no work. At each visit he entered a little farther, until only the tip of his tail was visible. Finally, he began to scratch at the entrance. Once he flew backward as he emerged from the burrow.

The male seemed to be slowly warming up to the point of helping to dig. By midmorning, he did so, at first for only a fraction of a minute at a time. Nevertheless, his zeal for the undertaking was increasing, and before noon he regularly alternated with his mate,

remaining at the task from two to four minutes at a stretch. Once he flew away while she was at work. While he was beyond view, she emerged from the tunnel and perched in front to await him. Returning, he alighted beside her and began to bow. He turned rapidly from side to side on his perch, bobbed his head up, down, and sideward, swung his tail up and down, and voiced low squealing notes. While he performed, the female trilled sweetly. Later, I watched the two perch side by side, spread their tails fanwise, revealing the chestnut outer feathers, and bow up and down to each other, very much in the manner of woodpeckers.

That afternoon was so warm that my clothes became soaked with sweat while I sat in the blind. Yet rarely have I seen birds work at a nest as long, as hard, or as continuously as these jacamars did. Perhaps they had lost a first nest elsewhere and were in a hurry to finish this, for neighboring jacamars were already feeding young. The male now took an almost equal share with his mate and fully compensated for his slight deficiency by continuing to feed her. Indeed, he kept her so well supplied with insects that she rarely had to catch one for herself. Once, when she had just started to enter the tunnel, he caught a small green beetle and called her back before she had passed beyond sight. After knocking it several times against the fern stipe, he passed it to her.

While the male was inside, his mate sometimes trilled, just as he did while she was at work. They had already begun to enlarge the nest chamber, which gave them room to turn around, and were coming out headfirst now. Sometimes the male paused a moment in the entrance as he emerged, making a most attractive picture with his black bill, green head, white throat, and green breastband framed in the round opening in the rust-colored earth. His mate was in such a hurry to continue to dig that she could hardly wait until he came out but dashed to the entrance before he had cleared it. Sometimes she went in while he was still there.

The jacamar's needlelike bill seemed more suitable for weaving a close-meshed fabric like an oriole's or a cacique's nest than for the coarse work of delving in the ground. This bill puzzled me greatly, for it seemed as poorly fitted for aerial insect catching as for digging burrows, although jacamars do both competently. After much pondering, I concluded that the long slender bill serves to reach past the fragile wings of a large butterfly or dragonfly, which may break and permit the insect to escape, in order to seize the solid body; also, it holds the fluttering wings at a distance from the face while the bird knocks them off. Likewise, its length is a safeguard against wounds from bees and the other stinging insects that jacamars sometimes catch. Incidentally, the long slender bill fits the jacamar's graceful form to perfection. It is as hard to imagine a jacamar with a motmot's heavy beak as it is to picture a tern with a pelican's pouched bill.

Although these jacamars used their bills chiefly for loosening the soil, which they kicked out of the burrow with their feet, sometimes one emerged bearing a lump in its bill. Once, while digging, the female found a grub or something of the kind, which she carried out of the tunnel and ate. The jacamars' bills became dusted with earth, but their glittering plumage remained remarkably fresh and clean throughout their labors.

On the third day after their burrow had been started, the jacamars were at work when I arrived at a quarter past eight in the morning. With short intermissions, they toiled throughout the day. When, at half past four in the afternoon, I left them to visit other nests, they were still digging, but their burrow appeared to be nearly finished. It went straight into the earth, without turning, and widened into the nest chamber at the rear. From the entrance to the back of the chamber, its length was 16½ inches (42 centimeters). The tunnel was only 2 inches (5 centimeters) in diameter, too narrow to admit my hand.

The Eggs and Incubation

Unfortunately for me, a root at the end of the tunnel forced the jacamars to dig their nest chamber downward, with the result that I could not see their eggs through the entrance tube. Fearful that the birds would desert, I did not open their burrow until after they began to incubate, which was about two weeks after they finished digging—a long delay, considering how eager they seemed to complete their work. Then, from a point a few inches to the side of their entrance, I dug a horizontal shaft obliquely into the hillside, until it met the nest chamber. I found the soil so soft and friable that the birds' task of excavation had not been arduous. When my shaft became wide enough to admit my hand, I drew forth four small pure white eggs, which were nearly spherical and appeared quite fresh, for the shells were slightly translucent and the yolks shone through them. Incubation could hardly have been in progress for more than two or three days. After measuring the eggs, I replaced them on the bare floor of the chamber, for the birds had brought in no softer lining. Then I closed my shaft with a stone and packed the earth around its entrance.

Although I could not see the eggs from the burrow's mouth because they rested so low, I soon discovered that, by approaching stealthily, I could peep in and see the greater part of the bird who warmed them. There at the back he sat, facing me, his sharp, pertly upturned bill covered with earth at the tip, his throat gleaming whitely in the glare of my flashlight, his deep brown eyes sparkling in the beam, his green cheeks and breast returning iridescent scintillations here and there as the light happened to strike them. Motionless and unblinking, he stared into the beam until I extinguished the light and silently departed.

After the stars began to shine, I again found the jacamar with the pure white throat in the burrow. It was always the same when I looked in. "Poor little overworked husband," I exclaimed to myself, "you not only feed your mate while she digs, take an almost equal share in the labor yourself, but sit on the eggs most of the day and all of the night!" I had already learned that male woodpeckers, anis, and Ringed Kingfishers incubate at night, and here was another species to add to the list!

I noticed that the female was less readily

frightened from the burrow than her mate by the vibrations of the soil when a person walked heavily near it; and, since in other species I had found that the partner whose attachment to the nest is stronger usually occupies it throughout the hours of darkness, this observation cast doubt upon my conclusion that the male incubated at night. After I had watched the female enter the burrow, I stole up and peeped in—to behold again the white-throated male! Then the truth dawned upon me: in the artificial light, the female's throat, which in daylight was distinctly buffy, appeared as white as the male's. To remove all doubt, I spent many hours in the blind, watching the jacamars enter and leave their burrow.

The jacamars arranged their turns in the nest in much the same manner as the Amazon and Green kingfishers, especially the latter. The female incubated every night. Her mate arrived before sunrise in the morning, alighted on his customary perch before the burrow, and called. She answered in a lower voice before she came to the entrance, where sometimes she paused briefly with her head framed in the aperture, then flew swiftly away. The male added another insect or two to his hastily snatched breakfast, then entered the burrow. His early entry into the nest had given him perhaps fifteen or twenty minutes with enough light to catch his morning meal. He came at about the same hour every day; on three consecutive mornings, he entered the burrow at 5:24, 5:24, and 5:37. Apparently, he was late on the third morning because the dark, overcast sky delayed his breakfast. His mate had become impatient and left the eggs six minutes before his arrival.

Between 7:00 and 7:30, the female returned to relieve her mate. She called him from the burrow, just as he had called her, and entered as soon as he left. Once she went in holding a fly in her bill. After the male flew down the bushy hillside he trilled, and she answered from the burrow with low rapid squeaks. From two to two and a half hours later, the male arrived for his second turn on the eggs. Thus they alternated throughout the day. The male took a long session of three or more hours in the late afternoon. Once the female appeared at 5:13 and called to him, but it was so unusually early for her to replace him that he remained in the burrow until she entered. On another day, she was much later; the male waited on the eggs until 6:20, then emerged with a lump of clay in his bill, probably because he was hungry. He called for his mate before he flew away. She entered nineteen minutes later, in the gathering dusk. Usually the sun had set before she went into the burrow for the night. This arrangement gave the male scant time for his evening meal; just as he had begun the day with a hasty breakfast, he ended it with a light supper.

While incubating, the jacamars regurgitated the chitinous parts of insects, including many glittering pieces of the exoskeletons of metallic green beetles, until the chamber's floor was thickly covered with them.

The Nestlings

Eighteen days after I first saw them (when they probably had already been incubated for a day or two), the four eggs hatched. In contrast to burrow-nesting kingfishers, motmots, and puffbirds, which are quite naked at birth, the nestling jacamars bore over most of their bodies copious natal down, long, soft, and white. The long filaments on chin and throat, hanging over their chests, made them appear prematurely bearded and aged. Their skins were pink, their eyes were tightly closed, and their lower mandibles projected slightly beyond the upper mandibles, like those of hatchling kingfishers. Both the outer and the inner toes were directed forward, although on older nestlings and adults these toes are turned backward. Their oval heel pads were already prominent and considerably broader than their legs; but, unlike the pads of young kingfishers, woodpeckers, and certain other birds that nest in unlined holes or burrows, they were nearly smooth. The hatchling jacamars could already stand erect and peep softly. While I held them in my hands, both parents arrived with small insects in their bills and perched nearby, uttering complaining squeals, but they neither darted threateningly at me nor tried to lure me away. Nevertheless, they were strongly attached to their nestlings. Two days later, their mother permitted me to touch her while she brooded them in the burrow. After remaining in the nest for several days, the empty shells disappeared, probably crushed into the growing accumulation of waste on the chamber's floor.

I watched the male as he perched on a leafless twig in front of my blind, catching insects for his family, while the female brooded. He was constantly turning his head from side to side, alert to pounce upon any sizable insect that came within his range. Tiny insects, such as might have attracted a swallow or a small flycatcher, were disdained, even when they passed a few inches from his perch. Nothing smaller than a housefly seemed worthy of his attention, and even insects of this size were too meager to take into the burrow but were promptly swallowed by him. He made long swift sallies after passing dragonflies and butterflies, from which he knocked the wings before he took them to the nestlings. When only four days old, they received slender-bodied dragonflies as long as themselves. Not without spirit, he drove away a Blue-diademed Motmot much bigger than himself.

When the nestlings were six days old, their eyes began to open and pinfeathers pushed out, most of them terminated, like dandelion seeds, by tufts of down. The upper mandible of each black bill was already longer than the lower. Their feet were yellow, with the first and fourth toes, which at birth were turned forward, already directed backward. The young jacamars huddled in the center of the nest chamber, facing outward and standing erect on each full foot like nestling kingfishers. While waiting for their meals, they uttered, in little faraway voices, the characteristic song of the adults:

be be be be be be be be be be be be be be

The development of the nestlings' voices was different from that of songbirds, who rarely sing before they have fledged. When the jacamars were only eight days old, with open eyes, they already voiced pleasant little trills, much like those of the parents but weaker. When I removed them from the burrow, they emerged with their pinfeathers, especially those on their heads and necks, standing on end, making their eyes scarcely visible in the pincushions that were their heads. While I continued to hold them, they slowly laid the pins flat and resumed their normal appearance.

When, at the age of twelve days, the nestlings' feathers started to escape from their horny sheaths, I could see that two would have pure white throats and two buffy throats; there were two brothers and two sisters in the family. They were bright, sprightly youngsters, constantly turning their heads from side to side, opening and closing their bills, and moving their wings. Now, toward the middle of June, heavy rains began. The burrow became damp and muddy, and the nestlings' bills and feet were soon caked with mud. As they preened their sprouting feathers, their natal down stuck stubbornly to the mud-tipped bills. To add to their troubles, small ants invaded their nursery, probably attracted by the maggots that bred in the filth on the floor, for jacamar parents are as careless of sanitation as kingfishers, motmots, and trogons are. Nevertheless, the young jacamars' plumage remained fresh and clean, because they stood erect and did not permit it to touch the soiled, muddy floor.

One morning, I found all four nestlings, already fully feathered, lying on the slope in front of their burrow, unable to fly. After I had cleaned the burrow and removed the ants that had driven them out, I replaced the young jacamars. The two males eventually died from this exposure, but their sisters survived to leave the nest at the age of twenty days, when they could fly well.

While these jacamars were incubating their eggs, I found the burrow of another pair along a steep bare slope in a little amphitheater in a precipitous hillside densely covered with second-growth woods. In this straight burrow, only 13 inches (33 centimeters) long, I could easily see with my flashlight four blind nestlings, who stood pressed together in the center of their nursery. While I sat on the hillside, 25 feet (7.6 meters) away, to watch their parents bring food, their

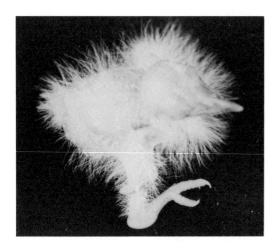

Rufous-tailed Jacamar: nestling two days old.

Rufous-tailed Jacamar: nestling thirteen days old.

constantly reiterated little cries emerged from the earth. Soon both parents brought butterflies, from which the wings had been removed. Their father, much less cautious than their mother, fidgeted around for only a few minutes before he delivered his insect, while she delayed for nearly half an hour. As I noticed also on later occasions, she was consistently more cautious than he was.

These parents had better fortune than the first pair: they brought all their young forth from the burrow early in May, before the rains began. This brood consisted of three males and one female, who when fully feathered closely resembled the parent of the same sex. They were truly gems from the earth, as scintillating as any diamond, emerald, or other precious stone. Pictures can hardly reproduce the fire and sparkle of the deep green plumage on their backs and wings, over which glints of bronze and gold and burnished copper played in wondrous fashion. But their loveliness was no cause for wonder, for loveliness was their daily fare. Beneath the branch where the parents prepared their food, I picked up the broad wings of a Morpho butterfly. Marvelous as was the play of blue and azure on this satiny expanse, it paled beside the iridescence of the jacamars' green coats. They had trans-

Rufous-tailed Jacamar: female nestling seventeen days old.

muted the butterfly's loveliness into a more animated, apparently more sentient loveliness. Nevertheless, I was saddened by the thought that so much beauty had been sacrificed to nourish their beauty, that it had been necessary to destroy in order to create.

Regretfully, I watched the parent jacamars lead their family into the depths of the thicket, where I could hardly follow. In voice, in mannerisms, in appearance, they were the most winsome nestlings that I have known.

Jacamars in Costa Rica and Venezuela

The Rufous-tailed Jacamar ranges over tropical America from southern Mexico to northwestern Ecuador, Bolivia, and northeastern Argentina. In various parts of this wide extension, it inhabits fairly arid as well as humid regions, high forest as well as thickets. From the warm lowlands where it is most abundant, it extends upward to about 3,000 feet (910 meters) in both Venezuela and Costa Rica, and once, in the extreme south of the latter country, I met a single individual about 1,000 feet (300 meters) higher. Over much of its range, the country people give the jacamar names that recognize its resemblance to an overgrown hummingbird: king hummingbird in Trinidad, *tucuso barranquero* ("hummingbird of the ravines") in Venezuela, *martín gorrión* ("martin hummingbird") in Guatemala. Brazilians apply the same name, *beija-flôr* ("kiss-flower") to both hummingbirds and jacamars.

When I settled at Los Cusingos in 1941, Rufous-tailed Jacamars were not rare in the high forest, where I found a number of nests. Ten years later, they had all but disappeared, along with a number of other conspicuous birds, evidently victims of the uncontrollable poachers and their dogs. Now, at long intervals, I hear the stirring calls of a solitary jacamar, apparently a wandering male seeking a mate that he cannot find. Without one, he does not stay. Before the resident jacamars vanished, I made observations that supplement my earlier studies in northern Central America.

The voices of the jacamars here in the Valley of El General seemed to me less sharp and more mellow than those I had heard farther north, so that it hardly seemed proper to call their notes squeals or squeaks. The Guatemalan birds sang a long series of ascending notes, at first rather widely spaced but with increasing tempo until a climax was reached, after which the notes were again more widely spaced. In the corresponding performance of Costa Rican jacamars, the increase in tempo was continued to the end, with no final retardation. One day in November, while wandering through the forest on a ridge above the Valley of El General, I found three jacamars perching in a fairly open space, about midheight of the great trees. Two males competed for a female with vocal outbursts so splendid that I listened enchanted. Their rapid, prolonged trills, clear and soft, rose in pitch to very high final notes. Other trills were dry rather than liquid. Single notes, more like whistles than squeals, were interspersed with the songs. At intervals, one of the males darted toward his rival, without ever striking him. After this delightful singing had continued for many minutes, the trio drifted off through the forest, more rapidly than I could follow through the tangled undergrowth.

Although the two burrows in Guatemala were in steep hillsides, none of the fifteen nests that I have seen in Costa Rica and Venezuela was in a similar site. Most were in more or less vertical banks, beside a stream, a woodland trail, or a seldom-used road. None of the banks was lofty; one was about 1 foot (30 centimeters) high, with the tunnel about 6 inches (15 centimeters) above its base. Often the tunnel's mouth was quite exposed; rather exceptional was a burrow halfway up the 5-foot (1.5-meter) bank of a gully, beneath an overhang of root-bound earth and screened by overarching vegetation. A special kind of bank is formed by a great uprooted tree, which raises a mass of clay, vertical on what was its underside, sometimes as much as 2 yards (1.8 meters) high, 2 or 3 yards (1.8 or 2.7 meters) long, and several feet thick. Five of the nests at Los Cusingos were in such masses of root-bound earth, which in tracts of forest poor in streambanks, escarpments, and the like offer

sites to burrow-nesting birds who might otherwise be unable to breed. On the whole, the
jacamars' tunnels that I have seen in these
walls of clay formed by uprooted trees appeared safer, less accessible to snakes and
small mammals, than those that I found in
trailside or streamside banks. One was 5 vertical feet (1.5 meters) above the depression in
the ground from which the mass was lifted.
The twelve burrows that I have measured
were 11½ to 19½ inches (29 to 49.5 centimeters) long. Seven of these were 12 to 13 inches
(30 to 33 centimeters) long. At Los Cusingos
I found no consistent difference in the lengths
of tunnels in banks and among the roots of
fallen trees. The two longest burrows, 17½
and 19½ inches (44 and 49.5 centimeters),
were in the Caribbean lowlands of Costa
Rica. Unless deflected by a root or stone, the
burrows are usually straight.

Although I have no knowledge of Rufous-
tailed Jacamars' nests in termitaries in Central America, in northern Venezuela I found
two, both in large termites' nests that
emerged from the ground in the form of
rough, black domes about 2 feet (60 centimeters) high. The excavations in these termitaries had the same shape as those in the
ground: they were horizontal tunnels 11½
and 12½ inches (29 and 32 centimeters) long
that expanded into low vaulted chambers at
the inner ends. As in some terrestrial tunnels, they were slightly wider than high at
the mouth, which in no case exceeded 1⅞
inches in width and 1¾ inches in height (4.8
by 4.5 centimeters). Improbable as it appears
that such apparently fragile bills as the jacamars' could dig into the hard laminated
substance of a termitary, the form and dimensions of the tunnels left no doubt that
they had done so. Close by one of these termitaries was a vertical bank such as jacamars commonly select as nest sites; but,
after long dry months, the soil was so hard
that the birds may have found the termitary
less refractory. In the Caribbean lowlands of
Costa Rica, I watched a pair of sturdier-
billed Great Jacamars carve into a similar
termitary, high in a tree instead of at ground
level (Skutch 1971c).

In the same locality where two pairs of

*Rufous-tailed Jacamar: terrestrial termitary in
which a brood was raised in northern Venezuela.*

Rufous-tailed Jacamars nested in termitaries,
a third pair had chosen a bank beside a dry
watercourse in a lightly wooded ravine.
Whatever the medium in which they dig
their burrows, the jacamars never line the
rounded chamber at its inner end. Sometimes they clean out and occupy the same
burrow in successive years. Occasionally they
must defend their burrows from Rough-
winged Swallows, which Gilliard (1959)
found nesting in a jacamars' excavation. He
did not learn whether the swallows had dis-
possessed the builders or waited until the latter had abandoned their burrow. He saw a
male jacamar feed the female, as I have done
in Costa Rica as well as Guatemala.

It will be recalled that the pair of jacamars in Guatemala who seemed in such a hurry to dig their burrow did not start to incubate until about two weeks after it was finished. At Los Cusingos, a burrow begun about February 24 did not contain an egg until April 8. The usual interval between the completion of a burrow and the start of laying was about ten days. To learn exactly when eggs were laid was difficult, because I often found a jacamar, female or male, in the burrow during the laying period, and it stubbornly refused to leave even when I pushed in a lighted electric bulb or stamped on the ground nearby; I never used more drastic means to make the birds uncover their eggs. Two to four days might elapse between the laying of successive eggs. Of eleven nests in Costa Rica, four contained two eggs, six held three eggs or nestlings, and one had four eggs. In northern Venezuela, at about the same latitude, one burrow held four eggs, and one had three nestlings. In Trinidad and Tobago, also at approximately the same latitude, two to four, usually three, eggs are laid (ffrench 1973). In Guatemala, about six degrees farther north, each of my nests had four eggs. In many kinds of birds, the size of the set increases with latitude, even in the tropics. The four pure white, nearly spherical eggs in my first nest measured 22.2 by 19.1, 22.2 by 19.1, 22.2 by 19.4, and 23 by 19.8 millimeters. Since I could not reach any eggs without altering burrows and increasing the risk of loss, I did not remove more; but I counted them by peering into straight burrows or inserting a small mirror into slightly curving tunnels, while they were illuminated by a flashlight.

In Costa Rica, eleven sets of eggs were laid from late March to late June, six of them in April, a month of usually light rains that usher in the wet season. One of the June sets was laid by parents who had lost nestlings a month earlier, and the other was probably the second brood of a pair whose young had flown three weeks earlier. In Trinidad, breeding has been recorded from February to June, principally in March and April.

A pair of jacamars whose incubation schedule I studied in Costa Rica followed much the same pattern as my first pair in Guatemala, but their sessions tended to be shorter. In the dim light of dawn, usually without waiting for her mate's arrival, the female flew from the burrow where she had passed the night. On seven mornings, the time of her departure varied only from 5:05 to 5:26, the latest when day dawned darkly clouded. On these seven mornings, the male arrived at times varying from 5:21 to 5:35, from zero to twenty-six minutes after the female emerged. Usually he delayed a few minutes before he entered the burrow. Throughout the day, the two alternated, sitting from 84 to 113 minutes at a stretch. Arriving to take its turn on the eggs, the partner announced its presence with calls that usually brought the other out promptly, although once the male kept the female waiting for twenty-three minutes before he emerged. Sometimes at the changeover the two perched side by side and trilled together, delaying the newcomer's entry. However, the eggs were rarely left unattended for more than five consecutive minutes. On a day when I watched for eleven hours, they were incubated for 95 percent of the time. As at the Guatemalan nest, the female began her nocturnal session late, usually between 5:30 and 6:00. Her mate did not always stay with the eggs until she came; when he did, he had little time to catch his supper in the failing light.

While studying incubation by jacamars and other burrow nesters, I usually set a little twig upright in the doorway after a bird entered. As long as this sentinel remained erect, I was confident that no bird had darted in or out while my attention wavered during the long uneventful hours. Sometimes, as he left the burrow, the male jacamar carried my twig away in his bill.

The incubation period was variable. My most accurate determination was between nineteen days and twenty days plus six hours, from the laying of the last egg to its hatching. At three other nests, it was twenty or twenty-one days, twenty-two days, and about twenty-three days.

Nestling jacamars at Los Cusingos were, if possible, even more loquacious than those in Guatemala. When they were only six days old and still had closed eyes, their little calls attracted attention as I passed along the roadway in front of their burrow. When two weeks old, bristling with pinfeathers, with open eyes, and no longer brooded, these voluble youngsters called through much of the day. Alone in the burrow, they continued their vocal exercises after all other diurnal birds had become silent. Before they fell quiet, the light in their earth-walled chamber must have been exceedingly dim, for it was almost dark outside. Likewise, in the morning, they raised their voices as soon as the first feeble rays of the new day penetrated their nursery, and they continued to call in low tones until their parents arrived with breakfast. By directing a flashlight's beam into the tunnel at any hour of the night, I could incite a new outburst of loud notes.

During the nestlings' third week, the trill that terminated their song became delightfully sweet and prolonged. From a slow, deliberate beginning, the whistles rose and rose in pitch, at the same time following each other more rapidly, until the trill seemed to taper off into a fine point. The young jacamars seemed to be practicing the musical scale. Now they used their voices more discriminatingly, reserving their songs to answer the notes of an approaching parent and to announce the times when they were very hungry. They were now clearly audible 70 feet (21 meters) from the burrow's mouth, above the loud clamor of the broad mountain torrent that flowed not far away. After their sixteenth day, the nestlings became more wary and silently shrank back in the chamber instead of calling when I illuminated their burrow. I feared that their loquacity might attract predators; but one day I watched a Coatimundi, that long-snouted, almost omnivorous relative of the raccoon, pass only about 10 feet (3 meters) from the burrow whence the young jacamars' songs were issuing, without seeming to notice them—or me, sitting unconcealed not far off. While the animal passed almost beneath the nestlings' father, who was perching in front of the burrow, he remained motionless and silent.

I have frequently been struck by the incongruity between the extreme wariness of tropical birds' approaches to their nests and the simultaneous loud calls that would seem to cancel all their caution. Probably the chief enemies of these nests find them by senses other than hearing: by sight or, especially at night, by scent. In the temperate zones as well as the tropics, snakes are nearly everywhere the chief pillagers of birds' nests.

The parents caught much of their nestlings' food where I could see them while watching the burrow. Insects comprised the whole diet of the young jacamars. They were always caught in the air and taken to the burrow one at a time. Perhaps the length of the jacamars' bills, or the size of their prey, made it difficult for them to add insect to insect until mouth and bill were laden, in the manner of songbirds feeding young. Prominent among the many butterflies caught were numerous skippers (Hesperioidea), with stout bodies and hooked antennae. Swallowtails were occasionally caught, but narrow-winged heliconians were ignored, even when they flew close to the jacamars, doubtless because they were distasteful. I did not see these jacamars capture a Morpho, rare at the time. Large dragonflies with filmy wings were occasionally taken into the burrow. Smaller items, more difficult to identify, included beetles, large diptera, and bees, some of which were shining green, long-tongued euglossids. This bee, the size of a horsefly, was among the smallest insects taken into the nest; still smaller insects, if not ignored, were swallowed at once. The amount of beating against the perch that an insect received, before delivery to a nestling, depended upon its size and hardness. Small soft insects might receive one or two knocks; large hard ones were pounded long and loudly. Often fairly large butterflies and dragonflies were taken to the nestlings with their wings intact.

The method of delivering meals changed as the nestlings grew older. While the chicks were still small, with only their natal down, the parents went all the way into the burrow, stayed to brood, and, after a while, emerged headfirst. After the first week, a parent often remained inside only long enough to deliver the food, then backed out tailfirst. Gradually, the young birds formed the habit of advancing down the tunnel to receive their meals, so that the parents could feed them with only their foreparts inside, then promptly back out and fly away. When the nestlings were twenty days old, the parent merely alighted at the burrow's mouth to deliver an insect. Apparently aware that with only its head inside, unable to see an approaching enemy but with most of its body exposed, it was in a precarious situation, the adult never delayed in this position. If a nestling did not take the food immediately, the parent would dart away, to return again and again until the item was delivered. Once the male flew to the burrow's mouth sixteen times with a butterfly, before a nestling received it.

During the chicks' last six days in the nest, and until the first to leave passed beyond my view, I watched them for twenty-five and one quarter hours. Their father fed them 88 times, their mother 34 times, making a total of 122 meals. Thus, two feathered nestlings were fed at the rate of 2.4 times each per hour. From every aspect, the father was the more industrious provider. Even after the mother ceased to spend the night in the burrow, he always arrived first with food, often while the dawn light was still dim. In the evening, either parent might bring the day's last meal. During the nestlings' final three days in the burrow, the female several times brought an insect, sat holding it for a while, then swallowed it herself and flew away. The nestlings' father spent much more time catching insects in sight of the burrow. If he had been as negligent as their mother became, they would have fared badly indeed. However, the first fledgling's emergence from the burrow stimulated her to greater activity, and she achieved her highest observed rate of feeding: five times in an hour. The male once brought seven meals in an hour. The maximum number by both parents was ten feedings in an hour.

The Fledglings' Departure

The departure of these two nestlings was accompanied by a surprising amount of vocal activity. Early in the morning, while the father trilled much from his usual perch in front of the doorway, the answering trills from within the burrow grew louder, and presently a male fledgling's head appeared in the entrance—the first time I saw a young bird there. During the next two hours, one or the other of the fledglings came to the doorway, where they received a number of meals. Finally, at 8:20, a fledgling stuck his head and breast through the doorway and peered all around—his first good look at the outside world, I believe. After a few minutes, he hopped down to the bare roadway, a drop of about 6 inches (15 centimeters). His first flight carried him only a few inches, to alight on an exposed root. Whistling and trilling delightfully, he gradually moved across the seldom-used roadway and flew into the light woods near the river.

Quite fearless of me, the fledgling continued to perch on a low twig while I stooped to pick him up. Much down still adhered to his iridescent plumage, especially on the sides of his head and breast, where he could not reach to preen. His tail was still stubby. While in my hand, he trilled, his whole body vibrating with the effort. When I smoothed his feathers with a fingertip, he looked around brightly. From the branch on which I set him, he flew about 20 feet (6 meters) on a descending course, which seemed to be the limit of his ability. Starting from the ground, he could with difficulty rise and fly 2 or 3 feet (60 or 90 centimeters).

Although I repeatedly placed the young jacamar on a perch, he persisted in flying or falling to the ground, where he passed at least two nights on fallen leaves before he vanished. He scarcely interrupted his trilling to take the food that his parents gave him on the ground. In his extremely vulnerable situation, so much revealing sound was certainly imprudent. What most amazed me was that, although unable to fly well, he squandered so much energy on trilling. But jacamars are irrepressibly vocal creatures. The departure of a brood of four Pale-headed Jacamars from a burrow in a Venezuelan bluff was likewise the occasion for much singing by both of the parents and their newly emerged fledglings, who from the moment of their exit flew very much better than the young Rufous-tailed Jacamars of this particular brood.

On the following morning, the second young male severed contact with the burrow, also to the accompaniment of much trilling. He could fly somewhat better than the first but nevertheless soon dropped down among the ground herbage, where I easily caught him. As in several cases when young of other species have left the nest on successive days, these two did so at about the same hour—8:23 and 8:34 A.M.—which convinced me that they emerged spontaneously, prompted by internal developments, rather than in response to any parental urging.

These two young jacamars left the burrow on July 3 and 4, when they were twenty-five and twenty-six days old. This exceptionally long nestling period was evidently caused by the lateness of the season; in June and July the ground was wet, and the large butterflies and dragonflies that enter prominently into jacamars' diets seemed less abundant than they had been a month or two earlier. In the following year, two young left this same burrow on May 12, at the ages of only twenty-one and twenty-two days; yet they were much more alert, and flew much better, than their predecessors when four days older. Evidently, these two broods had the same parents. In a growing number of avian species, it has been demonstrated that parental efficiency increases with age and experience. In a later year, two young who remained in the nest until mid July departed when twenty-four days old. At the other extreme, two or three jacamars raised in a termitary in dry weather in Venezuela emerged when only eighteen or nineteen days old, and the two survivors in my first nest in Guatemala left, flying well, at twenty days of age. Accordingly, the Rufous-tailed Jacamar's nestling period ranges from eighteen or nineteen to twenty-six days and appears to be shortest early in the season, before the rains become hard.

Although parent jacamars often stuck steadfastly to their nests when I found them within, they never protested or threatened while I examined their eggs or young, as many birds with open nests do. They never tried to lure me away by the broken-wing display. The reason why burrow nesters of many kinds consistently fail to give distraction displays seems clear. If a predator enters a burrow while a parent is within, the latter is trapped; if the parent arrives to find the enemy with its head already inside, the predator would not notice the display; if the animal has not yet found the burrow, to call attention to it by displaying would be folly. Distraction displays—which are not caused by delirious, uncontrollable outbursts but, to be successful, require complete control of all movements and a cool calculation of risks—are given chiefly by birds who have a good possibility of saving their progeny with this ruse, especially by those that nest on or near the ground. The absence of such displays does not signify weak attachment to the young. In strong contrast to the aloofness that makes many birds of tropical woodland extremely difficult to study, jacamars have often continued to attend their nests while I watched, unconcealed, at no great distance. This devoted attachment to their progeny, this confidence in my presence, together with their beauty, grace, vivacity, and pleasing songfulness, make jacamars among the most rewarding birds to watch.

In Venezuela, four young Pale-headed Jacamars returned every night, for at least eight weeks, to sleep with their parents in the burrow, twice as long as those of Rufous-tailed Jacamars, in which they grew up (Skutch 1968, 1977). In both Central America and Venezuela, I looked in vain for Rufous-tailed Jacamars to use their burrow as a dormitory. After the last fledgling departed, neither adults nor young returned to it.

29. Black-breasted Puffbird

Notharchus pectoralis

While I searched for nests in tall second-growth woods on Barro Colorado Island one morning in late March, tapping sounds led me to a pair of Black-breasted Puffbirds. They were stout, big-headed birds about 8½ inches (22 centimeters) long, mostly glossy blue-black, with a large white patch around the ears and a white throat separated from the white abdomen and under tail coverts by a broad black band across the breast. Their strong bills were black, their eyes dark, the legs and toes dusky. I could not distinguish the male from the female. This was my first meeting with Black-breasted Puffbirds, who usually stay high in the rain forests from central Panama through Darién and down the Pacific coast of Colombia to northwestern Ecuador.

Like other puffbirds, the Black-breasted sits for long intervals on the same exposed bough, its feathers puffed out, a picture of stupid lethargy. Although outwardly motionless, it is ever alert. Let an edible insect appear, flying through the air or creeping over leaf or bark—and the "stupid" puffbird darts out swiftly and straightly, seizes the insect in its bill, returns promptly to its perch, and pounds the victim loudly against the branch before gulping it down. Then the bird remains quietly perching until another insect tempts it into action.

Even with their voices, these puffbirds appear rarely to expend their energy needlessly. Although for many birds nest building is a songful time, the pair that I watched for many hours voiced only low whispered peeps while so engaged. When disturbed, they protested with weak nasal sounds. I never heard the loud song described by Ridgely (1976) as a long series of whistles usually ending with three drawling, descending couplets: *kweee-kweee-kweee-kweee-kweee; kweee-a, kwey-a, kyoo-a*—with sometimes as many as thirty whistles before the falling notes.

The Nest

The puffbirds whose tapping led me to them were starting to excavate a nest chamber in a very large black termitary, about 30 feet (9 meters) above the ground, far out on an ascending branch of a small leafless tree. The next morning, March 29, 1935, I returned before eight o'clock to watch them at work. Since they did not soon appear, I wandered through the surrounding woods, looking for birds and their nests, until the tapping sound recalled me to my observation post, a fallen log in a narrow opening which permitted a clear view of the termitary. Although I was wholly unconcealed at no great distance, the puffbirds, resting quietly on a slender leafless branch in front of the termitary, appeared not to notice me.

Soon one bird flew to the shallow depression they had already made in the side of the black mass, where it clung with its short tail propped against the side and its head bent forward into the hole. In this attitude it remained almost motionless, only at fairly long intervals pecking at the termitary, at most four times in succession. Each short spurt of activity was followed by a relatively long period of silence and immobility. I could not see the head of the bird, who may have been eating the termites that emerged to defend their nest. After clinging in this fashion for about fifteen minutes, the bird rejoined its mate on the leafless branch. The latter now flew to the termitary and behaved as the first had done. It hammered audibly more frequently than the first but still very little. It remained only six minutes and, upon leaving, darted to the trunk of the tree, plucked an insect from the bark, and flew with it to a horizontal swinging vine. It knocked the insect against the vine, then swallowed it. During the hour and a half that I watched them, the two partners alternated, remaining from less than one minute to about fifteen minutes clinging in front of their excavation. Sometimes they hammered more, sometimes less; but always their tapping came between long periods during which, as far as I could see or hear, they were inactive; and neither tapped audibly more than four times together.

The member of the pair not at work usually sat motionless on the bare limb with its feathers puffed out in the characteristic fashion of this family. At intervals it made a long dart to pick an insect from a distant branch or leaf. Both were silent, except for a whispered peep that I heard a few times. At 10:12 the bird who had been at the termitary flew out and away, and five minutes later the other followed. What a contrast these stolid birds made with lively, alert jacamars, timid trogons, noisy kingfishers, hardworking woodpeckers, and most other birds that I have watched dig their nest chambers in earth or wood or termites' houses!

By April 3 the hole in the side of the termitary had become so deep that, when the puffbirds worked in it, the tips of their tails just reached the rough black outer surface. They now devoted long hours to their task; I found them at the termitary both morning and afternoon. Just as I approached at about eight o'clock on April 3, they flew away, but their departure was evidently spontaneous, since they seemed wholly indifferent to my presence. In a quarter of an hour one returned and went promptly to work, while a moment later the second arrived on the perch where they always awaited their turns at the task. They alternated as before, but one spent considerably more time at the termitary than the other. Between 8:15 and 9:53, this bird gave fifty-seven minutes to the task,

while its mate, whom I could distinguish by a disarranged tail feather, remained at work a total of only thirty minutes. The greater time given by the first was accounted for by two long shifts of sixteen and seventeen minutes. The other periods of work by this bird were of five to seven minutes' duration. Those of its mate lasted from two to six minutes.

While at work, the puffbirds frequently uttered the low soft peeping, which was the only vocal sound that I had so far heard from them. The bird waiting outside sometimes darted after insects, at times to a considerable distance, but I never saw one feed its mate. During the longer shifts, the puffbird sometimes backed out of the cavity and rested briefly while it clung to the lower edge of the hole. Perhaps, when I first watched, I had underestimated the amount of work that they did while inside the cavity. With my ear pressed against the trunk of the supporting tree, I could hear sounds from within the termitary which were otherwise inaudible to me. The tapping was far more frequent than I had supposed from the louder taps which alone reached me where I sat. Other sounds suggested that the puffbirds crunched or tore at the termitary, in addition to pecking at it.

Returning late that afternoon, I found the puffbirds at work. They stayed in the termitary more briefly than they had that morning, and they alternated more frequently. In the morning I had to watch them against the sun, but now, with the sun behind me, the puffbirds' contrasting white and glossy bluish black plumage looked much more elegant.

The puffbirds were still working at their chamber in the termitary in the middle of the afternoon of April 10, at least fourteen days after they had started it. Three days later, I managed to reach their nest. I nailed cleats to the trunk to facilitate frequent visits; and, since the branch that supported the termitary seemed too weak to bear my own weight in addition, I braced it with a rope tied to the central trunk. Even after I had climbed to the termitary, I could not look into the puffbirds' nest, because the entrance was on the outer side, away from the trunk. To overcome this difficulty, I laid a stout pole between the nest tree and the crotch of a nearby tree. Then, standing upon the horizontal beam and steadying myself with one hand on the branch that supported the termitary, I could look into the opening. The next day I noticed that the termites were eating away the supporting rope and lashings, all of which I replaced with wire for greater safety.

When examined on April 13, the puffbirds' nest chamber appeared to be completed. A narrow horizontal tunnel, about 7 inches long by $1\frac{7}{8}$ inches in diameter (18 by 4.8 centimeters), led into the top of a spacious, neatly rounded cavity in the heart of the termitary. To examine the dark interior, it was necessary to insert an electric bulb and a small mirror.

When I started to nail cleats to the trunk of the tree, the puffbirds, who were resting on their favorite perch in front of their nest, remained where they were until the vibrations as I advanced higher drove them away. During the next ten days, I visited the nest on alternate days. Nearly always I found one puffbird standing guard on the perch in front of their nest. Despite the shaking of the slender branch as I climbed toward the bird, it stayed until I came within 2 or 3 yards (1.8 or 2.7 meters), then flew silently away. Twice I found a bird in the termitary, where it remained, shaken by my movements, until I had seated myself on the beam in front of the nest and started to arrange the lighting apparatus, when it shot out past my ears, uttering a nasal sound.

The Eggs and Incubation

On April 23 I was delighted to find the first egg, lying so far back in the chamber that, when I inserted the electric bulb, I could see it without the mirror. It was pure white, with a beautiful glossy shell, like a woodpecker's egg. It rested on chips of the hard black material of the termitary, with no softer lining. On April 24 I found the second egg. The third and last was laid on April 26, indicating that the eggs were deposited at two-day intervals. I noticed no termites in the cavity;

they had apparently sealed the galleries that abutted on it, as happens when trogons nest in termitaries. During the period of egg laying, one bird stood guard in front of the nest, as during the ten-day interval between the completion of the chamber and the deposition of the first egg. I made all my visits in the afternoons, in order to be less likely to disturb the female while she was laying.

On May 3 I started to watch the nest, just as the darkly overcast sky was brightening from black to gray. At 6:16 the puffbird who had passed the night on the eggs appeared in the doorway, where I could distinguish only its white throat, as it paused to look out upon the forest dripping after the night's hard showers and still dim beneath a dense mantle of clouds. After a minute's delay, the bird flew with short, swift wing strokes over the treetops and beyond my range of vision. At 6:33 a puffbird arrived and, after looking around briefly, entered the termitary. I could not tell whether this was the bird who had left sixteen minutes earlier or (as seemed likely) its mate. This bird sat in the nest for nearly three hours while I watched, drenched by heavy showers. At 9:15 it came to the doorway, looked around with its head framed in the aperture, then flew forth. It delayed for many minutes among the branches near the nest, then flew out of sight over the low trees. Since, without seeing one member of the pair relieve the other, I could not make certain whether one or both incubated, I decided to leave. Just as I was passing beneath the nest, at about 9:30, a puffbird arrived, apparently to enter it. I stood still to watch, but I was too near, and after a little hesitation the bird flew away.

Arriving at the nest at 1:57 P.M. on May 5, I found a puffbird perching in front of it. Here it remained for half an hour, sometimes stretching its wings, once catching a big flying insect, but mostly immobile. The record of the following hour and a half was this:

2:30 The puffbird entered the nest.
3:03 It left, paused a few minutes on the perch in front of the nest, then joined its mate in the next tree.

3:25   After pausing for some time in the vicinity of the nest and catching two insects, a bird entered.
3:32   It left and rested in front of the nest.
3:50   It entered again.
4:01   It left and perched in front of the nest.

This was most erratic behavior by birds who had been incubating for nine days and were capable of sitting for nearly three hours at a stretch. I decided to look into the nest and see whether anything was amiss. The puffbird who had just left the nest remained perching in front of it while I climbed the tree. When I was just 6 feet (1.8 meters) away, it flew to a more distant perch in the next tree and sat, silent and stolid, only turning its head from side to side as it watched me, during the whole time I was at the nest.

The electric light revealed the eggs safe and sound in their usual position. A few small black ants were crawling around the interior of the chamber and in and out through the entrance tube, but they had been present since before the eggs were laid and seemed innocuous. I could see no cause for the puffbirds' unrest, but perhaps their keen eyes detected some threat that escaped me.

When I arrived on the following afternoon, a parent was perching on the pole that I had fixed transversely in front of the termitary, where it remained, despite shaking, until I came within 6 feet (1.8 meters). At this distance I paused to look intently at the chubby little bird, so oddly marked with black and white, and to gaze into its large alert dark eyes. Only when I moved closer did it fly to the next tree, where it stayed to watch what I did. The eggs were not in their usual place, where I could see them the moment I switched on the light. I stuck in the mirror and turned it from side to side to scrutinize all the darker parts of the chamber. The eggs had vanished without a trace. Throughout the half hour that I spent at the nest, the puffbird lingered in the same spot, turning its big head from side to side, intently and silently watching me. Before I descended to the ground, its mate came to perch near it.

I had hardly reached the ground when the puffbirds flew to the perch in front of the nest. Then the first bird flew to the entrance and clung there, apparently wanting to enter but fearing to do so. It pushed its head in a little way, then backed out, then pushed in again, a little farther. Clearly, it was torn between conflicting impulses. At length, without having penetrated to the nest chamber, the bird retreated and joined its mate on the perch. The latter then went to the entrance, repeated the performance, and came away without having entered. Then the first flew again to the doorway, but it was no more courageous this time than last and rejoined its mate on the branch in front of the nest. Finally, the second bird went a second time to the entrance and, slowly, cautiously, alternately advancing and retreating, arrived at last at the empty chamber. While these explorations were in progress, the two puffbirds uttered an occasional peep, slightly louder than any I had heard them voice before.

After a minute, the puffbird emerged headfirst, proving that it had gone all the way into the chamber, where alone it had room to turn around. It flew to perch beside its mate, who after a few minutes also went inside, not without much hesitation. This was its third attempt to enter, and it remained within for two minutes, then came out headfirst, as the other had done. Then the second, who meanwhile had withdrawn to a more distant perch, flew again to the entrance, uttering a peculiar low nasal sound as it passed its mate. It entered, emerged a minute later, then after a pause went in once more, making three times in all. After its third exit, it flew to a more distant perch. The first puffbird went yet again to the doorway, where it clung while it repeated its weak peep, then flew off to join its mate, without having entered the nest. The birds devoted forty minutes to their apparent hunt for the vanished eggs, before at last they flew off over the treetops.

What could have taken the eggs? No hawk, large owl, or toucan could have entered the chamber or reached the eggs through the long narrow entrance tube. Any mammal slender enough to creep in would have been too small to remove the eggs, unbroken, in its mouth and must have devoured them where they lay, leaving telltale fragments of shell. But a snake could easily have slipped in and engulfed them whole, leaving no trace of its visit.

Bitterly disappointed by the loss of the puffbirds' eggs on May 6, I did not revisit their nest until May 30, when other business took me to their part of the forest. To my great surprise, the nest was again occupied. Despite the rather violent shaking caused by my climb up the slender supporting branch, the puffbird who was incubating did not dart out until I reached the termitary. Pushing in the electric bulb, I beheld three eggs resting where the first three had lain. Instead of being an immaculate white, as the first set had been when newly laid, these were heavily soiled with blackish speckles, just as happens to trogons' eggs in termitaries. Apparently, they had been laid a number of days earlier.

With only two more days on Barro Colorado, I made a last-minute effort to learn whether one or both members of the pair incubated. Late in the afternoon of May 31, I succeeded in witnessing the replacement of one by the other. One puffbird was within when I began my vigil at 3:40. Nothing noteworthy happened until 4:23, when the mate came flying through the treetops and alighted on a high bough about 20 feet (6 meters) from the termitary. I was more than twice this distance away and heard no sound, but the bird in the nest evidently did, for it appeared in the doorway. After looking out for a minute or two, it flew to a twig in front of the nest, where it delayed for several minutes, puffing out its plumage and repeating its low peep. Next it went to a more distant perch and rested longer, before it winged away above the treetops. The new arrival lingered where it had first alighted, then flew to the perch in front of the nest and delayed still more, knocking the sides of its bill alternately against the branch. Finally, twenty-three minutes after its arrival, it entered the nest to

stay—and at last I was certain that both sexes of the Black-breasted Puffbird share incubation. It sat in the nest for seventy-eight minutes (until 6:04), when it emerged and rested for nineteen minutes on the perch in front, then flew away through the treetops. At 6:50 this bird or, more probably, its mate approached through the forest and, after hesitating a minute or two, entered the termitary, when the fading light had become so dim that I could hardly distinguish it. This was my last glimpse of a Black-breasted Puffbird.

I had watched this nest for a total of seven hours while incubation was in progress. The five sessions on the eggs that I timed ranged from 7 to 162 minutes and averaged 58.2 minutes. Five intervals of neglect ranged from 17 to 46 minutes and averaged 25.2 minutes. The nest was occupied by one member of the pair or the other for only 70 percent of the seven hours. In their manner of incubation, these puffbirds resembled restless toucans more than patient White-whiskered Softwings, their close relatives.

Nesting Habits of Other Puffbirds
Many of the thirty-three species of puffbirds, distributed over the American continents from southern Mexico to northern Argentina, nest in termitaries. One March, in the dry woodland of northwestern Costa Rica, I watched a pair of White-necked Puffbirds take turns digging into a large black arboreal termitary. They worked for one to eight minutes at a stretch, were no more vocal than their close relatives, the Black-breasted Puffbirds, and were equally undisturbed by my unconcealed presence. In May, my son and I watched a pair of Pied Puffbirds alternately enter a dome-shaped termitary, about 90 feet (27 meters) up in a leafless treetop in the Caribbean rain forest; but observation was so difficult that we could not decide whether they were still excavating or preparing to incubate. Cherrie (1916) told how a Russet-throated Puffbird remained in its chamber in a termitary while he hacked it open and termites swarmed over the steadfast bird on its single fresh egg.

Other puffbirds nest in burrows in the

ground, which may be very long, like those of the White-fronted Nunbird and Swallow-wing, or short, like those of the White-whiskered Softwing. Unlike the nest chambers in termitaries, those at the ends of the subterranean tunnels are often lined with dead leaves or dry grass (Haverschmidt 1950; Skutch 1958a, 1972, 1980b). Other puffbirds have been found nesting in hollow trees, woodpeckers' holes, burrows of small mam-

mals, and the oven-shaped nests of clay built by Pale-legged Horneros. Puffbirds lay two or three, rarely four, glossy white eggs that, in the few species which have been studied, are incubated by both parents. Both attend the young, sometimes, as in the White-fronted Nunbird, assisted by one or more helpers. The habits of this ancient family, formerly much more widespread, are poorly known and would well repay further study.

30. Prong-billed Barbet
Semnornis frantzii

Soon after my arrival in Costa Rica nearly half a century ago, I visited a dairy farm on the northern slope of huge, sprawling Volcán Irazú. On sturdy mountain horses, the owner and I rode past the many-cratered summit, then down long treeless slopes covered with coarse grass and scattered low bushes. Below this, we passed through a zone of tall bamboos, which merged into an open wood of low, gnarled, moss-draped trees of fantastic aspect. Gradually increasing in stature as we descended, the trees formed a closed forest dominated by oaks and magnificently spreading alders up to 150 feet (45 meters) high. Still lower along the muddy trail, the forest of broad-leaved trees became more diverse, with many clustering tall palms and tree ferns and a profusion of bright-flowered shrubs in the undergrowth. The terrain was extremely broken, with towering precipices and bare rocky cliffs, over which poured many a slender waterfall. Between the escarpments were sloping or nearly level ter-

races that had been planted with pasture grass. On one of these the owner's little cottage stood, with a view over a chasmlike valley to the bare summit of neighboring Volcán Turrialba, now quiescent. Here I passed a day and a half; and, when rain and mist permitted, I began to become acquainted with the birds of Costa Rican cloud forests.

I had never been in a region where birds of many kinds tolerated such close approaches. A Hairy Woodpecker permitted me to watch him from only 6 feet (1.8 meters) away, and many other birds were almost equally confiding. It was easy to imagine that I had landed upon some uninhabited mountainous island, whose feathered denizens had as yet had no unhappy experience of humans. Along a trail through that lovely mist-shrouded forest, I met three brownish birds, about the size of Rose-breasted Grosbeaks, eating the large berries of a tree of the melastome family, which they held beneath a foot while they tore them apart with

thick bills. As fearless as nearly all the birds in this wild region, they continued calmly to eat their fruits, while I studied them at close range.

They were short-tailed birds, plainly attired, with big heads and dense plumage that made them look very stout. Their upper plumage was olive, their underparts chiefly grayish; but their crowns, throats, and breasts were a warm golden-brown. The feathers surrounding the base of the bill were black. On his hindhead the male wore a long tuft of glossy black feathers, which the female lacked. Their short, very thick bills were bluish, and their eyes were brown. I could not imagine what these strange birds might be, unless they were aberrant, grosbeaklike finches—although finches rarely hold food with their feet. Had I noticed that two toes on each foot were directed backward and that the lower mandible terminated in two sharp prongs, into the deep indentation between which fitted the slender tip of the upper mandible, I would have known at once that my conjecture was far from correct. Lacking one of the field guides that were published many years later, I was long in learning the name and classification of these peculiar birds. Familiarity with the sharp-billed, brightly colored Red-headed Barbet did not help me identify them; on the contrary, it threw me off the track. Months later, I learned that they were Prong-billed Barbets, little-known birds found only in Costa Rica and western Panama, chiefly between 2,000 and 7,500 feet (600 and 2,280 meters) above sea level on the storm-beaten Caribbean slopes of the cordilleras.

Two years after my first meeting with the barbets, I went to dwell at Montaña Azul, where I studied the Resplendent Quetzal and the Emerald Toucanet. Here barbets were abundant in the forest, where they usually foraged in the lower levels but often ventured forth into weedy pastures. Almost as tame and fearless as on Volcán Irazú, they permitted a close approach. Frequently they scolded with slight rattling notes while they watched me intently from the edge of a thicket. In July, I sometimes saw a solitary individual, sometimes two or more together. Sometimes one pursued another, voicing low harsh notes. Their utterances were mostly low and unmusical, of a rattling or rasping character. Largely vegetarian, they consumed great quantities of fruits of many kinds. Often I saw them cling beside heavy fruiting spikes of epiphytic aroids, to pluck the red or orange berries from a thick fleshy axis. They also ate the petals of large flowers, plucking the blossom and holding it against a branch with one foot, while they tore it with a thick bill.

At almost any hour of the day, I often heard a deep, far-carrying, rather throaty call floating out of the surrounding forests; not unmelodious in the distance, it sounded somewhat like the syllables *cwa cwa cwa*, rapidly repeated many times. This call always began as a sudden outburst of sound, in the production of which, to judge from its character, a number of voices joined. For many days I continued to hear this mysterious cry without learning its source. It always conjured up the vision of a fowl certainly no smaller than a quail, and I inclined to the opinion that it was of the gallinaceous order. My surprise was great when the true author of this utterance was revealed to me.

One morning, while I walked along the ever miry Sarapiquí trail, some birds at the edge of the forest, unseen by me, began to shout in the manner described. Soon a barbet perching in plain view in a young Cecropia tree beside the trail joined in the chorus. Presently two of the birds from the forest flew into the same low tree, where they faced each other on adjacent branches and called loudly as before. Their greatly out-swollen throats accounted for the production of such a loud, far-carrying sound by so small a bird. Later, in the breeding season, I sometimes watched a mated pair duetting with this loud call. The voice of the male was distinctly fuller and deeper than that of his consort. These sonorous calls earn for the barbet its inappropriate local name, *cacareón*, from the Spanish *cacarear* ("to cackle"). Duetting also appears to be widespread among the numerous Old World members of the barbet family.

Late in August, I discovered that seven barbets slept in a cavity about 75 feet (23 meters) up in a tall slender dead trunk at the forest's edge. The round entrance of their dormitory, shaded by bromeliads and other epiphytes, closely resembled the doorway of a woodpecker's hole. Emerging one by one, very early in the morning, while ease-loving woodpeckers delayed in their snug holes, the barbets gathered in the open and sounded their far-carrying chorus in the dim gray light of dawn. This high hole continued to be their dormitory until at least mid October. By February, when it had fallen, the barbets had moved to a huge blasted tree standing in the neighboring pasture. Watching this hole at daybreak, I stood amazed as more and more came out, until I had counted sixteen, the largest number of birds of any kind that I have found sleeping in the same dormitory. The cavity, about 25 feet (7.6 meters) up and screened by leafy shoots that made observation difficult, seemed too small to hold so many birds with comfort. Probably they massed together two or three deep.

These sixteen birds did not come and go as a single flock. After their morning emergence, they flew off in various directions; and in the evening they arrived, one by one, over an interval of about twenty minutes. Two quarreled briefly, with low grating notes, as they were about to enter. Evidently the good-companionship that prevailed in the flocks during the winter months was giving way to other feelings. In March, the number of lodgers in the big blasted tree gradually dwindled, until by early April it was abandoned.

Now the barbets entered a period of restlessness; the number of occupants and the holes they occupied changed frequently. One barbet might repulse another at the doorway or attack from the rear another who was about to enter. Finally, those who had quarreled might lodge together, retiring after the light had grown so dim that I could hardly see them. As late as April 6, I found four barbets sleeping in the same cavity. After this, all the old dormitories were abandoned. Out of so much restlessness and moving around emerged mated pairs, who soon be-

gan to carve new holes. In this month the barbets became more vocal; often a number of them, scattered through the woods or through trees and shrubs in the clearings, called back and forth with deep resonant voices, producing an impressive volume of sound.

The Nest

The shape of a bird's bill is a poor indication of the kind of nest it will make. If the jacamar's long thin beak appears ill fitted for digging a burrow in the ground or in a hard termitary, the barbet's short, swollen bill seems even less adequate for carving into wood. Until I found them doing so late in March, I assumed that they occupied old woodpecker holes, which they sometimes do for sleeping but never, as far as I know, for breeding. They choose for their nest cavities wood softened by decay but still firm and solid, in dead trees or dead branches of living trees. I saw none of their nests in wood so far advanced in decay that it had begun to crumble. The six occupied nests that I found ranged in height from 11 to over 60 feet (3.4 to 18 meters). In general, the sites chosen would have appealed to woodpeckers, with the difference that the barbets sometimes placed their nests where the doorway was screened by leafy shoots or epiphytic growths, whereas the woodpeckers that I know nearly always prefer exposed situations in clean, leafless trunks, where they enjoy a wide outlook from their doorways.

With a single exception, all the nests I discovered were in clearings, never far from the forest that covered most of the region. Four were in pastures, and one was beside the trail, in a low post that upheld the single telegraph wire that ran down to El Muelle de Sarapiquí. This was the lowest of all, only 11 feet (3.4 meters) up. Although I found only one nest in the forest, probably more careful searching would have revealed many more. Most of the forest birds whose nesting I greatly wanted to study—Resplendent Quetzals, Emerald Toucanets, Spotted-crowned Woodcreepers, Buffy Tuftedcheeks, and these barbets—took advantage of dead trees standing in the pastures as sites for

Clearing in subtropical forest at Montaña Azul, where Prong-billed Barbets, Resplendent Quetzals, and Emerald Toucanets nested.

their nests; and I soon located so many in the clearings that I had little time or need to hunt in the woodland for more.

The barbets worked principally early in the morning and late in the afternoon—at least, at these times I was most successful in watching them. The male and the female shared the labor, whether equally or not I could not learn, as the nests where I watched them carving into the wood were so high that it was difficult to distinguish the tuft of black feathers on the male's hindhead. While one member of the pair worked, its mate perched close by, often stretching a brownish wing, as though bored with waiting. I never saw one working while the other was out of sight, as woodpeckers frequently do. In their reluctance to work in the absence of a mate, barbets agree with trogons, jacamars, kingfishers, motmots, puffbirds, and certain parrots, all of which nest in holes or burrows excavated by themselves.

The most difficult part of nest carving was apparently making a start, when the barbets had to cling to the side of the trunk in a posture less natural to them than to woodpeckers. The carving, as far as I could see, was done chiefly by biting away the wood rather than by chiseling—a procedure for which their short, very thick bills were hardly adapted. Yet sometimes I distinctly heard a tapping sound from a hole in which a barbet was at work. It might be supposed that the delicate prongs at the ends of their mandibles would be broken by such use, but I found no evidence of this. The wood into which they carved, although still in those early stages of decay when it was neither discolored nor crumbling, was so soft that I could dig into it with my fingernails.

The barbets worked in short shifts. Eight minutes was the longest interval that one remained continuously in an unfinished hole, presumably working, while I watched them. More often they stayed in the hole only a few minutes at a stretch. At the beginning, they left the cavity tailfirst; but, after it grew wide enough to permit them to turn, they made their exit headfirst. Emerging, the barbet brought out a billful of loosened particles, which it took to a perch beside its waiting mate or often carried beyond my view among the trees, before it dropped them. Frequently a barbet entered the hole apparently for no other purpose than to carry away a billful of wood chips. Among hole- and burrow-nesting birds, barbets are rather unique in carrying away the excavated material, although certain titmice and chickadees sometimes do so. The form of a barbet's bill enables it to carry a larger load than seems feasible for woodpeckers, who usually throw the wood particles through the doorway.

One nest that I watched a pair of barbets excavate required no less than eight days to finish. As soon as the cavity was big enough, the male and the female slept together in it, deserting the sometimes crowded dormitories in which they had hitherto lodged. Now they emerged later in the morning than they had while they slept in larger companies. While one looked through the doorway upon awaking, the other might linger in the bottom, putting the finishing touches on the woodwork of their new bedroom—as I inferred from the tapping sounds, as of a woodpecker, that I heard coming from the nest before the morning departure of its inmates.

Viewed from the ground, the doorway of a barbet's nest was hardly distinguishable from that of a small woodpecker. But, at the first glimpse of the interior, I noticed obvious differences. The wood surrounding the orifice of a woodpecker's hole has little thickness, for the bird begins to carve downward as soon as it has penetrated the outer shell. The barbet continues to dig more deeply into the wood before turning downward, making an entranceway like a short horizontal tube, 2 or 3 inches (5 or 7.6 centimeters) long. The difference between the woodpecker's and the barbet's entranceways corresponds to that between the doorways of a thin-walled modern house and an ancient edifice with walls several feet thick. Once through the doorway, which is about 1⅞ inches (4.8 centimeters) in diameter and well into the heart of the trunk, the barbet turns abruptly downward, leaving little space in the top of its nest behind the aperture, while the top of a woodpecker's nest has a more spacious vestibule.

For the rest, barbets' and woodpeckers' holes are similar in shape, both being deep and relatively narrow, rounded on sides and bottom. The rotundity of some of the barbets' chambers was broken by ridges of wood projecting irregularly into the interior, these doubtless having been too hard for the birds to remove with their less efficient carving tools; but others, in wood of more uniform texture, were as neatly rounded as the best woodpeckers' work. The cavity in which sixteen barbets slept differed from all the others that I examined in being wider than deep, flat on the bottom, with very irregular instead of rounded sides. Its peculiar shape was apparently determined by the configuration of the softer portions of this still slightly decayed stub. I did not see barbets carve this cavity, but it was obviously the work of some bird, more likely barbets than woodpeckers.

The Eggs and Incubation

Soon after the pair of barbets began to sleep in their newly finished hole, the female started to lay her eggs. The earliest egg that I found appeared on April 9. Thereafter, one was laid daily in this nest until it contained five. Each of two other accessible nests had four eggs, also laid in April. These eggs were pure white and glossy, resembling those of woodpeckers. Since to open such a nest with saw and chisel decreases its chances of success, no matter how carefully it is closed again, I did not remove the eggs for measurement but viewed them with a mirror and an electric bulb. They lay on a bed of chips, no softer lining having been supplied for them.

At the nest to which I devoted most attention during this period, incubation began with the laying of the fourth of the five eggs. The pair continued to sleep together in the nest cavity during the laying period, throughout the incubation period, while the nestlings were present, and even after they emerged. Such an arrangement, although rare among birds, is by no means unknown in other species where both sexes incubate (Skutch 1976).

Awaking at dawn, the barbets sometimes uttered low rattling notes within their chamber. Soon one would occupy the doorway and linger a short while—at times as long as eight or nine minutes—gazing upon the growing daylight. Then it would emerge and fly away. The other might follow immediately or delay within for a few minutes more. The eggs were unattended for a brief interval, while the pair sought breakfast. Then, in from seven to sixteen minutes after the departure of the last, one would return to resume incubation. On the single morning when I succeeded in identifying the bird returning at this time, it was the female.

In the early morning, the barbets sat impatiently. The call of their kind coming from the neighboring forest would draw the incubating bird from its nest, even if it had been within for only a few minutes. Sometimes, after a spell on the eggs, the barbet would come out, perch on a convenient branch beside the doorway to look around, then reenter the nest. Or it would call until it received an answer, then fly off in the direction of the sound. Thus the eggs would be left uncovered again, but rarely for long, since one or the other member of the pair would soon return for a turn on them. When

one remained in the nest until the other arrived to replace it, the newcomer clung beside the doorway until its consort emerged. Rattling notes accompanied the changeover. As the morning grew older and the drowsy hours of the day approached, the barbets apparently became reconciled to longer spells at their lonely and possibly boring task— they sat for an hour or nearly two at a stretch. Sometimes, while incubating, the male barbet relieved his ennui by tearing or hammering at the walls around him, thereby enlarging the chamber.

On April 17, at the nest where incubation had been in progress for five days, I made a record of the parents' movements. I began to watch at 5:20, as day broke. At 5:25, I heard rattling notes from the nest. Two minutes later, one barbet looked through the doorway, where it lingered until it flew out at 5:36. The mate delayed inside for six minutes more, departing at 5:42. Sixteen minutes later, a member of the pair returned to incubate. Starting at 5:42, their sessions and absences in minutes, during nearly seven hours, are given in the accompanying table. If the figures are read from left to right, like the text of a book, the actual sequence of events can be followed.

The male attended the eggs for a total of at least 132 minutes, the female for 168 minutes, and 29 minutes were accounted for by members of the pair not recognized as they entered or left the hole. The total number of minutes devoted to incubation by both members of the pair was 329, and for 77 minutes the eggs were neglected. Accordingly, the eggs were unattended for slightly less than one-fifth of the nearly seven hours.

During the incubation period, mated barbets gave many tokens of mutual attachment. I saw a male feed his mate. Perching close together, they billed one another's feathers. Frequently they joined their voices in loud throaty duets, when it was evident that the female's tones were weaker than her mate's and somewhat hoarse in quality.

Although so gregarious through much of the year, now in the breeding season the barbets became strongly territorial. They re-

Incubation by a Pair of Prong-billed Barbets

Male	?	Female	Neither
			16
	15		2
	14		3
24			13
		32	
12			30
		26	
81			12
15			1
		110	
—	—	—	—
132	29	168	77

pulsed every trespassing barbet who ventured near their nest, flying at it with harsh rattles and rasping scolds. Rarely, two birds clinched and fell to the ground; but, on the single occasion when I witnessed such an encounter, neither contestant appeared to suffer injury. Birds of other kinds were also driven from near a nest. A female Hairy Woodpecker, who had been sleeping in a hole in the same small tree where a pair of barbets nested, abandoned her dormitory at about the time the barbets began to lay, possibly having been driven away by them.

'On the morning when I watched the pair of barbets incubate, the female alighted close beside a fairly large gray lizard which clung head downward on a hanging branch. The reptile immediately, apparently as a warning, protruded its pale pink gular pouch, which almost touched the barbet. Lightly she touched it with her bill, giving no indication of alarm, although the lizard was bigger than she was. This mutual confidence of two very dissimilar creatures was pleasing to witness.

Indeed, the barbets were fearless of most creatures, great or small. At their nests, as while foraging through the woods and bushy clearings, they seemed to know that I would not harm them. Even at low nests, much hammering and shaking of the trunk were needed to make a barbet leave when I wished to examine the contents. A few light taps might make it look out to see what was happening below, but it was rarely in a hurry to depart. Often it would watch while a helper and I sat a heavy 23-foot (7-meter) ladder against the trunk, only to fly reluctantly out when I had climbed to within a yard or two of its doorway. Often, too, a barbet would return to the eggs before we had time to remove the ladder. Even at the low nest in the telegraph pole, the barbets would enter while several people stood around it. One tried to go in before I removed the electric bulb that illuminated the interior but desisted when it struck the cord that passed through the doorway. With barbets, as with most of the birds whose nest life I studied in this montane forest, I did not need to use a blind—a fortunate circumstance, since the climate was so wet, and sitting for hours closely surrounded by wet cloth is neither comfortable nor healthful.

As I climbed toward a barbets' nest on the afternoon of April 26, I heard weak cries, as of nestlings, emerging from it. But, when I inserted the electric bulb and mirror and peered in, I beheld only the unbroken white surfaces of five eggs. The chicks were calling in their shells as they strove to escape from them. The parent who was in charge of the nest when I arrived became more excited than I had ever before seen either member of this pair. He flew back and forth between the two stubs of branches which were all that remained on the dead tree, a yard or two above my head, uttering loud cackling cries such as I had not hitherto heard. These soon drew his mate, who shared his agitation.

While I climbed the ladder toward the nest on the following afternoon, I heard similar cries coming from it, but now they were much louder and of a rather strident, squeaky nature. Hastening to illuminate the cavity and push in the little mirror, I saw my first barbet nestlings—perhaps the first nestlings of the Prong-billed Barbet that any naturalist had seen. The five eggs had hatched in thirteen or fourteen days, counting from the date on which the last was laid, and all within twenty-four hours, despite the fact that both parents had slept in the nest with them during the period of laying.

The Nestlings

The five hatchlings, pink-skinned and wholly devoid of down, huddled in a compact mass. Their eyes were tightly closed. The lower mandibles of their short bills were both longer and broader than the upper mandibles, as in newly hatched woodpeckers, toucans, and kingfishers. Their egg teeth were less prominent than those of woodpeckers. Their conspicuous heel pads were covered with long sharp papillae. The fleshy caudal protuberance, longer and more prominent than on most nestlings, was used as a third point of support by the little barbets as they stood upon the wood particles that carpeted their nursery floor. The parents had already removed all but a single fragment of the shells. They flew back and forth close above me, voicing the same loud and sharp cries of distress that I had first heard on the preceding day. I had hardly descended to the ground before one entered the nest.

One of the nestlings vanished within three days of hatching, another on the following day, leaving only three chicks. Possibly the prevailing stormy weather reduced the parents' ability to nourish them. The survivors always stood in the center of the floor, with their naked bodies pressed together and their slender necks intertwined, from time to time voicing sharp little cries of hunger.

During the first days, the parents brought the hatchlings tiny insects, some with wings, and other objects too small to be recognized while held in their thick bills. On each succeeding day the nestlings were given more fruits, until when over a week old they were nourished almost entirely with fruits, insects being very rarely brought. Whole small berries were sometimes delivered to them, and the red pulp of some larger, unidentified fruit was brought in great quantities. Once the male entered the nest with the green fruit of the Ira Rosa, a favorite food of the Resplen-

dent Quetzal. But this large hard item was obviously more than a nestling could swallow; after a minute or two, the parent reappeared in the doorway and with difficulty forced the fruit down his own throat. The two parents took about equal shares in feeding and brooding the nestlings. Although they continued to sleep together in the nest, by day I never saw one enter while the other was within.

The parents kept the nest scrupulously clean by removing droppings mixed with the wood fragments that covered the bottom of the chamber. Each time one left, it usually carried a large billful of this mixture to a good distance from the nest. By the time the nestlings were four or five days old, all the litter of fragments had disappeared; nevertheless, the parents continued to remove large billfuls of chips. Evidently, they dug fresh fragments from the wood surrounding the cavity, as I have seen woodpeckers do.

On the afternoon of May 6, a torrential rain was driven by a strong wind into the southward-facing doorway of this hole, flooding it and drowning the nestlings. At the age of nine or ten days, their pinfeathers were just becoming visible beneath the transparent skin, and their eyes were still tightly closed. Their development was so slow that they would probably have remained in the nest for a month or more, as certain African barbets do (Moreau and Moreau 1940).

With the loss of this and all my other accessible nests, I was unable to follow the later stages of the nestlings' development. But, on June 12, I found a nest only 20 feet (6 meters) above the ground, in a massive epiphyte-burdened stump in a pasture, favorably situated for watching. I did not need to bring a ladder to see what it contained, for the well-feathered nestlings showed their heads in the doorway, and to approach them too closely might have caused their premature departure.

Although these two young barbets spent most of the day looking, by turns, through the doorway, a parent arriving with food almost invariably pushed inside to feed them. Only once did I see a parent pass food to a nestling while clinging outside, as many other hole-nesting birds do when attending older nestlings. Small soft fruits and fruit pulp formed the great bulk of the young barbets' diet. Hard fruits, such as were preferred by the Resplendent Quetzals and Emerald Toucanets nesting in the neighborhood, were rarely brought by the barbets. They would arrive at the nest with their thick bills full to capacity with soft fruit pulp and apparently still more in their throats. The nestlings were fed very frequently and consumed prodigious quantities of fruits. Rarely, they received an insect. The parents cleaned their nest most actively between 6:00 and 6:15 in the evening, carrying to a distance such great quantities of fresh-looking wood particles that I was certain that they were newly torn from the solid wood surrounding the nest chamber. After this quarter hour devoted to preparing the nest for the night, both parents vanished for an equal interval, during which they probably found their own supper. Then, around half past six, both entered to sleep with their well-fed young.

The Fledglings' Return to the Nest

This low nest was the latest of all that I found. The two young barbets, hatched from eggs laid in early May, flew from it before nine o'clock on the morning of June 16. At this hour, I found them in a clump of epiphyte-laden trees 50 feet (15 meters) in front of the nest, where the parents were feeding them. These fledglings rather closely resembled the adults, but their foreheads and forenecks were a duller shade of brown. Their bills, instead of being bluish like those of the adults, were horn color, with a suffusion of black that was deepest in the middle of the upper mandible. Their eyes were conspicuously ringed with bare pale yellowish skin that gave them a facial expression quite different from that of their parents, who lacked such orbital rings. Neither of these fledglings bore on its hindhead the tuft of black feathers that distinguishes the male; but on the occiput of each was a little round gray spot, which both parents lacked. They were evidently both females, for about this

time I saw another young barbet, still being fed by his parents, who wore a black stripe on his hindhead, very much like that of the adult male.

Confident that the whole family, old and young, would return to sleep in the cavity from which the latter had just flown, I watched as the rainy afternoon ended. At a few minutes before five o'clock, the four barbets arrived, and a parent entered the hole, as though to show the way. Following the adult, the fledglings alighted on top of the trunk, but, not finding the doorway, they flew to nearby trees. For the next hour, the parents continued to go in and out of the hole, trying to guide the young to it, just as I have seen Southern House-Wrens, Banded-backed Wrens, and other birds do in similar circumstances. In this interval, the young made little effort to follow. Although they could fly 50 feet (15 meters) or more, one, after failing to find the doorway, grew tired and alighted on the close-cropped grass beside me; then, after a short rest, she rose to perch on a lovely Cavendishia shrub that grew on a neighboring tree. Wholly devoid of fear, she permitted me to touch her, even her bill, merely regarding me with curiosity, like a newborn calf.

As night approached, both parents entered the nest and stayed there. Soon after this, one of the fledglings, who had hitherto been quite silent, called *cwa cwa cwa* in tones weaker than those of the adults. Hearing this, both parents left the nest and joined the two young in a neighboring treetop. Then they flew back to the hole with the young following them, as for the last hour they had been trying, by example, to induce them to do. One fledgling reached the doorway and entered. The other became confused, slipped from the nest trunk to the ground, then wandered around as though completely bewildered. Following, I easily caught her, and for a quarter of an hour I held her in front of the hole on my open hand. When finally she flew, it was to a tree farther from the nest, where she flitted from bough to bough until lost to my view in the foliage and gloom, for daylight was waning fast. After they had one fledgling in the nest with them, the parents remained within, apparently forgetting the other, who passed the night amid dripping foliage.

On the following evening, both young barbets entered the dormitory. After their arrival on the third evening, the whole family rested quietly in a treetop for a quarter of an hour, without eating, as they appeared full and contented. Before the family retired, the parents removed two overflowing billfuls of wood particles; even after the young emerged, they were keeping their dormitory clean. Soon after six o'clock, both young barbets followed their parents through the doorway without difficulty. On subsequent evenings, the four members of the family went to rest in no set order. In the mornings, the young at first tended to linger in their dormitory after the parents' departure, especially when day dawned wet and blustery; but by early July, three weeks after the young barbets began to fly, the whole family became active at about the same time. By the month's end, this cavity was abandoned, and I could not discover what had happened to its occupants. A solitary barbet, who in August slept in a neighboring hole where Hairy Woodpeckers had raised a brood, may have been one of them.

Postscript

Birds that nest in holes and burrows are usually more successful than those that build open nests, but this was not true of the barbets. Of the six nests that I found, five of which had certainly contained eggs, only the last was successful, producing two young. One at a great height had been torn open, apparently by a Tayra or some other powerful arboreal mammal; one appeared to have been entered by a weasel or a rat; from one the nestlings were taken by people; and in one, as already told, two nestlings vanished and the others drowned. Fernando Gómez, the boy who helped me and who knew the birds well, saw an Emerald Toucanet tearing at the doorway of a barbets' nest that contained eggs, while the owners flitted around and protested. The thickness of the wood around the orifice thwarted the great-billed bird's attempt to open the nest.

One day I saw a fierce little Bat Falcon seize a full-grown Prong-billed Barbet, but no other instance of predation on adults came to my attention. A formidable enemy of these mountain birds is the prolonged period of rain, which occasionally so saturates their plumage that they cannot fly. During a spell of bad weather in December, some children found a barbet in this sad plight; but after a few days in a dry place, with an abundance of berries to eat, it recovered and flew away.

The forests amid which I studied Prong-billed Barbets were long since destroyed by the ax, and throughout their limited range woodland is yearly dwindling. Unless it is preserved in parks and reservations, this quaint bird may before long become only a memory.

31. Rainbow-billed Toucan

Ramphastos sulfuratus

No family of tropical American birds, with the possible exception of hummingbirds, receives so much publicity as toucans. These big birds with grotesquely large, vividly colored bills catch the fancy of artists, designers, and popular writers; they seem to symbolize the tropical American "jungles." Although for well over a century toucans have aroused wonder and interest among people who dwell far from the forests where they are at home, even today their habits are very inadequately known. Beebe (in Beebe et al. 1917) described the nests, eggs, or nestlings of several toucans of Guyana. The first careful study of the nesting of any toucan was that made by Van Tyne (1929) of the present species on Barro Colorado Island. Unfortunately, his observations were cut short by the loss of nestlings. Subsequently, a few other detailed studies of toucans have been made and will be mentioned in due course. We still know very little about the habits of the mountain toucans (*Andigena*); of the toucanets of the genus *Selenidera*, which differ from other toucans in that the sexes are unlike in coloration; and of the Saffron Toucanet of Brazil. And, for all other groups of toucans, our information is far from adequate.

Even without their enormous beaks, Rainbow-billed Toucans would be spectacular. From 17 to 22 inches (43 to 56 centimeters) long, they are largely black, washed with maroon on the hindneck and tinged with green elsewhere. Their upper tail coverts are white; bright yellow covers their cheeks, foreneck, and chest; and their under tail coverts are bright red. The bare skin around each dark eye is green and yellow. On their great bills one can distinguish tints of red, orange, yellow, green, and blue, all so delicately blended that the bird deserves to be known as the Rainbow-billed Toucan, although more prosaic books call it the Keel-billed Toucan. Males are larger on the average than females, especially in the size of their bills; but their measurements overlap, and it is usually difficult to distinguish the sexes.

The Rainbow-billed Toucan is a bird of the Caribbean rain forests from southern Mexico through Central America and northern Colombia to extreme northwestern Venezuela. In northern Costa Rica it spills over the low continental divide into the forests of the drier Pacific side, especially where they are kept verdant by high water tables. In southern Costa Rica, where rain forests similar to those of the Caribbean side are separated from the latter by the lofty Cordillera de Talamanca, Rainbow-billed Toucans have not been found on the Pacific side. In Mexico and Guatemala they are confined to low altitudes, chiefly below 2,000 feet (600 meters), but from Honduras southward they occasionally ascend much higher, even to 5,000 feet (1,500 meters) in the Santa Marta region of Colombia (Todd and Carriker 1922).

From the forests that are their true home, Rainbowbills roam through neighboring areas with scattered tall trees—shaded plantations of cacao or coffee, pastures, second-growth woods—to forage and sometimes even to nest. On these excursions one has opportunities to study their social organization and manner of flight such as are seldom enjoyed in the midst of high forest. The birds travel in small parties of up to a dozen individuals, rarely more, which exhibit none of the closely coordinated maneuvers of a flock of parrots or pigeons. When one takes wing, its companions linger behind, as though de-

bating whether to follow. Then, one after another, they straggle along, single file, behind the leader.

Each takes a number of rapid wingbeats, then completely closes its wings, whereupon it begins to fall, as though borne downward by its great forward-pointing beak. Immediately the black wings are spread widely again, converting the fall into a glide with a slight downward inclination, which is followed by a series of beats that recover the lost altitude. Thus the toucan traces an undulatory course from treetop to treetop. The sudden opening of the wings imparts to the toucan's flight its peculiar character, in keeping with the whole aspect and behavior of the bird—who is not so much grotesque and ungainly as unexpected, an artist's fantasy come to life in flesh and feathers. Clumsy in appearance, something of an avian clown, the toucan is sufficiently agile to meet all the demands of its arboreal life; it is hardly impeded, and in certain situations it is obviously aided, by its seemingly heavy bill, which is actually a light hollow shell of horny material strengthened by an interior network of thin bony rods.

Toucans are among the most frugivorous arboreal birds of tropical American forests. In addition to a number of unidentified fruits, I have seen the Rainbowbill eat the green fruiting spikes of the Cecropia tree; white objects that were probably seeds of *Inga* or *Protium* enclosed in soft coats; and the hard little seeds of *Alchornea costaricensis*, thinly covered by a digestible red aril. These last it shared with at least twenty-three other kinds of birds, including oropendolas, trogons, woodpeckers, tityras, flycatchers large and small, colorful little honeycreepers, and a variety of tanagers and finches. Van Tyne gave a list of eight species which he believed included most of the important food plants of this toucan on Barro Colorado Island. Among them are two palms, *Astrocaryum polystachyum* and *Iriartea exorrhiza*; a fig, *Ficus* species; the trees *Virola panamensis*, *Protium sessiliflorum*, and *Cupania seemanni*; and the liana *Cnestidium rufescens*. The palms and the fig provide edible fruits, but the other three trees

and the vine have capsular fruits with arillate seeds, which alone supply nourishment to the toucans, as in the case of *Alchornea*. On the same island, Chapman (1929) watched Rainbow-billed Toucans eating many of the small hard berries of the Mangabé (*Didymopanax morototoni*), a tall tree of the aralia family.

Rainbow-billed Toucans supplement their frugivorous diet with a small amount of animal protein in the form of insects, spiders, and an occasional small lizard or snake. Doubtless, like other members of their family, they are not above devouring eggs and nestlings. While I have not such definite evidence for this as I have in the case of certain other toucans, I once watched a Rainbowbill behave in a most incriminating fashion. The bird clung to the twig from which a Royal Flycatcher's nest hung above a woodland stream in Guatemala and pulled at the long pensile structure as though searching for something. But the nest was already empty.

Although a long bill helps a bird reach food, it creates a problem when it comes to swallowing, as is true of birds so diverse as tiny slender-billed hummingbirds and big swollen-billed toucans. The latter solve the problem by seizing the morsel in the tip of the bill, then giving the head an upward toss while opening the mouth, thereby throwing the berry or other item back between the parted mandibles into the throat. Once, while watching a nest, I witnessed an amusing display of this habit. A parent arrived with a white seed in the tip of its bill for its nestling, but it hesitated to deliver it in my presence. Perching nearby, it threw the seed back into its throat, probably swallowing it, then immediately brought it up into the tip of its bill again. It repeated this whole performance twenty-three times more, then flew away visibly carrying the seed.

On another occasion, a parent hesitating to take a large insect to the nest alternately held it beneath a foot and took it back into its bill, the whole while calling loudly. Holding things beneath a foot is a habit witnessed in only a minority of arboreal birds, but it seems to be general in the toucan family.

On Barro Colorado Island, one morning in

Rain forest of the foothills in northern Honduras, home of the Rainbow-billed Toucan.

Toucans, as a family, are far from being melodious, and the present species is no exception. Compared with certain trogons, motmots, and jacamars, it is a poor vocalist. Its harsh notes, which have been compared to the croaks of frogs, are often repeated so rapidly that they seem mechanical; the sound effect is much like that produced by winding a large cheap clock. Years ago, I tried to paraphrase the notes of some Rainbowbills that I heard "singing" in the forested foothills of northern Honduras. *Quenk quenk quok quok* they began, the notes sometimes so guttural that they resembled the croaking of a distant bullfrog, at other times higher-pitched and shriller. Little by little, the toucans warmed up to a continuous *quenky quenky quenky quok quok quok*, achieving a certain elementary rhythm and winning my admiration for their wholehearted effort if not for their voices. At a distance, a chorus of toucans reminded me of a spring chorus of frogs in a woodland pond in North America.

The Rainbowbills' vocabulary is extremely limited. In Costa Rica, I could detect no difference between the notes they poured out interminably, protesting our intrusion at their nest, and those which they used when "singing" unperturbed. While calling or singing, they throw their heads and great brilliant bills up and down and from side to side, restlessly bowing and turning. Aside from the croak, this toucan's only utterance appears to be a short castanetlike rattle, which one immediately assumes to be produced by clacking the mandibles rapidly together, although actually it is a vocal rather than a mechanical sound.

The sleeping posture of toucans has often been described, from observations of captive birds. They turn back the bill and lay it along the back, bring the tail forward until it covers the bill, and, fluffing out their plumage, transform their angular bodies into round balls of feathers. Thus they greatly reduce the space they occupy, and it has been widely assumed that this is an arrangement for sleeping in holes in trees. Although it has long been known that the middle-sized araçari toucans do sleep in holes (as will be told in the next two chapters), the only other

April, I watched a pair of Rainbowbills in the top of a tall tree. One held a bright red fruit in the tip of his multihued bill and offered it to his companion. The latter, evidently not hungry, moved away without accepting it, but the first followed and persisted in presenting it. Finally, the second toucan took the berry in her bill, apparently only to free herself of the importunities of the first, for in a minute she dropped the brilliant object to the ground. This was evidently an instance of nuptial feeding, which I have also seen in the Chestnut-mandibled Toucan, Fiery-billed Araçari, and Emerald Toucanet.

free toucan that has been reported to do so is, to my knowledge, the Guianan Toucanet (O'Brian 1979). My doubt, expressed long ago, that the big *Ramphastos* toucans sleep in cavities finds a measure of confirmation in an observation by Bourne (1974), who, shining his flashlight into the crown of a tree in Guyana, detected six Red-billed Toucans roosting side by side, in close contact, on a limb about 70 feet (21 meters) high.

The Nest and Eggs

The Rainbow-billed Toucans whose nests we studied were neighbors of the Great Tinamou, Black-throated Trogon, Broad-billed Motmot, and Rufous Motmot in the wet forests of northeastern Costa Rica. The first of these nests was called to my attention by Gordon Orians, who noticed it while he was censusing birds on a forested ridge at La Selva. The nest hole, 20 feet (6 meters) up in a smooth branchless trunk of a living Gavilán tree of moderate size, was apparently created by the decay of a knot rather than by a woodpecker or some other bird. From an opening only 2⅜ inches (6 centimeters) in diameter, the roughly cylindrical cavity extended straight downward for about 14 inches (36 centimeters). Its nearly smooth walls were almost constantly wet. Fifty feet (15 meters) away, in a trunk of a somewhat larger Gavilán tree, was another cavity that, outwardly at least, had much the same aspect. Here a pair of Chestnut-mandibled Toucans nested simultaneously with the Rainbowbills in both of the years when we studied them. The two big toucans appeared to ignore each other (Skutch 1972).

When first examined on May 5, 1967, the Rainbowbills' nest held a single nestling with pinfeathers just sprouting, who was successfully reared. On March 20 of the following year, this same cavity held four white roundish eggs, resting on a mosaic of seeds of various sizes, shapes, and colors, regurgitated by the toucans while sitting. Such a hard bed for their eggs is usual among toucans, who seem never to carry any soft lining into their nest holes. This nest with four eggs is the one that, with my son's help, I chiefly studied.

Later we found, at La Selva, another Rainbowbills' nest, which was not in the forest but several hundred yards distant from it, among the scattered trees of a cacao plantation. The nest was in the massive trunk of a living Burío tree, in a cavity evidently resulting from the enlargement by decay of a knothole in the smooth side of the trunk. The opening was 23 feet (7 meters) up, and the cavity was so deep and irregular that only part of the bottom was visible in a mirror when a lighted electric bulb was lowered inside. On May 17, 1968, this nest contained one or more naked nestlings, who were probably no older than two weeks.

The only other nests of the Rainbow-billed Toucan of which I know are five found by Van Tyne on forested Barro Colorado Island. All were in cavities resulting from decay in large trees, with openings at heights ranging from 9 to 90 feet (2.7 to 27 meters) above the ground. In the lowest nest, the hollow extended 6 feet (1.8 meters) below the doorway, so that the eggs rested only 3 feet (90 centimeters) above ground level—surprisingly low for a toucan. The other four nest holes were 3 to 16 inches (7.6 to 40 centimeters) deep. The openings of three of these cavities were only 3¼ inches (8.3 centimeters) in diameter, but those of the other two nests were about twice as wide. Three accessible nests contained one, three, and four eggs. Van Tyne described these eggs as dull white, "curiously sculptured with irregular pitted grooves extending lengthwise along the egg and becoming most prominent at the large end." The eggs measured 38 to 40.5 millimeters in length by 28 to 30 millimeters in transverse diameter. Van Tyne's first set of eggs was found on April 4, 1926, and hatched the next day. The following year, three eggs were laid on as many consecutive days, the last early in the morning of April 24. Van Tyne stated that on Barro Colorado this toucan breeds only in the dry season. However, if the young from these eggs survived, they would not leave the nests until May or June, which are usually rainy months on Barro Colorado, although rarely so wet as the latter part of the year. At La Selva, where the dry season is uncertain and at best short,

Rainbowbills must often nest in very wet weather.

Since toucans have a very limited ability to carve into even rotting wood, they are dependent upon ready-made holes for nesting. Small and middle-sized species often occupy the nest cavities of woodpeckers, sometimes evicting the birds who have laboriously carved them. The big species of *Ramphastos* seem to find the holes of even the largest woodpeckers in their territory too small for them and nearly always use "natural" cavities in living trees. If the cavity has solid walls of living wood, an opening barely large enough for the toucans to squeeze through, and sufficient depth, its contents may be inaccessible to large and medium-sized arboreal mammals—such as Ocelots, Tayras, Coatimundis, raccoons, and most monkeys—while squirrels and other quadrupeds small enough to enter may be held aloof by the toucans themselves. Cavities which meet all these requirements are not abundant in the forests, and their scarcity may limit the population of the larger toucans. When found, a first-class cavity appears to be occupied year after year. A month, or even six weeks, before laying begins, the toucans take possession of it, remain near it much of the day—although they do not sleep in it—clean out the rotten wood and debris that have accumulated in the bottom, and almost daily carry in small green leaves, which they remove when withered, as Van Tyne observed. Doubtless it was thanks to the possession of a first-class cavity that our pair of Rainbowbills succeeded in rearing young in both of the seasons that we watched them.

Incubation

At La Selva, where the birds had little experience of people and their destructive habits, we could watch most kinds, from antbirds, tanagers, and finches that nested in trees to motmots and nunbirds that raised their families underground, carry on their domestic activities without hiding ourselves. An outstanding exception was the toucan, whose nest surrounded by solid wood seemed safest of all; to watch it, a blind was indispensable. Indeed, even this was not adequate—we

found it advisable to camouflage the brown cloth of the blind with palm fronds. Despite this precaution, the Rainbowbills were distrustful, probably because they detected the lenses of our binoculars shining through the narrow aperture in the cloth. As the nestling found in 1967 grew up, the parents became increasingly reluctant to approach their nest in front of the blind; our repeated visits of inspection seemed to have made them more than ordinarily shy and suspicious. Finally, we abandoned our attempt to watch the parents attend the nestling.

On March 28, 1968, a day of intermittent showers and little sunshine, such as was typical of the weather at this period, my son, Edwin, and I took turns watching this nest from 6:10 A.M. until 5:10 P.M., when the light in the forest was growing dim beneath a heavily clouded, menacing sky. In this interval of eleven hours, we timed fourteen full sessions, by both parents, ranging from 4 to 86 minutes and averaging 32.9 minutes. The twelve intervals of neglect that were timed in full ranged from 2 to 44 minutes and averaged 14.7 minutes. The longest sessions, 86 and 60 minutes, came in the early afternoon; the longest interval of neglect, 44 minutes, occurred in the early morning. The eggs were attended for 70 percent of the eleven hours.

The toucan coming for a turn on the eggs approached through the treetops. Alighting high above the nest, it usually called for a while, then climbed down a stout liana that hung in a loop beside the trunk of the nest tree. The horizontal part of the loop passed a few inches in front of the doorway and provided a convenient perch for entering. Resting here, the toucan would turn its head from side to side, looking suspiciously all around. Then it would stick its great beak and head through the doorway, peering into the dark cavity, only to withdraw them and look around again. Often the wary bird did this repeatedly. Sometimes, for no apparent reason, unless it were distrustful of the innocuous blind, the bird would fly away again; but often it would enter after one or more of these inspections, struggling to force itself through the narrow aperture.

Sometimes, after sitting for a while, the toucan stuck its head through the doorway, looked out for a few minutes, then went down inside. Once, after incubating for only six minutes, the parent left the hole, returned four minutes later, stayed with the eggs another four minutes, then emerged again and disappeared. This was the only time that we saw the same bird take two consecutive turns on the eggs; but this could have happened on other occasions, when both partners were out of sight between sessions. Sometimes a parent came, looked into the hole and found its mate sitting there, then flew away, leaving the other within. Once the incubating bird left when its mate looked in, and then the latter, instead of taking its turn on the eggs, flew away, too. We witnessed only two changeovers in the course of the day, and both times the sitting partner emerged from the hole before the other entered; the two were never within together. The departing bird always climbed up the liana until lost to view amid the foliage, then flew away. One session was ended when a band of White-faced Monkeys, foraging noisily 50 yards (45 meters) from the nest, knocked down a dead branch that fell with a loud crash. After vanishing, this toucan or its mate reappeared and scolded the monkeys with its usual croaks.

The following morning, when the eggs were on the point of hatching, I watched from 5:50 until 9:45. The toucans appeared even more nervous and suspicious than on the preceding morning, and neither entered until 6:41, when one went in and sat for 109 minutes. After its departure, the eggs were neglected for only 8 minutes, before a parent entered; it remained until I left, 67 minutes later.

Although these Rainbowbills appeared distrustful of the blind during the early hours of March 28, for the rest of the day they seemed to ignore it, and the record we made doubtless gives a true picture of their mode of incubation. Nervous and restless, toucans are, for their size, surprisingly inconstant sitters. The Rainbowbills studied by Van Tyne took sessions of from 20 minutes to an hour. The session of 109 minutes (nearly two hours) on

the morning of March 29 is the longest that I have recorded for any toucan. In fifty-seven and one-half hours of watching at a nest of Red-billed Toucans in Guyana, Bourne recorded one session of 165 minutes, which was exceptionally long.

The incubation period of the Rainbowbill is unknown. The slightly larger Red-billed Toucan hatches its eggs in about fifteen and one-half days, which is close to the period of sixteen days of the much smaller Emerald Toucanet in a cooler climate.

The Nestlings

When we looked into the Rainbowbills' nest on the afternoon of March 30, it contained three nestlings, hatched since the morning of the preceding day, which resembled hatchling woodpeckers. Their pink skins were utterly naked, and their eyes were tightly closed. The lower mandible of each short bill was slightly longer than the upper mandible. Around each heel joint was a ring of light-colored projections, which fitted over and seemed to grasp some of the smaller seeds in the pebbly floor. The nestlings kept up an almost continuous sharp, squeaky buzz, much like that of recently hatched woodpeckers. While their nest was electrically lighted, they moved around a good deal. At times one tumbled on its back, legs waving in the air, but it promptly righted itself. The empty shells had already been removed.

The following afternoon, despite our intentionally noisy approach, a brooding parent stayed in the nest until we set our ladder against the trunk. Before the eggs hatched, the incubating toucan, always alert, would leave before we reached the base of the tree with the ladder. After abandoning its nestlings, the parent flew silently away and remained out of sight the whole time we were present, neither protesting our intrusion nor making feints of attack, as many a smaller bird has done in similar circumstances. When we looked into the hole, the nestlings, without interrupting their squeaky buzz, stretched up their open mouths, revealing an interior colored just like the outside of the body. After this exhausting effort, they sank down to huddle together. Their prominent uropygium served as a third point of support, along with their spiked heels. Their weak feet appeared to be useless appendages of the relatively stout legs terminating in the well-developed heels.

The fourth egg failed to hatch; and, after remaining in the nest for more than ten days, it disappeared, probably removed by a parent toucan. Before they were four days old, two of the nestlings vanished without a trace. Perhaps the parents had been unable to attend them adequately in the very wet weather that had prevailed since they hatched. In the preceding year, also, only one nestling was present when we first looked into the hole, after a rainy period. Van Tyne reported that the unusually rainy season finally destroyed the nests that he studied in 1927.

As long as it remained in the nest, we continued to visit the surviving nestling at intervals of three to five days, making notes on its development. Our examinations, made by inserting a small mirror into the top of the chamber—which was lighted by a small electric bulb attached by a cord to a flashlight—doubtless failed to reveal details that would have been evident had the nestling been taken in hand; but I did not wish to jeopardize it by enlarging the doorway, as I was above all desirous of learning the full length of the nestling period, which seemed never to have been achieved for any of the larger toucans. Perhaps I can best convey the extremely slow development of the young toucan by giving a selection of the notes made after each examination.

April 7. Eight days old. Except that it is bigger, the nestling has changed little since it hatched.

April 10. Eleven days old. Except that it is much bigger, the blind and naked nestling looks much as it did when newly hatched. Its abdomen has become relatively enormous. The only feather rudiments I can detect are those of the rectrices, which project possibly a millimeter from the long uropygium. The nestling seems to lie much of the time with its head on the floor, sideways. (At this age many small passerine birds are feathered and leave the nest.)

April 13. Fourteen days old. The nestling

grows rapidly but is still quite pink and naked. The rudiments of the rectrices are a little longer, and a darkening on the wings appears to be caused by the buds of the flight feathers. The eyes are still closed. The bill is becoming big, and the upper mandible is now as long as the lower.

April 16. Seventeen days old. The nestling's eyes are partly open (but see under April 29, beyond). The rudiments of body feathers are visible as dark points beneath the pink skin. The young toucan seems to lie most uncomfortably on its pebbly bed of decaying seeds, its head fallen over to one side. It still makes a squeaky buzz, which at times increases to a loud cry, somewhat like the wail of a human baby. It is especially likely to wail as the electric light is withdrawn from the nest, which might simulate the darkening of the hole as a parent coming with food fills the doorway. There is no accumulation of excrement, but an unpleasant odor of decay emanates from the damp cavity. (At this age the smaller trogons, which are also hole-nesting birds, are ready to fly or have already taken wing.)

April 21. Twenty-two days old. The nestling is still naked, but its skin has darkened. The pins of its body and wing feathers barely project from it. Its bill, a light horn color, is at least as long as its head, and the round nostrils on its base, at the top, are conspicuous. Its legs and toes have become dusky. It rests upright with less difficulty than formerly, on its heels and abdomen, with its prominent uropygium turned upward. The nestling kept its eyes closed the whole time its nest was illuminated.

April 25. Twenty-six days old. The pins of the nestling's body feathers project a few millimeters. Those of the remiges have become conspicuously long and are leaden blue in color. The young toucan kept its eyes closed while its nest was electrically lighted. At intervals, especially when we shifted the light or made a noise, it moved abruptly, making loud hollow thuds by striking its heels against the floor of the nest, on which the moldering seeds and other debris appear to have become compacted into a solid layer. Might not these knocks serve to frighten an intruder, like the hisses of titmice and certain other hole nesters? (At this age the larger trogons have flown from their holes, the smaller motmots from their deep burrows.)

April 29. Thirty days old. For the first time, the nestling had its eyes open and kept them so the whole time that I looked into its lighted nest. It crouched down as though in fear. On its wings both the remiges and the coverts are rapidly expanding from the ends of their sheaths. The body is still largely naked, the dorsal feathers just protruding from the ends of their short sheaths. There is a crest of pinfeathers along the top of the head, but the rest of the head is quite naked. The pale bill has become conspicuously keeled. The nestling moved with thumping sounds only once, and it could not be induced to repeat this. It seemed to be intimidated by the electric light and perhaps by the sight of my eyes reflected from the mirror above it. (At this age the larger motmots are ready to fly from their burrows, many woodpeckers from their holes.)

May 2. Thirty-three days old. The nestling is at last becoming feathered. It is largely black above, and yellow is appearing on its breast. The feathers on its crown are expanding, but its cheeks are widely bare. Its bill is becoming darker, with an orange tip. Its feet are now blackish. The nestling seemed curious rather than afraid, looking up at the mirror with wide-open eyes. At times it moved with the thumping sound.

May 6. Thirty-seven days old. The nestling is now decently clad. The red border between its yellow chest and black abdomen has become visible, and white is appearing on its rump. The rectrices, which were the first feathers to break through the skin, are at last expanding, after most of the others. The nestling made no vocal sound while we were at the nest, but sometimes it moved noisily. (At this age even the big Ringed Kingfisher has flown from its deep burrow.)

May 9. Forty days old. The nestling remained silent while we looked in. Its tail was turned up, and we could see that its under tail coverts were red, as in the adults.

May 12. Forty-three days old. Our last visit to the nestling in its hole found it still within.

To avoid causing premature departure, we did not again climb to the nest until after the young toucan had flown.

May 15. Forty-six days old. For the first time, the nestling was seen looking through the doorway. It was shy and drew back inside when it found itself observed.

May 17. At dawn the nest was empty. The young toucan had evidently flown during the preceding afternoon, at the age of forty-seven days. (This is the age at which Common Potoos first fly from the exposed stub where they hatched.) On the bottom of the nest chamber were decaying seeds and rotting fragments of wood but no visible droppings or maggots—in strong contrast to the nests of trogons, motmots, and puffbirds when their young leave. Parent toucans carry billfuls of waste from their nests.

The single nestling raised in this hole in the preceding year evidently stayed within to a still more advanced age. When first seen on May 5, its pinfeathers were sprouting, which would make it no less than twenty days old, according to the schedule of development just given. It left on June 9 or 10, when, by this reckoning, it was about fifty-five days old. Although in 1968 the nestling was first seen looking through its doorway only the day before it left, in the preceding year the young toucan was found looking out four or five days before it flew. Unlike its successor, it was not shy and remained with its head and shoulders projecting from the orifice while I approached and stood below it, in full view. It looked down at me with apparent interest. In the few minutes that I watched, the young toucan regurgitated four large seeds, apparently of *Virola*, dropping them outside the nest. Each act of regurgitation was preceded by opening and closing the bill several times. As a parent approached with food, the young bird repeated a whining note, then withdrew into the cavity. Its bill, nearing adult size, was pale greenish yellow, narrowly tipped with orange. The bare skin around its brown eyes was pale green. Its head looked much too big for its neck, and its crown feathers were still partly ensheathed.

The brood of Rainbow-billed Toucans studied by Van Tyne was taken from the nest by some predator when thirty-six days old. From their known rate of growth and measurements of other young collected immediately after leaving the nest, he estimated that his brood would have remained in the cavity ten days longer, to leave when about forty-five days old. I believe that even forty-seven days must be regarded as a minimum nestling period of this big toucan. When I approached the nest tree on the second young toucan's last afternoon in the cavity, the parents, as usual, became greatly excited, and possibly they were responsible for its departure after I walked away. In the preceding year, when we climbed to the nest only once, before the nestling was feathered, and all other observations were made from the ground, the parents had fewer alarming experiences with us. Probably for this reason they permitted their nestling to remain longer. The Red-billed Toucans studied by Bourne left the nest between their forty-fifth and forty-ninth day. Channel-billed Toucans in Trinidad remained in the nest for no less than forty-four but no more than fifty-one days (Lill 1970).

On the rainy morning of April 4, when the single surviving Rainbowbill was five days old, we watched from the blind from 5:53 to 11:22. The naked nestling was brooded only three times, by both parents, for intervals of thirty-eight, thirteen, and forty-one minutes. Six times the parents came with food visible in their bills. Five of the items were fruits or arillate seeds, and the sixth was an insect. Probably on these visits additional pieces were carried in the throat or deeper inside, to be brought up after the article in the bill had been delivered to the nestling. It was evident, however, that already fruits and seeds had become the chick's principal fare, as they continued to be throughout the nestling period.

After another two weeks, the parents had become so distrustful that they could no longer be profitably watched from the blind. Whenever, arriving with food, they found us standing near the nest or on the ladder looking in, they perched in the treetops high above us and continued interminably to complain—"winding their clocks," as my young helper said. Sometimes it was evident that the voice of one was pitched higher than that of its mate. I have already told how sometimes, in these circumstances, the parent would alternately swallow and disgorge a seed many times over or restlessly shift an insect between its bill and a foot. Never did one come near to threaten us by clacking its great bill or darting menacingly past us. Although they seemed greatly distressed when their nest was visited, they did not once jeopardize themselves to protect their young; self-preservation came first. Even after we walked away, they would sometimes continue to complain for many minutes, their voices carrying beyond any possible range of vision in the thick forest. They had such keen eyesight and were so wary that they would never go to their nest even when, screened by undergrowth, I watched at a distance of 50 yards (45 meters).

Although daytime brooding soon ceased, a single parent spent the night with the nestling for most, if not all, of its life in the nest. On the morning of May 9, the parent slept late. When no adult had appeared in the doorway by 5:20, when the feathered world was generally astir, I supposed that the nestling was alone. To make sure, I clapped my hands; but still no great bill was thrust through the doorway. Even light tapping and scratching on the trunk brought no response from this shy bird; but, when I hammered hard with the butt of my machete, an adult wriggled out and flew silently away. I hardly doubted that I had interrupted its sleep. On our next visit to the nest by moonlight, on May 17, it was unoccupied, the nestling having flown on the preceding afternoon. Thus, the young toucan was accompanied at night, by a single parent, until it was at least forty days old and well feathered. Bourne found that the female Red-billed Toucan sometimes brooded the nestling at night, but about four times as often it was the male, as in woodpeckers, some puffbirds, and anis. After the fledgling Rainbowbill's departure, neither parent nor young returned to sleep in the nest cavity.

32. Collared Araçari

Pteroglossus torquatus

After watching a solitary Olivaceous Flatbill dart into its pensile dormitory nest on an evening in February 1935, I wandered through the darkening forest on Barro Colorado Island, looking for other roosting birds. A sharp *penk* drew my attention to Collared Araçaris in the trees high above me; and, by rare good fortune, I managed to follow them to their lodging, about 100 feet (30 meters) above the ground, far out in a thick horizontal limb of an immense tree. The entrance to the hole, on the lower side of the bough and facing straight downward, was barely wide enough for the toucans to squeeze through. I watched their dark colorless figures, silhouetted against the last glow of daylight in the darkening sky, flutter below their narrow doorway and frequently turn back, to try again and perhaps a third time before they gained a foothold at the entrance. Having accomplished this difficult feat, they wriggled

slowly in, each long tail projecting stiffly outward after the body had vanished, then slowly following it.

I was not certain how many araçaris retired into this hole, so toward the night's end I went by moonlight to watch them leave. After the Crested Guans had soared drumming over the forest trees, and just as the great Rufous Motmots began their eerie hooting, a long bill shot out of the hole in the lower side of the high bough, and a slender body struggled out after it. Then, one by one, five bedmates emerged in the same laborious manner. All six araçaris flew off through the treetops, where I soon lost sight of them.

Apparently, I had found the dormitory of these six araçaris soon after they did, for their difficulty in entering came largely from lack of practice. On the evening of February 28, a week after I discovered them, all six slipped in without fluttering below the doorway or returning to a perch for a fresh start after a fruitless attempt. That the aperture had not been appreciably widened in the interval was obvious from the slowness with which the birds squeezed through it, their long projecting tails vibrating from their muscular exertions.

These Collared Araçaris were slender, middle-sized toucans, much of whose length of about 16 inches (40 centimeters) was occupied by their great beaks and long graduated tails. They were largely black or blackish. A narrow chestnut collar separated the glossy black of the hindneck from the greenish slate-black of the back. The rump and upper tail coverts were bright red. The ventral plumage, below the black foreneck, was mainly yellow tinged with red, with a large black spot on the breast and a black band, edged with red, between the breast and the abdomen. The thighs were chestnut. The long bill, black and grayish yellow or dull white, was very subdued for a toucan's beak. The upper mandible had a hooked tip and coarse serrations along the cutting edge; both mandibles were outlined at the base by a narrow whitish band. The birds had yellow eyes set amid bright red bare skin; their legs and feet were greenish olive. I could not distinguish their sexes.

These araçaris belonged to a species that ranges from southern Mexico through the length of Central America to northern Colombia and northwestern Venezuela. It occurs not only in the rain forests of the Caribbean side but likewise in the lighter, drier, highly seasonal woodlands of the Pacific side and the Yucatán Peninsula. In the rain forests of the Pacific slope, south of the Gulf of Nicoya, it is replaced by the closely related but more colorful Fiery-billed Araçari. From the lowlands it extends upward to about 4,000 feet (1,200 meters) in favorable localities.

By March 15, the number of araçaris who slept in the high hole had been reduced to five. During the second half of the month others left, until only one of the original six slept in it. Probably some of them had moved to a hollow in a decaying tree that stood in Gatún Lake near the island's wooded shore—a tree that had been drowned twenty years earlier when the Río Chagres was dammed to form the lake which became an important link in the Panama Canal. At various times from February to late May, I found from two to four araçaris lodging in this rotting tree, where none nested.

Nesting

The five araçaris evidently withdrew from the high hole in the forest to leave it free for breeding. By March 28, incubation had definitely begun in it. Whenever I stood in sight of the nest and loudly clapped my hands, a big pied bill was thrust forth from the narrow aperture. Despite the great height of this nest and despite the fact that I might be standing 100 feet (30 meters) from the tree's base, the araçari in charge of the eggs felt so unsafe that, on seeing me, it promptly squeezed through the doorway and flew off through the forest. Now for some nights only one bird slept with the eggs, but whether this was the male parent or the female I could not learn.

Incubation continued into early April. On April 11, when five araçaris again slept in the high hole, for the first time I saw one of them enter with food, thereby telling me that one or more nestlings had hatched. After a few days, the attendants of this nest became very shy and hesitated to approach it while I watched, unless I sat in a blind—although most birds who nest so high are indifferent to an earthbound observer, and later I found Fiery-billed Araçaris to be much less easily disturbed.

I soon became convinced that four of the five adults who slept with the nestlings were feeding them; I repeatedly had evidence of this. But it took long to prove what from the first seemed probable: all five did so. The best time for counting the attendants was the early morning, when, after leaving the nest together, a number returned with food at about the same time. On May 16, when the nestlings were at least thirty-five days old, the grown birds began to return soon after emerging at 5:45 A.M. In rapid succession, five entered the hole bearing food; and, since those who first delivered their offerings remained in view until the last of them entered, I was certain that I had not counted the same individual twice. At least two of the attendants brooded, but I did not learn whether more did so. By April 24, thirteen days after I noticed that the nestlings had hatched, they were brooded little by day.

The nestlings' food and the method of carrying and delivering it changed as they grew older. At all times the attendants were most wary in approaching the hole; they would usually perch on a high bough of a neighboring tree, turning their heads and great bills from side to side while they scrutinized their surroundings, before they advanced to the doorway. This pause often permitted me to see what they carried. During the first few days after the nestlings hatched, I noticed only insects, which were grasped in the tips of the adults' bills, the wings sometimes projecting from the sides. When the young were a month old, they still received many winged insects, but small fruits were becoming more prominent in their diet. Although I saw a large cicada taken into the nest in the tip of an attendant's bill when the young were almost ready to fly, toward the end of the nestling period most of the food was brought in the mouth or throat, and I rarely saw it. Apparently, this change in the manner of transporting the nestlings' meals was an adjustment to the larger quantities that were now needed. Until the young were over a month old, the attendants laboriously wriggled into the hole each time they brought food; but by May 16, at least thirty-five days after the nestlings hatched, I noticed that the young took a few of their meals through the doorway, while the attendant clung below it. Thereafter, an increasing proportion of their food was passed to them in this fashion.

Although this new way of feeding spared the attendants the effort of squeezing through the narrow orifice, to the detriment of their plumage, it brought fresh difficulties. Now they delivered food while clinging back downward, in which inverted position they could not regurgitate what they carried deeper in their alimentary tracts. The last article which an attendant had found for the nestlings was often held prominently in the tip of its bill when it arrived, and to deliver this caused no special difficulty, as was true also of items carried in the mouth or throat. But after passing these more available pieces to the nestlings the attendant often had to fly to a nearby perch, where, standing upright, it could bring to light certain objects that it had swallowed—a feat not accomplished without considerable effort, to judge by the contortions of the bird's neck, clearly visible through my binocular at a distance of 50 yards (45 meters). The newly available food was then carried to the nest for transfer to a nestling. The rate of feeding was very rapid, especially early in the morning; but, since I was ignorant of the number of mouths that were receiving these contributions, I did not count the feedings when so many other interesting details called for my attention.

Toward the end of the nestling period, one of the principal articles given to the young was the "wild nutmeg," the seed of a tall forest tree, probably *Virola panamensis*. The elongate grayish brown seed was brought to the nest still embraced by the bright red, corallike, branching aril, which resembled the mace of the true nutmeg and was the only digestible part; the seeds themselves were later regurgitated entire. Brown seed and red aril together formed a most attractive object, which measured about three-quarters of an inch in length by slightly over half an inch in transverse diameter (19 by 13 millimeters). When ripe, the oil-rich aril was pleasantly spicy to my taste, but when not quite mature it was forbiddingly hot and peppery; yet even at this stage it seemed to attract Massena Trogons as well as these toucans, who in the early morning flocked to a fruiting *Virola* tree at the forest's edge, where they swallowed these large objects whole.

After the young were a month old, the attendants carried large billfuls of waste from the nest. Apparently, they were keeping the chamber perfectly clean. Probably I had not noticed the removal of waste earlier because of the smaller amounts that were carried away.

One day while I watched the araçaris' nest, two Chestnut-mandibled Toucans flew into the nest tree. One of them soon discovered the hole, probably by hearing the nestlings within. It appeared to be interested and flew from branch to branch around it, but this big toucan had much more trouble reaching the downward-facing doorway than did the smaller, more agile araçaris. Presently it hovered beneath the hole and stuck in the tip of its great beak. After an interval, it repeated the performance and pushed its bill farther in. I doubted that it could reach the nestlings, for the entrance was far too narrow to admit its big body, and a cavity which provided space for six or more araçaris was obviously deep. But I also doubted that the visitor's intentions were benevolent, and I did not wish to risk losing this interesting nest. Accordingly, after the toucan's second attempt to reach the interior, I emerged from my blind and drove it away. The araçaris were not in sight while their larger cousin was present. Since the Chestnut-mandibled Toucan is a persistent nest robber, the araçaris did well to choose a hole with a doorway too narrow to admit it.

The Fledglings' Departure and Attempted Return

The attendance of a single nest by these five Collared Araçaris raised interesting questions. Did these birds nest communally, like anis? Did nonbreeding yearlings help older individuals attend their young, as I had seen at nests of the Brown Jay? Or was there an excess of males, who assisted mated pairs to raise their young, as with black-eared Bushtits? It was difficult to decide between these alternatives because the five attendants looked so much alike, with no differences that revealed age or sex. To know the number of young in the nest would help settle the problem. Since toucans generally lay only two or three eggs in a set, a larger number would make it appear probable that two or more females had laid in the same nest. Because the hole was inaccessibly situated about 100 feet (30 meters) above the ground, the only way to learn the number of nestlings was to count them as they emerged or, better, as they returned to sleep in the cavity. When adult birds of various species use the nest

space as a dormitory, they often lead their fledglings back to sleep in it, and I expected that the araçaris would do the same. Accordingly, I watched carefully for the young araçaris' departure.

Thirty-five days after I first saw an adult bring food to this nest, the attendants were passing some of the meals through the doorway, indicating that the nestlings had moved up close to it. Two days later, I first saw a nestling push its head outside to take its food. The young bird's bill already looked almost as big as that of the adults. When the nestlings were at least forty-two days old, one of them spent much time looking through the doorway, and I now first heard their voices, calling *pitit* like the adults but more weakly. The attendants had now become extremely excitable, calling much and appearing apprehensive.

At dawn on May 24, the five attendants left the high hole, as they had done since the nestlings hatched, and soon they returned with food for the young in the nest. Other birds claimed my attention throughout the day, but after supper I returned to watch the araçaris retire. One of the young birds had emerged since sunrise, and the attendants were helping it regain the hole for the night. While one of them hung, back downward, beneath the doorway, the fledgling clung momentarily to its back. Meanwhile, the other grown birds clustered around, crying *pitit pitit* in their high-pitched voices and displaying much excitement. I was reminded of the similar scene that I had witnessed two years earlier, when Banded-backed Wrens led newly emerged fledglings back to their bulky covered nest on the Sierra de Tecpán. But that episode had a happier ending.

The leaves were fast falling from the nest tree, and the araçaris were exposed to the open sky. I had just slipped into my blind to watch the animated proceedings when, without warning, a White Hawk swooped down from above and seized one of the unsuspecting toucans in its talons. The impetus of the raptor carried both birds down into the foliage of a lower tree; and meanwhile all the other araçaris had dispersed, along with a Black-cheeked Woodpecker and a pair of

Crimson-crested Woodpeckers, who had been clinging in the nest tree. As the hawk arose with the araçari in its grasp, the doomed bird cried piteously, reminding me of the wailing of a disconsolate child. These distressing notes continued, growing fainter with distance, as the bird of prey bore its victim across a deep ravine—followed by all the surviving araçaris, who had rallied to the defense of their companion, much as the toucans gathered around Bates (1863) when he picked up a wounded member of their party in Amazonia. Soon the trees interrupted my view and I could not see what the araçaris did, but doubtless they availed little against the larger and more powerful hawk.

The onslaught of the hawk had been so swift that I could not tell whether it captured the young araçari or one of the attendants. Later, when the sky had become very dim, all five adults cautiously returned to the nest tree and entered the cavity as rapidly as its narrow aperture would permit. It was the young bird who had succumbed so soon after its first flight. The White Hawk was reputed to subsist on snakes, lizards, and possibly fishes, but now it was clear that it also included birds among its prey.

The next morning I was present at daybreak to watch the araçaris leave their dormitory. Three darted out very early, soon after the Rufous Motmots began to hoot. The remaining two adults delayed much longer than usual, then stuck their heads through the doorway and for many minutes peered around carefully before they ventured forth. All through the morning the five attendants were in a highly nervous state. They approached the nest with the utmost caution, advancing gradually from branch to branch, on each of which they turned their heads from side to side as they looked in all directions for the approach of their enemy. They called much, and at times all those in the nest tree dashed off wildly together, repeating their shrill *pitit pitit pitit* as loudly and as rapidly as they could. Probably they spied the hawk soaring over the forest or resting in a treetop, although it was not visible from my station in the depths of the forest.

That evening, while I watched for the ara-

çaris to retire, the two or three who were in sight suddenly rushed toward a neighboring leafless tree, repeating *pitit* so rapidly that the notes seemed to stumble over each other. Emerging from the blind, I discovered the White Hawk perching on a lower limb of the leafless Roble de Sabana, while the araçaris rested above, watching its movements. The adult toucans appeared to have little fear of this slow and heavy raptor—their concern was largely for the safety of their young. But this evening I saw no newly emerged fledgling to be led back to the nest. When the sky was almost dark, two adults entered to sleep with the remaining nestlings. The others probably took shelter in a less harassed dormitory, possibly in the dead tree standing in the water by the island's shore.

The next morning, May 26, the hawk again returned, but a shot from my revolver drove it off. Soon another fledgling left the nest. Later, I watched two attendants offer it food simultaneously, while a third delivered a meal at the nest. The fledgling was almost as large as the mature birds but had a noticeably shorter tail. Before long, the attendants led it off through the treetops. That evening this young araçari failed to return to the nest, doubtless having been conducted to a safer lodging at a distance; but at least one young bird was still within. In the waning light, two adults came to sleep with it. On the following day I was obliged to be absent; but at dawn on May 28 a single adult left the hole, and I waited in vain for an attendant to bring food. The last fledgling had departed.

Apparently, three nestlings had been present. I first saw an attendant take food into this nest on April 11. At least one young fledgling left on May 24, the last on May 27. From this we may deduce that the fledgling who departed first was no less than forty-three days old. If the nestlings hatched on successive days, the last to emerge might not have been much older. Since I am not sure that the attendants had not been bringing food for a day or two before I saw them do so, the nestling period of the Collared Araçari may be placed conservatively at forty-four days, which is not unusually long for a toucan.

Postscript

On the evening of June 1, four adult araçaris retired into the high hole where the brood had been reared. The following day I left Barro Colorado, and I never learned where the surviving young lodged. My study of this busy nest proved conclusively that Collared Araçaris, like many other tropical birds of the most diverse families, sometimes have nest helpers or breed cooperatively, but it left many questions unanswered. How widespread are nests with multiple attendants? What is the relationship of the attendants to the breeding pair (or pairs)? In the many years that have passed since I watched this nest, including two seasons at La Selva, where these araçaris were not rare, I have searched for others with poor success. The only other Collared Araçaris' nest that I have seen was in the dry forest of Guanacaste, where I could not stay to watch. Despite the many professional and amateur bird watchers who have visited Barro Colorado over many years, only one other nest, at which adults were feeding nestlings in July, has been reported from the island (Willis and Eisenmann 1979). Long before, in El Petén, Guatemala, Van Tyne (1935) found a nest of the smaller Yucatán race of the Collared Araçari. It was about 45 feet (14 meters) high in a thick upright limb at the edge of a clearing, and on May 20 it contained three plain white eggs, on the point of hatching. This appears to be all that has been learned about the nesting of a widespread, once abundant bird who yearly becomes rarer as its forests succumb to ax and fire.

33. Fiery-billed Araçari
Pteroglossus frantzii

A few months after leaving Barro Colorado Island, I came to the Valley of El General in Costa Rica, where I have dwelt through most of the subsequent years. Here I found an araçari similar to the Collared in size and color pattern but brighter. The band across the middle of its ventral surface is broader, and it is red narrowly margined with black, instead of black edged with red. The Fiery-billed Araçari has the same dark chestnut collar across the hindneck, the same chestnut or deep cinnamon-rufous thighs, the same black patch in the center of the yellow, red-tinged breast. But the bill, which in all toucans is so conspicuous a feature, is strikingly different in the two species. That of the Fierybill is orange-red over the greater part of the upper mandible. Toward the base this color fades to yellow or greenish yellow, and a black band runs along the basal half or more of the ridge. The lower mandible is largely black, and both parts of the bill are outlined at the base by a narrow whitish band, which contrasts with the black head that it adjoins. The eye is bright yellow, with a triangular patch of bare red skin behind it. The feet and legs are olive-green.

This brilliant toucan, locally called the

cusingo, is confined to the Pacific side of Costa Rica, southward from the Gulf of Nicoya, and to the adjoining regions of western Panama, from sea level up to about 5,000 feet (1,500 meters). It lives chiefly in the upper levels of the tall rain forest of this wetter part of the Pacific littoral of Middle America, but it often forages, sleeps, and nests in neighboring clearings with scattered living or dead trees. Its flight is swift and direct; and it travels in loose straggling bands, which may contain as many as ten individuals but are usually smaller.

Sometimes a number of these araçaris—flying back and forth among the boughs in what appears to be a playful mood—strike their bills resoundingly against a trunk or branch, apparently merely to hear the report. From time to time, I have seen them engage in what seemed to be a more elaborate form of play, in a high treetop in or near the forest. In a typical episode, two araçaris, facing each other, struck their long bills together. Then they grasped one another's bill and pushed, until one of the contestants was forced backward and hung below the limb, after which it admitted defeat by withdrawing a short distance. The victor remained, and soon a third member of the flock approached to challenge it. Again the opponents struck their bills together, grasped, and pushed. This time the winner in the first bout was itself forced from the bough and retired, leaving the newcomer as uncontested champion. These contests appeared not to be entered in a hostile mood, and the loser was never pursued. I believe that they were undertaken wholly in a spirit of play, as in the neighboring pasture young calves bumped their knobby heads together and pushed. Such bill-pushing contests have been witnessed in several other species of toucans, including the Red-billed Toucan and the Yellow-eared Toucanet (Bourne 1974; West 1976).

While riding horseback through the great forest which fifty years ago covered most of the middle reach of the Térraba Valley, I watched a flock of araçaris bathe, one after another, in a pool of rainwater that filled a small cavity in the upper side of a thick hori-

zontal branch above the trail. I have also seen Chestnut-mandibled Toucans and Yellow-eared Toucanets bathe in high arboreal pools, but I have never seen toucans of any kind wet their plumage in a stream or pool at ground level.

Fiery-billed Araçaris subsist largely upon fruits of forest trees. They are strongly attracted to seeds partly or wholly covered by arils rich in oil, including those of *Protium* species, *Dipterodendron elegans*, *Lacistema aggregatum*, and the epiphytic vine *Souroubea guianensis* (Skutch 1980a). They descend into the low rank growth of new clearings, where—in company with a variety of tanagers, honeycreepers, manakins, and other birds smaller than themselves—they feast upon the juicy purple-black berries of the Jaboncillo (a species of Pokeweed) that springs up profusely on burnt ground. Seizing a little berry in the hooked tip of its great bill, the araçari tosses it into its throat by means of an upward jerk of its head.

Eggs and nestlings of other birds vary the largely frugivorous diet of this toucan. I surprised one removing a white egg from the hole of a pair of Golden-naped Woodpeckers, while the parents vainly protested; and at another time I saw a parent araçari bring a newly hatched nestling of some passerine bird to its own young. In the breeding season the araçaris periodically visit our dooryard, which adjoins the forest, to search through the shade trees and shrubbery—distressing all the parent birds and leaving empty nests, including one of Ruddy Ground-Doves from which they took two eggs. Accordingly, they are usually sent along their way with loud noises, before they can carry out their designs. Although they pass by the feeder where bananas are daily displayed, they have never been seen to alight on it.

Ornithologists have long wondered why toucans have such enormous and colorful bills. While I watched araçaris gather food, some of the uses of these bills became apparent to me. I was especially impressed by their efficiency while I watched birds of thirty species eat the arillate seeds of a *Diptero-dendron* tree, which were contained in thick pods that hung in long drooping panicles.

These pods opened slowly, a few at a time, each exposing usually a single seed, so that competition for them was keen. Some of the birds plucked seeds from the pods as they flew past, others while they hovered on beating wings. Still others clung below the pods, struggling to extract a seed from between the barely separated valves. Almost alone of the visitors, the araçaris could perch on fairly stout twigs, reach out or down, seize a pod in the tip of a long bill, force it open if necessary, and secure a seed in a trice. They ate so many in a short time that, unlike most of the other birds, they never stayed long in the tree.

Watching a toucan at a fruiting tree may convince one that its long bill serves it well yet still provide no explanation of the bill's thickness and color. The value of these features becomes more evident when one surprises a toucan plundering a nest. Vivid color emphasizes the size of a beak that intimidates the smaller birds whom toucans persecute. As far as I have seen, not the boldest of them dares to touch a perching araçari or other toucan and risk a nip from that terrifying beak. But the larger and more spirited flycatchers buffet toucans in flight, when the latter seem unable to turn their heads and defend their backs.

The highly colored bills probably also help toucans recognize other individuals of their species. Two species of toucans that inhabit the same forests, such as the Rainbow-billed and Chestnut-mandibled toucans of the Caribbean rain forests, are often more readily distinguished by their bills (and voices) than by their plumage. In this connection it is significant that seventeen of the forty-one toucans in Meyer de Schauensee's *Guide to the Birds of South America* (1970) are named (in English) for characteristics of their bills—an unusually high proportion.

The toucan's bill may, like colorful feathers, help it in courtship. This function is not incompatible with its role in intimidating the birds whose nests it robs; it will be recalled that, before warfare degenerated into mechanical and chemical slaughter, men decorated themselves lavishly to go to battle as well as to go courting. Although it has been suggested that, protected by the wooden walls of its nest cavity, the toucan employs its huge bill to repel predators from its doorway, this is fanciful. Few birds hurry from their nests on such slight provocation as quickly as the timid toucans. On the single occasion when I saw a small quadruped menace a toucan's nest—that of the big Chestnut-mandibled Toucan—the parent was not inside presenting its bill to the enemy but outside threatening the animal.

Vivid coloration makes hostile things more fearsome but friendly things more pleasing. A courtship offering may be more impressive if presented in an attractively colored bill than in a drab one. Courtship feeding is widespread in the toucan family. Early one March, I watched two araçaris eating the fruiting spikes of a Cecropia tree. Sometimes one would break off a small piece and, after pressing it a little between the tips of its mandibles, toss it back into its throat. When it detached a longer piece of the cylindrical green spike, the bird held it down against its perch with a foot, while it tore off fragments to swallow. Finally, one of the pair, doubtless the male, approached the other and gave her a piece. Then both flew off to the forest. In May I saw one araçari feed another with four items, three of which he regurgitated.

I was reminded of such incidents when I met a Fiery-billed Araçari with a strangely deformed bill. The brilliant upper mandible of this unfortunate bird was strongly bent both upward and sideward, so that there was a prominent gap between the two mandibles in the terminal half of the bill; moreover, the tip of the upper mandible was not above that of the lower but well to the side of it. I believe that such a deformity could have arisen only in the embryonic or at least the nestling stage of this bird's development, and I doubt whether it could have fed itself well enough to stay alive. Certainly it was seriously handicapped in eating; yet it was full-grown, in fine plumage, and apparently otherwise in good condition. I surmised that its companions, or possibly only its mate, helped nourish it; but, unfortunately, the flock did not remain in view long enough for me to see this.

The Fierybill's high sharp *pink*, *pitit*, or *pity* so greatly resembles the calls of the Collared Araçari that I doubt that I could distinguish the two species by their voices. When flying swiftly through a clearing, the Fierybill utters a piercing screech, which appears to be an expression of anxiety while the bird is vulnerable to attack by a raptor. Araçaris appear to have very limited vocabularies.

Sleeping

Most of my observations on the sleeping habits of the Fiery-billed Araçari were made in the Valley of El General from 1936 to 1943. In this period, new settlers were pouring into this originally forested region and making great inroads on the woodland. Usually when clearing forest they spared a few scattered trees, to avoid the labor of felling them or to preserve them as future sources of firewood. These isolated trees were killed by the fires set to prepare the land for sowing, and often the flames attacked other trees at the margin of the intact forest. Soon decaying, these dead or dying trees were drilled by woodpeckers—especially the Golden-naped, Red-crowned, Lineated, and Pale-billed—to make holes for roosting and nesting. When the woodpeckers abandoned these cavities, or sometimes before, they were claimed for nesting and sleeping by the araçaris. When, in 1941, I bought Los Cusingos, it contained a large new clearing that still smoked, with its usual quota of standing charred trees. Since then, no more old forest has been felled on this farm. After the fire-killed forest trees toppled over, I much more seldom found araçaris roosting in the smaller, faster-growing softwood trees that spring up in clearings or are planted to shade coffee, and I have not discovered them sleeping or nesting in the midst of intact forest, as probably they originally did and still often do.

Only the biggest of the woodpeckers, the Pale-billed and the Lineated, carve holes large enough to accommodate the araçaris. The latter woodpecker is the more abundant and, accordingly, the chief provider of lodgings and nest chambers for these toucans. As they wander through log-cluttered recent clearings with scattered standing trees, the araçaris, ever looking for good dormitories, examine the available cavities, often poking in their heads before the makers have abandoned them, much to the distress of the smaller hole nesters. The progress of a band of araçaris through such a clearing at the height of the nesting season is attended by the angry darts and complaining cries of the numerous other birds who breed there.

Apparently, it is chiefly as a safeguard against these great-billed intruders that the larger woodpeckers spend so much time with nestlings who are already feathered and no longer require brooding. At a Lineated Woodpeckers' nest that I watched for nine hours, the male spent half the time guarding his two daughters, almost as big as himself and nearly ready to fly. Twice during my vigil parties of araçaris came to the nest and were repulsed by the parent woodpeckers, once by the father from the inside and once by the mother from the outside. Whenever a heavy bird flew up to the charred trunk, the male drew down into the cavity, where he could not be seen from the front. Apparently not noticing that the hole was guarded, an araçari stuck in its head and received on its beak an audible tap from the sharp bill of the woodpecker, a happening which I witnessed twice at this nest, on different days.

Since the Lineated does not, like some other woodpeckers, regularly use its nest cavity as a dormitory after the young depart, these holes become available to the araçaris as soon as the brood has flown. The above-mentioned hole remained untenanted for at most two nights after the fledglings flew; on the third night I found araçaris sleeping in it. Another Lineated Woodpeckers' nest was also occupied by araçaris a few days after the brood left. In both of these holes five araçaris sometimes lodged; and later, in a different locality, I again discovered five araçaris roosting in a woodpecker's hole, apparently of this species. Five grown araçaris seems to be the limit of the capacity of the Lineated Woodpecker's nest, for some of these lodgers belonged to larger groups, the other members of which found shelter elsewhere. Thus, one evening when five araçaris entered a woodpecker's hole, three more went to rest in an older cavity nearby.

I have never found more than five Fiery-billed Araçaris sleeping together, but I have often seen from one to four enter a hole. Their sleeping arrangements change frequently. They seem usually to know a number of available lodgings, discovered on their periodical tours of investigation; and, if alarmed or ill at ease at one, they readily fly off to another as the day ends. Often there is much cautious inspection of the holes while clinging in front, much going in and out of the cavities, much flying back and forth in the waning light, before all the members of a flock are comfortably installed for the night. Compared with woodpeckers, araçaris retire late in the evening and arise early in the morning.

Abandoned woodpecker holes are also in demand by other birds, especially Gray-breasted Martins and Masked Tityras, for their eggs and young; and this brings these birds into competition with the araçaris. Elsewhere (1946, 1969) I have told about some of the troubles which the timid tityra has with her huge-beaked, greatly feared neighbors, who often sleep or breed in another cavity in the dead tree that holds her nest, even when they do not contend for the same hole.

Sometimes the araçaris are the aggrieved party. In a narrow clearing between two strips of forest, I watched a hole in the top of a tall dead tree into which a female tityra was carrying inflorescence stalks and dead leaves for her nest. In the evening, when three araçaris arrived to sleep in this hole—where they may well have been lodging before the tityra claimed it—she and her mate pursued them in flight and darted at them while they clung at the doorway, inspecting the interior before they entered. But the toucans paid slight attention to the tityras, who remained watching the hole until after the larger birds had retired, then flew off in the dusk to sleep in the forest. This continued for a number of evenings, on some of which the tityras' pursuits showed great spirit, although I doubt that they ever found courage enough to strike the toucans.

By day, when the araçaris were absent, the female tityra busily filled the cavity with coarse material. One evening, the lodgers arrived to find the space so reduced that they had difficulty accommodating themselves. The first went in without trouble, but the second tried several times to enter and then flew to the edge of the forest. The first araçari emerged, whereupon the second returned to the hole, stuck in its head, pulled out a bunch of material—consisting largely of dry leaves—carried it to a neighboring tree, and dropped it. Finally, two birds entered the cavity to sleep; the third went elsewhere.

On the following evening, two araçaris entered the hole without difficulty. Then the tityras stood side by side on top of the tall stub, peering over the edge to see what was happening below them. Presently, as it grew dark, the male flew away, leaving the female alone on the stub. While she stood there, the third araçari arrived very late; and, finding it hard to enter the reduced space headfirst, it turned around and inserted itself forcibly tail foremost, as woodpeckers sometimes enter narrow dormitories. As it went in, I clearly saw it turn its long tail forward over its back, and on subsequent evenings I repeatedly witnessed this procedure. In these circumstances, the value of this space-saving arrangement was obvious.

On the morning of April 26, the female tityra, after much hesitation, entered the disputed hole and stayed for about twenty minutes, probably laying an egg. This was doubtless broken when three araçaris squeezed in above it that evening. A few days later, this hole was abandoned by both araçaris and tityras. If, as I suspect, one or more eggs were broken in it, ants probably arrived and made it untenantable by the birds. However, by mid May, the tityras were nesting in this hole, which the ants may have abandoned. Mild-mannered as they are, tityras often gain their objectives by great persistence. Higher in this same trunk, a pair of Golden-naped Woodpeckers nested while the dispute was going on; and one evening, before the araçaris arrived, eight small bats dropped, one by one, from a neighboring hole, where they had slept throughout the day.

The parties of from four to eight araçaris, which even at the height of the nesting season in April and May wander through the clearings and lodge either together or, in the case of the larger groups, in neighboring holes, appear to be composed largely if not wholly of nonbreeding birds. Their presence suggests that Fiery-billed Araçaris do not begin to nest until the second spring following that in which they hatched or, possibly, at a still more advanced age. These observations on a related species support the conclusion that three of the five attendants at the Collared Araçaris' nest were young unmated helpers.

One rainy afternoon last September, the top of a tall, massive decaying trunk on the hillside behind our house broke off. The fracture occurred at the level of a thin-walled chamber, carved by Lineated Woodpeckers, where four Fiery-billed Araçaris had been sleeping for weeks. It was amusing to watch them when they arrived in the evening to find that a shallow bowl, open to the sky, was all that remained of their dormitory. Two promptly flew off to the forest, while two tried to make themselves comfortable in the hollow at the top of the trunk. They fidgeted around and around, with bills and tails sticking up above the shallow rim. Finally, one flew away in the dusk. The other stayed, crouched down in the hollow, its great bill projecting beyond the edge into the outer air, where after nightfall I saw it silhouetted against the moonlit, overcast sky. Fortunately, the night was rainless. On the following night, all four araçaris slept elsewhere.

A Pair Followed for over a Year

At the end of my first February in El General, a flock of from five to eight Fiery-billed Araçaris came in the evenings to an abandoned cornfield at the edge of the forest, on a slope high above the Río Buena Vista at an altitude of 3,000 feet (910 meters). Here a number of tall fire-killed trees stood above the bushes

and vines that were fast growing up into an impenetrable tangle over the steep mountainside. In these trees were many woodpeckers' holes, some unfinished, some with eggs or nestlings, others newly abandoned by their makers, yet others in all stages of decay. The araçaris examined many of these cavities, but they were chiefly interested in one vacated only a day or two earlier by a brood of Lineated Woodpeckers. On the evening of February 26, four entered this lofty hole, while one clung beside the doorway; then all swarmed out and flew to the forest; and finally one returned to sleep alone in the cavity. These araçaris appeared very unsettled; during the next week the number of lodgers in this hole fluctuated capriciously from none to five, with sometimes one in a neighboring older hole.

By March 10, one member of this group had begun to sleep in another hole, with a doorway so narrow that it could barely squeeze through, about 100 feet (30 meters) up in a great dead tree, standing a short way down the slope from that in which the others lodged. This woodpecker's hole with a narrow orifice was selected to contain the araçari's eggs. Now the flock rapidly dwindled, until the old cornfield on the mountainside was left in the possession of two individuals, who soon clearly showed that they were a mated pair. The two slept apart, one in the tree lower on the slope, where incubation began about the end of March; the other slept 50 feet (15 meters) away in the Lineated Woodpeckers' hole which not long before had sheltered the five araçaris. Since the male and the female were so similar, I could not tell who was in charge of the eggs throughout the night and who slept in the nearby hole. By day, they sat alternately on the eggs. By mid April, both were carrying small insects into this high nest; but, before the young fledged, somebody cut down the tree.

After the loss of their nest, the pair slept together in the Lineated Woodpeckers' hole. Now they emerged so unusually late in the morning that I concluded they were feeling broody and would nest again, but I am fairly certain that they laid no more eggs that year.

With the araçaris' usual wavering attachment to their dormitory, they slept in the woodpeckers' hole on and off until, in August, the owner of the land also cut down this tree for firewood. Then for two months I lost track of them. In October I found a pair, most probably the same, lodging in a hole recently carved by a woodpecker in a Cecropia trunk in the same clearing. This cavity was only 20 feet (6 meters) above the ground, with a doorway so wide that in the morning, when the araçaris lingered in their dormitory, both could look out together, with the end of the great bill of one beside or above the projecting head of its mate. Although they did not sleep here consistently, this was a principal lodging until the following February. These two araçaris, once mated, seemed never to rejoin the flock from which they had separated in the preceding March; they kept apart, at least by night, and preserved their domain through all the months when they did not breed. Yet they were not strictly intolerant of others of their kind on their territory, and for a while they permitted a third araçari to sleep not far from themselves in a hole that they had formerly occupied.

In February, the mated Fierybills, whom I had now known for a full year, took possession of a hole from which a pair of Pale-billed Woodpeckers had not long before lost newly hatched nestlings to some predatory creature—probably not to the araçaris, who would hardly have dared confront that powerful white chisel-beak. In this low hole the pair slept together, with occasional inexplicable absences in true araçari style, until the female laid in it at the end of March. Now, as in the preceding year, a single parent slept in the nest, while the other lodged again in the Cecropia trunk where formerly both had found shelter. This time the nest was plundered even before the eggs hatched, as told in more detail beyond. Nevertheless, the araçaris did not abandon the clearing where in two successive years they had had such bad luck. As after the loss of their nest in the preceding year, both now slept in the dormitory of the member of the pair who had not incubated by night, in this case the

low hole in the Cecropia trunk that had so long been their lodging. Again, I discovered no attempt to replace their lost eggs. In mid June I left the locality, and my acquaintance with these araçaris, which had continued for more than fifteen months, came to an end.

The Eggs and Incubation

I did not try to reach the 100-foot-high (30-meter) hole in which the pair nested in 1936; but the following year, when they occupied a hole only 20 feet (6 meters) high carved by Pale-billed Woodpeckers, I made a ladder with poles from the neighboring forest and climbed up to the nest on April 1. When the interior was illuminated with an electric bulb, my mirror, stuck through the doorway, revealed two pure white eggs, resting on a layer of regurgitated seeds which covered the whole floor and looked like a bed of assorted beans. Since I could barely touch these eggs with my fingertips, I did not jeopardize future studies by trying to remove them for closer examination and measurement. These were the only eggs of the Fiery-billed Araçari that I have seen or of which I can find a record.

In both years, I watched these araçaris while they incubated, calling the one who passed the night with the eggs A, the other B. In 1936 their behavior in the early morning varied considerably from day to day. On April 4, A left the nest and flew into the woods at 5:28 A.M., returning to the eggs ten minutes later. B did not emerge from its dormitory until 5:42, when it flew directly into the forest. The following morning, however, B flew from the dormitory at 5:20, while A remained in the nest until B returned and entered it at 5:44. On April 12, B left the dormitory at 5:32 A.M. Araçari A emerged from the nest at 5:45 but perched in front of it until B came to incubate a minute later. Often, as B flew from the old woodpecker hole in the morning, it was pursued as far as the forest by one or both of the Masked Tityras whose nest was in the same trunk. Sometimes it was chased again as it approached its lodging in the evening.

In addition to my vigils at dawn, I watched this nest while incubation was in progress from 5:18 to 10:38 A.M. on April 5 and from 2:12 to 6:06 P.M. on April 7. Araçari A left the nest at 5:44 A.M. on April 5 and entered for the night at 5:25 on April 7. In the slightly over eight hours during which the partners alternated on the nest while I watched, I timed twelve sessions by both of them, ranging from 2 to 102 minutes and averaging 25.6 minutes. Only one session, in the afternoon, was over an hour long. Since I could not distinguish the parents, I could not tell how equally they shared incubation. Only exceptionally did one remain sitting until the other arrived to replace it. I saw these changeovers most frequently in the early morning, when the newcomer often entered before the other emerged. Sometimes the incubating bird left the hole, perched in front for two or three minutes, then returned to its task. Once one member of the pair did this thrice in eighty-one minutes, breaking what might have been one long session into four short ones, lasting twenty-four, twenty-one, twenty-one, and seven minutes, which were counted separately in computing the average. As a result of all this restlessness, the nest was unattended for eleven intervals ranging from 2 to 53 minutes and averaging 15.9 minutes. The eggs were incubated for only 63.6 percent of the over eight hours—a poor record for so large a bird.

On April 9 of the following year, I watched the lower nest from 5:20 to 11:12 A.M.; but, since A did not leave until 6:13, my record covers only five hours of the active period. The araçaris were now so restless that neither stayed at its post until its mate arrived, and I did not see a single changeover. Once, however, one partner came to the doorway while the other was within, only to fly away again as the latter tried to push past it. Doubtless both sexes participated in incubation, as in the previous year. Seven sessions ranged from 12 to 53 and averaged 28.1 minutes. An equal number of periods when the eggs were neglected varied from 2 to 31 and averaged 14.6 minutes. The eggs were covered for 65.9 percent of the five hours. The two records, made in different years, are surprisingly similar, especially if we take only the earlier part of that made in 1936. In this

year, from 5:44 to 10:38 A.M., the eggs were attended for a total of 199 minutes and left alone for 95 minutes; in 1937, from 6:13 to 11:12 A.M., the corresponding figures were 197 and 102 minutes.

One wonders why araçaris—and other toucans—taking turns on the nest sit so restlessly that the two parents together keep their eggs covered less constantly than many a small passerine female incubating alone. It is not only because, being largely frugivorous, the toucans need to eat more frequently than birds whose diets are richer in proteins; often they interrupt their sessions on the eggs without going for food. Tiny manakins, also frugivorous, incubate far more steadfastly than toucans many times their size. Compared with other nonpasserines of about their size, including pigeons, trogons, motmots, kingfishers, and puffbirds, whose sessions on the eggs usually continue for hours, toucans incubate fitfully. The contrast between the araçaris and the Pale-billed Woodpeckers whose hole they occupied was striking: the woodpeckers kept their eggs almost constantly covered, with only two changeovers in a whole day's watching. The only explanation that I can offer for the toucans' instability is temperament. They are restless birds, whose mercurial disposition contrasts strongly with the restful nature of most trogons, kingfishers, and puffbirds. Perhaps for this reason they find it difficult to remain sitting quietly in a narrow chamber. But jays and jacamars, also vivacious birds, stay on their eggs for long periods, so that additional factors appear to influence constancy of incubation.

When approaching their nest, the araçaris often carried a small object in the tips of their bills. Sometimes they dropped this before going to their eggs; at other times they took it inside. When they stuck their heads through the doorway or flew from the nest, they likewise often held something in the bill, only to drop it after a short while. These objects were probably regurgitated seeds of forest fruits, with which they toyed before relinquishing and which were so prominent on the floor of the low nest. During my afternoon vigil in 1936, a family of four Red-crowned Woodpeckers, including two young who had recently left a nest in a neighboring dead trunk, climbed and pecked over the araçaris' nest tree. The young male cautiously peered into the hole where an araçari was incubating. Later, when the nest was unattended, he went to the orifice and—after much hesitation—entered, only to emerge a moment later. Apparently, he was prospecting for a dormitory, since Red-crowned Woodpeckers, unlike Goldennapes and some other species, do not lead their fledglings to sleep in a hole but leave them to find lodgings for themselves.

At dawn on April 10, I was distressed to find that the araçaris' eggs had vanished from the low nest, apparently taken in the night by the same mammalian predator that enlarged the entrance of the Golden-naped Woodpeckers' hole higher in the same trunk and carried off their nestlings. Although the pair of araçaris survived, I followed their activities for the next two months without noticing another attempt to rear a brood.

The Young and Their Return to the Nest
By April 16, 1936, the Fierybills were bringing food to the high, inaccessible nest. The small insects that they now carried in the tips of their bills—contrasting with the big regurgitated seeds which at an earlier stage they often held—were not so easy to see. A few days later, in the early morning, a flock of five araçaris flew into the clearing and were joined by the nesting pair, making seven great-bills in all. Some of the newcomers came near the nest but did not visit it. Although I saw no quarreling between the residents and the visitors (I have never seen toucans fight), I sensed tension. After the whole party went to perch at the forest's edge, I heard sounds that suggested a dispute; but, before I could get a clear view of the araçaris, the momentary flare-up had subsided, and soon the visitors vanished. A week later, the nest tree had been felled, for firewood or to take what was left of the nestling araçaris after a fall of well over 100 feet (30 meters), when the tree crashed down the steep slope. At no time did I see more than two adults attending this nest.

My third and last nest was about 45 feet (14 meters) up in an old hole, probably carved by Lineated Woodpeckers, in a tall, branching, fire-killed tree standing in a newly made pasture. When I found it on April 24, 1943, the parents were feeding nestlings. This nest was in plain view of the pedestrians and horseback riders who passed along the unpaved road that led to the nearest village, and perhaps for this reason the araçaris were much more shy than those in the more secluded clearing where the first two nests were situated. I could watch the parents approach the nest only if I stationed myself a long way off, behind screening bushes. They brought insects, fruits, and once a newly hatched passerine nestling. I saw no indication that other individuals helped them care for the young. By May 7 the nestlings, already with big bills, had begun to look through their doorway; sometimes two stood there together. Both parents now slept in the nest; but if they noticed me watching, even from afar, they would, unlike most other araçaris that I have known, go elsewhere to pass the night.

Early on May 10, I saw only one nestling in the doorway, and continued watching convinced me that the other had flown. By the evening of the following day, the second young bird had not yet emerged. While it looked through the doorway, both parents flew down from the neighboring forest, excitedly calling *pitit pitit* in high sharp voices, at the same time twitching their great bills up and down. Presently the fledgling who had emerged on the preceding day came down from the forest to join them. It flew fairly well but landed clumsily and hung for a moment below the branch, before it succeeded in righting itself. One of the parents entered the hole but promptly returned to the lower tree where the young bird rested. Soon an adult went into the cavity to stay, while the other flew to a more distant tree. Left alone, the fledgling started toward the nest, only to veer to one side of the trunk and continue its flight unbroken to the forest's edge, where it remained for its second night in the open. Later, the other parent retired into the nest. Thus, on this night the two adults slept in the hole with the remaining nestling, while the more advanced young araçari was exposed to the elements.

Continuous rain interfered with my observations on the evening of May 12; but the following dawn two adults and two young were in the nest, whence it was evident that one of the latter had entered after two nights outside. It left three-quarters of an hour after its parents and easily flew to the forest. Until six o'clock, the second young stayed inside and called *pit pit* in a high slight voice, in answer to the reiterated *pitit* of its parents at the forest's edge. Then I went to breakfast. When I returned an hour later, the second fledgling had flown and was resting on a charred fallen log between the nest and the woodland, where the parents' excited behavior called my attention to it. I approached quite close before it flew with directness and force, but it could not rise as steeply as the slope ahead—with the result that it landed abruptly in deep sticky Calinguero grass, among charred logs and stumps, 50 feet (15 meters) from its takeoff. Advancing cautiously, I captured it by throwing my cloth cap over it, while the parents looked down from dead trees with obvious concern. Taken in hand, it struggled forcefully to escape and once bit me hard enough to hurt. After I had written a description, I left the fledgling to resume its journey to the forest. It had emerged three days later than its nest mate, and after its departure the cavity was empty.

During a lull in the afternoon rain at five o'clock on the same day, I found a young araçari, doubtless the older, already in the hole, looking out. Half an hour later, both parents flew down from the forest, soon followed by the other fledgling, whose skill on the wing had improved during its first day in the open. After a parent entered the hole, the fledgling tried to follow, but it aimed too high and clung to the trunk above the doorway. While it rested there, the other parent slipped into the hole below it, without giving the least encouragement. After another unsuccessful attempt to join its family in the hole, the young araçari started toward the forest but dropped down into the pasture, where I lost sight of it in the drizzle and

deepening gloom. A few moments later, both parents emerged from the dormitory, flew toward the fledgling, but passed above it to the woodland, where they remained until it was dark. The more advanced fledgling slept alone in the nest cavity, while the younger one, repeating the experience of the other, was forced by its weak flight to sleep in the open on its first night out of the nest. On the following evening, none of the family came in sight of the nest tree, which thereafter was deserted. Probably the parents had not tried harder to guide their offspring to the nest hole because they were themselves ill at ease in this exposed situation.

The newly emerged fledgling that I held in my hand rather closely resembled the adults in plumage, but its colors were duller. Its bill was much less vivid, the upper mandible being yellow clouded with dusky, with the ridge blackish at the base and greenish toward the center of its length. The lower mandible was dusky, but both parts of the bill were brighter yellow at the tip. The inside of its bill was yellow. Its iris was straw color, instead of bright yellow as in the adults. The bare skin around the eye was bright yellow behind the orbit (where it is red on the adults), greenish yellow above it, and greenish in front, on the lores. The legs and feet were yellowish green, with black toenails. The heel pads were still quite evident, with five prominent projections in a ring around each heel.

Araçaris as Neighbors

Although araçaris occasionally eat eggs and nestlings, they do not systematically prey upon other birds that breed in holes near their own nests. The inspection of many of the cavities in a clearing with dead trees appears to be done chiefly by the parties of nonbreeding birds which wander about at all seasons and by mated pairs seeking a nest site and a lodging. After the pair of araçaris that I watched in 1936 and 1937 had become comfortably established, I did not see them pay attention to the many holes in their clearing, other than the two in which they nested and slept.

I have repeatedly seen other hole nesters,

including Masked Tityras, Gray-breasted Martins, Golden-naped Woodpeckers, Red-crowned Woodpeckers, and Lineated Woodpeckers, raise their families within sight of an araçaris' nest, often in the same trunk with it. The immunity of the smaller woodpeckers might be attributed to the depth of their holes combined with the narrowness of their doorways, which places the eggs beyond reach of the araçaris' beaks, while the safety of a Lineated Woodpecker's brood may be due to the rather constant guard kept by these parents with powerful bills. But neither of these explanations would account for the immunity of the tityra and the martin, who often lay in old holes with doorways wide enough to admit an araçari. The only instance of predation on a hole-nesting bird that I have witnessed was the removal of a single egg from a Golden-naped Woodpeckers' nest, which appeared to be exceptionally shallow, for the toucan managed to reach the egg while clinging in front of the doorway. Yet in this same hole, only 1 yard (90 centimeters) above an occupied araçaris' nest, the woodpeckers hatched one or more remaining eggs, only to lose their nestlings to the mammalian predator that also took the toucans' eggs. Although all these hole nesters, as well as other birds, are fearful of the araçaris and greatly perturbed by their approach, the toucans are not such dangerous neighbors as their predatory habits might lead one to suppose.

Postscript
Although the big Chestnut-mandibled Toucans long ago vanished from the forest at Los Cusingos, where they were formerly abundant, the smaller, swifter, more agile Fiery-billed Araçaris remain in the nature reserve that was named for them. Since they probably could not survive in wholly deforested country, they are doomed to diminish or vanish unless some of the sadly shrunken rain forest within their limited range can be preserved.

34. Emerald Toucanet
Aulacorhynchus prasinus

In the mountains of tropical America, from Mexico to Bolivia, dwell seven or eight species of small green toucans known as toucanets. While I studied Mountain Trogons and Blue-throated Green Motmots on the Sierra de Tecpán, I often heard about the *cucharón*, as the northernmost of these green toucans, a white-throated race of the Emerald Toucanet, was locally called; but it was rare and elusive, and I learned little about it.

In my travels about Guatemala, I found it ranging vertically from heavy subtropical forests at 3,500 feet to temperate zone woods of oaks, pines, and cypresses, even up to 10,000 feet (1,050 to 3,000 meters). It also occurs sparingly in the lowlands of El Petén.

When I came to Costa Rica, I found a blue-throated race that has been regarded as a distinct species, the Blue-throated Toucanet—here called *curré*—much more

abundant from high oak forests down to 3,500 feet (1,050 meters) and sporadically 1,000 feet (300 meters) lower. They rarely visit Los Cusingos at 2,500 feet (760 meters); but last December we were delighted to see one of these birds, after much hesitation, alight on the feeder in front of our house and eat freely of bananas—probably its first taste of this fruit, for, unlike our regular attendants, it did not distinguish the pulp from the peel. This toucanet and its companion, who was too distrustful to stand on the board while we watched, must have crossed several miles of sugarcane, pastures, and other open country to reach us from the forests higher on the mountain slopes. Only once before, in late November years ago, had I seen a lone toucanet here on the farm. November to February is the season when we are most likely to meet wandering individuals of certain species whose true home may begin only 1,000 feet (300 meters) higher. Most tropical birds stick closely to their altitudinal life zones.

The blue-throated toucanet of Costa Rica and western Panama is about 12 inches (30 centimeters) long and nearly everywhere green of a moderately bright shade, but not metallic and glittering like trogons, jacamars, and hummingbirds. Its throat and lower cheeks are blue, and its under tail coverts are cinnamon. Its strongly graduated tail feathers, largely green, become bluish toward the ends and are tipped with cinnamon. Its four-color bill, although much smaller than those of the big lowland toucans, is huge in proportion to the bird that bears it. The greater part of the upper mandible is yellow with a greenish tinge, but its base and cutting edge are black, as is the entire lower mandible. At the base of the culmen is a small patch of dull red. The whole bill is outlined, where it joins the head, by a broad white stripe. The sexes are colored alike, but some pairs may be distinguished by their bills, that of the male being noticeably bigger.

Toucanets travel in small straggling flocks which rarely consist of more than six or eight individuals. Not infrequently, a solitary bird is met. Although the mossy mountain forest is their preferred habitat, they wander through adjoining clearings with scattered trees and often nest in them. Restless, excitable birds, they scold a human watcher in tones that at times resemble the chatter of an angry squirrel, while they hold their tails and great-billed heads in various angular, ungraceful attitudes. Their language, although varied, is nearly always unmelodious; throaty croaks, dull barks, and dry harsh rattles are their most frequent utterances. While nesting, they sometimes give voice to softer notes. Their food, like that of other toucans, consists of a variety of fruits and insects, with occasionally a nestling of some other bird. Like the larger toucans, they seize a fruit in the tip of the bill and throw it back into the throat with an upward toss of the head.

The boy who helped me find nests at Montaña Azul saw a blue-throated toucanet fall prey to a Bat Falcon, a raptor no larger than its victim but fierce out of all proportion to its size. Aside from this, I have discovered no dangerous enemies of adult toucanets. But, if they have few enemies, they likewise have few friends. Their nest-robbing habits make them intensely disliked by the small birds among whom they dwell. Dark Pewees have as strong an antipathy to toucanets as Boat-billed Flycatchers have to the big toucans of lower altitudes; they become greatly excited whenever a toucanet appears anywhere in the vicinity of their mossy nests.

Although the behavior of other birds toward the toucanets stigmatizes the latter as nest robbers, I only once saw one of them plunder a nest. One afternoon in May, my attention was drawn by a Mountain Thrush who was very much upset. She perched on the ends of the branches of a wide-spreading, dense epiphytic shrub attached high above the ground to the trunk of a lofty tree, where she nervously twitched her wings and uttered sharp, robinlike cries of distress. She flew back and forth around the shrub, in which she evidently had a nest, darting at something that was screened from my view by the compact foliage and the mist that shrouded the trees. Presently a toucanet flew out of the shrub with the thrush in hot pursuit. I hurried to a toucanets' nest not far from the scene of this episode. Soon a parent toucanet arrived with the legs of a passerine nestling dangling from its bill, in which the victim's body was largely concealed. This seemed to be a nestling that it had taken from the thrush.

The Nest

The toucanets that I studied in most detail were neighbors of the Resplendent Quetzal and Prong-billed Barbet in the tall, epiphyte-laden forest at Montaña Azul. When I arrived there in July 1937, I found them very abundant, roaming in small flocks through the forests and shady pastures around the cottage. Thereafter, they became increasingly rare, so that in September and October I saw few. Probably many descended to lower, warmer levels, in search of food and sunshine, like those that I have occasionally seen late in the year on the slopes surrounding the Valley of El General. In Chiapas, white-throated Emerald Toucanets likewise migrate up and down the mountains (Wagner 1944). In the opening months of the following year, blue-throated toucanets gradually became more prominent at Montaña Azul; by March, when their breeding season approached, they were again abundant and conspicuous. In the following months, I found six of their nests, and many years later, in southern Costa Rica near the frontier of Panama, I found four more nests and filled gaps in my knowledge of the habits of this bird. In this locality, near the lower limit of their altitudinal range, the toucanets mingled with Vermilion-breasted Trogons, Blue-diademed Motmots, Fiery-billed Araçaris, and other birds of the tropical zone.

Toucanets appear usually to nest in holes that have been made and abandoned by woodpeckers or that they steal from them. Occasionally they try to carve holes for themselves, probably rarely with success. In late March of 1964 I witnessed one such attempt near Cañas Gordas in extreme southern Costa Rica. In the trunk of a living tree standing in a pasture near forest was a vertical band of decaying wood. Here, 15 feet (4.5 meters) above the ground, an irregular roundish opening, too narrow to admit a toucanet, gave access to a cavity which penetrated rather deeply in a horizontal direction but seemed not to descend below the doorway. The excavation appeared to be newly begun, apparently by the toucanets themselves.

While I watched these birds enlarging the hole from 9:19 to 10:49 A.M. on March 23, the female took eleven spells at work, ranging from two to ten minutes and totaling fifty-six minutes. Her partner with a bigger bill took only three spells, lasting three, five, and five minutes. Even while at the hole, he rarely exerted himself as much as his companion, whose shorter bill seemed a more effective tool for this work. While carving, she clung with her feet clasping the trunk below the doorway and her tail pressing against the trunk for much of its length. She pecked and hammered much at the wood, so hard that I could hear the sound 100 feet (30 meters) away. She often, perhaps always, delivered the blows with her mandibles slightly parted. Instead of throwing her whole body into each stroke, as woodpeckers do, she moved only her foreparts when she struck the wood. She also seemed to bite away the rotting wood with her bill; but this was difficult to see, for her head was inside the hole. The loosened particles dropped out on her breast, from which they slipped off to the ground. While one partner worked, the other rested much of the time in a tall shrub of *Ardisia* that grew in front of their hole, from time to time eating the juicy purple berries.

After 10:49 I saw no more work done in the morning; but in the afternoon of the same day I watched the female work for three spells lasting five, three, and three minutes, while her mate looked on. The following morning I watched for the toucanets to resume their task without seeing them, probably because of the strong wind that blew all day. A few days later it was evident that this undertaking had been abandoned unfinished, apparently because the wood proved to be too hard for toucanets to work.

On March 29, I learned that a toucanet had slept the preceding night in a hole about 30 feet (9 meters) up in a massive decaying trunk in the pasture, a few hundred feet from the excavation that was abandoned. The doorway of this hole, which looked old, was partly screened by the great, glossy, perforated leaves of *Monstera*, an epiphytic aroid. Later that same morning, I watched the female toucanet remove five overflowing billfuls of wood particles from this cavity, carrying each load to a neighboring tree before she shook it from her bill. It interested me greatly to see the toucanet remove the excavated material to a distance, just as hole-carving barbets do, instead of simply throwing the wood particles through the doorway, as, in my experience, woodpeckers invariably do. While the female toucanet worked, her mate—sometimes preening and gaping—rested on a petiole of the *Monstera* below the doorway. Then he clung to the doorway and looked around but did not enter. Later in the morning, he did go inside and stayed for four minutes, during which the female twice entered and left the hole and once clung to the doorway without going in. When finally he emerged, I detected nothing in his bill.

While I sat in my blind watching a Collared Redstart's nest at Montaña Azul on April 23, 1938, a pair of toucanets came repeatedly to an old hole, apparently made by a Golden-olive Woodpecker, only 7 feet (2.1 meters) up in a nearby stub far advanced in decay. While the warbler sat quietly on her eggs, I enjoyed an exceptional opportunity to watch toucanets at close range, myself unseen. At intervals one of them clung in front of this cavity and looked in, while its mate rested on a dangling vine nearby. They uttered low, soft, murmurous sounds, surprisingly different from their usual froglike croaks and dry rattles. They made these notes in their throats, with closed bills, so that it took me a while to trace to their source sounds so unexpected. When a squirrel climbed over the base of a neighboring trunk, one of the *currés* flew at it with harsh notes and drove it away. But when, after retreating a short distance, the rodent returned to the same place in the presence of the toucanets, they ignored it. One of them alighted on the ground, apparently to pick up something edible, as toucans of all kinds seem very rarely to do. Although I did not see the toucanets remove material from this hole,

I later found many large, freshly detached flakes of decaying wood on the ground below. The toucanets deepened the shallow cavity; in the following days, I sometimes found one of them looking through the doorway. Then, for about two weeks, I failed to find them present. Later they returned, and on May 13 the first of a set of three eggs was laid.

Not always content with old abandoned woodpecker holes, toucanets sometimes displace the industrious carvers from holes that they have just made. At the end of April, I watched a pair of Hairy Woodpeckers working by turns at a hole 14 feet (4.3 meters) up in an old decaying trunk in a pasture, close by the forest at Montaña Azul. The woodpeckers, who had already lost an earlier nest, rapidly enlarged this chamber in the soft wood. They had hardly finished their undertaking before the larger, stronger toucanets wrested the hole from them. Although I did not see the toucanets remove wood, they evidently enlarged the doorway, which was substantially wider and slightly higher than that of a neighboring hole still occupied by the Hairy Woodpeckers who had carved it. After the toucanets took possession of the woodpeckers' chamber, I repeatedly found one of them within it, before an egg was laid. They prudently guarded their stolen cavity, lest it be retaken by the rightful owners. In a hole higher in the same trunk, a Buffy Tuftedcheek successfully nested.

When they nest at lower altitudes, toucanets find holes, large enough to accommodate them without alteration, made by such big woodpeckers as the Pale-billed and the Lineated. Above 5,000 feet (1,500 meters) in Costa Rica, the chief hole carvers are Hairy and Golden-olive woodpeckers and Prong-billed Barbets. As already told, barbets excavate holes like those of woodpeckers in shape, with the important difference that they leave a greater thickness of wood around their doorways. Fernando Gómez, the lad who helped me at Montaña Azul, saw a pair of *currés* tearing at the entrance of a barbets' nest containing eggs, while the owners flitted around and protested. The would-be pirates made so little progress that they soon left the barbets in possession of their home.

The eleven nests of the blue-throated toucanet that I have seen over the years, at altitudes ranging from 3,800 to 7,000 feet (1,160 to 2,150 meters) above sea level, were from 7 to about 90 feet (2.1 to 27 meters) above the ground, with an average of 35 feet (10.6 meters). All were in holes in dead or dying trees, most of which stood in clearings a short flight from the forest, although a few were just within the woodland's edge. My failure to find a nest deep in the forest probably reflects merely the greater difficulty of discovering nests high in closed stands of trees. One nest cavity was 18½ inches (47 centimeters) deep, measured from the lower edge of the doorway. This is oval in form, with the long axis horizontal; the width varies from 2⅛ to 2½ inches, the height from 1¾ to 2 inches (5.4 to 6.4 by 4.5 to 5 centimeters). Often it is barely large enough for the toucanets to squeeze through. The bottom of the cavity may be covered with wood particles but is never softly lined.

The Eggs and Incubation

Three accessible nests contained four, four, and three plain white eggs, which I viewed only in a mirror as they lay in nests lighted with an electric bulb. In two of these nests, the eggs were laid on consecutive days. Laying often begins early in April. These highland toucanets, like highland Resplendent Quetzals, raise second broods, although the lowland members of the toucan and the trogon family are not known to do so. Young of second broods remain in their nests through much of July.

As already told, by day I frequently found a toucanet in the nest captured from Hairy Woodpeckers at the end of April. Nevertheless, neither member of the pair slept in it as late as the night of May 5 to 6. The first egg was laid on May 6, and a toucanet remained with it throughout the night that followed. On the next day the second egg was laid; and, although two more were to follow, the incomplete set was apparently incubated more or less throughout the day.

Halfway through the incubation period, I passed a long morning in my blind watching the low hole near the Collared Redstart's nest. As I had already seen at a high, inaccessible nest, both sexes incubated, but one rarely remained until the other came to relieve it, so that I witnessed only one changeover all morning. On this occasion, the newcomer clung before the doorway; the sitting partner looked out; they uttered low rattling notes; then the one inside pushed past the other and flew away before the newcomer entered. Early in the morning, the noisy fall of a large leaf in the neighboring woods sent the easily alarmed toucanet from its nest, but more often it left for no apparent reason. During the first six hours of the day, eight sessions of both sexes ranged from less than 1 to 81 minutes and averaged 33.3 minutes. Eight intervals of neglect varied from 1 to 18 minutes and averaged 11.9 minutes. The eggs were incubated for a total of 266 minutes and neglected for 94 minutes. Thus, the eggs were attended for only 73.9 percent of the morning, which is about normal constancy for the mercurial toucans.

At this nest I could not distinguish the sexes. In the pair that tried to dig a cavity and failed, then nested in an old hole screened by an epiphytic *Monstera*, the male's bill was so much bigger than his mate's that I easily told them apart. On the evening of April 1, the male rested in a tree near this nest, at intervals stretching his wings. When his mate arrived, he accompanied her to the aroid in front of the doorway. She entered to stay for the night; he flew away. Soon afterward, three Fiery-billed Araçaris entered a hole higher in the same trunk, where for some nights they had been lodging. On succeeding evenings, events occurred in the same sequence. The female toucanet did not even look from her doorway when the larger toucans entered their dormitory several yards above her. Each evening, after seeing his mate installed in the nest chamber, the male toucanet flew off through the pasture until beyond my view. If he roosted in a hole, I could not find it. I have never known a toucanet to sleep in a cavity except when attending a nest, at which time only a single parent is present, even when nestlings are being brooded. Apparently they usually roost in trees, like the big *Ramphastos* toucans.

One evening, while the pair of toucanets rested near the hole behind the *Monstera*, the large-billed bird tried to mount the small-billed bird before the latter entered for the night. The next morning, near the nest, the large-billed member of the pair gave the other a fruit from a tree of the laurel family, which she ate. Then he billed her neck and tried to mount her, but she resisted. Thus, I had confirmation from behavior that my identification of the sexes by bill size was correct. After the feeding, one of the toucanets scratched its head by raising its foot outside its wing, which it held folded against its body, just as woodpeckers do. In piciform birds, I have not noticed the over-the-wing (or inside-the-wing) head scratching prevalent in passerine birds and hummingbirds.

Incubation evidently began in the hole screened by the aroid about April 4, but the attendance of the parents was at first so desultory that I was not convinced that they had eggs until some days later. I watched these toucanets incubate through the afternoon of April 15 and the mornings of April 16 and 18, but the record made in the afternoon is imperfect because I failed to notice all the birds' movements. The incubation pattern of toucanets is more complicated than that of birds who sit more patiently, and for clarity I have summarized the records of the two mornings in the accompanying table. When the record for each morning is read across and downward, as one reads a book, it gives the actual sequence of sessions by the two parents and the intervals when both were absent, all in minutes. On the morning of April 16, the female, who had occupied the nest throughout the night, sat until her mate came at 5:39, long before sunrise, to replace her. He sat for only ten minutes. On April 18 he arrived at 5:40; but, instead of staying to incubate after the female left, he followed her from the nest tree and did not return to attend the eggs until seven minutes later. Then on both mornings the two partners alternated on the nest, with intervening periods of neglect.

After the male replaced the female at 8:10 on April 16, he alone was in charge of the nest for the next four hours and twelve minutes. But far from incubating continuously, as many a smaller bird would have done, he broke this long period into eight sessions on the eggs, separated by recesses. The first session lasted fifty-three minutes, but the others were much shorter. The decreasing length of his sessions revealed his increasing restlessness as his mate's absence was prolonged. Sometimes he passed his whole recess, often stretching and preening, on a petiole of the *Monstera* in front of the doorway. At other times he perched in a neighboring tree, from which he could see the nest, but occasionally he flew farther off. His longest interval off the eggs was twenty-two minutes, for only half of which was he out of sight of the nest. Although too restless to sit for even an hour at a stretch, he was obviously ill at ease away from the nest, unless he knew that his mate was there.

On April 18, the toucanets divided the task of incubation more equally. From 7:17 to 9:24 the male was in charge, taking four sessions separated by short outings. Then at 9:33 the female took over and sat for six intervals, broken by five rests lasting from two to ten minutes. At 12:10 the male returned, and at 12:19 he entered the nest. When not in the nest, the female also spent much time resting in front, guarding it, but sometimes she was out of sight for the whole of a brief recess. Taking the two mornings together, in nearly thirteen and a half hours the male incubated a total of 376 minutes, the female 252 minutes, and the eggs were neglected for 175 minutes. The male covered the eggs for seventeen sessions, ranging from 1 to 53 minutes and averaging 22.1 minutes; the female's eleven sessions ranged from 13 to 37 minutes with an average of 22.9 minutes; and the eggs were neglected for twenty-four intervals ranging from 1 to 22 minutes and averaging 7.3. The two parents together kept their eggs covered for only 78.3 percent of the time, which is no better than many a small bird does alone. Nevertheless, they were slightly more attentive than the pair of toucanets that I watched incubate in the very low hole by

Incubation by a Pair of Emerald Toucanets

April 16, 5:39 A.M. to 12:22 P.M.			April 18, 5:40 A.M. to 12:19 P.M.		
Male	Female	Neither	Male	Female	Neither
10		5			7
	21	5	5		7
1		4		37	
48	25	4	11	30	
	28		38		9
53		4	27		1
21		7	29		2
27		10	21		9
25		22		18	4
20		12		14	2
21		3		13	9
6		8		28	10
13		1		19	9
	began			19	21
			began		
245	74	85	131	178	90

the redstart's nest; and they did much better than the Fiery-billed Araçaris and Rainbow-billed Toucans.

One question of long standing was answered at this nest: which sex among toucans takes charge of the eggs at night? I would not have been surprised if, as in the related woodpeckers, the male had incubated throughout the night; but repeated observations proved that the female toucanet did so. The order Piciformes is far from uniform in this matter. We now know that in at least one jacamar, the Rufous-tailed, and one toucan, the Emerald Toucanet, the female alone occupies the nest by night while it contains eggs and young. A male Red-billed Toucan brooded nestlings about four times as often as the female (Bourne 1974). In at least one puffbird, the White-whiskered Softwing, the male occupies the nest at night (Skutch 1958a), as appears to be universally true of woodpeckers, except in those genera (*Trip-*

surus, *Picumnus*) in which the mated pair sleep together in the hole at all times (Skutch 1969). In the Prong-billed Barbet, the male and the female also sleep together in the nest with eggs and young.

While the blue-throated toucanets incubated in the daytime, I sometimes heard tapping or hammering coming from their trunk. After she entered the hole for the night, the female tapped much while daylight faded. From the character of these sounds, I suspected that the toucanets were enlarging their nest chamber. However, considering their evident distaste for the task of incubation, they may have been tapping on their wall merely to relieve boredom, as a man beats a tattoo with his fingers on the table. When one partner came for a turn at incubation and found the other inside, I heard a rattling sound as the latter emerged, pushing past the newcomer. I could not tell whether one sex or both made this noise. In the afternoon, when the sun shone hotly, the toucanet in charge of the eggs spent much time with its head in the doorway, instead of incubating.

At the lowest nest, eggs were laid on May 13, 14, and 15. Two hatched on May 30, the third on May 31. The distribution of hatching supports the conclusion, drawn from casual watching, that fairly constant incubation began with the laying of the second egg. The incubation period of the last egg was sixteen days.

The Nestlings

The nestlings in the lowest nest died when about two weeks old, apparently as a result of the seepage of rainwater into their dilapidated chamber. The toucanets who stole the Hairy Woodpeckers' hole also had bad luck: a few days after they started to incubate their four eggs, only broken shells lay in the cavity. I believe that a weasel which lurked in the pasture grass was responsible for this destruction. My third low nest fared better. It was situated 15 feet (4.5 meters) above the ground, in a slender rotting stub in the pasture, near the forest. To prevent the access of snakes and small mammals to the nest, I surrounded the trunk with a metal band 14 inches (36 centimeters) wide—a five-gallon kerosene tin flattened out—placed head-high. I can recommend to bird watchers this method, which is commonly employed in warm countries for the protection of open-air hen roosts. Above this metallic guard—which gave no purchase to the sharp claws of weasels, squirrels, or Tayras or to the scales of serpents—the young toucanets remained safe in their low exposed nursery through all the six weeks of their nest life.

When first examined on May 5, this fortunate nest contained three hatchlings and one egg that did not hatch until the following day. The hatchlings were pink-skinned, with no slightest trace of feathers. Their eyes were tightly closed; their bills were short and somewhat flattened, with the lower mandible both longer and broader than the upper. The heel pads, studded with high prominent papillae, were grotesquely large when compared with the tiny feet that seemed mere

appendages to them. This was appropriate, for during many days these pads would bear much more of the nestlings' weight than the toes themselves. The day-old toucanets so closely resembled the hatchling Prong-billed Barbets whom I was studying at the same time that, had the two broods been mixed together, I am not sure that I could have separated them. Their resemblance to day-old woodpeckers and kingfishers was also strong, but not quite so close.

Unlike Fiery-billed Araçaris and Rainbow-billed Toucans, the parent toucanets did not permit regurgitated seeds of the fruits they ate to accumulate in the nest until they formed a rough bumpy layer over the bottom. Whether or not they regurgitated while incubating I could not see. Also, the parents removed the empty shells within a day or two after the emergence of their occupants. Thus, the young toucanets began life in a clean nursery, carpeted with a layer of fine wood particles. This condition was maintained through most of their long nestlinghood, for the parents were careful of sanitation—they carried away large billfuls of waste when they left the hole at daybreak, others at intervals through the day. In this process all the loose chips were eventually removed, leaving the floor bare. Only during the young toucanets' last few days in the chamber did the parents relax their attention and permit waste to accumulate.

Whenever I looked into the hole with my electric light and mirror, I found the nestlings huddled close together, their long scrawny necks interlocked. One of the four vanished before it was five days old. The remaining three often arranged themselves in a symmetrical pattern, each with the head of a sibling resting on its neck and its own head supported on the neck of the other sibling. They were noisy, uttering a variety of little squeaks and squeals, especially when I lightly shook their trunk, as though one of the parents, returning with food, had alighted upon it. During their first few days, they were brooded much by both parents. When one arrived with food, it clung beside the doorway until the other emerged. I did not at any time see both together in the nest;

and only one stayed with the nestlings at night, not two or more adults, as at nests of araçaris.

The young toucanets developed very slowly. They were two weeks old when, with the mirror, I detected the first rudiments of feathers beneath their transparent skins. The difference in the lengths of the mandibles now began to disappear. When the nestlings were twenty days old, the sheaths of their body feathers were just breaking through their skins, but those of the wing plumes were distinctly longer. The bill was now acquiring the shape of that on an adult toucanet. Not until May 30, when the nestlings were twenty-five days old, did I see them with open eyelids; but the eyes still appeared cloudy, as though covered by a delicate membrane. By June 1, the eyes were both open and clear. Both the remiges and the body feathers, but not those on the head, were now beginning to erupt from their sheaths, which never became as long and conspicuous as those of kingfishers, motmots, jacamars, and lowland trogons. From their first appearance, the feathers were green, like those of the adults. The twenty-seven-day-old toucanets were very noisy, uttering such a variety of grunts and squeals that their nursery reminded me of a miniature piggery.

Even after their feathers began to expand, the young toucanets were long in becoming completely covered; on June 5, when they were a full month old, much of their skin was still exposed. At thirty-five days of age they were at last fully clad, at least on their upper parts, which were all I could see; but their tails were still quite stubby. They were thirty-nine days old before I saw one looking out through the doorway. And still they lingered within.

Before they flew, the young toucanets closely resembled their parents in plumage, even to their blue throats. But their eyes were ringed by pale bare skin, lacking in the adults; and their bills, which had gradually been approaching adult size, were still smaller and differently colored. The upper mandible was much like that of the adults— black at the base and along the cutting edge, elsewhere light yellow—but it lacked the red patch at the base of the culmen. The lower mandible was black only along the cutting edge; elsewhere it was yellow clouded with black. The white line around the base of the bill, conspicuous on the grown birds, was lacking in the young.

In strong contrast to toucans of other species that I have watched attend far higher nests, at this nest the parents were so fearless that they would enter their low hole with food while I stood close beside the rotting stub. When I wished to watch them for long periods, I had only to sit on a stump at a convenient distance, unconcealed. In their fearlessness, they resembled most of the birds in this wild region.

From the age of a few days, the nestling toucanets were nourished principally with fruits, brought in the tips of the parents' bills. Small at first, these morsels gradually increased in size as the young grew larger. After they were well grown, the chicks received many of the big hard green fruits of a tree of the laurel family that grew near the nest. These were about 1½ inches long by ¾ inch in diameter (3.8 by 1.9 centimeters); each had thin olive-colored flesh between the green skin and the single large seed. It could not have taken many such fruits to fill a nestling; but each yielded only a relatively small amount of nourishment, since the hard seed was indigestible. Rarely, the parents came with articles so small that they were nearly or quite enclosed in their bills and thus difficult to distinguish. At least some of these small items were insects. I watched the adults try to catch insects on the wing, within the edge of the neighboring forest, and at times their clumsy efforts appeared to be successful. Once, as already told, a parent entered the hole with a naked passerine nestling, apparently a Mountain Thrush.

The nestling toucanets received rather infrequent meals. In the first four hours of their forty-second day, food was brought to the two survivors only sixteen times, at the rate of one meal for each nestling every half hour. Although the young toucanets now spent much time looking through their doorway, their parents usually pushed inside to feed them. On the few occasions when they delivered food while clinging in front of the entrance, I could see that, when smaller fruits were brought, in addition to the single one held in the tip of the bill, the parent produced others—usually two—that it carried in deeper regions and now brought to light, one by one.

Early in the morning, a parent arrived with one of the big lauraceous fruits already described. It entered the nest and, after a minute or so, started to come out; but, when halfway through the doorway, it stuck and could go no farther. With its head and breast outside, its big bill wide open in a ludicrous attitude, it struggled to squirm through but could not. Then it seemed to realize what the trouble was: it regurgitated the big fruit that it had swallowed inside the nest when it found that the nestlings could not. Holding the fruit in its bill, as it had done when it entered, it passed through the doorway without difficulty, since it was now considerably thinner. For about twenty-five minutes, the toucanet continued to hold the big fruit, while resting near the nest. At intervals it went inside to offer it once more to a nestling, and finally, on the third offering, one of the young managed to swallow it—as I infer from the fact that the parent entered the nest with the fruit in its bill and emerged without embarrassment, with no fruit visible. Later that same morning, a parent again took in a big fruit, which the nestlings were too full to swallow just then, stuck in the doorway when it tried to come out, and had to regurgitate the fruit in order to reduce its girth. This time, it carried the fruit away for its own consumption.

These amusing incidents demonstrated that the doorway of the nest was barely large enough to permit the adult toucanets to pass through. One could also see this plainly by watching from directly in front while a bird emerged. The form of the orifice, an oval broader than high, matched the shape of the bird's body and permitted it to pass through an opening no larger than was necessary.

A single parent slept nightly with the nestlings until they were at least forty-one days old; not knowing when they would depart, I did not check this point on their final two nights in the nest. The two surviving toucanets left their nest before nine o'clock on the morning of June 17, when they were forty-three days old. Arriving at that hour, I found one of them perching in a low tree at the edge of the woods, where the parents fed it. It took a leaf in its bill, as though to test its edibility, but decided that this item was not good to eat. I failed to find the other fledgling, who had apparently wandered farther into the woods.

On the evening after the young toucanets' first flight, I watched for their return to the nest; but no member of the family came near it, and thereafter the hole was abandoned. The same was true at a second, much higher nest. A slight deposit of droppings on the floor of the nest when the fledglings left was not subsequently removed by the parents, as birds who continue to sleep in the nest space usually do. These facts strengthened my conviction that toucanets, unlike araçaris, do not sleep in holes when not attending eggs or young.

Years later, at the nest screened by the *Monstera* leaves, I saw more of the care of nestlings. Here the parents were bringing food by April 20, when I passed the afternoon watching them attend their newly hatched young, of unknown number. From 1:05 until the female entered the hole for the night at 5:55, the male brooded for seven intervals, ranging from 2 to 23 minutes and totaling 56 minutes. The female brooded the nestlings eleven times, for periods ranging from 2 to 29 minutes and totaling 113 minutes. The nestlings were alone for eleven intervals, ranging from 1 to 31 minutes and totaling 121 minutes.

On this afternoon, the female took food to the nest ten times, the male seven times. At times the article held in the tip of the parent's bill was unrecognizable, but often it was clearly a small fruit, sometimes an insect. The female's contributions tended to be smaller and better mashed than the male's, which on two occasions were too big for the nestlings to swallow, so that he emerged from the nest still holding the food and then ate it himself. Another time he came with an empty bill, perched in a tree near the nest, and regurgitated a large green fruit. He held it in his bill, as though considering whether it would be suitable for a nestling, then swallowed it again, flew away, and in a few minutes returned with a much smaller fruit, which he took inside the nest. This reminded me of the incident that I had witnessed long before, when a parent was trapped in the nest after swallowing the big fruit that it had failed to deliver to a nestling.

That afternoon, in a tree 50 yards (45 meters) from the nest behind the *Monstera*, I watched the parent toucanets croak at a Fiery-billed Araçari, probably one of the three who slept in the hole above their nest. Then the toucanets tried to drive the larger toucan away, but it turned the tables and chased them from branch to branch. These toucanets also worried a pair of Golden-naped Woodpeckers nesting high in a neighboring tree. On several occasions they chased the woodpeckers as the latter approached their own nest hole. The male toucanet repeatedly stuck his head into the woodpeckers' doorway, trying to reach the nestlings. Finding that he could not, he tried to enlarge the doorway so that he could enter; but the wood around it was too solid for him to tear away. As I have repeatedly seen, hole-nesting birds do well to make their doorways barely large enough for themselves to pass through, in the hardest material that they can work.

These toucanets also worried the Chestnut-headed Oropendolas in a neighboring small colony. One afternoon I watched a toucanet investigating the long woven nests that hung in a high treetop. The toucanet clung to the sides of the swinging pouches, sometimes upright and sometimes with head downward, and once it entered a nest but apparently did not descend to the bottom. While the toucanet searched among the pouches, a pair of Piratic Flycatchers, preparing to nest in one of them, protested violently. Again and again they darted, with snapping mandibles, close by the bird so much bigger than themselves, and one of them knocked out some of its green feathers. But the oropendolas had already finished breeding, and the would-be nest robber, finding neither eggs nor nestlings in the pouches, finally flew off, leaving the flycatchers calling vociferously.

Long before they were old enough to fly, the nestlings vanished from the nest behind the aroid. After this occurred, I saw the male of this pair give two articles of food to his mate. Evidently they were preparing to try again to rear a brood; but, if they started another nest, I could not find it. Although replacement of a lost brood is not known in the larger toucans, it is to be expected in the double-brooded toucanet. All three pairs whose young successfully fledged at Montaña Azul were soon afterward found nesting again. The fecundity of blue-throated toucanets accounts for their abundance in Costa Rican mountain forests, where the great variety of fruit-bearing trees can support a large population.

Bibliography

Alvarez del Toro, M. 1948. Polygamy at a Groove-billed Ani nest. *Auk* 65: 449–450.

———. 1971. El bienparado ó pájaro estaca (*Nyctibius griseus mexicanus* Nelson). *Icach* 2: 7–13.

Bates, H. W. 1863. *A naturalist of the river Amazon.*

Beebe, W., G. I. Hartley, and P. G. Howes. 1917. *Tropical wild life in British Guiana.* Vol. 1. New York: New York Zool. Soc.

Belcher, C., and G. D. Smooker. 1936. Birds of the colony of Trinidad and Tobago. Pts. III and IV. *Ibis* ser. 13 (6): 1–35, 792–813.

Bent, A. C. 1932. Life histories of North American gallinaceous birds. *Bull. U.S. Natl. Mus.* 162: i–xi, 1–490.

———. 1940. Life histories of North American cuckoos, goatsuckers, hummingbirds and their allies. *Bull. U.S. Natl. Mus.* 176: i–vii, 1–506.

Borrero H., J. I. 1970. A photographic study of the Potoo in Colombia. *Living Bird* 9: 257–263.

———. 1974. Notes on the structure of the upper eyelid of Potoos. *Condor* 76: 210–211.

Bourne, G. R. 1974. The Red-billed Toucan in Guyana. *Living Bird* 13: 99–126.

Carriker, M. A., Jr. 1910. An annotated list of the birds of Costa Rica, including Cocos Island. *Ann. Carnegie Mus.* 6: 314–915.

Chapman, F. M. 1929. *My tropical air castle.* New York and London: D. Appleton and Co.

Cherrie, G. K. 1916. A contribution to the ornithology of the Orinoco region. *Bull. Brooklyn Inst. Arts Sci.* 2: 133a–374.

Davis, D. E. 1940. Social nesting habits of the Smooth-billed Ani. *Auk* 57: 179–218.

Eisenmann, E. 1952. Annotated list of birds of Barro Colorado Island, Panama Canal Zone. *Smithsonian Misc. Coll.* 117 (5): 1–62.

ffrench, R. 1973. *A guide to the birds of Trinidad and Tobago.* Wynnewood, Pa.: Livingston Publishing Co.

Friedmann, H., and F. D. Smith, Jr. 1955. A further contribution to the ornithology of northeastern Venezuela. *Proc. U.S. Natl. Mus.* 104: 463–524.

Gaumer, G. P. 1881–1882. Notes on the habits of certain Momotidae. *Trans. Kansas Acad. Sci.* 8: 63–66.

Gilliard, E. T. 1959. Notes on some birds of northern Venezuela. *Amer. Mus. Novitates* no. 1927: 1–33.

Goodwin, D. 1967. *Pigeons and doves of the world.* London: British Museum (Natural History).

Gosse, P. H. 1847. *The birds of Jamaica.* London: John van Voorst.

Haverschmidt, F. 1950. Notes on the Swallow-wing, *Chelidoptera tenebrosa*, in Surinam. *Condor* 52: 74–77.

———. 1953. Notes on the life history of *Columbigallina talpacoti* in Surinam. *Condor* 55: 21–25.

———. 1958. Notes on *Nyctibius griseus* in Surinam. *Ardea* 46: 144–148.

———. 1968. *Birds of Surinam.* Wynnewood, Pa.: Livingston Publishing Co.

Haydock, E. L. 1950. Supplementary notes on African cuckoos. *Ibis* 92: 149–150.

Herrick, F. H. 1910. Life and behavior of the cuckoo. *Journ. Expt. Zool.* 9: 169–234.

Hudson, W. H. 1920. *Birds of La Plata.* 2 vols. London: J. M. Dent and Sons.

Hundley, M. H., and C. R. Mason. 1965. Birds develop a taste for sugar. *Wilson Bull.* 77: 408.

Johnson, R. E. 1937. Hunting for the "Poor-me-one." *Illustrated London News*, March 13.

Kendeigh, S. C. 1952. Parental care and its evolution in birds. *Illinois Biol. Monogr.* 22: i–x, 1–356.

Köster, F. 1971. Zum Nistverhalten des Ani, *Crotophaga ani. Bonn. Zool. Beitr.* 22: 4–27.

LaBastille, A., D. G. Allen, and L. W. Durrell. 1972. Behavior and feather structure of the Quetzal. *Auk* 89: 339–348.

Lill, A. 1970. Nidification of the Channel-billed Toucan (*Ramphastos vitellinus*) in Trinidad, West Indies. *Condor* 72: 235–236.

Lockley, R. M. 1953. *Puffins*. London: J. M. Dent and Sons.

Luther, D. M. 1979. An intensive study of parental behavior in the Mourning Dove. *Indiana Audubon Quart.* 57: 209–232.

Marchant, S. 1960. The breeding of some S. W. Ecuadorian birds. *Ibis* 102: 349–382, 584–599.

Marion, W. R., and R. J. Fleetwood. 1978. Nesting ecology of the Plain Chachalaca in south Texas. *Wilson Bull.* 90: 386–395.

Martin, R. F., and M. W. Martin. 1980. Observations on the breeding of Turquoise-browed Motmots in Yucatán. *Condor* 82: 109.

Merritt, J. H. 1951. Little orphan ani. *Audubon Mag.* 53: 225–231.

Meyer de Schauensee, R. 1970. *Guide to the birds of South America*. Wynnewood, Pa.: Livingston Publishing Co.

———, and W. H. Phelps, Jr. 1978. *A guide to the birds of Venezuela*. Princeton, N.J.: Princeton University Press.

Miller, A. H. 1932. Observations on some breeding birds of El Salvador, Central America. *Condor* 34: 8–17.

Mitchell, M. H. 1957. *Observations on birds of southeastern Brazil*. Toronto: University of Toronto Press.

Moreau, R. E. 1944. The Half-collared Kingfisher (*Alcedo semitorquata*) at the nest. *Ostrich* 15: 161–177.

———, and W. M. Moreau. 1940. Incubation and fledging periods of African birds. *Auk* 57: 313–325.

Neff, J. A., and R. J. Niedrach. 1946. Nesting of the Band-tailed Pigeon in Colorado. *Condor* 48: 72–74.

O'Brian, P. 1979. Breeding activities of Waved Woodpeckers in Surinam. *Wilson Bull.* 91: 338–344.

Orejuela, J. E. 1977. Comparative biology of Turquoise-browed and Blue-crowned motmots in the Yucatán Peninsula, Mexico. *Living Bird* 16: 193–206.

Peeters, H. J. 1962. Nuptial behavior of the Band-tailed Pigeon in the San Francisco Bay Area. *Condor* 64: 445–470.

Rand, A. L. 1953. Factors affecting feeding rates of anis. *Auk* 70: 26–30.

Ridgely, R. S. 1976. *A guide to the birds of Panama*. Princeton, N.J.: Princeton University Press.

Ridgway, R. 1911. The birds of North and Middle America. *Bull. U.S. Natl. Mus.* 50, pt. V: i–xxiii, 1–859.

Rowley, J. S. 1962. Nesting of birds of Morelos, Mexico. *Condor* 64: 253–272.

———. 1966. Breeding records of birds of the Sierra Madre del Sur, Oaxaca, Mexico. *Proc. Western Foundation Vertebrate Zool.* 1 (3): 107–204.

Russell, S. M. 1964. A distributional study of the birds of British Honduras. *Amer. Ornith. Union, Ornith. Monogr.* no. 1: 1–195.

Salvin, O. 1861. Quesal-shooting in Vera Paz. *Ibis*, 1961: 138–149.

———, and F. D. Godman. 1879–1904. *Biologia Centrali-Americana. Aves.* 3 vols. of text, 1 of plates. London: Taylor and Francis.

Skutch, A. F. 1937. Life history of the Black-chinned Jacamar. *Auk* 54: 135–146.

———. 1942. Life history of the Mexican Trogon. *Auk* 59: 341–363.

———. 1944a. Life history of the Blue-throated Toucanet. *Wilson Bull.* 56: 133–151.

———. 1944b. The life history of the Prong-billed Barbet. *Auk* 61: 61–88.

———. 1944c. Life history of the Quetzal. *Condor* 46: 213–235.

———. 1945. Life history of the Blue-throated Green Motmot. *Auk* 62: 489–517.

———. 1946. Life history of the Costa Rican

Tityra. *Auk* 63: 327–362.

———. 1947a. Life history of the Marbled Wood-Quail. *Condor* 49: 217–232.

———. 1947b. Life history of the Turquoise-browed Motmot. *Auk* 64: 201–217.

———. 1948a. Life history notes on puffbirds. *Wilson Bull.* 60: 81–97.

———. 1948b. Life history of the Citreoline Trogon. *Condor* 50: 137–147.

———. 1949. Life history of the Ruddy Quail-Dove. *Condor* 51: 3–19.

———. 1953. How the male bird discovers the nestlings. *Ibis* 95: 1–37, 505–542.

———. 1956a. Life history of the Ruddy Ground Dove. *Condor* 58: 188–205.

———. 1956b. A nesting of the Collared Trogon. *Auk* 73: 354–366.

———. 1957. Life history of the Amazon Kingfisher. *Condor* 59: 217–229.

———. 1958a. Life history of the White-whiskered Softwing *Malacoptila panamensis*. *Ibis* 100: 209–231.

———. 1958b. Roosting and nesting of araçari toucans. *Condor* 60: 201–219.

———. 1959a. The Great Tinamou of the tropical forest. *Animal Kingdom* 62: 179–183.

———. 1959b. Life history of the Black-throated Trogon. *Wilson Bull.* 71: 5–18.

———. 1959c. Life history of the Groove-billed Ani. *Auk* 76: 281–317.

———. 1962. Life history of the White-tailed Trogon *Trogon viridis*. *Ibis* 104: 301–313.

———. 1963a. Habits of the Chestnut-winged Chachalaca. *Wilson Bull.* 75: 262–269.

———. 1963b. Life history of the Little Tinamou. *Condor* 65: 224–231.

———. 1963c. Life history of the Rufous-tailed Jacamar *Galbula ruficauda* in Costa Rica. *Ibis* 105: 354–368.

———. 1964a. Life histories of Central American pigeons. *Wilson Bull.* 76: 211–247.

———. 1964b. Life history of the Blue-diademed Motmot *Momotus momota*. *Ibis* 106: 321–332.

———. 1966. Life history notes on three tropical American cuckoos. *Wilson Bull.* 78: 139–165.

———. 1967. *Life histories of Central American highland birds.* Cambridge, Mass.: Nuttall Ornithological Club.

———. 1968. The nesting of some Venezuelan birds. *Condor* 70: 66–82.

———. 1969. *Life histories of Central American birds.* Vol. III. *Pacific Coast Avif.*, no. 35. Berkeley: Cooper Ornithological Society.

———. 1970. Life history of the Common Potoo. *Living Bird* 9: 265–280.

———. 1971a. Life history of the Broad-billed Motmot, with notes on the Rufous Motmot. *Wilson Bull.* 83: 74–94.

———. 1971b. Life history of the Keel-billed Toucan. *Auk* 88: 381–396.

———. 1971c. *A naturalist in Costa Rica.* Gainesville: University of Florida Press.

———. 1972. *Studies of tropical American birds.* Cambridge, Mass.: Nuttall Ornithological Club.

———. 1976. *Parent birds and their young.* Austin and London: University of Texas Press.

———. 1977. *A bird watcher's adventures in tropical America.* Austin and London: University of Texas Press.

———. 1979. *The imperative call.* Gainesville: University Presses of Florida.

———. 1980a. Arils as food of tropical American birds. *Condor* 82: 31–42.

———. 1980b. *A naturalist on a tropical farm.* Berkeley, Los Angeles, and London: University of California Press.

———. 1981. *New studies of tropical American birds.* Cambridge, Mass.: Nuttall Ornithological Club.

Smith, S. M. 1971. The relationship of grazing cattle to foraging rates in anis. *Auk* 88: 876–880.

Smithe, F. B. 1966. *The birds of Tikal.* Garden City, N.Y.: Natural History Press.

Spence, L. 1945. *The religion of ancient Mexico.* London: Watts and Co.

Taylor, C. 1980. *The Coppery-tailed Trogon: Arizona's "bird of paradise."* Portal, Ariz.: Borderland Productions.

Todd, W. E. C., and M. A. Carriker, Jr. 1922. The birds of the Santa Marta region of Colombia: A study in altitudinal distribution. *Ann. Carnegie Mus.* 14: i–viii, 1–611.

Van Tyne, J. 1929. The life history of the

toucan *Ramphastos brevicarinatus. University of Michigan Mus. Zool. Misc. Publ.* no. 19: 1–43.

———. 1935. The birds of northern Petén, Guatemala. *University of Michigan Mus. Zool. Misc. Publ.* no. 27: 1–46.

Vehrencamp, S. L. 1977. Relative fecundity and parental effort in communally nesting anis, *Crotophaga sulcirostris. Science* 197: 403–405.

———. 1978. The adaptive significance of communal nesting in Groove-billed Anis (*Crotophaga sulcirostris*). *Behavioral Ecology and Sociobiology* 4: 1–33.

———, F. G. Stiles, and J. W. Bradbury. 1977. Observations on the foraging behavior and avian prey of the Neotropical carnivorous bat *Vampyrum spectrum. Journ. Mammalogy* 58: 469–478.

Wagner, H. O. 1944. Notes on the life history of the Emerald Toucanet. *Wilson Bull.* 56: 65–76.

West, S. 1976. Observations on the Yellow-eared Toucanet. *Auk* 93: 381–382.

Wetmore, A. 1968. The birds of the Republic of Panamá. Pt. 2. *Smithsonian Misc. Coll.* 150 (2): i–v, 1–605.

———, and B. H. Swales. 1931. The birds of Haiti and the Dominican Republic. *Bull. U.S. Natl. Mus.* 155: i–iv, 1–483.

Willis, E. O., and E. Eisenmann. 1979. A revised list of birds of Barro Colorado Island, Panama. *Smithsonian Contrib. Zool.* no. 291: i–iii, 1–31.

Index

Illustrations are indicated by boldfaced numbers.